Relationship Sabotage

RELATIONSHIP SABOTAGE

Unconscious Factors that Destroy Couples, Marriages, and Family

William J. Matta

Sex, Love, and Psychology
Judy Kuriansky, Series Editor

Westport, Connecticut
London

Library of Congress Cataloging-in-Publication Data

Relationship sabotage : unconscious factors that destroy couples, marriages, and family /
William J. Matta.
     p. cm. — (Sex, love, and psychology, ISSN 1554–222X)
  Includes bibliographical references and index.
  ISBN 0–275–98921–6 (alk. paper)
  1. Interpersonal relations.   2. Family.   3. Marriage.
  I. Matta, William J. II. Series.
  HM1106.R45   2006
  155.9'24—dc22   2006009158

British Library Cataloguing in Publication Data is available.

Library of Congress Catalog Card Number: 2006009158
ISBN: 0–275–98921–6
ISSN: 1554–222X

First published in 2006

Praeger Publishers, 88 Post Road West, Westport, CT 06881
An imprint of Greenwood Publishing Group, Inc.
www.praeger.com

Printed in the United States of America

The paper used in this book complies with the
Permanent Paper Standard issued by the National
Information Standards Organization (Z39.48–1984).

10 9 8 7 6 5 4 3 2 1

The book is dedicated to my brother,
Dr. Joseph E. Matta (1948–1991).

Dr. Joseph Matta was an exceptional researcher who made significant contributions to the Army. He impacted everyone he met. He was a warm, sensitive person, a good friend to many of us, and an exceptional family man. Joe received his PhD degree in Physics in 1974 from Leigh University. He came to Aberdeen Proving Grounds in 1978 as a research physicist following a brief assignment at the U.S. Bureau of Mines. He became an international authority on the relation between the physical properties of non-Newtonian fluids and their breakup into liquid aerosols when subjected to various shear forces. His work has led to 40 publications and 7 patents. In 1983 he was selected for an Army Research and Development Achievement Award for his work on characterizing the breakup of viscoelastic fluids. Most importantly, he developed a small-scale dissemination device to develop data to predict liquid breakup. The Munitions Directorate used this method to select the polymer and concentration for the chemical fill for the MLRS Binary Chemical Warhead, a major program that helped convince the Soviet Union to seek a chemical weapons treaty. Later, his recent efforts have been directed toward support of the Strategic Defense Initiative.

Aberdeen Proving Grounds was very fortunate to have Dr. Matta as an employee for a dozen years. The outstanding research that Joseph produced will continue to contribute to programs for many years. Moreover, his high professional standards, his quiet, unpretentious manner, and his approach to solving rather than creating problems serve as a model for all employees.

Dr. Joseph Matta is survived by his wife, Karen, and three lovely children, Joseph, LeAnn, and John.

CONTENTS

FOREWORD

Much has been said about what's wrong with relationships today, helping couples and families realize the forces and stress in their daily lives that impact—and interfere—with their happiness. But many times, knowing what the problem is, and specific exercises as solutions, does not fully solve what's wrong. Why? Because there are deeper issues at work, boiling beneath the surface, lurking in the time-honored but too-lately-neglected "unconscious." In other words, what you don't know *can* hurt you! In this age of quick fixes and behavioral solutions, unconscious factors at play in relationships need to be honored, recognized, and dealt with. Fortunately, Dr. William Matta brings these unconscious dynamics to light in this engaging and refreshing insight into how to solve relationship problems by becoming aware of the underlying issues that escape the conscious mind. As an eclectic therapist myself, I appreciate the cognitive-behavioral exercises to approach and solve problems that are included in the book for a full perspective. After three decades of experience I am convinced that the deeper understanding of analytic concepts of the unconscious, the underlying premise and focus in this book, placed in a perspective of relational therapy and other theoretical approaches, is crucial to good therapeutic practice and also to clients' lasting change. This integration makes this book a valuable resource for professionals and the public, to "make the unconscious conscious" and to recognize and therefore overcome the dynamics at play that can sabotage relationships between couples and in families.

Dr. Judy Kuriansky
Series Editor

ACKNOWLEDGMENTS

I would like to thank Mr. Ed Igle, LCSW, for his contribution by writing chapter 9, "Extramarital Affairs—Silence, Secrets, and Self-Disclosure."

I also thank Mr. Daniel Hoffman, LCSW, and Mrs. Tami Grovatt-Dawkins, LPC: Daniel Hoffman for his contribution by writing chapter 10, "Addictions— A Vain Attempt to Make Us Feel Whole," and Mrs. Tami Grovatt for the partial submission and research of chapter 12, "Emotional Detachment—The Ultimate Relational Destroyer."

Special thanks to my office personnel, Ms. Megan Nisula, for her patience and ability to make sense of my notes and for the endless hours transcribing the manuscript.

Thanks to Mrs. Gloria DiStefano for the technical review of the manuscript.

Last, I am grateful to the following for making the book possible: Mr. Martin Edsell, Mr. Michael Haas, Mrs. Alexia Matta, Mr. Kyle Matta, Mr. Lee Matta, Mr. James O'Rourke, and Mr. Lou Procacci.

PREFACE

Many people get divorced or destroy relationships, and they don't even know why. This disturbing reality is the pivotal concept of this book.

In this book the focus is on unconscious factors that can eventually destroy a marriage or relationship. The repressed feelings and emotions that lie just beneath the surface of our awareness often play havoc with, or can even obliterate, relationships.

The idea for the book developed from a small seed six years ago. I was in a meeting with a number of therapists, and one of the therapists was describing a scenario regarding a case where a husband was screaming at his wife and even actually threw an ashtray at her. The police were called in by the neighbors to calm down the domestic incident. As the officers arrested the man and took him away, neither spouse really understood what had happened. Why did he become so violent? All they were doing at the time was cooking dinner together. The couple had been married for two years, and although they had disagreements, there was never any earlier physical abuse.

As therapists in the meeting discussed the case, it became apparent that what was being played out was a clear example of projective identification. He was unconsciously projecting onto his spouse unresolved anger toward his mother. When he was a child, his mother was often emotionally abusive when he "didn't do things just right." While they were cooking, his wife inadvertently criticized him, and he reacted angrily.

In reality, he never confronted his mother for the harsh treatment, but he was more than able to take his hostility out on his wife.

As we discussed this case, it occurred to me that most partners are not aware that such unconscious mechanisms exist, let alone understand how hidden forces can sabotage and destroy normal, healthy, functioning relationships. Many therapists' therapeutic training and orientation focuses on conscious, overt behaviors and interactions between couples, and they fail to fully understand the true latent meaning behind seemingly bizarre behavior.

Here you will discover how our unconscious imprints can be the hidden driving forces behind our children's acting-out behaviors, marital games, extramarital affairs, addictions, and even emotional detachment disorders.

This book will not only identify the unconscious forces that ruin relationships, it will expose these forces and make them transparent. The book also provides proven techniques and interventions to help you acquire and sustain rewarding and meaningful relationships.

Included are real-life case studies. The contributing authors and I discuss proven techniques and material that we have, over the years, gathered from noted professionals in the mental health field.

Chapter One

WHAT PEOPLE BRING TO COUNSELING IS OFTEN NOT THE REAL PROBLEM

John, age 46, and Mary, age 42, wanted family counseling because their 16-year-old daughter was out of control; she was fighting with others and was cutting classes.

Another man, Joe, age 42, entered the office because his wife demanded that he seek counseling—she caught him leaving a porn shop.

Luis and Carmella initiated counseling because according to Luis, he had an affair and felt tremendous guilt, and he wanted to save the marriage.

All three of these cases are the result of unconscious forces at work—the repressed feelings and emotions that lie just beneath the surface of awareness. In this book I will often refer to these unconscious forces as negative "psychological imprints." I call them imprints because these feelings are strongly etched into our psyches. These negative psychological imprints often wreak havoc with interpersonal relationships.

In the case of John and Mary, adolescents will revolt against their parents as part of their natural development. The revolt is part of the normal maturational process translated into a struggle for power with their parents. Adolescents, in an attempt to gain little measures of control over the rules that govern them, are supposed to look for ways to circumvent the authority of their parents. The agenda of the adolescents is to reform the parent. In my practice I see many teenagers and tell the parents not to take their child's revolt personally, but to direct it in socially acceptable ways. Adolescents are attempting to create their own realities. When they find vulnerable areas in the boundaries set by their parents, they rush to seize power and overthrow parental control. At times like this the father and mother need to align and back each other in setting limits and boundaries.

However, I too often see parents undermine each other's authority. For unconscious reasons beneath his or her awareness, a parent will side with the child to help the child win power struggles. For example, a father whose mother was too controlling may unconsciously join the mother-child clashes on the side of the child to defeat the mother. A mother whose father was abusive may unconsciously rescue the child from the father whenever the father attempts to set limits for the child.

In the case of John and Mary, Mary's alcoholic father emotionally abused her, and no one came to her rescue. In her adult family, when John would move to correct his teenage daughter, Mary would often side with her daughter. Such actions would infuriate John, and this would only serve to reinforce Mary's negative feeling of men as role models. In the meantime, the daughter, by dividing and conquering, was able to "get her way" and do what she wanted to do.

John and Mary initiated counseling because they were constantly arguing, and their daughter was out of control. However, in reality, on the unconscious level Mary was undermining John's authority as a father. The coalition that Mary and her daughter had developed would be difficult to dissolve, and this alignment would weigh heavily on John and Mary's marriage. On the conscious level Mary was only doing what she thought was best for her daughter. On the unconscious level she was trying to rescue herself.

Joe, like many addicts, came from a dysfunctional family. Joe's father was an alcoholic, and he was unable to offer love to Joe. On the other hand, Joe's mother's emotional time was preoccupied in vain attempts to please her husband. Joe came from an emotionally deprived family, in which love was not expressed and was conditional. "Conditional" in this context means that Joe had to achieve the aspirations his parents had for themselves but never realized. The parents fell short of their own goals and required that Joe reach for what they did not achieve. Joe did not receive love and approval, and he lacked self-esteem. His self-worth became based on the opinions others held of him. In Joe's family, compliments were rare and were seen as a form of weakness, and as a result, Joe felt he was a bad, unworthy person. Joe was also labeled in the family as lazy and inept and became shrouded in a story that said he would never amount to anything. Joe, at an early age, was on his way to becoming some kind of an addict: he had a void that needed to be filled. Addiction has to do with searching for something outside of us to make us feel whole. Remember, what people present at counseling is often not the real problem. Joe's sexual addiction was not about pornography; it was about repressed feelings of loneliness, unworthiness, and powerlessness. Joe was trying to fill those holes with the phony validation he would get from viewing pornography but to no avail because the holes remain.

Luis, age 34, and Carmella, age 32, were married for 11 years, and they had a child that was three years old. Luis initiated counseling because he felt guilty that he had had an extramarital affair. As the story evolved, I was surprised to learn that the affair took place 14 years ago, three years before they were engaged. Luis related that they had had a good marriage but that the affair was causing stress in their marriage. Actually, all was going smoothly for the couple before their child, Ramon, was born. Naturally, Carmella, being a nurturing mother, had to spend a lot of time taking care of Ramon. The time that used to be exclusively dedicated to Luis was now lavished onto the baby. This reduction of care from Carmella was perceived as abandonment and neglect. It just so happened that Luis's parents had migrated from Central America to New York when he was three years old and had left him in the care of his aunt, who had little time for him. Consequently, those unconscious and repressed feelings of abandonment were surfacing once again. What he was presenting as the problem, the affair, was actually a plea for attention from his wife. Had Luis and Carmella been able to organize problem-solving conversations regarding his need for more attention, they could have avoided a long, unproductive journey down memory lane and addressed their real issues.

People are not stupid. Most of my clients are gainfully employed, intelligent, and are able to deal with life. Why are they not consciously aware of their problems? They have repressed into their unconscious anxiety or guilt about certain impulses, ideas, or memories that they feel are unacceptable or dangerous to express. In essence, the unconscious protects us, pushing painful or dangerous thoughts out of consciousness, thus keeping them unconscious. Therefore, often, the problems that people present in counseling are masking the true meaning of their anxieties and the true nature of their troubles.

A classic example of the facts that both what people present to counseling is often not the problem and how unconscious forces can destroy a marriage is that of John, age 54, and Kristen, age 52. They entered counseling because, as they described it, their relationship was "like a roller coaster ride." Initially, I was not sure what they meant by that statement, but it became clear as the essence of their marital problems revealed itself.

Kristen was married two times before she met John. Her first marriage lasted three years, and her second marriage lasted five years. John was married once prior to Kristen. He was first married at age 16, and this marriage lasted 18 years. Kristen and John had been married for 19 years. They had two children of their own, ages 16 and 18. They both had children from their previous marriages that were older and out of the house.

What Kristen presented in counseling as the major problem was that when she and John argued, John not only withdrew emotionally, but withdrew from the family, and that he left the home and buried himself in work.

John complained that Kristen was not taking him seriously. He often related that Kristen would ignore him and that she would often scream at him.

Issues in the relationship were never resolved. When a problem needed to be discussed, typically, John withdrew, and Kristen pursued. Therefore in Kristen's eyes John was apathetic toward their marriage, and in John's eyes Kristen was always nagging him.

Without intervention, this unconscious pattern of self-defeating behavior eventually would have destroyed their marriage. Each partner would blame the other, and they both would leave the arguments feeling unheard and unloved.

As a therapist, I needed to uncover the hidden, underlying conflicts at the core of their relationship. Some of the questions that needed to be answered were, Why had their previous marriages failed? What did they mean by the statement that their relationship was "like a roller coaster ride"? What purpose did John's obsession with work serve? Why couldn't they resolve their issues? What were the unconscious dynamics that threatened to destroy their marriage?

Within a few sessions I gradually learned that Kristen's father abandoned the family when she was seven years old. Early emotional scars tend to taint our perception and discolor our reality unless they are resolved. We tend to see things as we are and not as they are. In this case Kristen learned to make preemptive strikes against abandonment by asserting her needs and proclaiming her self-sufficiency.

John, on the other hand, came from a large family. He had two brothers and four sisters, and John was the middle child. He felt lost and, as he put it, "insignificant." As a child, John would often lose in arguments with his more articulate sisters. He learned to protect himself from hurt by shutting down and becoming uncommunicative.

Whenever the couple needed to discuss emotionally charged issues, John would withdraw, become quiet, and feel isolated. Under similar circumstances Kristen would feel inadequate and abandoned. Kristen also felt a desperate need to try to solve the problems because she didn't want another failed marriage.

On the unconscious level, whenever there was a dispute, John would protect himself by withdrawing, and Kristen would protect herself by attacking John. Then John would become even more distancing in order to avoid her wrath.

After a while, this self-defeating cycle became their way of dealing with problems. This pattern would repeat itself over and over again. No wonder they described their relationship as a roller coaster ride.

In essence, Kristen's abandonment issues and John's fear of obliteration were the unconscious imprints at the core of their past and present relationship problems. It was the primary cause of Kristen's previously failed marriage. It was also at the core of John's long hours at work: volunteering extra hours made him feel significant.

As their therapy progressed, Kristen and John became more and more aware of how the negative imprints that lay beneath their conscious levels almost destroyed their marriage. They also learned through counseling, as I will discuss in chapter 8, how to organize problem-solving conversations.

A dramatic and often fatal example of the fact that what people bring to counseling is often not the real problem is the case of Sharon. Sharon, age 19, was brought to counseling by her mother. Sharon was eating irregularly and rapidly losing weight. After a few sessions Sharon was diagnosed as having anorexia nervosa.

Anorexia nervosa is about more than food. It has to do with being a perfectionist, all-or-none thinking, and control.

A few of the symptoms of anorexia nervosa are the refusal to maintain body weight at or above a normal weight for age and height, an intense fear of gaining weight, even though underweight, a denial of the seriousness of the current low body weight, and, in postmenarcheal females, the absence of at least three menstrual cycles.

Sharon lived with her biological parents and had two younger sisters. Her father was an alcoholic. He owned a small chain of clothing stores. Her mother was a homemaker. Sharon was highly intelligent and a good student. Sharon was a college student majoring in biology. She planned to go to medical school. Sharon's mother initiated counseling. At first Sharon was hesitant to seek help. However, I was able to establish rapport during the initial session, and Sharon agreed to continue. When I first met her, she weighed 98 pounds and was 5' 10" tall. She was exercising two to three hours a day, which is typical for anorexia nervosa. She felt obsessed about losing weight because when she looked in the mirror, she saw a 200-pound fat lady, also typical for this disorder. She would normally sit with a salad and push the salad around with a fork, rarely taking a bite. She didn't have her menstrual cycle for months, and her body hair was growing longer. Sharon was not in denial: she knew she had a problem but didn't know how to solve it.

Like most anorexic persons, Sharon was a perfectionist. She had to be perfect at everything she did. She was an A student, a good athlete, and she wanted the perfect body. In her mind the perfect body weighed 80 pounds. (Incidentally, I often counsel people who think there is a big difference between being perfect and doing the best that you can. Being perfect is obsessive, while doing the best you can is human.)

Also, people with anorexia need to be in control. Many come from dysfunctional, out-of-control families, and therefore as adults, they need to be in control. Eventually, they discover that they can't control their outer worlds, so they control their food intake, or better yet, their lack of intake.

People with anorexia are difficult to counsel. They are as difficult or more difficult to counsel than people with alcoholism. Most are in denial, and they see the world from a distorted perspective. Many even die from lack of nourishment. Luckily, Sharon eventually decided that she wanted to change and also to live. For Sharon, as for most people suffering from anorexia, it would be an uphill struggle.

However, Sharon's treatment progressed at a steady rate. In addition to counseling, she was seeing a nutritionist, and she was medicated with Prozac. Prozac is often the medication of choice for these types of obsessive-compulsive disorders. Today, Sharon is doing fine. She has learned to cope with her disorder, she has gained weight, and she is happy with her life. She is presently attending medical school.

Last, one of the most astounding examples of the idea of what people present to counseling is not often the problem is that of Joey, age 12. Joey was in the 5th grade at a local parochial school. Joey's father died in a car accident when he was seven years old. His mother was a college professor. Joey had two younger brothers. Being the older brother, Joey was very responsible since he naturally had to take care of his younger brothers. Joey was an excellent student, a good athlete, and was very popular.

All was going well for Joey until, during the 5th grade, he came down with a case of mononucleosis, an illness that kept him out of school for more than three weeks. After three weeks Joey was all set to return to school, but the night before he returned to school, he accidentally slipped on a rug in the family room. The next morning, when he got out of bed to go to school, he collapsed on the floor. Apparently, he also suffered from anxiety, and his hands would continually quiver. It was disastrous—Joey couldn't return to school in that condition. The whole family was in a panic.

When I initially saw Joey, he had been out of school for six weeks. When his mother made the appointment, she described her son as having anxiety and panic attacks. However, when I escorted Joey into the office, I was surprised to see that Joey could barely walk. He literally was crippled. During the initial session I learned that Joey did have an extensive evaluation by a neurosurgeon and a medical doctor. The evaluation indicated that there was no physiological or neurological damage. The report confirmed what I had expected: Joey was suffering from a rare disorder called conversion disorder. Conversion disorder is a form of neurosis in which anxiety is unconsciously converted to a significant physical loss such as paralysis, deafness, and so forth. However, there is no organic basis for the problem.

It's very natural for a therapist in private practice to encounter such a disorder. It is a defense mechanism that usually occurs in wartime. For example, a soldier has a choice to fight or possibly get killed and be called a coward, ergo the person goes blind—the conflict is resolved.

In Joey's case he had been out of school for so long that he feared the ramifications of his absence. In his mind the ramifications of possible conflict were numerous. What also contributed to Joey's problem is that the avoidance of anything feared is reinforcing in itself; that is, the longer he avoided going to school, the more difficult it became for him to go back.

What people bring to counseling is often not the real problem; they are looking for a solution for their present conflicts, while the therapist is searching for a solution to the conflicts embedded in their past. The task of therapy is to bridge the gap between their current conflicts and their embedded, unconscious conflicts. The therapist's task is, also, to uncover the latent meaning behind the unconscious conflicts that ruin relationships. The therapist attempts to make unconscious transactions transparent and provide techniques and interventions to help clients acquire and sustain meaningful relationships.

Chapter Two

THE UNCONSCIOUS MIND—FRIEND OR FOE?

The unconscious mind contains memories, wishes, and feelings of which we are not aware.

Sigmund Freud theorized that people have three levels of awareness: the conscious, the preconscious, and the unconscious.[1] The conscious mind consists of whatever one is aware of at a particular time. For example, you are consciously aware that you and your spouse are arguing again. The preconscious contains material just beneath the surface but nonetheless exerts great influence on behavior. For example, a wife is still angry at her husband for getting drunk at their wedding. The unconscious withholds feelings, memories, and desires that are well buried below the surface of conscious awareness. Psychological conflicts, tensions, and anxieties stem, in large part, from these unconscious sources.

Carl Jung, like Freud, placed great emphasis on the unconscious role in determining one's personality. However, he viewed the unconscious as having two layers: the personal unconscious and the collective unconscious. The personal unconscious encompasses all personal experiences and feelings not within one's conscious awareness that are repressed or forgotten. The collective unconscious is the storehouse of mythological associations or latent memory traces inherited from people's ancestral past. According to Jung, every individual shares the collective unconscious with the entire human race.

Jung also states, "It is certain that consciousness consists not only of wishes and fears, but of vastly more than these, and it is highly probable that the unconscious psyche contains a wealth of contents and living forms equal to or even greater than does consciousness, which is characterized by concentration, limitation and exclusion."[2] This wealth of content that lies just beneath our awareness can be responsible for numerous relationship conflicts on the conscious level.

Many mental activities and contents exist partly or wholly below conscious awareness, and much of our behavior is determined by them. Marital conflicts, tensions, and anxieties stem, in a large part, from these unconscious sources. Many marital feelings, decisions, and behaviors as well as our impassive and frequently unexplained reactions to other people stem from the unconscious mind.

Many of our conflicts are played out entirely beneath our conscious awareness. These safety devices are automatically called to action to protect ourselves from anxiety, guilt, or loss of self-esteem. These reactions serve a number of purposes. They reduce emotional conflict, protect the self against its own dangerous impulses, alleviate the effects of traumatic experiences, soften our disappointments, and, in general, help us maintain a sense of personal worth. Generally, we are not aware of this defensive behavior, and we have little, if any, realization of the anxiety and "ego threat" that lie behind it. A goal of psychotherapy is to bring these unconscious ego defense mechanisms into the open since this is an important means of increasing the individual's insight into himself.

At the root of the unconscious are the ego defense mechanisms. The ego defense mechanisms, as the name implies, are self-regulating, automatic attempts to defend the ego when it feels threatened. They are a common, often healthy way to reduce anxiety. However, these complex transactions are played out beneath our conscious awareness. Obviously, if many behaviors and relationship transactions are evoked at the unconscious level, it is no wonder why so many relationships are self-defeating. One of the defense mechanisms is called repression. Repression is the automatic psychological process that functions to protect us from experiencing extreme anxiety or guilt. Repression protects us from feelings and memories that are extremely harmful and hurtful. During my experiences as a therapist, many women have expressed to me that they suspected they had been sexually abused and that they only saw the true picture when they were in a hospital for some sort of operation. It appears that the anesthetic often serves as a hypnotic drug, and the horrific, repressed experience surfaces to the conscious level. It is unfortunate that recent research suggests that one in three girls and one in five boys are sexually abused by the age of 18.[3] More often than not, the abuser is a relative: a stepfather, uncle, or stepbrother.

Reaction formation is another defense mechanism that prevents unacceptable or dangerous desires from being expressed by acting in a manner opposite to one's true feelings.[4] For example, a mother unconsciously resents her child, but such feelings are unacceptable by society, and the mother unconsciously masks these feelings by becoming overindulgent. The overindulgence is not undertaken for the sake of the child but rather as a psychological necessity for the sake of the mother. The crusaders against pornography, alcohol, and homosexuality may also be inwardly fighting their own repressed urges. By utilizing reaction formation, we are protecting ourselves from our own unacceptable feelings and desires through behavior that is opposite to our hidden unconscious feelings.

Not all zealous behavior and righteous concerns are expressions of reaction formation. As in most areas of psychology, there are fine lines that distinguish terms. The key indicator of reaction formation is usually clear: the behavior is exaggerated, uncompromising, and often inappropriate. Reaction formation behavior is unending, oversolicitous, and fanatical. In reality, our feelings toward our loved ones—as well as toward most things in life—fluctuate. At times we feel close to our spouse and children, and at other times we don't. Moreover, the overt behavior may provide a disguise or an outlet for the very tendencies it appears to oppose. The stark opposer of homosexuality may actually enjoy reading male pornographic magazines.

Reaction formation not only leads to behavior that interferes with relationships but also infringes on other people because its overzealous expression often alienates other people.

As a marriage and family therapist, an unconscious self-defeating behavior that I encounter is one spouse's unconscious projection onto the other spouse's unresolved issues from his family of origin. For example, when Joan and Fred would have an argument, Joan would get quiet and withdraw emotionally from Fred. Fred, on the other hand, would get furious over her withdrawal, and in turn, Joan would further withdraw and withhold her love. Every time they had a heated argument, this self-defeating cycle would repeat itself. What was revealed during counseling was that as a child, when Joan would misbehave, her father would retaliate by exploding and then withholding his love. Fred's explosion served to resurrect Joan's unresolved, unconscious abandonment feelings. Because of the unconscious dynamic involved in their interactions, this couple was not able to organize problem-solving conversations and resolve their issues without counseling.

Lin and Ming-Sue were a professional couple in their mid-forties that had been married for two years. Ming-Sue was married once before meeting Lin, and Lin was married once prior to this marriage. They also learned poor ways of dealing with problems because frequently, their arguments developed into days of not talking to each other. When they fought, Lin would often get loud and demonstrative. This behavioral pattern would only infuriate Ming-Sue, and then Lin would storm out of the house and stay away for hours. This act of leaving home would only serve to reinforce her feelings that when life got tough, the man would take off, just as her dad did to her and her mother when she was a small child. On the unconscious level Ming-Sue was still hurt and angry that her father deserted her and her mother years ago. She hadn't seen her dad in years and was not given the opportunity to vent her anger directly to him. However, when her husband demonstrated similar behavioral patterns, she unconsciously projected those unresolved feelings onto her husband. In fact, Ming-Sue unconsciously engineered altercations to relieve this repressed rage.

These are examples of projective identification. This defense mechanism enables us to express unresolved family-of-origin anger but, unfortunately, at the expense of the partner. Many therapists feel that a couple's relationship inevitably resembles the parent-child relationship that the partners experienced in their families of origin. Troubled marriages often carry negative imprints or memories from past relationships with members of the previous generations residing in each partner. These unresolved imprints not only cause marital conflicts within the couple, but these conflicts tend to be passed along to their own children, who will also have similar problems in their own relationships.

Only by gaining insight into their destructive, unconscious, dynamic forces can a couple learn to develop healthy adult relationships and parenting skills. Otherwise, this self-defeating behavioral cycle will continue to repeat itself over and over again.

As a therapist, I observe how destructive, relational patterns are transmitted unconsciously from generation to generation. I have seen many examples of how mothers who lacked adequate mothering or fathers who lacked satisfactory fathering behave inappropriately as parents because they have no internal model to follow. These parenting deficiencies repeat themselves over several generations.

These parents also develop unrealistic expectations toward others. Quite often, the deficient woman or man will select a spouse that she or he imagines will fill in the void. Each partner seeks to create, through marriage, a way to heal his or her childhood wounds. In such an arrangement, both partners want to play the role of the wounded child, which often leads to frustration and struggles for weakness. One consequence of the struggle is that when these partners become parents, they often project the deficiencies onto their child, and they attempt to save the marriage at the expense of the child. Also, the child feels an unconscious responsibility for saving the marriage and the family.

A case in point is the marriage of Maria, age 36, and Lawrence, age 40. They had two children, Kathy, age 14, and Larry, age 12. After taking their case history I learned that both Maria and Lawrence came from unnurturing families and that both Maria and Lawrence, in a self-defeating way, were attempting to heal their childhood wounds. They projected their misgivings onto Kathy, who was the more emotionally sensitive of the two children. Kathy was acting out in school, her grades were slipping, she was disruptive in the classroom, and she had many altercations with other children.

On the unconscious level Kathy was acting out to draw attention away from the parents' discord onto herself. The concept of acting out is best understood by the statement, "we often relate to others to dissolve difficult emotions from within ourselves." Kathy, for example, was laden with unconscious tension and fear about what was going on between her parents, but she could not put it into words. Her acting out served two purposes: relieving her tension, while at the same time drawing attention away from the conflict between her parents. Kathy's acting out was self-defeating behavior. It did not resolve the conflict between the parents and only added to her own distress. Without therapy, parenting deficiencies will repeat themselves over generations.

Scapegoating is another unconscious mechanism that I often encounter in marriage and family counseling. Many children are assigned roles in the family that distinguish them from the other children. Examples of such roles would be the people-pleaser, the overachiever, the underachiever, the disturbed child, and the loner. Many therapists feel that unconsciously, the family serves to further perpetuate pathology by assigning and scripting these roles. The dynamics involved in the following case revolve around the homeostasis or balance in the family. The family is unknowingly driven to perpetuate the pathology.

One such example involved a 15-year-old boy from one of the local high schools. Johnny was acting out in school, he was failing many of his subjects, he was cutting his classes, and he was caught smoking marijuana. Up to age 13, Johnny was a good student. Also, he had a high IQ and as a child, he wanted to be a doctor.

Johnny lived with his biological parents. He had a younger brother, Albert, age 13, and a sister, Alicia, age 10. The role that Johnny played in the family was that of the underachiever and the troublemaker. Albert was a good student and did not give the parents any real problems. Alicia was the ideal child. She was an A student, a cheerleader, and was extremely popular.

Johnny was scapegoated as the "problem child." Johnny was very successful in playing the role. He hung around a bad crowd that would, on a daily basis, smoke marijuana and steal from local stores. When his parents would confront him about his behavior, he would often have outbursts, punch holes in the wall, throw furniture, and storm out of the house.

What was revealed in family therapy was that Johnny was scapegoated for problems that existed between the mother and the father, and Johnny got used to playing the role of the "troubled child." Under the surface it was revealed that the husband was tired of hearing the wife complain and got satisfaction from the conflict between mother and child. On the other hand, the mother, who always doubted herself and went to the husband for advice, was projecting part of her anger onto Johnny. In this family these self-defeating transactions were a safer way to deal with problems than having a conversation that might open up Pandora's box.

Johnny's behavior was purposeful and, in a self-defeating way, effective. It served to focus attention onto him and away from the underlying conflicts between the husband and wife. Also, he was carrying the pathology for the entire family. However, all members benefit from the pathological dynamics in the family. The parents displace their discord onto the child, and the child struggles to keep the family together. As in so many cases of acting out behavior, the symptomatic behavior maintained the operation of the family. Both Albert and Alicia benefited as well since both children's minor flaws and petty mistakes were easily overshadowed by Johnny's vivid and dramatic problems.

Our unconscious can protect us from unwanted feelings and emotions but can also be the driving force behind divorce, extramarital affairs, addictions, marital games, and feelings of loneliness and isolation.

In future chapters you will not only become aware of your own unconscious, destructive forces that can play havoc with your interpersonal relationships, but you will also learn practical methods to end the psychological need to sabotage close relationships.

Chapter Three

THE MIXTURE OF UNCONSCIOUS FORCES AND CHILDHOOD WOUNDS CAN BE LETHAL TO A MARRIAGE

Jack, age 46, and Theresa, age 38, were a working middle-class couple. John was a schoolteacher, and Theresa was a nurse's aide. They had been married for nine years. They had two small girls, one age six and one nine months. Theresa complained that Jack was immature for his age, that he would forget to pay household bills, and that he would sleep late on the weekends, while she would have to get up and take care of the little one. Jack complained that Theresa was too controlling, was always angry, and never wanted to have fun. Their scenario fit perfectly into a fascinating unconscious relationship cycle that therapists often encounter called the pursuer-distancer pattern. In this dance, when problems arise, the distancer, usually the male, acts unconsciously to distance himself from the female. By the act of distancing himself, he unconsciously chooses a childlike position in the marriage.[1] All too often, I hear complaints from the wife regarding household responsibilities and chores. The pursuer, who often has been parentified in her own family of origin, is all too willing to take on the job of caretaking the distancer. Eventually, however, the pursuer becomes exhausted, angry, overwhelmed, disappointed, and aggressive to the distancer. The distancing husband runs or avoids the pursuing wife when he perceives that she is trying to dominate him.

In essence, the pursuer has once again failed to change her own father into a mature, responsible, sensitive man. The childlike distancer is perfect for the dance. The distancer, once again, unconsciously attempts to escape the perceived controlling mother, who is trying to replace her own distant or absent father. The distancer wants a mother figure, but at a distance.[2]

Interestingly enough, the couple feels comfortable carrying out these fixed behavioral patterns. Unfortunately, this dysfunctional relationship and the accompanying transactional patterns will be continued by their children.

To better understand and appreciate how family-of-origin wounds can devastate a relationship, we must travel back to our own early childhood days. As we journey through childhood, we proceed through developmental psychosocial stages.

How our parents responded to our needs greatly affects the outcome of our maturational processes. Many of us grew up with parents who met most of our needs, or they met at least some of them. All adults enter a relationship or marriage with emotional needs that were not met when they were children.[3]

Our partners make us feel anxious by stirring up forbidden parts of ourselves, especially if our partners have or are perceived to have the same negative traits as our parents.

Most mental health practitioners would agree with famous psychoanalysts like Sigmund Freud and Carl Jung that our basic personality is formed by the age of six. The building blocks of personality are analogous to the foundation on a house. If the foundation is shaky, the whole house is shaky. Therefore the first six years, and especially the first two years, are critical for healthy relational development. Do I believe people change? Yes, or I wouldn't be in this business. However, we have to realize that change is difficult, that we have to want to change, and that sometimes we need to get professional help.

To better understand this concept, one needs to become familiar with the theories of Erik Erikson.

Erikson divided the life-span into eight stages.[4] The eight stages of social and cognitive development are determined by the types of learning and social interaction that take place at each developmental stage. The individual must resolve conflicts at each stage. If the conflicts are not resolved, detrimental psychosocial traits are acquired. I personally have found the first four stages of Erikson's model to be the most crucial to understanding how these unresolved family-of-origin issues can be lethal to a marriage (table 3.1).

Erikson's first stage, trust versus mistrust, encompasses the first year of a baby's life. During this stage the baby is completely helpless and dependent on the parents to have his basic needs met. If the baby's basic biological and emotional needs are met by the caregivers, the child develops an optimistic and trusting perception of the world. However, if the child's basic needs at this stage are neglected, a more pessimistic, distrusting view of the world may result.

Erikson's second stage, autonomy versus doubt, unfolds during the second and third years of the child's life. During this time, parents begin to lead the child into taking more responsibility for himself. The child starts to feed and dress himself as well as to master toilet training. If all goes well, the child

Table 3.1
Erikson's Psychological Stages

Approximate age	Crisis	Adequate resolution	Inadequate resolution
0–1½	Trust vs. mistrust	Basic sense of safety	Insecurity, anxiety
1½–3	Autonomy vs. self-doubt	Perception of self as agent capable of controlling own body and making things happen	Feelings of inadequacy to control events
3–6	Initiative vs. guilt	Confidence in oneself as initiator, creator	Feelings of lack of self-worth
6–Puberty	Competence vs. Inferiority	Adequacy in basic social and intellectual skills	Lack of self-confidence, feelings of failure

Source: Wayne Weiton, *Psychology: Themes and Variations*, 6th ed. (Belmont, Calif.: Wadsworth, 2004), p. 639, figure 1.

develops a sense of self-sufficiency. However, if the parents are too critical or demanding of the child's efforts, the child may develop a sense of personal shame and doubt. As an adult, he may feel anxious, have low self-esteem, feel insecure, and constantly second-guess himself. Frequently, as a result of low self-esteem, the child may underestimate his abilities in all aspects of his life, including career, friends, and even the person he chooses to marry. All too often, I see teenagers with low self-esteem, and they gravitate toward other low-self-esteem teens who use drugs to bolster their egos.

Erikson's third stage, initiative versus guilt, encompasses ages three through six. In this stage the child starts to use his imagination and takes initiative for his own behavior. At this stage the child's behavior will sometimes conflict with the rules of the parents. If the parents are overcontrolling, the child may develop feelings of guilt and low self-worth. During this stage, parents need to support their child's emerging independence, while maintaining appropriate control. From my experience this is where the parents need to establish mutually agreeable, consistently applied rules with natural, logical consequences. It is crucial that the parents do not undermine each other and that they be consistent. An eye-opening recent occurrence was a couple that came in to the office and were upset because they couldn't control their two boys' bedtime. Virtually the boys would go to bed when they wanted. When I asked the mom the ages of their boys, she replied two and four. Obviously, this lack of control reflected serious problems between the husband and wife. The parents' discord and power struggle reflected their unwillingness to work together, and consequently, they were unable to properly discipline their children.

Erikson's fourth stage, industry versus inferiority, encompasses ages six through puberty. It entails learning social skills beyond the family setting to broadened realms such as the neighborhood, church, and school. In this stage the child learns the value of achievement and learns to take pride and achieve a sense of competence.

A typical example of how I would apply Erikson's concepts to marital therapy is the case of Charles, age 50, and Marion, age 42. They had been married for 20 years, and they had two girls, ages 14 and 16. As the counseling progressed, I discovered that Charles had learned not to trust others, while Marion suffered from low self-esteem. Their first two years of marriage were happy, but matters got complicated, and their marriage deteriorated when Marion decided she wanted to return to college and complete her degree. One night, Charles picked her up at school and saw her talking to a male student. Charles became outraged and badgered her until she stopped going to school. They fought for weeks over this matter. Unconsciously, what was happening was that Charles's lack of trust, which he learned by the age of one, surfaced when he saw Marion talking to another man, and Marion's lack of self-esteem was exacerbated by not furthering her education.

Instead of executing this self-defeating cycle, their relationship would have improved if Charles had sanctioned Marion's need for an education and if Marion had discussed Charles's misconceptions about her colleague, thereby allaying Charles's insecurity. But once again, unconscious forces, left to run rampant by each spouse's difficulty in negotiating early life stages, made such a rational compromise impossible.

From my experience as a marriage counselor, when spouses attempt to heal each other's childhood wounds, the relationship is enhanced. For example, if the husband's primary wound in his family of origin is insecurity, as long as the wife makes him feel more secure, he is content. Conversely, if the wife's primary wound is a need for love and belonging, as long as the husband makes her feel loved, she feels more content. If each partner does not attempt to heal each other's childhood wounds, the relationship will feel unfulfilling and unsatisfactory to both parties.

Howard, age 24, and Melanie, age 21, were only married for a year when they entered marriage counseling. They had no children, and Howard wasn't sure if he even wanted children, even though prior to getting married, he often talked about having a family.

During the sessions Howard would often make comments to the effect that his marriage "will never last," while Melanie's retort would be "he doesn't care about me." Eventually, I learned that Howard's parents divorced when he was only three years old. He and his younger sister lived with their mother in a one-bedroom apartment. Howard's mother struggled financially during his early childhood and throughout his adolescence. At times his mother would get laid off from the factory. What made matters worse is that Howard's father claimed bankruptcy, and he rarely paid child support. Howard's mother often took his father to court. He would pay child support for a while, then stop paying. What Howard always needed during his early years—but rarely received—was security.

Melanie came from a large family. She had three older brothers and a younger sister. Melanie's family emigrated from Europe when Melanie was five years of age. Her father was an engineer, and her mother was a homemaker. Melanie's older brothers were good students, however, Melanie struggled academically. Education was an important value to her parents. She tried to compensate for her academic deficiencies in other ways. She was very popular, a cheerleader, and participated in many school activities. However, this was not good enough for her parents, especially for her mom. Her mother had a need for Melanie to be an excellent student like her brothers. Although Melanie tried to be a good student, she was "never good enough."

What Howard needed as a child and rarely received was security; what Melanie needed as a child and rarely received was validation. Remember, relationships will perpetuate as long as we attempt to heal each other's childhood wounds. Therefore whenever Howard argued with Melanie or implied she wasn't good enough, those negative family-of-origin imprints would be resurrected in Melanie. Conversely, whenever Melanie would behave in such a way as to make Howard feel insecure, his negative childhood imprints would resurface.

As a case in point, Melanie, on occasion, when they would have an argument that they could not resolve, would not talk to Howard for days. This withdrawal of her love would confuse Howard, and he would question whether she planned to leave him. These feelings served to deepen embedded wounds of insecurity. Also, these quiet spells would frustrate Howard, and he would, at times, resort to calling her names, like "stupid." These transactional patterns would serve to further emotionally distance the couple.

As a therapist, I observe that most couples are not consciously aware of how their unconscious imprints can negatively impact their relationship. Their repressed feelings, lying beneath the surface of awareness, play havoc with relationships.

In order to reverse their path of destruction, Melanie and Howard had first to become consciously aware of their own childhood wounds and then become willing to help heal each other's wounds.

UNRESOLVED WOUNDS AND A MARRIAGE THAT NEVER TOOK PLACE

Recently, a young man, Thomas, age 30, commenced counseling, and he related a distressing scenario regarding his wife-to-be, Jackie, age 28. Thomas was extremely distraught, anxious, and clinically depressed over the upcoming marriage. Thomas and Jackie had dated for over two years, were recently engaged, and were soon to be married. Jackie's family had even paid for the reception and other expenses.

Even though Thomas and Jackie were constantly arguing, Jackie was anxiously planning for her wedding day. Jackie often explained to Thomas that she was raised to vent her angry feelings and that after these explosions she felt better, and then the situation was forgotten. However, her explosive nature was not easily forgotten by Thomas. All too often, Jackie, in the heat of the argument, would say things that she would later regret. Thomas was having second thoughts about the marriage because of these frequent, hostile altercations. Also, Thomas was starting to feel smothered by Jackie's constant need for reassurance. They had a major blowup over the fact that for years Thomas would take a four-day fishing trip with his family once a year, and Jackie would not hear of it. Jackie felt that they should spend all of their free time together, and when they weren't together, she would call him sometimes as many as five to seven times a day.

Jackie came from critical and demanding parents. Jackie had an older sister, who excelled at most endeavors. In addition to being an honor student, the sister was a good athlete and later became a successful businesswoman. Jackie's mother especially would make derogatory comparisons between Jackie and her sister. Over the years Jackie developed low self-esteem as well as a sense of personal shame and doubt.

From the information that Thomas was relating it appeared that Jackie's negative imprints beneath her conscious awareness were causing grave emotional conflict in her relationship with Thomas. What made matters worse was that when she experienced these negative feelings, she would get even more possessive in an attempt to manage her own anger and fear. Such behaviors only served to further distance Thomas, and his distance would only further fuel her desperate attempts to meet her unconscious needs—and the cycle would go on and on.

At the same time, another dynamic was taking place. As we'll see in chapter 4, people tend to select a mate who is on the same level of self-differentiation; that is, emotional people marry emotional people, and the more intellectual types marry intellectuals. In the case of Thomas and Jackie, Jackie was extremely emotional, and Thomas scored high on the intellectual scale. As a result of such differences, the prognosis for a successful marriage was poor.

What further complicated matters was that Jackie did not believe in counseling, and she would have no part of it. Jackie would never learn how her unconscious needs would negatively impact her life. She would never really understand why the marriage would never take place.

Chapter Four

YOUR FAMILY PROBLEMS MAY HAVE STARTED BACK IN MEDIEVAL TIMES

Our emotional stability is at the mercy of our ancestors. Dysfunctional behavior is transmitted from generation to generation without the awareness of the participants. Pathology often correlates to the emotional composite of our descendants.

Murray Bowen's model of family therapy focuses on the concept of differentiation of self.[1] Bowen focuses on the importance of self-development, intergenerational issues, and the significance of the past to the present-day interactions of the family unit. The differentiation of self is the ability to separate our thoughts about ourselves and others from our feelings about them. Self-differentiation enables an individual to resist being consumed by the emotional reactivity of his or her family. Bowen proposed that self-differentiation can actually be quantified and scaled from 0 to 100 (figure 4.1).

People on the lower level of the scale, "fusion," are likely to be very emotional when they are in a situation in which everybody else is very emotional. Fusion represents a lack of self-differentiation. Decisions are based on feelings rather than on facts and beliefs. People at this lower end of the scale are likely to have problems in every aspect of their lives. People at this fused end are dominated by the needs of those around them. They are controlled by emotions that dominate the family and react automatically on an emotional level to situations.

Individuals on the higher level of self-differentiation are more prone to use their intellect and sort out their feelings from the feelings of the people around them. These people can allow themselves to respond emotionally but are capable of using their intellect when necessary. They are more able to separate their

Figure 4.1
Bowen's Continuum of Self-differentiation

thoughts from their feelings. However, they are not afraid to lose themselves in intimacy and close relationships.

At the higher level of self-differentiation, important life decisions are carefully considered. There is a greater ability to delay gratification. On the other hand, people on the lower level of self-differentiation are more impulsive in life, and long-term goals are chosen haphazardly.[2]

Integral to how family problems may have started back in medieval times is the concept of triangulation, as also developed by Bowen.

A two-party system is very unstable. For example, if you are having problems with your boss, you are likely to pull in another coworker on your side to confirm your opinion that the boss is at fault. Or, if you are having problems with a friend, you might encourage other friends to align with you against the person. This new alignment is called triangulation, and it serves to dilute anxiety.[3]

The process of triangulation is completely unconscious and virtually inevitable in families. Yet, sometimes families can pay a very high price for the emotional relief it provides. A classic example is the mother-father-child triangle.

A mother and father may be having marital difficulties that they cannot discuss openly and honestly. The fact that the difficulties are present in the marital relationship creates tension in each parent. Some children are more sensitive to tension in their parents than other children and may even select themselves to unconsciously "help" the parents by acting out and drawing negative emotion toward themselves. One parent or the other—sadly, in my experience it is usually the mother—discharges (marital) tension toward the child rather than toward the marital partner, often by projecting blame onto the child for her own lack of support from the other parent.

This process facilitates emotional stability between the parents but has devastating effects on the child's development. It has always intrigued me that such dysfunctional interactions can become systematic and serve the whole family because the child unconsciously learns to play a useful but inappropriate role in regulating the stress between the parents. However, when the stress decreases, emotional stability returns to the couple, and the child often feels lonely and isolated. The cycle plays itself out over and over again, so when anxiety increases between the couple, and they experience stress, they find fault not with each other, but with a child. Many systems will have more than one scapegoat, who will automatically be blamed when something goes wrong and stress rises within the family.

Generally speaking, the higher the degree of family fusion, the more intense are the efforts to triangulate a child, and the least well-differentiated person is particularly vulnerable to being drawn in to reduce the tension within the family. Usually, within the family the most sensitive child is triangulated. If the situation is intense enough, other siblings can be involved. The invested child develops a heightened sensitivity to emotional pain in the parents, who react in the manner described previously. Other brothers and sisters tend to be less sensitive to parental emotions. They grow up with a greater degree of separation between thinking and feeling. They are somewhat more differentiated than the more compromised sibling. They tend to learn more from the parents' strengths. The involved child learns about and simulates the parents' emotional immaturity, and the cycle is projected onto the next generation. Thus the legacy of dysfunction is perpetuated.

Bowen postulates that people will marry on the same level of self-differentiation; emotional individuals will tend to marry a more emotional spouse, and more intellectual types marry a higher level of self-differentiated individuals. As each generation produces individuals with poor differentiation, these people become increasingly vulnerable to anxiety and fusion.[4] Over generations this type of family dysfunction can eventually lead to severe mental disorders and chronic substance abuse.

A case that exemplifies the concepts of poor self-differentiation and triangulation is that of the D family. Billy D was a 14-year-old ninth-grader, who came to the office with his mother, Kathy D. He was referred by his school counselor. Billy had received numerous detentions. He had been a discipline problem both at school and at home. He had stolen valuable baseball cards from his father.

The family consisted of Billy, the mother, Kathy, age 46, and the father, Dan, age 50. The Ds also had a daughter, age 28, who was married and lived in Florida. Mr. and Mrs. D had been married for 28 years. Mrs. D worked part-time as a secretary, while Mr. D was a truck driver. Mrs. D was an only child. Her father was a sheet metal worker. Her mother, who was deceased, was a housewife. Dan came from a large family. His father worked in a factory in Camden, New Jersey, and his mother was a seamstress. Mrs. D described her husband's upbringing as difficult because it was a large family, and they did not have much money. The kids took care of themselves because both parents worked long hours to make ends meet.

Mrs. D came across as a caring and concerned parent who didn't know how to handle Billy. She set rules for Billy to follow, but he often broke them. According to Mrs. D, Dan was like most fathers and didn't get too involved with children's matters. Billy, during the initial sessions, was quiet and indifferent. Mrs. D was concerned that if he didn't change his behavior, he would be expelled from school.

The questions of concern to me were, What role did Billy's symptomatic behavior play in the operation of the family? Why was Billy acting out? What purpose did stealing the baseball cards serve?

Mr. D initially resisted participation in counseling but eventually agreed to get involved for "the sake of his child."

It became increasingly obvious that both Mr. and Mrs. D had numerous unresolved marital issues, the major issue being that Mr. D was nonavailable: nonavailable to his wife and also to his son. When he wasn't working, he would be with his buddies at sporting events or frequenting a bar. Both Mr. and Mrs. D came from poorly differentiated families that taught them to avoid talking about marital disappointment. To alleviate the stress, Mrs. D would unconsciously take it out on Billy. Consequently, Billy's behavior would deteriorate at home and at school. He even stole his dad's baseball cards in an unconscious, futile attempt to ease marital tensions.

Billy's symptomatic behavior was not only an unhealthy way of dealing with his own anxieties, it also served to dilute the anxiety between his mom and dad. In a self-defeating way, all the family members benefited from this dysfunctional pattern.

During the father's absences Billy would unconsciously act up—refuse to do his chores, battle with his mom over homework, access forbidden Web sites, and not abide by his curfew. Mrs. D would enter into fierce power struggles with him over these issues, expending lots of energy and eventually "forgetting" all about her marital disappointments.

If the Ds had been more differentiated, they could have better identified what was happening and could have controlled the urge to participate in the triangle. Also, Billy's fusion and poor level of self-differentiation, in all likelihood, would be transmitted to his family when he got married and had children.

We all utilize triangulation. How about the times you spoke ill of your friend or partner to another friend?

Triangulation constantly happens in marriage counseling. Repeatedly, one spouse wants me to side with him or her against the other spouse. My siding with the spouse, in his or her mind, confirms that he or she holds the truth and that the other spouse is wrong. Usually, my response is that both are accountable for the situation. Always, my goal is to enhance the relationship and remain as impartial as possible

A tragic example of triangulation that is played out in numerous divorcing families is that of the K family. Mrs. K brought her son, Joseph, age 12, and her daughter, Alicia, age 10, in for "child counseling." Mrs. K recently separated from her husband; Mr. K moved out of the house and went to live with his brother 10 miles away. Although it wasn't clear to me why the parents separated, it was clear that her children blamed her for the separation. It was also clear that she was triangulating the children. She was attempting to triangulate each child against their dad. Unfortunately for the children, she would speak badly of the father to the children. She blamed the father for everything. However, her attempt to have the children align with her against the father, as it so often does, backfired. Even though she loathed her husband, he was still the father of her children. The children became increasingly aggressive, defiant, and even hostile to Mrs. K. Joseph would even curse at her, and on one occasion he even struck his mother. The children were also acting out in school. Joseph got into numerous fights, and Alicia, who previously was an A student, was failing two subjects.

When the mother attempted to discipline them, they would threaten that they would go live with their dad. These young children, in a short period of time, learned how to divide and conquer in an attempt to do what they wanted to do.

Separation and divorce are extremely difficult for the children. Parents need to make this transition as stress-free as possible for their children. Some rules that I have found effective in helping to protect children from the devastation of separation and divorce follow.[5]

1. Children should not hear parents talk against each other.
2. When one parent has a complaint against the other parent, it should be discussed between only the parents.
3. Children should not be questioned about the other parent.
4. When difficulties arise between a parent and child, that parent should work on the problem without intrusion from the other parent.
5. Children should not be caught in the middle or used as go-betweens by the parents.
6. Parents need to establish and reinforce mutually agreeable rules with natural, logical consequences. They still need to support each other regarding discipline matters.
7. The parents must not encourage misbehavior in an attempt to get back at the other spouse.
8. Children should be free to contact the other parent when they want to do so.
9. Don't judge your child's feelings, complaints, or concerns about the separation or divorce.
10. Don't withhold information about your child's school performance and social activities from the other parent. By doing so, you aren't only getting back at your spouse, you're also hurting your child.

Generally, if the parents can keep the best interests of their children as their top priority, everything will fall into place. A lot of the turmoil of separation and divorce would be less devastating if each parent made decisions based on what's best for the children and not based on self-service.

Many family therapists feel that the triangle, a three-person system, is the basic emotional system. It is the fundamental emotional system for not only families but all groups. A two-party system may function in a "normal fashion," but when anxiety escalates, the most vulnerable member seeks to pull in another to form a triangle. When the anxiety decreases, the twosome returns to its "normal" state, while the third party feels isolated and alone.

I included this chapter in the book because I wanted the reader to become more consciously aware of the impact and often negative consequences of triangulation, especially the negative impact of the father-mother-child conflict on the family.

These conditioned, automatic, unconscious responses can play havoc not only with the adult relationship, but also with the children. The children are harmless pawns, and the triangulation is an expression of much deeper needs: a need for couples to express and openly communicate their needs, anxieties, and concerns to each other.

BREAKING THE CYCLE

After my clients become aware of the concept of self-differentiation, and especially of the harm that triangulation can inflict on their children, they want to break the cycle.

In my opinion, without intense psychotherapy, it is very difficult—after years of conditioning and programming—to transform oneself into a less emotionally reactive person. I feel the best chance of disrupting the cycle is to focus on the process of triangulation. When the spouses learn how to better deal with their own issues and not pull their children into their problems, the self-defeating emotional cycle is terminated.

To break the cycle, we must first become aware that we are participants in our automatic unconscious reactions to stress. When the stress between you and your partner builds up when emotions are high, you must consciously become aware of the probability of triangulating your child in an attempt to diffuse the stress. Take a moment, and reflect on stressful moments with your spouse and how you pulled a child into your problems. Some of the stressful situations may have been financial, not being validated by your partner, working too hard, not having enough time for each other, in-laws, and so forth.

When stress escalates between you and your spouse, you must stop your old patterns of behavior or transactions, you must calm yourself down or take a time out and—for a short time—get away from each other. Later, you need to reapproach each other and, in a more calm and rational manner, attempt to discuss your issues. It's imperative that you make an effort to discuss the issue at hand and not involve the children in your problems. You have to make the previously unconscious dysfunctional behavior conscious. You must learn to act and not react. Also, if your child attempts to get involved, you must direct him or her not to get involved in adult problems.

Couples that want to stop the triangulation need to make a conscious effort to work out their problems in adult-to-adult conversations. It's not so much what we say, but how we say things to each other. More specific step-by-step information regarding healthy ways of communication is provided in chapter 8.

CHANGE

Change is difficult, and most people resist change mostly because of fear: fear of the unknown and the unfamiliar. Even positive change is stressful. There is even overwhelming stress in taking a relaxed vacation: saving money, packing, airport hassle, renting a car, and so forth. Even a positive change, for example, when one of the alcoholic spouses stops drinking, is difficult. A case in point is the K family. Mr. K drank for 20 of his 22 years of marriage. It was not until Mr. K stopped drinking and went to counseling and Alcoholics Anonymous that Mr. K threatened divorce. What happens in so many alcoholic families is that the disease is insidious and gradually infects the family. In the case of the Ks, Mrs. K assumed responsibility for the family: she took the kids to their sporting events, paid the bills, made excuses for her husband's absenteeism, and so forth. In other words she had to take on a lot of responsibility and had control over family matters. However, once Mr. K wasn't drinking and became sober and more cognizant of family matters, he wanted to become more involved in family matters and have more control. His positive change disrupted the homeostasis, or balance, in the relationship and generated surprisingly high levels of anxiety in his wife, and almost led to divorce.

Change is difficult, but for the sake of your children and your marriage, it's worth it. In order to implement change, I recommend that you and your spouse write, "I will not involve my children in our problems," and keep it in a personal place, where you can frequently remind yourself of this promise. Also, fast forward your life, and ask yourself the following questions: How does it feel to look back and see how triangulation has negatively impacted your children? How does it feel to look forward and see how becoming better able to face and resolve your marital problems has benefited every member of your family?

In a marriage or relationship, there will always be problems that need to be resolved, not avoided in the hopes they will somehow go away. Part of the reason why problems become power struggles or we involve our children in adult problems is the belief that life is not supposed to be difficult. The unconscious theory is that personal defects, such as bad choices, poor self-control, and impulsive behavior, lie at the root of each of life's misfortunes and that if the spouses were only good enough, problems would pass us by, and we would forever live happier.

If we bought into this myth, we would be constantly trying to correct our spouses' faults so that we did not have to face our problems. This would likely become a problem in itself, but even if it didn't, whenever we were faced with a problem, our first inclination would be to battle with our partners over whose defects would have to be corrected before we could arrive at a solution.

On the other hand, if we subscribe to a different theory, one in which we assume that life is supposed to be difficult, and if we think communally, not individually, we can find solutions to our problems. Additionally, if we organize conversations with our spouses into contests over who's to blame for the problem, we only construct temporary solutions that are often sabotaged by the resentment of the blamed and defeated party.

The strongest families are not the ones that don't have problems or have not been affected by illness, loss, or trauma. The strongest families are those families that both face the problems and, together, find solutions to the problems without blaming each other.

In my opinion, attitude is 90 percent of the impetus for change. The brain is much like a computer: what we input into our brains is what we experience. If we say "I'll try," we'll fail. You and your spouse must approach problems together as a win-win, nonblaming process and not as survival of the fittest.

THE W FAMILY BREAKS THE CYCLE

An example of a family that was able to break the cycle of triangulation is the W family. Tom W and Elizabeth W had been married for 14 years. They had two children, Lisa, age 10, and Thomas, age 13. The parents initiated counseling because Thomas was nearly expelled from school because he slashed the seats on the bus. Interestingly, he slashed the seats on the way home from school, not going to school, strongly indicating that the acting-out behavior was his unconscious attempt to deal with his emotions due to the problems at home.

Mr. and Mrs. W were extremely upset over the incident. Not only was the school involved, the police were involved, and they had to go to court.

Thomas was a good student, and he did not have a history of behavioral problems at school. However, in the four months leading up to the incident Thomas was angry and displayed aggressive behavior, especially toward his mother and younger sister, Lisa.

All the family members were involved in the counseling sessions. Eventually, it was revealed that Mr. and Mrs. W were having marital difficulties. Mrs. W recently took a part-time position as an accountant, and Mr. W wanted her to be a stay-at-home mom. Most of their arguments eventually centered on her getting a job. Mr. W would then try to shout and have his son join in in an attempt to defeat the mom. Eventually, Mrs. W would feel guilty and retort by saying that she would resign. However, when it came down to resigning, she couldn't because she felt a need to do the work she was educated and trained to do.

Over time their behavioral transactions became fixed and predictable: when the parents would disagree, Mrs. W would organize the situation in such a way as to triangulate Thomas and align with him against the father. As a result of the unnatural family structure and the emotional instability, Thomas would act out his repressed, volatile feelings.

Initially, Mr. W found it difficult not to elicit the support of his son, Thomas. However, he did want to save the marriage. Also, after he became aware of the negative consequences that were reflected in his son's behavior he wanted to make changes. The Ws became proficient in becoming consciously aware when the stress between them escalated, and they learned to step away and approach each other at a later time and not attempt to discuss emotionally charged issues when they were angry. They also become increasingly aware of the attempt to engage Thomas in the process, and they would stop the process immediately. They even became adept at ushering Thomas out of the conversation when he attempted to intervene. Once Thomas was exited from the marital dyad, he became less anxious and more free to concentrate on his own development.

Unconscious forces hidden from our conscious awareness are so imprinted in our psyches that they can even devastate our relationships with our beloved children. The role of the therapist is to first assist the clients in becoming aware of the existence of these negative imprints and then to help them to reprogram their scripts so that they are more able to develop healthier relationships with their children.

Chapter Five

UNCONSCIOUS FORCES CAN DESTROY NOT ONLY RELATIONSHIPS, BUT WHOLE FAMILIES

A case that I found intriguing and initially baffling was that of the E family. The family consisted of Mr. E, age 40, Mrs. E, age 38, and their three children, Thomas, age 15, JoAnn, age 10, and Kyle, age six. Mrs. E's mother also lived with them. Mr. E worked for Federal Express. Mrs. E was a full-time mother.

The E family initiated counseling because Thomas was becoming increasingly aggressive. The police were even called in to break up a physical fight between Mr. E and Thomas.

Mr. and Mrs. E were both caring and nurturing parents. When I first met Thomas, I found him to be angry and even hostile, especially toward his father.

As I further gathered data regarding the family, a few of the questions that needed to be answered were, Why was Thomas so obviously hostile toward his father? Was this an example of typical adolescent revolt to parental authority? Were Mr. and Mrs. E undermining each other's authority? Why was Thomas acting out and not JoAnn or Kyle?

After our first few sessions Thomas's behavior deteriorated even more. The police were called in again when Thomas punched the father in the face. As a result, Thomas spent a few nights in a juvenile detention center.

Eventually, I discovered the unconscious motive for Thomas's aggressive and hostile acting out. In a family session I noticed that almost every conversation between Mr. and Mrs. E, while starting out about Thomas's need for correction, ended up being a battle between the parents about the role of Mrs. E's mother in the discipline process. It seems that not only was the grandmother supporting Thomas's insubordination by rolling her eyes and making jokes about the father's competence during power struggles, but she was also complaining to Thomas about his father's faults to the family behind the parents' backs.

It became clear to me that Thomas's acting out behavior was generated by his unconscious rage over his father's reluctance to take charge of the family. From that point onward my course of treatment was to establish Mr. and Mrs. E as the authoritative parents and to get them to work together to reduce the grandmother's interference in discipline transactions. Every time the grandmother attempted to step in and undermine the father, both parents escorted the grandmother away.

Family therapists are quite aware that when behavioral or emotional problems erupt in one member of the family system, these problems are really unconscious communications about others in the family system. Symptoms are communication about situations.[1] The person in the family who displays the symptoms is called the *symptom-bearer*, but she or he is by no means the only one involved in constructing the situation that has made a symptom necessary, and she or he is by no means the only one looking for a new family arrangement that will make the symptoms unnecessary. In the case of the E family Thomas's aggressive behavior was an adolescent attempt at establishing a new family arrangement, that is, to expel the grandmother as a parent and to place his parents in control.

When children are symptom-bearers in families, the situation around a child often contains elements of hierarchical confusion. The family may be confused by being ambiguous so that no one quite knows who is the peer and who is the parent. The confusion may stem from one member of the hierarchy forming an alliance with a child against his or her hierarchical partner. This means that the family leadership, generally entrusted to the adults in the household, has for one reason or another become ineffective. Sudden illness or disability, substance abuse, unemployment, marital distress, and many other stressors can divert the attention of the adults in a family away from leadership and create a powerful vacuum that sucks a child into a leadership position for which she or he has no preparation and which, in turn, diverts the attention of the child away from age-appropriate interests like friends, sports, and school.

A classic example of how hierarchical confusion contributes to unconscious acting-out behavior is seen in the unhappy world of the *parentified child*.[2] Parentification occurs in families when a parent or parent figure stops paying attention to the overall regulation of the life of the family and when a child steps in to invent or execute the rules for family operations. In extreme situations, parentified children decide everything from what the family eats, to when (if ever) homework gets done, to who goes to school, to what time is bedtime. While enacting some parental functions toward younger siblings is appropriate for children during certain family life cycle sequences, perpetual positioning in adult roles is detrimental. Frequently, adolescent substance abusers come from families wherein hierarchical rules are reversed, that is, where the adolescents are as influential or more influential than the parents in setting the family's leadership agenda.[3] I personally find this scenario to be particularly true of single-parent families.

In an equally complex and dysfunctional hierarchical role is the *spousified child*. Spousified children are children who have been inducted into quasi-marital roles in the lives of parents with an unavailable spouse. They may have become unavailable through marital disintegration, sickness, or death or from overinvolvement with jobs and the like. Often, the spousified children carry the entire weight of family responsibility for the emotional equilibrium of a very lonesome parent. The spousified child can be observed to unconsciously discharge this emotional duty from a position of equal authority as a parent and can become the focus of clinical attention in school when she or he generalizes this equality to school officials through comments and gestures that are disrespectful and emotionally intrusive.

A case in point is the B family. Mr. and Mrs. B, at the school's request, brought their 14-year-old son, Emmanuel, in for counseling because the school mandated that he get help. Emmanuel was acting inappropriately at school, bossing other students around and being disrespectful toward teachers. Emmanuel was also bullying his younger brother, Ralph, age 10. Ralph, also, was starting to act out at home and at school. The situation was getting out of control, and the parents had no idea how to solve the problem. Mr. B attempted to discipline Emmanuel, but the situation only got worse. Mr. B worked 80 miles from home and would often stay at hotels closer to work from Monday through Friday. As a result of his absence, Mrs. B would rely on Emmanuel for many of the parental responsibilities, including governing over his younger brother, Ralph. Emmanuel gradually, in a subtle way, became inducted into the quasi-parental role of the father. This role became so dysfunctional that at one point in the session Mr. B said, "Either he goes, or I go." Emmanuel was becoming Mr. B's parental rival. Even little Ralph was starting to act out because of the evolving dysfunctional hierarchical reversal. Mr. and Mrs. B, via family counseling, became consciously aware of how Emmanuel's symptomatic behavior was maintained by the inadequate hierarchy and boundaries. They learned how to work together and take charge of their children. They learned how to establish mutually agreeable rules with natural, logical consequences.

For a therapist the assessment of the *hierarchical arrangement* in the family is critical in discovering who is deciding what gets the family's attention and how attention is distributed in the life of a family. It is critical in understanding behavior, but particularly of students who are acting out in school. A student who is paying more attention to how his parents are getting along (emotionally, economically, or medically) than he is to academics may make unconscious choices in school that decelerate the pace of academic advancement. Acting-out behaviors in school—like not handing in homework, misbehaving, and other attention-seeking activities—that result in poor grades can make the family leaders direct their attention back to the leadership of the family. Before these behaviors are clustered into a full-blown psychiatric diagnosis it is a good idea to take a look at how they may be unconscious attempts to stabilize or even improve the quality of life in the child's family.

Families, like individuals, proceed through predictable life cycle phases.[4] They add members through births and adoptions, launch members into relationships, school, and jobs, and relinquish members to relocations, in-laws, and death. The appearance of a symptom-bearer often coincides with the approach of a new life cycle phase and, in family therapy terms, often signals that the family is stuck and is having difficulty moving on to its next life cycle phase.[5] Life cycle advancement is a function of family leadership, and when the family leaders have their attention focused elsewhere and expect previous family arrangements to carry the complexity of new biological, social, or intellectual circumstances too long, the family is at risk for requiring a family member to produce an attention-getting symptom.

For example, at the beginning of junior high, Jeff, who had done reasonably well in school, suddenly began to act out in class. He developed a pattern of not completing his assignments, daydreaming in class, and reacting disrespectfully when confronted by his teachers. Appeals to Jeff from administrators and guidance personnel only increased his oppositional demeanor, and his grades began to deteriorate. Parent-teacher conferences were held, and Jeff's highly motivated and loving parents attempted to intervene, which resulted in the parents joining the school in both frustration and ineffectiveness in relation to his problem. Was Jeff's acting-out behavior unconsciously serving his family by slowing down the pace of developmental change? Could this adolescent have been displaying acting-out behavior that unconsciously demonstrated that his family was not ready to deal with a member who is about to leave the nest? Is it possible that Jeff's sudden need for more attention from his parents in school was unconsciously another way to divert their attention from a marital conflict over Mom returning to the world of work now that her children were more autonomous? Could it be that Jeff's problems in school were providing one or both of his parents with an ironclad rationale for not being able to spend more time with their own aged parents?

According to Minuchin, families establish patterns of transaction over time, and these transactional patterns maintain the family as a system.[6] Developmental advances on the part of a family member challenge familiar patterns and introduce crisis into the family system. These crises are managed homeostatically; that is, the family unconsciously reaches back into its repertoire of previous successful problem-solving tools and applies a solution that worked well in the past, but often does not work in the present. In Jeff's case, for example, news of an academic or behavioral problem in school may have been handled swiftly and effectively by a serious talk with an extended family member, by a few hours in the "bad chair," or by added attention at home each evening from Mom or Dad. Now, perhaps, Jeff's family had become disconnected for one reason or another from its extended family, or Jeff had just gotten too big for the "bad chair," or Jeff's parents were too laden with work-related fatigue, health and fitness preoccupations, or marital conflicts to pay enough attention to his school performance on a regular basis.

It is precisely the fact that no previous solution seems to be working that signals that the family is approaching a developmental milestone in its life cycle. Yet, the disturbance of customary rituals and routines as well as a generalized sense of suspense in the family as to whether family leadership can negotiate the rough seas of conflict and change sends unconscious emotional shock waves through the entire family system. Vulnerable family members may become anxious or even physically ill when family life cycle transitions are approaching, especially when it is likely that the transition will require unspoken conflict to become overt in the leadership unit itself.

The dynamics of the psychological tensions underlying family life cycle transitions were well articulated in the work of the founders of the family therapy movement. Bowen concluded that family anxieties about life cycle transitions are transmitted to children through a process of projection that is outside the conscious awareness of family members. He theorized that regressed, immature parents unconsciously select their most infantile and most sensitive child as the container of their anxieties.[7] As in the present case, Jeff became the object of his parents' unconscious projections at the price of his own developmental advancement. The more terrified the parents are of family life cycle movement, the more they project their fears onto the child and the more likely the child is to develop an advancement-delaying symptom dysfunction.

SINGLE-PARENT FAMILIES

Single-parent families are also susceptible to unconscious forces. A typical case that comes to mind is that of the Z family. The family consisted of 15-year-old Jennifer and single-parent mother Gloria, age 42. Gloria and her husband divorced 12 years ago, after he left Gloria for another woman. After the divorce Mr. Z did not see Jennifer for three years. Even though Mr. Z and his new wife lived close to Jennifer, Mr. Z rarely saw Jennifer, and they only communicated by telephone occasionally. Mr. Z and Gloria hadn't spoken to each other in years. As far as Gloria was concerned, their relationship had been severed a long time ago.

Jennifer and her mother agreed, during the intake, that Jennifer was spoiled and manipulative. For example, if her mother wanted her home at 12:30 on Saturday night, Jennifer would sometimes stay out until 3:00 A.M. Or, if her mother drew the line in an attempt to discipline her, Jennifer would call her father for his support and in turn relay his comments back to her mother.

Gloria was working as a lawyer's secretary and made a good income of over $50,000 annually. She was dating another man named Tony. Tony and Gloria intended to get married in the spring of 2004. Tony and Jennifer tended to get along, and she didn't object to him being a future stepfather.

Gloria's father was an alcoholic, and his behavior had discouraged her from drinking or from trying other drugs. Gloria's parents moved to San Diego years ago. According to Jennifer, she had tried drugs as a freshman, but she hadn't taken them since that time. Jennifer was a good student, and she wanted to be a lawyer.

By observing the peer-like interactions between Gloria and Jennifer in family therapy sessions, I learned that there was no functioning hierarchy in the family. The relationship was enmeshed, and the boundaries were blurred. Jennifer was attempting to establish herself as an independent adult, at age 16, while still under the care of the mother. The mother needed to establish a more delineated parent-child boundary. It was necessary for the mother to set and implement firm rules and guidelines for her daughter to follow.

My hypothesis was informed by the structural model, and I formulated my treatment plan accordingly. My treatment plan was to empower the mother, to place her in charge of the family. It was necessary to assist her in establishing firmer child limits and in setting age-appropriate rules and consequences. My goal was to support the mother's right to make certain demands and to take charge of her daughter. I intended to take the mother beyond her routine, unworkable transactional patterns and to help her feel more confident in restructuring new patterns. It was also necessary for Mrs. B not to be unconsciously influenced by her daughter's moods and to free herself from Jennifer's efforts to triangulate her father against her mother.

The plan to support Mom's position as the parental authority created a healthy hierarchy in the family. One of the unconscious forces that Mrs. Z had to first learn to be consciously aware of and consistently cope with was "control by guilt." As with so many single parents, Mrs. Z felt guilty and remorseful for Jennifer's lack of an alternate parent figure—in this case an absent father. Jennifer also became an expert at manipulating the situation, and when she didn't get her way, she would threaten to run away and live with her dad. A coalition existed between Jennifer and the father—triangulation—against the mother. Jennifer further escalated resistance to the new structure by reassuring threats to use Dad to dilute mom. Mom needed to free herself from the pattern of triangulation.

Mrs. Z grew tired of being blackmailed. She decided that either Jennifer was going to follow her rules or move in with her father. Jennifer did move in with her dad, which only lasted two months. Jennifer came back to live with her mom, but this time under her mom's leadership. Both Mrs. Z and Jennifer learned that rules define family, and dysfunctional families follow dysfunctional rules.

HEALTHY PARENTING

Parents need to work together and back one another up in the tough role of setting limits and rules with natural, logical consequences. The parents must work as a team to win the struggle for power that inevitably arises during the course of raising children. It takes extra effort to enforce the consequences and to be consistent in enforcing consequences. As I mentioned earlier, the agenda of the adolescent is to reform the parents. Children need parents who will see one another through the temporary loss of approval and affection by the children where rules are enforced. This temporary loss of approval and affection is especially difficult for single parents because the parent already has a history of feeling guilty for not providing a so-called normal life.

Adolescence is a difficult emotional time. Most teens don't have the experiences and critical thinking skills necessary to make good choices. They are naturally self-centered, impulsive, and of course, feel indestructible and take many risks. Many of their negative behaviors can be resolved, but some behaviors have lifelong consequences. It is our job as parents to help assure that their behaviors don't result in unresolvable predicaments such as lawbreaking and even homicide.

Parents must establish rules with natural, logical consequences. Establishing rules with natural, logical consequences modifies unacceptable behavior, which guarantees that the child will arrive safely at independence without the trauma of having to invent limits for himself. It is developmentally necessary that the parents be in charge because the children are not ready for self-governing.

Natural, logical consequences are discernibly different from punishment. Punishment takes place in the past tense. It is punitive, threatening, and rarely related to the misbehavior. Also, usually at the time of the misbehavior, we get angry and blurt out a punishment that is outlandish, laden with unconscious resentments and fears, and impossible to carry out, for example, "You failed algebra, and you are grounded for the remainder of school." This punishment is purely irrational, unconsciously self-punishing, and places too much responsibility on the parent figure for enforcement. It denies the child the opportunity to make his own decisions and take responsibility for his own behavior.

On the other hand, natural, logical consequences teach a child to become more responsible. They teach a child accountability, that is, to be accountable for his own actions and choices. In my experience the child is never too young to learn to be accountable. Natural, logical consequences are those that permit children to learn from the natural order of things. For example, if you speed when driving, you can get a ticket. Rules with natural, logical consequences should be age-appropriate. The rules for a 16-year-old should be different from those for a 12-year-old.

STEPPARENTING

The strategies for stepparenting are different. Central to the combined family is the couple's lack of an equal relationship to the children. Only the biological parent fully understands the emotional tie between him or her and the child. On an unconscious level the child often experiences terrible emotional pain and a feeling of loss from the separated natural parent.[8]

Some of the strategies that I encourage follow.

- If you are a new stepparent, don't try or even expect to have a major hand in disciplining right away. If you do, your involvement will be greeted by anger and resentment.
- Recognize and respect the child's love for the other biological parent.
- Encourage, don't discourage, the relationship with an absent parent.
- Include the other biological parent in all family events that revolve around celebrations of the child, such as religious rituals, graduations, awards ceremonies, school plays, birthdays, and so forth.
- Allow time (at least a few years) for a relationship with stepchildren to solidify.
- Be aware of your stepchildren's stages of development and how they impact their relationships with you.
- Focus on small successes in building the relationship.
- Don't force the relationship or demand love from your stepchildren to solidify it.
- Control feelings of resentment and jealousy when faced with the close biological bond between your spouse and his or her children.
- Don't expect to feel equally toward your children and your stepchildren.
- Build the relationship with each stepchild individually.
- Accept that stepfamily life is not smooth sailing.

FAMILY ROAD MAPS

People often comment that there are no road maps for families to follow. But there are firm guidelines, and if couples would follow them, it would assure healthy development of the child. Consider these:

- As in the case of Mr. and Mrs. E, there must be clearly defined generational boundaries so that the parents form a subsystem with executive power.
- There must be alignments between parents among issues such as discipline.
- Parents must establish agreeable, age-appropriate rules with natural, logical consequences.
- Couples must validate each other and learn to communicate with each other.
- Don't take adolescent revolt personally. If they didn't revolt, they wouldn't detach from us. Don't blame yourself for the unsettled nature of the relationship.
- Don't waste your time trying to convince teenagers of their inconsistency or illogical thinking. Share your feelings, but don't lecture.
- Give up control over little things, and accept behaviors over which you have little control.
- Usually begin to deal with a problem by discussion and natural problem solving. Expect communication.

Additional traits of a healthy family can be found in appendix A at the end of this chapter.

As we have seen, whole families are susceptible to hidden forces that can wear at the fabric of the family. The role of the therapist is to discover the hidden forces and make them cognizant to the parents so that positive changes and growth can be fostered.

In chapter 6 we will discuss various marital games that are really unconscious methods of deception.

APPENDIX A

Here are the 15 traits commonly perceived in the healthy family by those people who work with families. (The trait listed first was selected most often by respondents, the trait listed second received the next largest number of votes, and so on.)

The healthy family . . .

1. communicates and listens.
2. affirms and supports one another.
3. teaches respect for others.
4. develops a sense of trust.
5. has a sense of play and humor.
6. exhibits a sense of shared responsibility.
7. teaches a sense of right and wrong.
8. has a strong sense of family, in which rituals and traditions abound.
9. has a balance of interaction among members.
10. has a shared religious core.

11. respects the privacy of one another.
12. values service to others.
13. fosters family table time and conversation.
14. shares leisure time.
15. admits to and seeks help with problems.

Chapter Six

PEOPLE WHO FEEL DIVORCED BUT ARE STILL MARRIED

Many couples that I counsel feel isolated and distant from one another. They feel lonely, as if no one cares for them. They don't feel emotionally close to one another, and they have lost their intimacy. Intimacy refers to a sense of feeling close and connected and having a sense of welfare for the other. It also encompasses sharing oneself, giving and receiving emotional support, and trusting the spouse.

Consider Sternberg's triangular theory of love (figure 6.1).[1] According to Sternberg, enduring love does not start with passionate romance. It starts with commitment to the development of a relationship. This commitment leads to intimacy, which in turn fuels passion. The passion serves to intensify commitment to the relationship, and intimacy and passions continue to nurture love. Intimacy is a sense of feeling close, connected, or bonded, having a sense of welfare for the other, and wanting happiness for the other.

In my opinion, people often confuse the concepts of intimacy and infatuation. People often comment that they have lost their intimacy in the relationship. Intimacy is different than infatuation. Infatuation is the first stage of love. When we are first attracted to another, we become infatuated with that person. We see only the good in the person and do not see his or her faults. We put the person on a pedestal. When people have extramarital affairs, they become infatuated with the person and operate out of an unrealistic perception of the other. I often tell the person that having the affair is likened to temporary insanity. Infatuation can last weeks or even years, but eventually, it fades away, and we see the person in a more realistic fashion. Intimacy, on the

Figure 6.1
Triangle of Love

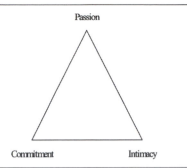

other hand, is a by-product of communication. It is no surprise that the highest rate of divorce is in the first two years of marriage, but people are surprised to learn that the second highest rate of divorce occurs during the empty nest stage, when the children become adults and leave the house. The culprit is lack of communication. In my experience, roughly 80 percent of a couple's conversations revolve around the children, and when the children are gone, the couple finally realizes that they have lost their identity as a couple and that they have become less intimate.

You become intimate by having honest, open conversations. As the years go by, if the couple does not work at validating each other by communicating about their relational needs and expectations, they grow farther and farther apart, and they lose their identity as a couple.

Over the years, people get lost in their parenting responsibilities, jobs, hobbies, and clubs. I tell people that we have to take our spouses more seriously than our jobs and hobbies. We have to treat our spouses as real people. We have to learn to work at a marriage. We have to work at validating the other, developing more sensitivity, and changing some priorities or simply learning how to listen to one another. Couples need to understand that their behaviors influence their relationships. Their behaviors can make the relationship supportive or stressful.[2]

After 30 years of marriage Alexia wanted to end her union with Thomas. She and Thomas had raised three children. Alexia had been a homemaker. She felt forced to go to work, and she had always resented her husband for it. Alexia was first in sales and later was promoted to a management position. She made new friends, got more promotions, and she got a different sense of self. As the years went by, Alexia and Thomas grew farther and farther apart. Thomas wasn't really interested in her career path, but he still wanted to discuss his work and problems with her. Alexia felt that her husband didn't view her job as being as important as his and that her income was insignificant. Although Alexia had changed, Thomas had not. Thomas still viewed her as dependent on him, and she wasn't; she had become independent. Thomas was shocked when she asked for a divorce. Thomas felt that he was married, and Alexia felt like she had been divorced for two years. Alexia and Thomas had lost their intimacy. They became like two separate corporations rather than a unified, intimate couple.

In every marriage, there will be problems. Unconscious family-of-origin issues too often come into play. For example, one spouse may have come from a dysfunctional family. As a child, he witnessed nothing but chaos in the family, and therefore as an adult, that spouse needs to be in control. When he is not in control, uneasy, anxious feelings then take over.

Edward, age 29, and Susan, age 31, came to the office because most of their conversations led to full-blown, destructive arguments. Like many people, after a near-atomic-like explosion, they would not talk to each other for days. Susan unconsciously feared getting too intimate because if she did, she would lose control of her life and her husband. Susan unconsciously feared that Edward would take too parental a role. The dynamics involved are a result of Susan's family-of-origin issues. Susan's parents, especially her dad, were very controlling, and as a child, she developed a poor sense of identity. Susan feared that she would be engulfed by her partner. Ironically, Susan searched for and found in Edward a man to complete her sense of self, but she would also retreat from the relationship to preserve whatever fragile sense of self she already possessed.

I have also encountered many couples in which one or both partners hold a fear of abandonment or rejection. If a partner was abandoned or was continuously rejected by a parent, these childhood wounds can permeate his or her adult relationships. William, age 32, was needy, and he felt that his wife, Nicole, age 28, was not giving him the attention that he deserved. Things got even worse when they had children. Naturally, there was a need to take care of the children, and often, William resented his wife for spending so much time taking care of them.

Again, you enhance intimacy by being honest and open and sharing feelings. Self-disclosure and the willingness to listen are important ingredients in the development of close, satisfying, and adaptive marital relationships.[3] However, many people have a fear of intense emotion and have difficulty sharing their feelings with their spouses. Partners who have obsessive-compulsive disorders often use their defenses to mask or avoid feelings. These types of people think rather than feel. They are devoid of emotion and, what makes matters worse, they often project their uncomfortable feelings onto the spouse. The reason for this fear of intense emotion can be traced to times during which their childhood feelings were discounted by their parents. The parents would ignore, criticize, or punish the child for displaying emotions such as anger, sadness, or frustration.

According to Luciano L'Abate, the components of intimacy are as follow.[4]

1. Seeing the Good—Each partner should be able to see the good, in himself and in his partner. Each should be able to say what is good about himself and be able to express what he likes about his partner.

2. Caring—A caring attitude toward oneself and the other is vital to a healthy relationship. Caring, which may be defined differently by each spouse, can be shown in many ways.

3. Protectiveness—The couple must take care of each other. When children are involved in the family, the couple must first take care of the couple's relationship. Any discord between the husband and wife will reverberate throughout the family. In order to have a happy and nurturing family, it is essential that the relational partners see to the needs of their own relationship. The couple must also protect themselves from outside forces, such as work, in-laws, employers, and hobbies. I see too many couples who don't take the time for each other. No wonder these relationships are strained over a period of time.

4. Enjoyment—Enjoyment refers to giving pleasure to oneself and to one another. Couples need to take time to enjoy activities that they *both* enjoy just for the sake of pleasure. Too often, one partner will play golf and the other partner will play tennis, and they rarely enjoy activities together. If a relationship is to grow, the couple has to do things as a couple and have fun, like they did when they first got married.

5. Responsibility—In an intimate relationship, each person must take responsibility for problems that might occur in the relationship. Both partners are accountable for the relationship. Each partner is responsible for resolving problems in the marriage. Therefore it takes both parties to work out the difficulties. Too often, one partner blames the other for a problem. For example, a husband prefers to stay in the house and not to do things together outside the home. The wife needs to get out of the house once in awhile. I tell each spouse that she has not just the right but the relational duty to tell her mate what she needs from the relationship that she's not getting. Having "good reasons" to avoid the partner's needs—like exhaustion from working or parenting, lack of imagination, or an unwillingness to reexperience things—will not do the trick. Intimacy will only grow if you challenge yourself to move beyond your own comfort zone.

6. Sharing Hurt—Intense levels of anger are often characteristic of troubled relationships. Suppressing feelings such as hurt, anger, resentment, frustration, and guilt only tends to fracture the relationship. The couple needs to learn that in a good marriage it's okay to talk about anything. Learning to share hurt rather than burying it is critical in promoting the understanding and empathy that underlie intimacy. Talking to others helps to dissolve unwelcome feelings within ourselves. Not talking to others about our difficult feelings leads to acting out our feelings in pantomime. The partner that feels angry needs to discuss these feelings with the other partner.

7. Forgiveness—In a marriage we will, from time to time, hurt the other partner. It is impossible to be in a relationship for a period of time without occasionally hurting the partner. Also, at times, we create necessary emotional distance from one another by fighting with the partner. I tell couples that forgiveness is a natural outgrowth of love. All of us are human, and we need to learn how to forgive one another. I believe that if we don't let go of anger and forgive one another, the resentment will eventually eat us alive.

RITUALS

Rituals are emotional dances that both partners unconsciously perform to satisfy psychological needs. The purpose of rituals on the unconscious level is to allow the couple to become closer emotionally, to enhance self-acceptance, and to help heal childhood wounds.

A case in point is Martha, age 38, and George, age 42. The couple entered counseling at Martha's request. George and Martha were married for five years. They opted not to have children, a decision they later regretted.

Martha related that most of the time, they got along, but all too often, they became emotionally distant from one another. At these times they felt divorced, even though they were married. Specifically, Martha complained that George, when they would discuss difficult issues, would withdraw and become quiet and isolate himself. George complained that he felt like he was being punished.

Again, what people present in counseling is often not the true problem, and I needed to uncover the underlying meaning of their interactions. I wanted to help the partners identify the ritual of connection and disconnection that they had invented and also to help them discover its unconscious meaning.

George was an only child. His father was a college professor, and his mother was an attorney. As a child, George was quite hyperactive. He was so hyper in preschool that he was expelled when he was five years old. He had poor grades in both elementary and high school. According to George, he was a real disappointment to his parents, and he was often disciplined for not getting good grades. George did not go to college and pursued a career as a mechanic. As an adult, George was diagnosed with attention deficit disorder with hyperactivity. When George was a child, attention deficit disorder was not fully understood and was rarely diagnosed and treated. However, the lasting negative imprint in George was that he "couldn't do anything right." Even today, I find that many professionals do not recognize the symptoms of attention deficit disorder, especially with hyperactivity. Refer to appendix B at the end of this chapter for a list of symptoms.

Martha came from a small family. She had a brother that was two years older than she. According to Martha, her parents, especially her father, favored her brother and would give him privileges that she never received. For instance, her father would only take his son to sporting events. Also, the father would often go fishing with the son, and he would buy the son neat things like go-carts and four-wheelers. Martha grew up feeling that "life was not fair."

Figure 6.2
Martha and George's Ritual

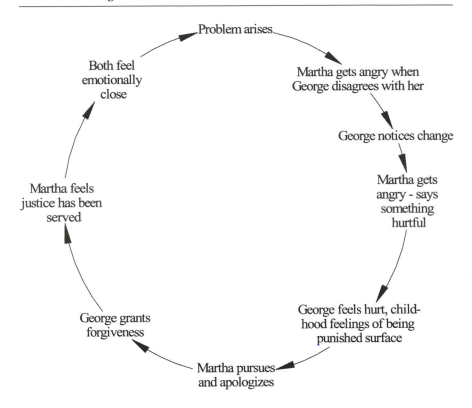

When George and Martha were confronted with difficult issues, the pattern or ritual that they would act out involved Martha getting angry at George for disagreeing with her and often saying something hurtful to George; George would feel hurt, feel that he was being punished, and withdraw emotionally. Martha eventually would pursue George and apologize, George would grant forgiveness, Martha would feel that justice had been served, and both would feel emotionally close to each other (figure 6.2).

Again, the ritual would be played out and unconsciously serve its purpose. The purpose was to allow the couple to become emotionally close, enhance self-acceptance, and help to heal childhood wounds. In George's case, Martha apologizing seemed to function as parental contrition for being so critical and punitive. Conversely, George was granting forgiveness to Martha for childhood injustices.

Another example depicting the unconscious dynamics of rituals is that of Gordon and Jenny. Gordon, age 36, and Jenny, age 30, were both eager to engage in the counseling process. They were eager to initiate counseling for the sake of their children, Jennifer, age six, and Zachary, age three. Undoubtedly, both parents wanted what was best for their children. Ironically, most of their arguments revolved around the children; however, their children had little to do with the deeper unconscious reasons for their arguments.

Gordon came from a large family. He had five siblings, and he was the middle child. Often, the middle child is the lost child, the child that seeks attention. During the sessions Gordon often commented that as a child, nothing he did was "good enough." From his perspective, being an honor student and a good athlete did little to get the attention of his father. His father was too busy providing for the family to attend Gordon's sporting events.

Jenny, on the other hand, came from a small family; she had only one brother, three years her senior. Both her parents were alcoholics, and the generational boundaries in the family were blurred. Her parents could hardly take care of themselves, let alone the children. Her childhood years were full of turmoil and chaos. Things were out of control. No wonder so many children that come from chaotic, dysfunctional families bring exaggerated needs for control into their adult lives.

Gordon's need for approval and Jenny's need to be in control were the focal points of their unconscious ritual. In their relationship, when a problem arose, and quite often it would revolve around parenting issues, the following ritual or pattern would evolve. An unresolved problem or issue would come up. Gordon, in attempting to please Jenny, would offer a resolution to the problem; Jenny, in turn, perceived such gestures as Gordon taking control, and she would frantically seek to regain control. Often, her retorts were irrational, demanding, and critical. Gordon's unconscious feeling of rejection would surface, and in order to suppress his intolerable emotions, he would appease his wife (figure 6.3).

Jenny then would feel guilty for her nasty demeanor. Gordon would forgive Jenny, and thereby both their unconscious childhood needs were temporarily satisfied; that is, Jenny was back in control, and Gordon's need for approval was met. Now, Gordon and Jenny felt intimate again, and they felt a sense of mutual acceptance. But at a price.

As anticipated, this cycle would consistently repeat itself as their preferred way of problem solving. No wonder their issues were never resolved. As so many couples fail to do, they weren't problem solving; rather, they were resolving their childhood emotional needs.

Once this couple consciously understood the unconscious purpose of their ritual, they were quite willing to learn how to organize problem-solving conversations to resolve their differences.

Figure 6.3
Jenny and Gordon's Ritual

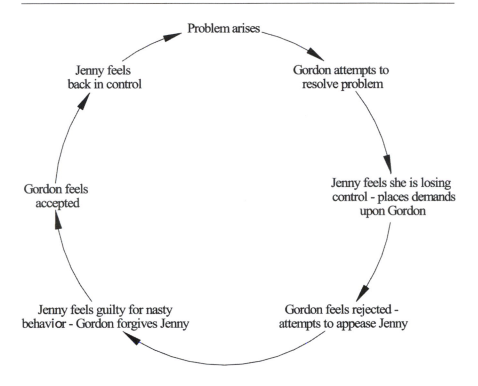

APPENDIX B

Attention–Deficit/Hyperactivity Disorder[5]

A.   Either (1) or (2):
    1.   six (or more) of the following symptoms of inattention have persisted
        for at least 6 months to a degree that is maladaptive and inconsistent
        with developmental level:

Inattention

      a.   often fails to give close attention to details or makes careless mis-
        takes in schoolwork, work, or other activities
      b.   often has difficulty sustaining attention in tasks or play activities
      c.   often does not seem to listen when spoken to directly
      d.   often does not follow through on instructions and fails to finish school-
        work, chores, or duties in the workplace (not due to oppositional
        behavior or failure to understand instructions)
      e.   often has difficulty organizing tasks and activities
      f.   often avoids, dislikes, or is reluctant to engage in tasks that require
        sustained mental effort (such as schoolwork or homework)

g. often loses things necessary for tasks or activities (e.g., toys, school assignments, pencils, books, or tools)

h. is often easily distracted by extraneous stimuli

i. is often forgetful in daily activities

2. six (or more) of the following symptoms of hyperactivity-impulsivity have persisted for at least six months to a degree that is maladaptive and inconsistent with developmental level:

Hyperactivity

a. often fidgets with hands or feet or squirms in seat

b. often leaves seat in classroom or in other situations in which remaining seated is expected

c. often runs about or climbs excessively in situations in which it is inappropriate (in adolescents or adults, may be limited to subjective feelings or restlessness)

d. often has difficulty playing or engaging in leisure activities quietly

e. is often "on the go" or often acts as if "driven by a motor"

f. often talks excessively

Impulsivity

g. often blurts out answers before questions have been completed

h. often has difficulty awaiting turn

i. often interrupts or intrudes on others (e.g., butts into conversations or games)

B. Some hyperactive-impulsive or inattentive symptoms that caused impairment were present before age seven years.

C. Some impairment from the symptoms is present in two or more settings (e.g., at school or work and at home).

D. There must be clear evidence of clinically significant impairment in social, academic, or occupational functioning.

Chapter Seven

GAMES PEOPLE PLAY IN RELATIONSHIPS

Often, clients are skeptical when I relate that many people are clueless as to why their relationships are self-destructing before their eyes. They don't understand, as Salvador Dali, the great surrealist painter, would comment, because "People don't see the latent secret repertoire among things." In order to fully understand the hidden, unconscious dynamics behind unhealthy relationships and communication styles, we need to investigate *Games People Play*, by Eric Berne, MD.[1]

When I was in college, taking a psychology course on relationships, we were required to present a topic about relationships. I had recently read *Games People Play*, and I found the book to be intriguing and insightful. At that time, little did I know that the material I presented in a basic psychology class would be so useful to me in my professional career.

Basic to an understanding of the dynamics of a game is Berne's concept of ego states (figure 7.1). Ego states are systems of feelings accompanied by a related set of behavioral patterns. The ego states can be divided into three categories: (1) ego states that resemble those of parental figures (parent); (2) ego states that are grounded in reality (adult); and (3) those ego states that are fixated in childhood (child). At any given moment, in a social situation or when communicating with your partner, you will exhibit a parent, adult, or child ego state, and you can shift with varying degrees from one ego state to another.

Interestingly, when we shift from one ego state to another, we emotionally reexperience the feelings of that state. For example, everyone has had a parent or substitute parent, and we incorporate into our psyche a set of ego states that

Figure 7.1
Berne's Ego States

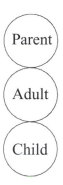

Source: From Erik Berne, *Games People Play* (New York: Grove Press, 1964), p. 30.

reproduce the ego states of those parental figures. These parental ego states become activated under certain conditions. In essence, everyone carries his parents inside of him. The parent ego state enables a person to act effectively as the parent of actual children; that is, we parent as we were parented.

Most everyone learns how to process data objectively and how to deal effectively with the outside world. The adult ego state is necessary for survival, and it enables one to reality test to indicate what is dangerous and what is safe. For example, it calculates the danger in crossing a busy street. The adult ego state also mediates between the parent and child ego states to find a healthy balance.

Every mature individual was once a child. Many of our behavioral traits are learned at an early age. For example, according to Erikson, we learn to trust or not trust by 18 months, we learn to overcome shame and self-doubt and to act on our own by age four, and we learn to keep guilt at bay and set goals for ourselves by age five or six.[2] In the child resides creativity, spontaneous behavior, and enjoyment.

Communication will proceed smoothly as long as the transactions are complementary. In transactional analysis a transaction consists of a stimulus and a response between two ego states. One example is a transaction between two parent ego states: I feel that our son's curfew should be 11 P.M. on Saturday, and my spouse agrees. The response is appropriate and expected, and it follows the natural order of healthy human communication. For example, if you and your spouse are clowning around together, this would be an example of child-to-child transaction, and communication will proceed smoothly. If you and your spouse are discussing ways to pay the bills, this would be an example of an adult-to-adult transaction.

Figure 7.2
Communication on the Same Ego State Plane

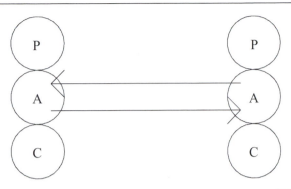

Source: From Erik Berne, *Games People Play* (New York: Grove Press, 1964), p. 30.

Figure 7.3
A Parent-to-Child Communication Transaction

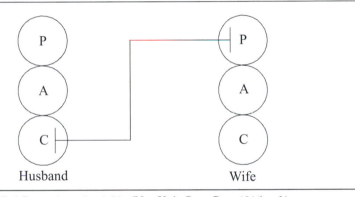

Husband   Wife

Source: From Erik Berne, *Games People Play* (New York: Grove Press, 1964), p. 31.

Communication will proceed smoothly as long as we communicate on the same ego state plane (figure 7.2). Communication is broken off when the transactions are crossed. For example, a wife (parent) telling her husband (child), "You are going to learn to pick up the clothes or else" is an example of a parent-to-child cross transaction, and there is a strong likelihood that as a result of this transaction, an altercation will transpire (figure 7.3).

Another example of a parent-to-child transaction would be if the parents are discussing child-rearing techniques, and one of the parents says, "I hate you, I don't care what you think, little Johnny should be able to stay out late with his friends." In my experience as a marriage/family therapist, the number one reason why conversations escalate into full-blown arguments is that a transactional ego state has been crossed. No one likes to be talked down to—in addition to the conversation becoming condescending, those unconscious family-of-origin feelings of inferiority come to the surface. When people are screaming at each other to be heard, no one is listening, and everyone is frustrated.

What happens over a period of time is that these transactions become predictable and follow a predetermined course. Then, couples find themselves in the same faulty communication rut and are rarely able to organize effective problem-solving conversations.

THE GAME

A game, according to Berne, is an ongoing series of complementary ulterior transactions pr ogressing to a well-defined, predictable outcome. Every game uses deception, and every game has a payoff. Every game is basically dishonest, and the outcome or payoff has a serious negative consequence for the relationship.

"If It Weren't for You"

The most common game played, according to Berne, is "if it weren't for you." In my counseling practice I often see this game played out. One couple that were experts at playing the game were Lance, age 50, and Marion, age 46. After a couple of sessions it was revealed that Lance was very controlling (parent) and that he would limit Marion's hobbies and social activities. It was later revealed that Marion suffered from social anxiety disorder, and now she could unconsciously rationalize her social inhibition by saying "if it weren't for you" (child).

The underlying dynamics involved in this were intriguing but purposeful. Marion was very shy and socially awkward before marrying Lance, and she picked a domineering man for a husband. She was then in a position to complain (child) that she could have done all sorts of things "if it weren't for you."

However, contrary to her complaints, Lance was inadvertently performing a real service for her by forbidding her to do something that she deeply feared—social interactions. In addition to having an available psychological excuse to avoid feared social situations, she also had the self-assurance that it wasn't her problem because "he wouldn't let me get involved" (child).

It was later revealed in the sessions that Marion was physically abused as a child, and from her perspective Lance's domineering behavior only confirmed her opinion that men were tyrants and abusive. Again, this dynamic gives credence to the statement, "We don't see things as they are, we see things as we are."

What people present in counseling is rarely the true issue or problem. In the case of Lance and Marion, covertly, both profited from the game; that is, Marion had an excuse not to deal with her neurotic fears, and Lance could continue to be controlling. Both parties became very comfortable with their dysfunctional homeostasis.

Playing by New Rules

The game can only be stopped if the players first become aware that such a game is being played, and then at least one of the players needs to refuse to continue playing the game. For example, if through self-help books or counseling Marion started to realize that she was suffering from social anxiety disorder, she might have proceeded to get the proper treatment.

In my experience the controlling partner does not usually want to change because he is used to being in charge and in control. Also, unless the controlling partner becomes involved in individual or marriage counseling, it is unlikely that he will even be cognizant of the fact that he is controlling. Too often, I observe one spouse calling the other spouse controlling, and yet the controlling person still denies it, even in the face of obvious truth. However, in this case Lance was involved in marriage counseling, and he did eventually come to realize that he was domineering and to recognize the role that he played in their dysfunctional interactions.

A good part of the counseling process revolved around the balance of power. Lance, who was in control of the direction and lifestyle of the relationship, learned to give up some power and control to Marion. Marion eventually learned how to ask for and take more ownership of her fears and anxieties. Both had to redistribute how power was arranged in their relationship.

"Guess What I Want"

What I'll call the "guess what I want" game is one of the most frequent scenarios that I see played out in the office, and I'm sure you have seen this sequence of interaction in your relationship or in those of others. In this scenario, one of the partners sets the other partner up to guess what his or her needs are. A case in point is that of Justin, age 28, and Samantha, age 24. They were married for four years and had a daughter, Kayley, age three. Justin repeatedly set Samantha up for defeat. Both were extremely busy: Justin was a marketing executive, and Samantha went back to teaching third grade after a leave of absence of three years to raise Kayley. During one initial session Justin commented that he was disgusted with the relationship, which came as a complete surprise to Samantha. When further questioned, Justin angrily blurted out, "She's not affectionate, and she doesn't know when I want sex." Samantha couldn't believe what she was hearing. Justin also exclaimed that by this time, she should know what he wants. The outcome of this game is predictable. All too often, Samantha would try to "guess" (child) what would please Justin, and she would frantically stumble to please him, but to no avail. Hence the payoff: "See, you don't love me, and you don't understand what I want."

Underlying this game was Justin's unconscious need for love and belonging. Justin came from a family of origin that did not or was not psychologically capable of providing a nurturing environment. Justin was sentenced to a life of seeking love and approval. Unfortunately, Justin didn't really believe that he deserved love, and he married a partner who had difficulty in providing nurturing behavior. Samantha's somewhat unemotional disposition served to confirm her husband's inadequacies.

Playing by New Rules

As we'll further learn in chapter 8 regarding communication, couples have the right and obligation to tell the other person what they need and are not getting. All of us view the world through tainted filters, filters that are tainted by our childhood experiences. We see what we expect to see. We tend to seek information to reinforce our beliefs and avoid information to the contrary. For example, a spouse could be nurturing and loving the majority of the time, but the partner does not see it.

In the case of Justin and Samantha, both came to understand the dynamics of the hidden meaning of the payoff, "See, you don't love me or don't understand me." They also learned more how their family-of-origin issues played a part in their relationship. They learned, as I have discussed in chapter 3, the importance of emotionally taking care of each other to mollify childhood wounds. But most importantly, they learned to discuss the concept of telling the other person what they need that they are not getting.

"Look How Hard I've Tried"

Over the years I have seen many cases that exemplify the "look how hard I've tried" game. In the past it was usually the husband who had become adept at playing the game, but today, I find the wife to be playing this game just as much, if not more often. When I initially meet a couple, or even when the spouse calls for an appointment—it is always the spouse that wants to try to save the marriage that calls—I tell him or her that for marriage counseling to work they both must make a commitment to the marriage, or at least to the counseling process. If one is playing the "look how hard I've tried" game, the one that really wants out of the marriage will halfheartedly enter the counseling process.

A recent case that illustrates such a game is that of Trevor, age 32, and Jennifer, age 28. The couple had a little girl, Jennifer, age six. After the initial sessions it was obvious that for whatever reason Jennifer wanted out of the marriage. During the second session Jennifer commented to Trevor, "I love you, but I'm not in love with you." I often hear this, in my estimation, nonsensical comment; I asked her what she meant by it, and, as I typically find, she wasn't quite sure what it meant. Usually, I find it means that that spouse is having an affair. What I found peculiar was that overtly, the couple enjoyed sports and social events together, but they were rarely passionate. Jennifer even commented that Trevor was a great provider (adult). However, both parties said that they wanted to make the marriage work. Jennifer was clever; she didn't protest the counseling, but it was obvious that she wasn't willing to devote herself to the process.

After a few sessions it was obvious that Jennifer was getting increasingly angry, not only at Trevor, but at me. In addition to her comment about loving him but not being in love with him, the anger directed toward her spouse often indicated that she was experiencing guilt, and guilt is projected as anger toward the betrayed spouse. Finally, in the sixth session Jennifer commented that counseling was not working and that she had "tried so hard" (child). In her mind she was blameless; she had tried to save the marriage by participating in counseling. From her perspective she could now say to her parents, child, friends, relatives, judge, and attorney, "Look how hard I've tried."

Playing by New Rules

Some weeks later, Trevor made an individual appointment with me. He did discover that Jennifer was having an affair. She was obviously playing the game in a vain attempt to unconsciously reduce her guilt and rationalize her affair. The outcome could have been different if during the sessions Jennifer had been more open and honest. I later learned that Jennifer's father left the family when she was very young. Consequently, Jennifer's childhood need for security and approval was insatiable. However, couples' counseling was doomed from the start because Jennifer withheld the truth.

Jennifer eventually ran off with Frank, a relationship that lasted six months after the infatuation period wore off. Trevor and Jennifer divorced. However, as Jennifer would eventually learn, only 10 percent of couples believe that they are better off five years postdivorce.[3]

GAMES OF INTIMACY THAT REFLECT POOR PROBLEM SOLVING

Nancy and Robert

Just as we learned in chapter 6, we may perform dances that enhance intimacy, and many people play games that serve to avoid intimacy. One such game involved a pleasant couple named Nancy, age 32, and Robert, age 37. They had one child, Kelsey, age 10.

After a few sessions, when Nancy felt comfortable, she discouragingly related that all Robert was interested in was sex. She exclaimed that he didn't really love her and that she was around only for his sexual enjoyment. Often, Robert would abide by her seemingly honest wishes, and they would not have sex for weeks. Nancy learned to play the game well; she learned how to subtly tease Robert, especially when they had had a few drinks. When she made advances and became flirtatious, he would reciprocate, and she would become repulsed. Then she was in a position to exclaim, "All men are alike, all you want is sex—I want affection!" What is most interesting is that once this scenario was enacted, it set the stage for a vain attempt to avoid their real problems—their in-laws and financial troubles.

In addition, the game served to protect Robert's fragile male ego in that Robert was also afraid of sexual intimacy, and he unconsciously chose a mate who wouldn't readily respond to his sexual advances.

Johnny and Susan

Another game of intimacy that at its core encompassed pure manipulation was a game that Johnny and Susan learned to master. Johnny and Susan were married for over 30 years. They had three children, and all three were out of the house. The game would be played out as follows. Susan would make a request of her husband, such as going out for dinner, and Johnny would oblige her. During dinner Susan would have his undivided attention, and she found it to be an appropriate time to plead for things she wanted him to do, such as fix up the house or pay for major purchases—Susan was particularly fond of expensive antiques. Johnny, on the other hand, was thrifty, and he usually found her requests to be untimely, expensive, and annoying.

At other times Johnny would manipulate the conversation and would subtly bring up things that needed Susan's attention around the house. Susan would then eagerly want to discuss Johnny's shortcomings, but Johnny would rudely dismiss her requests, and he would abruptly terminate the conversation.

After such transactions Johnny would get angry, take Susan home, and go to a bar, where he would see his buddies.

The relational purpose of the game that both played so well was to provide each spouse with an unconscious way to avoid intimacy. Whenever Johnny or Susan wanted to avoid intimacy, they became apt at rudely introducing domestic issues, and the game was launched into motion.

Cycil and Alicia

Another example of a game that I often see played out is, unfortunately, a result of repressed sexual abuse as a child. Again, it is a sad fact that one out of three girls is sexually abused as a child. Often, such horrific psychological trauma is not without devastating consequences within adult relationships. From my years of counseling I could cite numerous examples, but the one that comes particularly to mind is that of Cycil and Alicia.

Cycil, age 24, and Alicia, age 21, were only married for one year when they initiated counseling. Alicia would complain that Cycil was not passionate and that his sexual advances were rude and crude. At his wife's request he would attempt to modify his sexual aggressiveness, but all too often, sex became a major issue and a source of marital conflict. It became such a volatile conflict that the couple did not have sex for six months. It even got to the point that Alicia would cringe whenever Cycil would even casually touch her.

Alicia eventually confessed that she was repeatedly sexually abused by a stepbrother as a child. She, for years, unconsciously repressed the abuse, but Cycil's sexual advances served to resurface the abuse. From her perspective, any sexual contact was unconsciously perceived as a threat, and she would protect herself emotionally and sexually by shutting down. On the unconscious level her payoff was to be able to avoid sexual contact and even blame her husband for her sexual fears. The more psychologically painful the early life trauma, the greater the likelihood that as an adult, the person will engage in an unconscious effort to make close relationships fit an internal negative scheme of things.[4]

Playing by New Rules

In the case of Nancy and Robert the perpetuators of the game were utilizing the defense mechanisms of denial, projection, and rationalization: denial in that both parties, on the conscious level, did not face their sexual inadequacies; projection in that each would project onto the partner his or her own sexual inadequacies; and rationalization in that they learned to utilize their game as an excuse for not dealing with delicate issues that needed to be discussed and resolved.

As I mentioned previously, marriage counseling has to do with how people organize the space between each other, how they go about solving problems. In the case of Nancy and Robert the couple had to first become cognizant of the fact that they were playing a game, then understand the underlying meaning of the game in order to deal with their sexual problems. They also had to learn healthier ways of dealing with emotional and delicate issues.

In the case of Johnny and Susan the spouses had years to orchestrate their game, a game that enabled them to avoid intimacy and to facilitate Susan's eventually purchasing her precious antiques and for Johnny to participate in barroom activities. In this case, both parties had to become aware of the nature of the game, and at least one of the parties needed to refuse to play the game. Once the nature and the consequences of the game were outlined, both were able to more clearly understand the manipulation and deceitfulness of the unconscious motives of their hidden transactions. Also, both learned more open and effective ways to work through and deal with issues of intimacy.

Unfortunately, the outcome for Cycil and Alicia wasn't as favorable as was hoped. Alicia was resistant to getting involved with individual counseling and to dealing with her sexual abuse. The trauma was too painful. Alicia and Cycil eventually separated and divorced.

ENDING GAME PLAYING

During the course of this chapter I have provided a brief analysis of how each couple could learn to operate out of a healthier set of rules. However, there are some general rules to help terminate game playing.

For the games in a relationship and marriage to end, an agreement between the partners must be reached to end all power plays.[5] Both partners need to be aware of power plays in their transactions and must be willing to stop them as soon as they take place.

We will discuss further, in chapter 9, the importance of not keeping secrets from our partners, especially secrets about what we want. We have the right and, I feel, an obligation to tell the other person what we need that we are not getting. We must ask for everything we want 100 percent of the time. The tendency to use games to get what we want is a result of the inability to be honest, open, and clearly request what we want from our partners. We don't always have to agree with our partners' desires, and sometimes we can't accommodate our partners. However, if we at least express our wants, we give the partner at least a chance of obliging. We eliminate the need for games, hidden communication, and power plays, and it fosters honest, open communication.

Another way to move toward ending destructive game playing in a relationship is to examine what S. B. Karpman calls the victim/rescuer dynamic.[6]

Figure 7.4
Karpman's Triangle: Removing the Victim

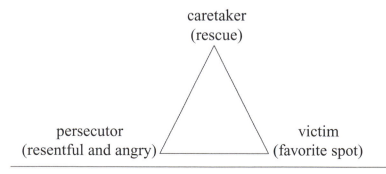

caretaker
(rescue)

persecutor
(resentful and angry)

victim
(favorite spot)

Karpman advocates that marital partners remove both the victim and rescuer roles from their relationship (figure 7.4).

According to Karpman, we can learn to recognize a rescue, refuse to rescue, and refuse to let people rescue us. Surely we will continue to alternate between the three positions until we become consciously aware that we are placing ourselves in a position of disempowerment and we decide to change it and take action.[7]

Removing the Victim

A practical way to help you remove the victim proceeds as follows.

1. On a sheet of paper, detail all the things you consider your responsibilities. Do this for your participation at work and with children, friends, family, and your spouse or boyfriend.
2. Now, list, detail by detail, what responsibilities belong to the other people in your life. If any responsibilities are shared, list what percentage you think is appropriate for each person.
3. Become familiar with Karpman's triangle and how you got through the process in your life. When you find yourself rescuing, watch for the role and mood shifts, and when you catch yourself feeling resentful or used, figure out how you rescued.

Do things you want to do. Say no when you want to say no. Refuse to guess what people want and need; instead, insist they ask you directly for what they want and need. When you initially stop taking care of people who are used to it, they become frustrated and angry. Explain to them that you need to change the system.

Last, in order to eliminate the power struggle in games, you must equalize the power. That means there must be equal rights in a relationship. The word "partner" denotes just that—partner.

Power struggles fuel games. I too often witness one of the parties in therapy struggle for control, and he or she wants the other one to change. Often, there is a hidden, unconscious reason why one partner needs to be in control. And usually, the partner that needs to be in control as an adult came from a dysfunctional family. As a child, his developing years were chaotic, ergo as an adult, he needs to be in control.

SOME IDEAS ON FAIR PLAY

When I first started out as a couples' therapist, I came across a practical little book that profoundly influenced my work. The book was Susan Campbell's *Beyond the Power Struggle*. Dr. Campbell listed some guidelines that I have adopted over the years to help couples who are locked in struggles for power.

Some guidelines that I have found successful in dealing with power struggles include the following.[8]

- The power struggles between people reflect the inner struggles within people. We don't get emotionally involved in a power struggle unless we are in a state of inner conflict, ourselves.

- In any close relationship, where interdependence is essential, all attempts at controlling the other eventually backfire. Communication should be directed toward understanding and empathy, and not controlling one another.

- Each of us sees the world through the filter of his own desires, preferences, values, and past experiences. One person's view represents only one's perspective of "truth" or reality.

- Expanding your perspective to include other viewpoints does not mean you are abandoning your own perspective; you now are thinking in terms of "marital best interest" and you can better see your partner's realities.

- It's not what happens to you that makes you happy or unhappy with your life, but how your interpretation of what happens to you.

- Many couples are attracted to one another because each partner has qualities the other admires; and perhaps unconsciously wishes to possess.

- We can't make other people change; if you want to change your partner, change yourself.

- If you wish another person to treat you in a certain manner, try treating that person in the same manner. Respect engenders respect. Love engenders love.

- Each of us is responsible for the quality of his own inner state, and peace of mind, no matter what happens to him in the external world. Only you control your emotions. Don't utilize *first-impulse* reactions—think.

- Positive expectations about another's motives or intentions engender positive outcomes.

- To expand your range of choices, experiment with *non-habitual* ways of dealing with negative emotional reactions. Attempt to expand your emotional comfort zone.

Chapter Eight

ORGANIZING PROBLEM-SOLVING CONVERSATIONS

All too often, I receive frantic calls pleading to make a marriage counseling appointment for that very day or evening. The callers often comment that if I don't see them immediately, their marriage is doomed. Their hope, of course, is that someone outside of them will save the marriage. In reality, only they have control over their destinies. Also, usually, one spouse believes that if only the other spouse would change, everything would be all right. However, as you peel away their defenses, you discover that often, marital difficulties have to do with the couple's inability to organize problem-solving conversations. I tell my clients that marital difficulty is kind of like stress: it goes away when you are dead. There will be financial problems, in-laws, children, job stress, and so forth. Couples need to learn how they organize the space between themselves and how to approach each other to solve their problems in a healthy, effective way. In fact, a recent study found that 96 percent of the time, the first three minutes of a couple's dialogue predicts whether or not problem resolution will take place.[1]

Popular wisdom tells us that most men withdraw from conflict and difficult conversations, while most women pursue communication. The more the woman pursues, the more the man withdraws. The woman is perceived by the man as a nag, and the man is perceived as not caring or being apathetic. The couple then moves farther and farther apart, and problems are never resolved. Spouses need to learn how to approach each other and resolve their problems. All couples need to learn how to organize problem-solving conversations.

It is no surprise that the highest rate of divorce is during the first and second years of marriage; however, people are often amazed to learn that the second highest rate of divorce occurs during the midlife years.[2] The empty nest stage is, of course, when the children grow up, and they have left the house to pursue their own lives. The reason for the high rate of divorce during the empty nest stage is a lack of communication. In my opinion the majority of a couple's conversations revolve around the children: disciplining them, helping them with schoolwork, engaging them in sports, helping them find the right friends, and so forth. The children leave the house, and unfortunately, the couple finds that they have little in common. They are surprised to learn that they really don't know each other anymore. They are certainly not the same people that they were when they first fell in love. Often, the couple discovers that they are not intimate. You become intimate by having honest, open conversations. If a couple does not work at validating each other, they grow farther and farther apart, and they lose their identity as a couple.

Also, as the years go by, we tend to take our partners for granted. We stop putting our partners first, and many times, we stop doing things as a couple. We may do things as a family, but we also need to do things as a couple. Couples need to get away from the children occasionally and take care of each other. As a family therapist, I tell people that any discord between the husband and wife will reverberate throughout the family. The husband and wife must first take care of each other for the children to feel secure and nurtured. Quite often, the relational arrangement of the family is dysfunctional; that is, the children always come first. If a healthy family is to flourish, it is imperative that the husband and wife first take care of each other, and as a result, the children's emotional needs will be met.

In this chapter I want to offer a blueprint for effective communication and problem solving. So many times, marital partners leave the content and processes of their day-to-day conversations to the mercy of haphazard, unproductive communication habits that are completely governed by unconscious processes. Borrowing on the work of Harville Hendrix and others, I want to show you how to free your communication from these unconscious processes and put it in service to your relational happiness.[3]

GUIDELINES FOR EFFECTIVE COMMUNICATION

When working with couples, in the initial session I stress the need for the couple to utilize healthy communication techniques. Early in my career as a marriage and family therapist, I came across a set of guidelines for effective communication that I would like to share with you. I am not sure who authored them, but I am sure that they have been useful to many of the couples I have treated over the years.

1. Express what you are thinking, feeling, or wanting *now* in your relationship with one another. References to the past tend to confuse issues.
2. Express your feelings in positive terms (that is, say what you're for rather than what you're against): replace "I hate it when you leave the toothpaste in the sink" with "I just like the sink to be clean." Thus the conversation becomes less defensive, opens one's mind, and allows one to be more open to experience.
3. Allow each person to express himself fully before the other talks.
4. If you want the person to behave differently, express yourself in terms of "would you please," or "I would like you to," rather than in terms of "you should." It is imperative that one use "I feel" statements, for example, "I feel hurt when you come home late and don't call in advance."
5. When expressing feelings you know will be upsetting to your partner, describe your own mixed feelings, for example, "I know you are close to your mother, but I feel angry because she is intruding in our family business."
6. No name calling.
7. Don't use generalizations; that is, don't use such words as "never" or "always." For example, don't complain, "You're always so emotional; I can never talk to you."
8. Do not be condescending. No one likes to be ridiculed.
9. As we discussed in chapter 7, when communicating with your partner, do not cross ego states:
   child–child;
   adult–adult;
   parent–parent.
10. Be gentle with each other; your spouse can be your best friend.

PHILLIP AND DOLORES

Phillip, age 26, and Dolores, age 28, entered the office yelling at each other. After the screaming subsided I learned that they intended to get married in eight months. Both were concerned that the relationship wouldn't last because they were constantly fighting and their arguments were never resolved. Their altercations would get so emotionally charged that they wouldn't talk to each other for days. Both would walk away from each other angry, isolated, and frustrated.

As we discussed in chapter 4, relational processes are controlled by unconscious forces that flow directly from the partners' levels of self-differentiation. Phillip and Dolores were working from a low level of self-differentiation; both were very emotionally reactive. Their decisions were based on feelings rather than facts. They also tended to act without thinking things through.

I found that both Phillip and Dolores violated many of the 10 basic rules of healthy communication. Both would constantly interrupt each other, and this intrusion would further escalate their arguments into full-blown personal attacks and name-calling.

Both rarely used "I feel" statements to express themselves. For example, Dolores was habitually late, and instead of Phillip saying, "I feel frustrated because I thought you would be on time," he would exclaim, "You tick me off, you're always late." It's not so much what we say as how we say it. For example, if a spouse is late and we respond with, "You're always late," I guarantee that there will be a fight. More effective communications would start with, "I feel hurt," "I feel lonely," "I feel frustrated," and so forth.

I have found in my counseling experience that it's not so important what we say as how we say it. In a healthy relationship a couple should have the right to talk about anything. Sometimes the topics are emotionally charged, such as sex, in-laws, finances, and so forth, and we have to be careful how we talk to our partners.

Phillip and Dolores would habitually alternate between ego states. Both became apt at calling each other children (parent to child). I, on a number of occasions, would overhear one state to the other that the other was acting like a child. What was most frustrating to the couple was the fact that the issues that needed to be resolved were never resolved. How could one thing be resolved when they couldn't stick to one topic and constantly made references to the past? Specifically, Dolores would bring up the fact that two years ago, Phillip looked at another woman in a restaurant, while Phillip would constantly remind Dolores about a serious financial blunder she had made in the past.

MARITAL FIGHTS SHOULDN'T BE SURVIVAL OF THE FITTEST

For many couples the initial infatuation of romance eventually gives way to a struggle for power in the relationship. I observe many couples that organize their disagreements into "survival of the fittest." Hopefully, when they take their wedding vows, they regard themselves as a relational unit, develop a sexual agreement to terminate passion for others, and develop an interpersonal agreement to establish the priority of their relationship among all their commitments to others.

Because couples enter an emotionally charged relationship, married couples are bound to fight about things. They fight to find out what the relationship can endure, to test each other, to learn where each other's loyalty lies, and to determine whether each participant will be regarded by the other as a competent adult.

Sometimes couples fight for a more primitive reason. They lock themselves into a lifelong struggle, which only the fittest mate will survive. The goal of their sadistic arrangement is not commitment, but conquest; they fight not to change the rules of their relationship, but to succeed in forcing improvements onto one another. They lock themselves into a war of wills, wits, and wounds, from which only one party will emerge victorious, while the other party will be defeated.

The problem is that individual victory in a marital fight, though temporarily appealing in terms of proving gender superiority, defeats the victor in the long run. The conquered mate stops fighting, and the important relational issues that the fights are supposed to clarify never get addressed. The primitive victor in the struggle for power becomes the undisputed master of a domestic situation wherein important issues remain in suspense, loyalty is shaky and shallow, and respect for adult competence is virtually unknown.

The struggle for power in marriage should not be individual, but communal. Fights find their way into marriages not to prove who is the stronger or the better mate, but to strengthen and improve the way both mates arrange the rules of their marital connection.

A case in point is that of Nate, age 56, and Melinda, age 52. Both partners were married once before. They had a boy, Nathan, age 13. The couple was married for 16 years. The last five years had been laden with conflict and power struggles. According to them, the core of their conflicts stemmed from the fact that six years ago, Nate had an extramarital affair, and it was never resolved, while at the same time Melinda quit a well-paying job as an accountant due to extreme job stress. It was difficult for Melinda to find another well-paying position. Both parties were bitter, wanted to prove the other wrong, and were in a struggle for survival of the fittest. Nate eventually won the struggle for dominance, but as so many intense, righteous conflicts end up, he lost the cause. Melinda, after years of emotional abuse and succumbing to his dominance, felt defeated and emotionally withdrew into herself. These issues were never addressed or resolved. After a few sessions Melinda felt that their relationship was hopeless, and they eventually separated. Nate may have won the battle, but he lost the war. Sadly, Nate was so distraught over the breakup that he eventually attempted suicide.

Couples also need to validate each other. Everyone wants his feelings and opinions to be validated. For the speaker to perceive the interaction as intimate, the listener must be responsive, accepting, and validating.[4] We all want to be heard—this goes for in the work environment as well as in our married lives. If our feelings are not validated, we become frustrated and angry. As the years go by, we become more and more angry at the withholding partner. We become more apathetic and more lonely and isolated. We drift apart, and we really don't know the partner anymore. When a discussion escalates into a full-blown fight, we stop listening to each other, and we scream at each other in a futile attempt to be heard.

This technique always backfires. Once the argument escalates and a couple is fighting, it might take hours or even days for the couple to reapproach each other and generate a new attempt to "win the battle."

A more effective technique of communication from the work of developmental psychologist Harville Hendrix is the speaker-listener technique.[5] Basically, this technique involves paraphrasing what the other person is saying. It's based on the premise that we really don't hear or validate each other because we are busy formulating what we will say next. We are planning our defense. The steps involve not interrupting the other person; in fact, we paraphrase each statement that our spouses make. For example, the wife wants to do more things as a couple. The wife starts by using "I feel" statements such as, "I feel frustrated because we need to spend more time with each other." When the wife completes her sentence or short statement, the husband reflects by saying, "I hear what you're saying" or "I understand that you." After the wife completes her thought it is the husband's turn to verbalize. He might comment, "I agree, but we have little time available." The wife paraphrases his comment, for example, saying, "I hear you say we have little time," and so forth.

Some basic rules regarding this technique include the following: stay on one topic, don't jump all over the place, use short, clear statements, and stop often—every sentence or two or if the statements are too long and too difficult to paraphrase. For a more thorough description of the speaker-listener technique, refer to appendix C at the end of this chapter.

When expressing feelings that you know will be upsetting to the other person, describe your own mixed feelings, for example, "I know you are close to your mother, but I feel angry because she is intruding in our family business."

In line with healthy communication I also tell couples that they have the right to tell the other partner what they need that they are not getting. If couples would follow this simple rule, it would help each partner to feel validated, and there would be no second-guessing what the other person wants from the relationship.

Too often, for some unconscious psychological reason, one spouse wants the other spouse to guess what he wants, as if the spouse is a mind reader. If the spouse doesn't guess right, she loses the game. Such a transaction is called a communication double bind. Again, basic communication dictates that we have the right to tell the other person what we need that we are not getting.

STEPS TO FAIR FIGHTING

Once the couple has mastered the 10 specific guidelines for effective communication and is proficient at utilizing the speaker-listener technique, we advance to the more sophisticated, healthy communication steps of "steps to fair fighting." The steps that I have listed here are steps that I first learned from other professional colleagues and that I have refined over the years based on feedback from clients.

1. The person who has the problem is responsible for bringing it up as soon as possible. Before you bring the problem up, think it through in your own mind.
2. State the problem to your partner as clearly and concretely as possible. Use the following format:
   "I am feeling_____ (for example, angry) because of_____ (for example, the way you put me down at your parents' house last Sunday)."

3. It is important that you both understand the problem being brought up. The partner who is on the receiving end should reflect back what was said using the following format:

   "I hear you saying you_____ because of _____."
4. When both partners agree on what is being said, the first partner may proceed.
5. The partner who brings up the problem should take responsibility for offering a possible solution:

   "I would like to suggest_____."
6. This solution can be discussed, and then the other partner may offer a counter-proposal.
7. Discuss several options until you agree that one proposal is most *workable* (not right or wrong, but workable).
8. Once you have agreed on a plan, proceed to talk about how you will put it into action. This means being able to clearly answer the question, Who will do what, when, and how?
9. Now that you have reached an agreement, think about what could happen to undermine it. Who could sabotage this agreement, and how?
10. Working through a conflict stirs up a lot of feelings and means you had to give up something. Congratulate each other for the hard work and willingness to compromise. Reaffirm your relationship in as many ways as possible. You have good reason to celebrate.
11. Agree to come back to this problem after some specific period of time to reassess how the agreement is working. You may need to change it or fine-tune part of it.

ADDITIONAL SUGGESTIONS FOR CONSTRUCTIVE CONFLICT

In addition to these first 11 steps, here are some guidelines suggested by my clients themselves.

1. Be specific when you introduce a gripe.
2. Don't just complain, no matter how specifically; ask for a reasonable change that will relieve one gripe.
3. Confine yourself to one issue at a time. Otherwise, without professional guidance, you may skip back and forth, evading the hard ones.
4. Always consider compromise. Remember, your partner's view of reality feels just as real as yours, even though you may differ. There are, in relationships, no totally objective realities.
5. Do not allow counterdemands to enter the picture until the original demands are clearly understood and there has been a clear-cut response to them.
6. Never assume that you know what your partner is thinking or predict how he will react or what he will accept or reject until you have checked out the assumption in plain language.
7. Never put labels on a partner. Call him or her neither a coward, nor a neurotic, nor a child. If you really believed that he or she was incompetent or suffered from some basic flaw, you probably would not be with him or her. Do not make sweeping, labeling judgments about your partner's feelings, especially about whether or not your partner is real or important.

8. Sarcasm is dirty fighting.
9. Forget the past, and stay with the here and now. What either of you did last year or month or that morning is not as important as what you are doing and feeling now. The changes you ask cannot possibly be retroactive. Hurts, grievances, and irritations should be brought up at the very earliest moment, or the partner has the right to suspect that they may have been saved carefully as weapons.
10. Meditate. Take time to consult your real thoughts and feelings before speaking. Your surface reactions may mask something deeper and more important. Don't be afraid to ask your partner for some time to think.

Remember: constructive conflict resolution takes time. Schedule plenty of time for those conflicts that keep coming up. A time limit is useful (for example, one-half hour), and if you haven't reached an agreement after that period of time, come back to the problem in your next session at home.

The most important thing to remember is that in fair fighting you both begin the process with a win-win attitude. This means that you must be willing to give up something for yourself and your relationship.

THINK IN TERMS OF MARITAL BEST INTEREST

One technique that I utilize in my practice that helps temper how partners react and communicate with each other is to think in terms of marital best interest—not necessarily what is best for each partner, but what's best for the relationship or marriage. If fact, when I first initially meet clients for relationship or marriage counseling, I explain to my clients that I attempt to take the side of the relationship. When we think in such terms, everything falls in place.

A case in point is that of Theresa, age 26, and Mario, age 26. Both were recently married, and the Christmas holidays were approaching, which presented problems. Both their families wanted them to spend Christmas Eve with their families. Theresa was close to her family, and she always spent Christmas Eve with her entire family. Mario was an only child, and if he didn't spend time with his parents, his parents would be all alone, except for an aunt. Both Mario and Theresa loved their families, and they fought for weeks as to with which of the families they would spend Christmas. Thinking in terms of marital best interest sheds a new light on old problems. It also implies that the relationship between two people is more important than either individual. This decision was not based on what was best for Theresa or Mario, but on what was best for the relationship. I am pleased to report that Mario and Theresa found their decision to be an easy one. Both agreed to share their time with both families; they would go to Theresa's home for dinner and later to Mario's home to open presents.

Another case utilizing the principle of marital best interest is that of Latanya, age 28, and Clarence, age 29. This case also involved family gatherings. For the most part Latanya and Clarence had a happy marriage, except when it came to Latanya's family, especially her father. Latanya had two older sisters and an older brother. From Clarence's first meeting with the extended family, there would be problems. Latanya's father, for whatever reason, didn't accept Clarence into the family, and so Latanya's siblings aligned with the father against Clarence. The father would actually insult Clarence and overtly display his disdain for him. Latanya's siblings, although they did not overtly insult Clarence, would ignore him and subtly ridicule him. It was not long before Clarence wanted to avoid the family at all costs. Eventually, his attempts to avoid family functions became an issue of major contention between Latanya and Clarence. It got to the point where Clarence would not attend any of Latanya's family functions. As so often happens, Latanya's family couldn't possibly understand why Clarence was "so standoffish."

After learning of the dynamics of their situation it appeared that neither Clarence nor Latanya would be willing to compromise. Latanya couldn't understand why he disliked her beloved family. Clarence couldn't understand why she wouldn't side with him against such miserable people.

During one of the sessions we discussed the concept of marital best interest: not what's best for Clarence or what's best for Latanya, or even what's best for Latanya's family, but what's best for the relationship. Although, at times, the conversations became intense and emotional, eventually, both agreed upon the following: even though Clarence disliked Latanya's family, it was still Latanya's family, and for the best interest of the marriage he would attend family functions for a specified period of time. He would then be able to leave, and Latanya could stay for as long as she wanted.

It appeared that Latanya and Clarence successfully negotiated, and they were able to compromise for the sake of marital best interest. Clarence never learned to love her family, but he did learn to tolerate them. Clarence learned that we can't control others' actions, only our reactions to their actions. Clarence also learned that we can transcend our environment. When we transcend our environment, we are truly free to behave as we choose, not as other people choose for us.

MARITAL BEST INTEREST AND EARLY RECOLLECTIONS

During counseling sessions, when we are discussing the concept of marital best interest, I often incorporate a technique called "early recollections" to help the couple elicit pleasant memories from their past. Early recollections is basically a projective technique developed by the famous psychologist, Alfred Adler.

This technique is formulated on the belief, as I have related in this book, that our perceptions are subjective and selective and that we often view our partner's behavior through tainted filters. The intervention enables me to uncover lifestyles, relational attitudes, values, and beliefs.[6]

The procedure involves requesting each partner to recall earlier situations that he or she can recollect and to describe them as if they were happening in the present.

Some of the questions that I usually ask follow.

- Can you recall the first time you met your partner? What attracted you to him or her? What most impressed you?
- In earlier years, what kinds of things did you like to do together?
- Before having children, what did you enjoy doing as a couple?
- In earlier times, what was it like to have a sense of wellness? Remember how good it felt?

One particular case that illustrates the use of early recollections to help formulate behaviors that facilitate marital best interest is that of Richard and Claudia.

Richard, age 42, and Claudia, age 39, had three children. As we saw in previous cases, it is very easy for couples to lose their way in the midst of children, careers, families, and so forth. Richard and Claudia got caught up in the fast pace of life, and they forgot what was really important, that is, to think and act in terms of marital best interest. They had taken their marriage for granted; they stopped working at the marriage. Emotionally, they became distant, ergo there were few moments of intimacy and passion.

Via the technique of early recollections, I helped Richard and Claudia rediscover what was really important for them and to recognize what was inadvertently lost. Richard wanted Claudia as she was earlier in the marriage: to initiate things to do as a couple, to be warm and friendly, and to pay more attention to him. Claudia, on the other hand, also wanted Richard to be warm and friendly and wanted him to surprise her with gifts on occasion, to hold her hand more often, and to be less critical of her.

As we discussed these earlier behaviors, we were able to formulate ways to incorporate these requested behaviors into action to enhance their marital best interest.

GETTING WHAT YOU WANT

Earlier, I briefly discussed the necessity, and even obligation, of telling the other partner what you need that you are not getting. This concept is crucial for effective communication and validation of one's feelings. If couples would follow this rule, there would be no need to second-guess what the partner wants and needs. There would be no communication double bind, that is, trying to guess what the partner wants. Telling the partner what you need and are not getting is fair play and enhances open, honest communication, which in turn enhances intimacy and, eventually, passion. As we have learned from previous chapters, various, unconscious forces underlie one's need to orchestrate communication double binds.

Such is the case of Donna, age 48, and Tim, age 50. Tim, due to his childhood experiences, was very insecure. As a result of his insecurity, he was always testing Donna, that is, testing to reassure himself that Donna would not leave him. For example, Donna would go out, on occasion, with the girls, and when she came home, Tim would sulk for days. In essence, Tim was establishing two double binds: "She should have known I'm insecure, and I don't want her to go out with the girls" and "I'm sulking, and she should know that I'm angry." Via counseling, Donna and especially Tim learned the importance of having open and honest discussions about his insecurities. They were able to put an end to the mind reading and an end to the guessing games.

Other statements that I frequently hear that signal to me that one is utilizing mind reading follow:

- "If you loved me, you would know what I want."
- "By now, you should know that. . . ."
- "I know what you want; you should know what I want."
- "If you took the time to understand me, you would know that. . . ."
- "All my life, I've tried to please you, and you should know that. . . ."
- "After all these years you should know that. . . ."

GETTING WHAT YOU WANT AND POSITIVE EXCHANGES

A technique that I used with Donna and Tim to enhance positive relationship feelings and cooperative behaviors is called the "intervention of positive exchanges." This intervention guides the partners through a set of communications that feel rewarding, deepen intimacy, and directly address what each partner wants. As outlined by Robert Sherman and Norman Fredman, the procedure is as follows:[7]

1. Identify clearly and specifically what each person wants.
2. The couple is requested to state these wants in a direct, positive way rather than stating what is not wanted.
3. Surprise the partner regularly with positive behaviors.

I asked each spouse to list three activities the other spouse could perform to please each other. I requested that the activities be specific and be stated in positive terms rather than in a negative or complaining manner. I reinforced the concept that it's not what we say, it's how we say it.

Donna, for example, in an amiable, positive way, requested that she would appreciate having lunch and going shopping with her friends on occasion.

Tim, on the other hand, in a positive, direct fashion, requested that they spend more time together, specifically by having dinner out once a week.

Each partner was instructed to agree to perform at least three tasks prior to the next session.[8] I then followed up on their ability and willingness to complete the tasks.

Tim and especially Donna were resistant to performing various tasks, but eventually, they found the activities to be rewarding. In the beginning, Donna felt that Tim was requesting more of her than she was of him, but we were able to negotiate and resolve this issue. Eventually, however, both learned how to, in a specific and amicable way, ask the other person for what they wanted that they were not getting. They learned to interact in a healthy, positive manner and to modify their self-defeating transactions. They shifted the responsibility for change onto themselves rather than waiting for the partner to change first. They both became more accountable for the happiness of their marriage.

YOU CAN'T MAKE OTHERS CHANGE UNLESS YOU CHANGE

A major factor in facilitating healthy and effective communication is attitude. I find that many couples that I counsel feel defeated. They feel that their relational situation is hopeless, and they feel helpless: no matter what they do, nothing will change. However, the truth of the matter is that we have control and ultimate power more than we realize. A story that I often relate to my clients that exemplifies this point is that for years I taught a psychology course from 2:00 P.M. to 5:00 P.M. on Friday. Frankly, on Friday, I'm exhausted, and I would rather be anywhere than working. However, the same goes for the students. I would project exhaustion onto the class, they would pick up on it, and they would become bored and inattentive. In turn, I would pick up on their negativity, which would make me feel more negative and invalidated—and so forth and so on. I realized that if I purposefully and consciously projected enthusiasm and energy, in turn, the class would become energized, enthusiastic, and eager to learn. Be assured that this technique worked on the vast majority of the class; however, a few students, under any circumstances, will never get enthusiastic about learning.

This scenario is the same for couples. If you want your spouse to change, you change. If you want your spouse to be more considerate, you be considerate. In fact, I'm convinced what we try to control in a spouse usually backfires. If we want people to change, we must change. *When we change, it changes the way we view things, and the things we view change.*

I even, at times, relate a few golden rules from Dale Carnegie, including the following:[9]

- Become genuinely interested in the other person.
- Be a good listener. Encourage others to talk about themselves.
- Make the other person feel important—and do it sincerely.
- Try honestly to see things from the other person's point of view.
- Talk about your own mistakes before criticizing the other person.
- Praise the slightest improvement, and praise every improvement. Be "hearty in your approbation and lavish in your praise."[10]

A case that exemplifies that you can't make others change unless you change is that of Michael, age 56, and Margaret, age 52. Michael and Margaret had been married for 30 years. The couple had three children, and all three lived on their own. Especially after the children left, the couple found their lives to be monotonous. Both would go to work, come home, and watch TV. They even ate their dinner in front of the TV set. Both found themselves in a marriage of convenience, and both were becoming disillusioned with their marital arrangement. Both were extremely unhappy, and after 30 years they thought things would never change.

Even their weekends were uneventful. Michael would play golf, and Margaret would go to garage sales. They rarely did anything together. For example, they hadn't gone out to dinner for nine months.

Michael and Margaret couldn't see the forest from the trees. Over the years their transactions became fixed, negative, and self-reinforcing. They lost sight of what worked well for them. Neither partner attempted to make positive change and gestures to facilitate change, nor did they know how to go about change.

YOU CAN'T MAKE OTHERS CHANGE UNLESS YOU CHANGE AND CARING DAYS

A technique that I found effective in enhancing mutual feelings of security and nurturance between Michael and Margaret was the intervention called "caring days." Caring days is a behavioral therapy technique devised by Richard Stuart based on social learning theory.[11] It enhances positive emotional feelings by encouraging couples to promote small positive changes in their relationship with one another.

In this intervention, couples are asked to initiate transactional changes by acting as if they really do care for one another. The concept is based on the premise of the famous psychologist, Norman Vincent Peale: "throw your heart over the hurdle and the mind will follow."[12] Initiate the action, and the feelings will follow.

In the case of Margaret and Michael I conveyed to them that they must be vested in the process and that they must be willing to change independently of the other. Too often in the past, they were locked in a futile, self-defeating power struggle of waiting for the other person to initiate change.

I asked each one, "Exactly what would you like your partner to do as a way of showing that your partner cares for you?" As outlined by Stuart, it's imperative that the request be positive, specific, small, and not involve present emotional conflicts.[13] Emotionally charged issues would be handled at later sessions, once the couple's relationship was enhanced.

The statements must be formulated in a positive fashion. For example, "don't be late for dinner" was not acceptable, while "please be on time for dinner" was acceptable. Also, statements such as "be nice to me" were too vague, while pressuring the partner for a specific behavior, such as washing the dishes, was acceptable and could be part of the lists.

I then asked each partner to note these items for the week. My intent was to revive and celebrate their progress during the next weekly session and add a few requested items each week as we felt necessary and appropriate.

The list for Margaret and Michael progressed as follows:

Margaret Dates Performed	Agreements	Michael Dates Performed
	Say good morning after waking up.	
	Give me a hug before leaving the house.	
	Bring me a surprise.	
	Eat dinner at the dinner table.	
	Take a walk and converse after dinner.	
	Rub my back.	
	Listen when I talk about work.	
	Take me out for lunch during the week.	
	Hold my hand.	
	Go out for ice cream.	

Deep down, the couple loved each other, but during the course of their hurried lives they had lost sight of each other as soul mates, and they didn't know how to gain back the close emotional feelings that they had in the past. The caring days technique taught them how to make clear, direct requests of one another and what they wanted in the relationship. It was rewarding for me when both expressed that they were feeling more appreciative, emotionally closer, and even more passionate toward each other.

DISILLUSIONMENT AND POSITIVE GESTURES

We all get disillusioned with our partners, and even with our friends. People who fall in love believe that there is another person in the world who thinks ahead about their needs and emotions and who chooses to do things for their best interests. This "special" person is supposed to do things that nurture and protect these feelings.

As time passes, partners take each other for granted. Partners forget that thinking ahead about emotions, choosing not to do annoying things, and choosing to be protective are gifts that partners give to one another. Partners unconsciously begin to regard these gestures as entitlements and start making the exact set of demands for them, which will decrease their frequency and set the stage for disillusionment.

Disillusionment is the relational moment when a person realizes that a relational partner cannot possibly, consistently sustain and fulfill all of one's nurturance and emotional needs. Some relationships are not able to deal with disillusionment, while others learn that they should not expect their partners to be responsible for fulfilling all of their emotional and nurturance needs.

The truth is that disillusionment signals the real beginning of relational commitment. Like the love it supports, commitment rests on the mystery of freedom to choose to deliver to a relationship the gestures that make it thrive.

PROBLEM SOLVING

Once a couple is convinced of the importance of thinking in terms of marital best interest and is proficient in utilizing effective communication skills, they are in a better position to organize problem-solving conversations.

The steps that I utilize in organizing problem-solving conversations are as follow: I have the couple define the problem. After getting each person's perspective of the problem, I ask each person what he or she wants to happen to resolve the problem. Then the couple develops a list of all possible solutions. From that list they discuss conflicts in each person's "want to happen" list. Then the couple generates alternative ways to meet each person's "want to happen" items, and then they pick a final set of alternative actions. Last, they summarize the responsibilities of each person, and then I have them formalize the responsibilities in a written agreement.

One of the most frequent issues that couples need to compromise on is the setting aside of time exclusively for each other. For example, in chapter 1 we discussed the case of Luis and Carmella. Luis, age 34, and Carmella, age 32, were married for 11 years. They had one child, Ramon, age four. Luis ostensibly initiated counseling because in his mind he had had an affair and was experiencing tremendous guilt, while in reality he had no affair. He dated a girl before he met his wife, Carmella. What he was presenting as the problem, "the affair," was actually a plea for attention from his wife.

The first step in problem solving was to define the problem. From Luis's perspective the problem was Carmella's inattentiveness. From Carmella's perspective the problem was Luis's inability to see that working a part-time job, managing a household, and caring for a child were exhausting her.

Carmella wanted to spend more time with Luis but didn't know how she would get the time. Their compromise statement regarding the problem was "we need time for each other, and we need to evaluate our schedules (especially Carmella's hectic schedule) to determine what we need to do to make time for each other."

Their list of wanted solutions included the following:

- Carmella would quit her part-time job.
- Carmella's mother was to watch the baby so they could go out as a couple.
- They would take walks with their child after dinner.
- Luis would not work any more overtime.
- Luis would wash and put away the clean clothes.
- Luis would vacuum the house.
- Luis would cook a few meals a week.
- hey could take out an equity loan to compensate for lost money if Carmella quit her job.
- They would save more money if they stopped doing their hobbies (Carmella liked knitting, and Luis enjoyed activities at the local YMCA).

We reviewed the list in an amiable, problem-solving manner, and both saw conflicts in the "want" lists. Both realized that they couldn't make it financially if Carmella quit her job; however, if necessary, Luis could cut back on overtime. Luis's notion of joining a local swim club was decided to be excessive, but he would continue to enjoy the low-cost YMCA facility. Luis didn't feel that he should be cooking meals since he never cooked, but he did agree to wash and put away the clothes on weekends.

In the end they compromised and agreed in writing to the following resolutions: both Luis and Carmella needed the additional income provided by Carmella's part-time job and Luis's overtime. Luis agreed to help Carmella by vacuuming the house, and on weekends he would do the wash and fold and put away the clothes.

As a way of spending more time together, on Wednesdays and Saturdays Luis and Carmella would cook a meal together. On Mondays, Wednesdays, and Fridays they would walk after dinner. Every two weeks, on Saturday, they agreed to go out alone for a meal at the local diner or go to a movie. Regarding hobbies, they agreed to swim together at the local YMCA at least twice a week. They could leave their child with Carmella's mother.

This chapter is one of the longest in the book because in my experience, what is lacking in troubled relationships and marriages is not so much communication, but the ability to organize problem-solving conversations. Hopefully, this chapter has enabled the reader to not only understand the necessity of effective communication, but also specific steps to enhance it.

APPENDIX C

Checklist for Couples' Dialogue

Two reasons it would be wise to use *couples' dialogue:*

1. To discuss something about which you are upset.
2. To discuss a topic that you think might be "touchy."

The *receiver* is the listening partner. The *sender* is the partner who wants to send a message.

It is the receiver's job to grant a couples' dialogue as soon as possible—preferably right away. If it is not possible to participate fully in a couples' dialogue right away, arrange an appointment so that the sender knows when he or she will be heard. This appointment needs to be made as soon as possible.

SENDER: Ask for an appointment: "I would like to have a dialogue about something. Is now okay?"

RECEIVER: Grant the appointment as soon as possible: "I am available now. What's going on?'

SENDER: Send message.

RECEIVER:

1. Mirroring:
   a. "If I got it right, you are saying. . . ."
   b. "Is that accurate?"
   c. "Is there more about that?"
2. Validation:
   a. "I can understand you would think. . . ."
   b. "Based on what you said, that makes sense to me."
3. Empathy: "I can imagine that you must feel. . . ."

Once the sender feels that he or she has been heard completely, partners trade places as the receiver becomes the sender and the dialogue becomes reciprocal and continues as above.

The Couples' Dialogue

Effective Communication is Essential to a Good Relationship

Communication is the act of transmitting ideas or information. Communication can be non-verbal or the verbal exchange of information, ideas and feelings between at least two people.

In my practice, I have found the couples' dialogue to be one of the most effective techniques to enhance communication between partners. The couples' dialogue provides structure and provides safe means of communication for difficult and emotionally charged issues. It consists of three processes including mirroring, validation and empathy.

Mirroring is the process of accurately feeding or reflecting back the content of a message from one partner. Paraphrasing is the most frequently used form of mirroring. A "paraphrase" is a statement in your own words of what the message of your partner is saying to you. Mirroring signifies to your partner that you are attempting to "truly" listen and understand your partner's point of view. Mirroring eliminates misunderstanding of a message. Too often we don't "hear" the person because we are too busy thinking of our response. In the mirroring exercise, each partner has the opportunity to send his or her message again, and to be paraphrased until it's clear that the message has been accurately understood.

Validation is communication to the sending partner that the content of the message has been received, and is understood by the receiver. It indicates that you understand the message from your partner's perspective, and accept that the information has validity. Validation is a temporary suppression of your feelings regarding the message. Validation indicates that you not only hear, but are truly listening to your partner's point of view. It allows your partner to express her reality. It does not necessarily mean that you agree with the message. It merely recognizes the fact that realities can be different, and it's alright to have different realities. In any communication between two people, there may be two points of view, and every report of any experience is an "interpretation" of what is the "truth" for that person. The process of mirroring with validation enhances trust, open communication and intimacy between partners. Typical validating phrases are: "I can see that," "I hear you saying," "It makes sense to me," and "I get it." Such comments send a message to your partner that these feelings are not discounted or that they are absurd.

Empathy is the process in which the receiving or listening partner attempts to imagine or experience the feeling the sending partner is feeling about the situation being discussed. In this close level of communication, you attempt not only to recognize what your partner is expressing, but attempt to actually experience the emotions your partner is sending. Empathy allows the couple, if only for a moment, to put aside their differences, and see the world as each other sees it. Such a close emotional experience has remarkable healing power and enhances intimacy. Typical phrases for empathetic communication include: "that must feel awful," "I understand how you feel," and "those feelings must really be painful."

A complete dialogue may sound as follows: "So I understand you to be saying that I don't listen to you. I can understand that; I'm glad you brought that to my attention, and I realize that it made you feel angry and isolated because I was not listening to you. That must be a terrible feeling."

After a demonstration of the couple's dialogue, your therapist may ask you to practice it in all conflicted transactions with your partner for the remainder of your therapy.

Chapter Nine

EXTRAMARITAL AFFAIRS—SILENCE, SECRETS, AND SELF-DISCLOSURE

Edward Igle

Rose Castorini:	Well then, why do men need more than one woman?
Johnny Cammareri:	I guess it's because they fear death.
Rose Castorini:	That's it!

When John Shanley wrote the above dialogue into the screenplay of MGM's 1987 production of *Moonstruck,* he put into words the painful, unconscious reality that couples' therapists confront so often with clients who come to them for help in the aftermath of extrarelational affairs. The powerful forces that drive people to break their sexual agreements with one another—and inflict untold damage on their closest relationships—are largely unconscious and heavily denied.

Very few people enter into committed relationships with the conscious expectation that the relationship will be anything other than sexually exclusive. The language of sexual exclusivity is woven into the recited marital vows of many religious traditions and is a cultural given, even in secular wedding ceremonies. Infidelity is grounds for divorce for traditional marriages and legalized domestic partnerships alike. Who, on the day of his wedding, imagines himself or his beloved wrapped in the arms of another?

So why do people cheat on their mates?

JUAN AND MARIA

Consider the case of Juan and Maria. Juan and Maria met in high school and started dating one another exclusively in their junior year. Awkwardly, yet with great emotion, they sexualized their relationship toward the end of their senior year. On their graduation, they announced their engagement, and they married—with the blessings of both of their original families—after they had saved up enough money to afford to get a place of their own.

In the third year of their marriage Juan and Maria became the proud parents of healthy twin boys. By mutual agreement, Maria, who was a bank clerk, stopped working outside the home, and Juan, who was a roofer by day, took a second job as a security guard at night.

Fern was a dispatcher at the security firm. She was around the same age as Juan, slightly overweight, and terrifically lonely. Fern lived with her single-parent mother and three younger brothers. She had never been married and had no children. Out of loyalty and love for her mother, Fern had delayed going to college to help her family financially. Her deadbeat father could not be counted on for child support. He could be counted on, however, to offer Fern long and pathetic tales about his failed efforts to please his ex-wife, Fern's hapless mother.

Juan's security job was structured in such a way as to require him to check in with Fern several times during his shift and to check out with her when the shift ended. Their chats were all business at first but gradually became more and more personal. Fern talked about the miseries of her mom and the chronic probation troubles of her brothers. Juan talked about the fatigue of his wife, the demands of his sons, and the stresses of working two jobs.

Without Juan ever intending it he began talking more openly and honestly about his personal life with Fern than with Maria. Maria sensed the growing relational distance between herself and her husband but chalked it off as exhaustion. Maria and Juan continued to talk to each other, but their conversations were centering more and more on their schedules and their children and less and less on their relationship and their emotional needs.

Fern and Juan's blossoming psychological intimacy became clandestine sexual intimacy about three months after Juan started working as a security guard. In the beginning the intimacy consisted of exchanges of oral sex at the workplace, but soon the couple was meeting furtively at motels, parks, and clubs for more thorough sexual activity. Juan's explanations to Maria about his whereabouts became more convoluted and less plausible, and finally, during an emotional confrontation with Maria, Juan admitted that he was having an extramarital affair. To keep his family, Juan agreed to quit the security job, stop seeing Fern, and participate in marital therapy.

The marital work I did with this couple was painful and maturing for both spouses. I used treatment paradigm, developed by psychiatrist Frank Pittman.[1] I also utilized some of the more contemporary concepts offered by psychologist Janis Abrahms Spring. The first task was to stabilize the spouses' conversations (so that every conversation did not lead to a rehash of the pain associated with the disclosure of the affair) and then to help the spouses identify the unconscious forces that placed their marriage at risk for intrusions by sexual raiders in the future.[2]

For Juan the unconscious forces that fueled his participation in an illicit affair were embedded in his beliefs about talking. Somehow, he came to believe that he was not supposed to voice feelings of exhaustion and stress to his wife. He made up a story in his head that Maria was exhausted too and that talking to her about his own troubles would just make her troubles worse. Moreover, Juan supported his silence by telling himself that Maria would think that he was less of a man if he complained about his jobs, his kids, and his life.

Juan could not imagine a conversation between himself and his wife (about the stressors they were confronting) that could lead to either of them feeling better about their circumstances or closer to one another. He could, however, imagine that talking about these stressors with his affairee instead of his wife was a good way of protecting his wife from unwelcome duress. What Juan did not anticipate, however, was that psychological intimacy would grow between himself and Fern and that this intimacy would feel like relief from a nagging sense that he was not man enough to stand up to the pressures of life. Neither did he anticipate that his relief would push him toward the kind of sexualized relationship that would completely erase his feelings of being less than a man.

For Maria the unconscious forces that organized her into the hapless role of the cuckold were likewise embedded in her beliefs about talking. Somehow, she too had come to the belief that voicing her feelings of exhaustion and stress to her husband would only make things worse. Maria made up a story in her head that Juan would experience her concerns as more work for him, and she supported her silence by telling herself that to pretend not to notice their growing relational distance was a favor she was doing for her husband and for their marriage.

In marital therapy Juan and Maria began to talk together about the unconscious rules that each of them was obeying when it came to deciding what could be discussed and what had to remain unspoken. Maria recalled the way her own parents relied on highly ambiguous, nonverbal signals (sighing, eye rolling, and so forth) to express exasperation, exhaustion, and disappointment to one another. Juan recalled that his own father chose to suffer in silence, for fear that the slightest complaint would send his wife into emotional orbit and lead to threats of marital dissolution.

Both spouses found that they had entered their marriage with virtually no language to use to talk about dissatisfaction. They found that they were slavishly obeying unconscious rules of silence and nondisclosure that made their marriage open to external emotional intrusion. Happily, Juan and Maria eventually found that working together to invent a language for this side of their experience was a good way to affair-proof their relationship in the future.

ELLEN AND TED

The situation of Ellen and Ted was somewhat more complex. Ellen and Ted met in college, when both were working toward bachelor's degrees in elementary education. They began dating one another exclusively in their senior year and married soon after graduation. They were lucky enough to go to work for the same school district, and even though they taught in different schools (because of school board policy), they were both satisfied that this arrangement would be good for their relationship and good for their professional development.

Five years into their marriage, Ellen and Ted decided it was time to start a family. After two years of trying to conceive a child (one year of which was devoted to the rigors of fertility counseling) the partners received the unwelcome news that Ted was unable to have children. Their grief was intense, but their love was strong, and Ellen and Ted decided to make the best of the situation and move on with their life as a childless couple.

That is, until Ellen met Alan. Alan was a new teacher at Ellen's school. He was fresh out of college, handsome, and full of energy and enthusiasm. Ellen befriended Alan almost immediately, telling herself that he reminded her very much of Ted in their college days. Ellen introduced Alan to Ted, and the three of them became great friends. They went out to dinner together often, enjoyed the same kinds of music and plays, and shared the same (critical) attitudes toward school board politics and policies.

Ellen and Alan worked together on various extracurricular projects at their school, just as Ted was doing at his school. Sometimes Ellen and Alan would work late into the night at Ted and Ellen's apartment to finish an important project before the next day of school. One night, Ted, who had gone to bed early and left Ellen and Alan in the living room of the apartment working on a project, unexpectedly came out of his bedroom, only to discover Ellen and Alan having sex on the living room floor. Alan gathered up his clothes, apologized profusely to Ted, and left the apartment in haste. Ted and Ellen sat for a long time in silence, each waiting for the other to speak. When they did begin to talk, the talk was about pain, humiliation, betrayal, and lost trust.

Many couples would have collapsed under the weight of this kind of problem, but not Ellen and Ted. Ellen and Ted decided to seek out marital therapy to help them figure out how to work through the terrible feelings of hurt and resentment that were blocking them in their attempts to reconnect with one another. They knew they wanted to stay together, and they wanted staying together to feel safe and secure.

My work with Ellen and Ted, and their traumatized relationship, was complicated by the fact that both of them wanted their friendship with Alan to continue. They did not view him as a predator out to invade their relationship, but as a young, impulsive man who had made a terrible mistake. Alan, too, reportedly wanted to remain friends with both Ted and Ellen, and he was appropriately contrite and had pledged to respect the sexual boundaries of the marriage from now on.

Since Alan was going to be something of a permanent fixture in their lives for years to come, the couple was going to have to embark on a psychological and emotional journey together of considerable depth and in considerable pain. Much of the journey would be about the unconscious forces that were organizing Ted and Ellen into having and keeping sexual secrets.

Ellen was the second oldest of four children, born to parents who were married and who lived under the same roof until Ellen was nine years old. She had one older brother and two younger sisters. After Ellen's parents divorced Ellen and her sisters lived with her mother in the marital home, while her older brother went to live with her father in a nearby town. According to Ellen, the separation and divorce of her parents was accomplished painfully but without the destructive rancor and sabotage that accompanies so many marital dissolutions. In the years following the split-up of the household Ellen stayed in touch with her father and even established a workable bond with the woman who would become her stepmother.

Ellen's bond with her mother was complicated by Ellen's mistrust of her mother's judgment when it came to men. Ellen viewed the men her mother dated as "losers" who were seeking to save a damsel in distress and secure a ready-made family for themselves. These men, according to Ellen, were impulsive, self-centered, and immature. In one of our sessions of marital therapy, as the spouses were talking to one another about the beliefs about gender that each had carried into the marriage, Ellen singled out one of her mother's suitors in particular as an illustration of her mother's stupidity and went into an unbridled tirade against her mother for having had a relationship with such a man.

I wondered to myself whether Ellen's anger toward her mother was protecting her own ego from a less conscious, more powerful anger toward herself. I directed Ted, who was shrinking back from Ellen's display of outrage against her mother, to ask Ellen if it would be all right with her if he asked her to talk more about this man and less about her mother. Ellen took a deep breath and agreed. I helped Ted find the words to ask his wife if there was anything about this man that Ellen would like to tell him, perhaps something that would help both of them understand their marital circumstances. Ellen slowly and tearfully disclosed to her husband that this man, who was only in Ellen's life for less than six months when she was 11 years old, had molested her sexually on at least five separate occasions.

Ted received Ellen's disclosure with a mixture of terror and tenderness. It made sense to him, he told Ellen, that she was furious toward her mother for not protecting her and that she was loathe to talk about this horrible experience with others. It meant a lot to him, he continued, that Ellen had chosen to reveal this part of her pain to him. He pledged to accompany Ellen through all the mandatory reporting procedures required by our state, and, more importantly, to never hold the secret or the silence against her.

SILENCE AND SECRECY

Ellen had kept this sexual secret to herself for over 20 years and had essentially decided that she would carry the secret with her to the grave. She had come close to yelling the secret at her mother during a fight just before Ellen went off to college, but she did not let go of it. Ellen had another close call with disclosure during the infertility procedures—believing, of course, that the infertility problem was her fault and somehow associated with the molestation—but her interest in disclosure evaporated once she found out that Ted was the one with the problem.

It is worth noting at this point that Ted was less than free of sexual secrets himself. Ellen's disclosures somehow made it possible for him to talk openly to her about his own troubling, beer-saturated experiments with homoerotic activities during his middle and later adolescence. He was able to disclose that for a long time he secretly worried that he might be gay and that his discovery that he was infertile had reactivated these same nagging worries. He, too, had decided to carry this secret—and all its anxiety—with him to the grave.

Now, the sexual secrets were out in the open, and Ellen and Ted could work together to unbind their marital happiness from their secrets' terrible grip. Ellen and Ted could begin to figure out why having or being a sexual secret was such familiar territory for both of them. They could develop a language that would help them talk more openly and honestly about their sexual histories, needs, and interests. Now, they could make healthy decisions together to protect their relationship from future sexual traumas.

The beliefs about silence and secrecy that compounded the miseries of these two couples had their roots in the less conscious aspects of their marital contracts. Marital contracts are relational premises that regulate each partner's participation in a marital system. Some of these premises are conscious and publicly articulated, like ceremonial vows about being true to one another in good times and in bad, and in sickness and in health. Other premises are conscious and privately articulated, like agreements between relational partners about where they will live, how they will earn and control money, how they will organize their work schedules, and so forth.

Couples draw information about what sorts of conscious expectations to include in their marital contracts from their cultural and social environments. Among other things, these environments assure them that they rightly expect their mates to be loyal, loving, devoted, and sexually exclusive. They can also expect their mates to provide a kind of insurance against loneliness as well as socially sanctioned, readily accessible sex. More dramatically, partners can rightly expect that their marital contracts will be based on strong levels of conscious agreement that the marital relationship will serve as a launching pad for the creation of a family, will provide both mates with a strong ally in pursuit of economic security, and will protect both mates against the chaos and stress of everyday life.

SEXUAL SECRETS

The problem is that relational problems like infidelity usually do not come from the conscious aspects of a couple's marital contract. They come from the less conscious needs and relational premises that flow beneath the surface of relational functioning, especially in the murky regions of human sexuality.

For both of the men in the clinical examples above, marriage was supposed to suppress fears of gender inadequacy. We may never know what kinds of early developmental insults to his masculinity organized Juan to believe that if he complained about the hectic and draining pace of his life to his wife, she would think that he was less than a man and that her thinking that he was less than a man would make it true. Was Juan taught silly pet names for his genitals as a child that make being a male seem ridiculous? Was his father's masculinity constantly berated or ridiculed in his family of origin? Did he learn to view masculinity solely through the eyes of a mother who was profoundly disappointed in a man, as Frank Pittman would put it?[3]

What we do know is that Juan unconsciously operated out of the premise that his masculine identity was in the head of his wife and not in his own head. Thus at all costs he had to work hard to organize and preserve her sense that he had what it took to be a man. He had to avoid any conversation that might have placed her vision of his masculinity in jeopardy, and—even if he felt hollow and alone within—he had to keep his fears about not being enough of a man to himself.

In a way, that's what made the relationship with Fern so appealing, and so compelling, to Juan. He certainly did not consciously intend their conversations about life's pressures and stresses to lead to erotic exchanges, but the intimacy that began to grow between them, once Juan convinced himself that Fern could be trusted not to pass a negative judgment on his masculinity, generated an erotic life of its own. She was presenting him with a sexual opportunity, and no real man could turn down a sexual opportunity. In a way, that was completely unconscious to Juan—sex with Fern could do what talking to Maria could not do: convince Juan that he was still a real man.

The unconscious relational premises that compounded the gender issues for Ted were equally complex and controlling. Unlike Juan, Ted was keenly aware that his sense of gender adequacy had been injured. Ted's homoerotic experiences in college haunted his male ego all the time, and he had taught himself to integrate them into his emotional system in a homophobic way, as "bad things" he would "never be led into again." This conscious resolution seemed to work well for Ted, until it was shattered by the news that he was infertile.

Ted's internalized homophobia established an unconscious matrix that led him right from infertility to self-rejection. Even though there was no real connection between Ted's sexual experimentation and his inability to have children, Ted felt like there was, and this feeling became the linchpin of his sexual secrecy.

Ted was not gay, or even bisexual. Even during the heyday of Ted and Ellen's burgeoning friendship with Alan, Ted felt no erotic attraction toward Alan. It is possible that the proximity to Alan was stirring up some less conscious homoerotic feelings, but these feelings did not seem to be the ones that were organizing Ted to keep this one piece of sexual history a secret from his wife. It was his unconscious premise that when it comes to preserving a marriage, some things are better left unsaid.

David Schnarch, a psychologist and sex therapist from Evergreen, Colorado, has written and lectured extensively on the issues surrounding relational self-disclosure. Dr. Schnarch talks about the difference between reciprocity and what he calls "self validating intimacy"[4] in intimate relationships. Reciprocity, according to Schnarch, has to do with the belief that one's relational partner controls how much information one gives about the self. When you hear someone say, "I would love to tell my wife about this (behavior, mood, or belief), but I can't because if I did, she would get too upset," you know he is operating out of what Schnarch calls "a reflected sense of self."[5]

In a reflected-sense-of-self scenario, one relational partner subtly blames the other for what has to be hidden about the self. My openness depends on your tolerance. In reality, according to Schnarch, my openness about myself does not depend on your tolerance at all; it depends on my own tolerance for self-disclosure, that is, the extent to which I can challenge my own fears of rejection in order to be honest with myself first (and subsequently, with the other) about my life, my sexual needs and interests, and my biography.

Self-validating intimacy is just the opposite. In this scenario I do not blame the moods and hysteria level of the other for my secrecy; I view my secrets, especially my sexual secrets, as a challenge to myself. I ask myself to ferret out the unconscious premises that lead me to think of them as unspeakable. I challenge myself to hold on to myself emotionally, whether my partner expresses revulsion and disgust or acceptance and empathy. The central question in intimacy becomes not "what can my partner stand to know about me?" but "what can I stand to say about my true self?"

Think about Ellen. It makes sense that she had decided to protect Ted from the pain of learning that she had endured sexual molestation as a child. But was she really doing him a favor? Was she helping her marriage? What was she doing to herself?

In our culture, people keep sexual secrets for the same reason that they tell lies. People never lie to people whom they perceive as relational equals. They only lie to people whom they perceive to be either too powerful or too vulnerable to know the truth: too powerful because they may use the truth about them to obliterate them; too vulnerable because the truth about them may obliterate them.

It's the same with sexual secrets. They are only necessary in relationships that are structured around inequality. Ellen's secrecy about molestation, and all the shame that was accumulating on the secret like barnacles on an ocean liner, were keeping her below Ted in the marital relationship. Compounding the burden of the molestation secret was the secret extramarital affair with Alan.

Therapists who work with the adult survivors of childhood sexual abuse often find that many survivors are experts in not noticing or denying that sexual boundaries have been or are being crossed in a relationship. This is because children tend to disperceive that a trusted grown-up could be using them for his or her sexual gratification and because children naturally tend to use denial when they do not understand what is happening to them. For many adult survivors, actions that are obviously sexual in nature and in content just do not feel that way, largely because their denial systems are active in protecting them from a reiteration of childhood trauma.

Ellen's innocent exchanges of affection with Alan were indeed sexual long before she recognized them as such. What made her realize that she was in fact involved in an extramarital affair was not so much the erotic activity taking place between herself and Alan, but the fact that she felt required to keep the activities a secret from Ted. A terrible conflict was (once again) taking place inside her soul as she struggled with the gap between her perception ("Alan and I are just very affectionate friends") and her behavior ("I can't tell Ted just how affectionate Alan and I have become").

In a way, having a sexual secret of her own, and being Alan's sexual secret in their affair, was familiar territory for Ellen. The same unconscious, very self-effacing relational premises were governing both aspects of her relational life: "My silence about the pain I endure as I keep my sexual secrets is a favor I am doing for someone I care about," Ellen would say to herself unconsciously. "I cannot withstand the emotional effect that telling my sexual secrets would have on my husband."

The unconscious belief idea that keeping silent about pain is a favor one does for one's relational partner also afflicted Maria. Recall that her parents were quite indirect when it came to expressing marital frustration and that, like them, Maria came to rely on highly ambiguous, nonverbal signals (sighs, winces, moans about physical aches and pains) to communicate her troubles to her husband. Recall, too, that Juan had a father who was an expert in trying to avoid responsibility for a woman's next bad mood and that Juan was therefore not very good at seeing negative, nonverbal signals as information about his wife; he thought they were all about him.

PREOCCUPATION WITH THE AFFAIREE

Yet Maria carried another, more lethal relational premise into marital therapy with her, a premise that could have torpedoed both the therapy and, more importantly, the marriage from the start.

When couples come for therapy in the aftermath of the disclosure of an extramarital affair, they usually have talked themselves into sad and painful impasses of frustration by talking too much about the affairee, the mechanics of secrecy, and the appropriate levels of outrage and contrition. One of the first things a couples' counselor has to do is emancipate the couple from the belief that talking about the affairee—especially her or his personality defects and moral turpitude—is a good way to restore marital balance.

At the beginning of my work with Juan and Maria it was virtually impossible for Maria to stop talking about Fern. She wanted to know all about Fern, everything from her bra size to her unabridged sexual history. When Juan would come up with weak answers to her questions, Maria would blast him for "holding back the truth." Juan would then respond with something that sounded to Maria as though he was defending Fern's privacy, and Maria would fly into emotional orbit in a way that was reminiscent of Juan's mother. Juan would freeze, look at the door of my office, and then look to me for help. I told Juan to explain to Maria that the things he did not know about Fern were the same things he did not know about Maria.

As the battles over Fern began to lose their intensity, Maria slowly became interested in exploring the deeper meaning of her curiosity about Fern. What unconscious premises were organizing Maria to the belief that the only way she could find relief from her feelings of disappointment and betrayal was to scour Juan's perceptions of the affairee's life for a list of Fern's weaknesses and defects?

Maria, it turned out, was drawing her entire identity as a woman from being selected as a partner by a man. She was only attractive if a man said she was. She was only competent if a man said she was. Intelligence, intuition, imagination, and importance could not be permanently achieved; they had to be temporarily assigned to her by a man. For Maria the loss of a man's validation meant the loss of her identity as a woman.

It was Maria's unconscious belief that Juan's breaking of the sexual agreement was information about her and not about him. Her pain at being betrayed in the marriage was compounded by all the fear and shock that comes with a loss of identity, an unconscious suspicion that her life had lost its grounding. To reground, Maria had to obey an unconscious rule that required her to know what made Fern "superior" to her in Juan's mind. This, at a time when Juan's mind was not on Maria, but on his own feelings of male inadequacy.

I am happy to report that by working together in couples' therapy, both Maria and Juan were about to surface and think through and discard the highly sexist, unconscious premises that destructively skewed the balanced power in the relationship against Maria even as they set Juan up for masculine failure. They were able to move past battling about Fern and to begin talking about their own relational needs and expectations, and more than that, they were able to talk as equals, whose senses of gender adequacy came from within and not from outside.

RAIDING OTHER PEOPLE'S MARRIAGES

Before we move on to ways that couples can protect their relationships from sexual raids from outsiders, let's think about the two sexual raiders in our case examples, Fern and Alan. Why do people raid other people's marriages?

Some people forgetfully leave their keys in their cars or the doors to their houses unlocked. Most people walk right by cars with their keys in them without attempting to steal them, and most people walk by unlocked houses without entitling themselves to the contents therein. But some people do not.

Fern was not a client, so my understanding of her role in the marital crisis between Juan and Maria is based largely on their narratives about her. She seems to have been primed, however, for a role in an unhappy marriage by her role in her family of origin, which, as you recall, placed her in something of a parentified role toward her overburdened mother and which may have unconsciously kept her searching for a way in which she could cure her irresponsible father.

I am guessing that Fern listened to Juan's story about his personal miseries with a sympathy that was familiar to her. I am guessing, too, that this familiarity activated a need to be needed by him that was completely unconscious to her. This need to be needed organized Fern into the role of affairee in incremental steps, first as a good listener, then as an emotional soother, and ultimately, as a sexual partner.

As for Alan, it would be easy just to chalk off his intrusion into the emotional space between Ted and Ellen as boyish impulsivity or male inability to turn down a sexual opportunity. But Alan was propelled into the role of affairee by more than unbridled energy and blind pursuit of sexual gratification. He was in love.

Alan's employment at the same school where Ellen taught was his first real job. After living at home during his college years he was happy to be able to afford a place of his own and to be able to come and go as he pleased without having to generate explanations that would satisfy his critical and somewhat hypervigilant parents. During college Alan had had a few girlfriends, but none of them passed the family muster: each one was either too fat or too thin, the wrong religion or ethnicity, or the wrong something else. His college flames would easily be extinguished by gusts of parental disapproval.

Alan approached his first job with enthusiasm, high hopes for success in being able to get through to his students, and a hole in his life where companionship was supposed to be. When Ellen befriended him and introduced him into her life with Ted, Alan was ecstatic. He loved the feeling of being with a slightly older couple who accepted him for who he was, and he gloried in the experiences of being respected as a peer by more experienced colleagues in his chosen profession. Most of all, he love being treated as an adult.

Alan did not befriend Ellen and Ted with a conscious wish to become Ellen's sexual secret. It was, as he explained, the farthest thing from his mind that he would actually fall in love with Ellen, let alone enter into a sexual relationship with her. Those long nights of working together with Ellen on school projects, basking in the glow of her admiration and acceptance, lit a fire inside him, and the fire, which he called "love," had a course and mind of its own.

Alan knew he was in love with Ellen long before he acted on it. Once he realized what was happening, he still participated in merry events with Ted and Ellen together: he still laughed at Ted's jokes, he still took Ted's professional advice seriously, he still joined Ted and Ellen in hilarious conversations about the foibles of the authority figures that they had in common. He soon began to long for little moments of time alone with Ellen—when Ted went to the men's room at a restaurant, when Ted had to take a telephone call, when Ted would have to go to bed early, and so forth.

Soon, Alan began to engineer these little moments of alone time. He volunteered for extra projects at school that required Ellen's attention and participation. He generated power struggles with uncooperative and arbitrary authority figures at work that would get him so worked up emotionally that only Ellen could soothe him into viewing the situation calmly and rationally.

During these alone times Alan found himself getting more and more tactile during his conversations with Ellen. At first, they just held hands. Friends hold hands, he told himself. Then they started kissing. Friends kiss, he told himself. Then sexual arousal started to accompany the kissing. This is only natural, he thought. Then the secretive, undeniable sex started taking place. This must be what happens, Alan told himself, when people are in love.

What Alan did not tell himself was that Ellen was married to another man. Of course, he "knew" that she was Ted's wife, but somehow this knowledge was not available to him when he was immersed in his own experience of being in love. Granted that Ted and Ellen had left the door to their intimate marital space wide open, but why did Alan need to enter it?

It is likely that on an unconscious level Alan selected Ellen for romance precisely because she was married and therefore unavailable. Perhaps he had unwittingly internalized his parents' critical stance toward his selection of girl-friends in college. This internalization would have thoroughly organized Alan to unconsciously expect that falling in love was something that happened just before a relationship collapsed. It would also protect him from an unconscious fear that if left to his own devices, he would pick the wrong relational partner. The unconscious is a great architect of safety: what better way is there to prepare yourself for a relational demise and to escape responsibility for a relational failure than to raid somebody else's marriage?

CONSTRUCTING AN AFFAIR-PROOF RELATIONSHIP

The disastrous impact of extramarital affairs on couples and families cannot be underestimated. Somewhere between 17 and 60 percent of all divorces take place in the aftermath of the discovery of infidelity.[6] The children of divorce are well, if not overrepresented among the consumers of mental health care in America, are among the subjects of child study teams in virtually every school district, and, of course, are among the pathetic individuals involved with the juvenile justice system.

Thus it is a good idea for couples to develop effective ways to prevent infidelity from creeping into their relational structures.

The best way to affair-proof a relationship is to have a clear, conscious, and communicated sexual agreement. Sexual agreements set the sexual boundaries in and around a relationship. They are articulations of what the relational partners agree are their acceptable sexual behaviors together and what the relational partners agree are the acceptable sexual limits that must be set in relationships with others. Sexual agreements govern all kinds of sexual behaviors, including autoeroticism, pornography, oral and anal sex, conventional sex, birth control, kissing, fondling, cuddling, sadistic and masochistic endeavors, the use of prostitutes, and more.

There are no official sexual agreements. There is only the sexual agreement negotiated between the partners themselves, guided by whatever moral, spiritual, religious, philosophical, or cultural resources are available to the partners at any given point in their development. Some partners may agree, for example, that masturbation is sanctioned by their sexual agreement as long as it is done in solitude, while others may agree on just the opposite. Some may agree that pornography may be used to enhance sexual enjoyment, and others may detest pornography as an affront to the dignity of human sexuality. Some may agree that kissing a nonspouse is okay but that fondling a nonspouse breaks the sexual agreement.

The point is that not having a clear, conscious, and communicated sexual agreement creates a dangerous level of ambiguity about what really constitutes infidelity. The preinfidelity problem for many couples is that they either have no sexual agreement at all or that they have left too much of their sexual agreement unspoken and therefore unconscious and unnegotiated.

What makes it hard for couples to have the set of conversations that will give them the gift of a clear, mutually agreeable, and effective sexual agreement? In a culture where sex drips from every corner of advertising and where the "private" sexual antics of celebrities have just as much exposure as the public performances of their crafts, you would think it would be easy for relational partners to talk openly and honestly about their own sexual interests, needs, and tastes, but it is not.

Many couples that set out to negotiate a sexual agreement find their voices choked off by unconscious fears of rejection. Somehow, the partners are governed by an unconscious premise that tells them that if the partner really knew what was sexually interesting to him or her, the partner would run away shrieking in disgust. In reality, sexual needs and interests are no more character-revealing than a person's interest in diet and exercise, TV shows and Broadway plays, or hip-hop and country music, but disclosures about the self in these domains certainly do not feel the same as disclosures about sex.

Disclosures about sex do not feel the same as other revelations about the self because the unconscious premise of rejection is layered with shame and self-loathing. Shame is the name of an emotional force that keeps us convinced that some mistakes we made in the past are so powerful that they forever determine our futures. Self-loathing is a management of shame, a foreclosure on the rejection that would surely come from others if they knew the terrible things one had done. For many people their first excursions into sex were so awkward, so isolative, and so inexpressible in words—especially to the people closest to them—that the unconscious premise of rejection became their best psychological friend.

For couples who want to protect their relationship by developing a clear, conscious, and communicated sexual agreement the unconscious premise of rejection is a friend that needs to be left behind. Negotiating a clear, conscious, and communicated sexual agreement is no easy task, but the failure to negotiate such an agreement greases the skids to marital disaster.

Another good way to affair-proof a relationship is to observe when and why the relational partners stop talking to each other about their relationship. It is true that not everyone appreciates talking about relational themes, and marital researcher and therapist John Gottman has described an entire coterie of married couples who seem to thrive on avoiding talk about relational problems and minimizing relational conflicts.[7] It is also true that almost every couple can look back on the early days of its formation and find a time when talking about the relationship itself felt safe and informative. During those early, privileged days of romantic attachment and interpersonal enchantment, relational partners freely disclosed their dreams and desires to one another, and the flow of mutual feedback felt effortless and welcomed by both partners, but apparently not for long.

One of the first things that couples tell their relational therapists is that they haven't talked about their relationship in a nonconfrontational way in a very long time. The partners go on to say that jobs, or children, or money, or possessions, or travel, or hobbies became more interesting topics of conversation and that talking about each other's relational needs and expectations just took a backseat to more pressing issues. There was no conscious shift away from talking about the relationship—it just happened.

Relationships exist in the heads of relational partners and in the heads of the people who make up a relationship's audience (children, relatives, friends, employers, work mates, and others). Relationships therefore exist in language; that is, they come into being, generate meanings, and advance in their development when the partners take their ideas about the relationship out of their heads and talk about them with one another. In addition, the ways that people talk about their relationships to one another and to the members of their audiences send powerful signals to the members of their audiences about the health and viability of the relationships themselves.

When partners stop talking to one another about their relationship, two things happen: (1) relational ideas in the heads of the partners get more and more saturated with distortions about one another's needs and expectations and (2) distortions invariably lead to overt conflicts or deadly silences that are supposed to clear things up, but that only compound the distortions. When certain members of the relational audience unconsciously experience the conflict or the silence as a vacuum, they feel sucked in to the midst of it and are primed for tragic roles as relational intruders and affairees.

The processes that control couples when they stop talking about what is happening between them are largely unconscious. Often, the partners are aware of surface rationalizations like "every time we talk about our marriage, he gets upset" or "the less said the better" or some other similar pattern of thought. They are less aware of deeper, more controlling beliefs about sexual shame, fear of rage, or terror in the face of rejection that reinforce the avoidance of conversations about the partners' shared relational experience.[8]

That's why it's a good idea for relational partners to build opportunities to talk about their needs and expectations into the infrastructure of their life together. Many good ideas about how to do this are found elsewhere in this book. Granted, conversations about needs and expectations are laden with anxiety and sometimes lead to emotional distress but are certainly not as stressful as the conversations with therapists, lawyers, and judges that inevitably take place when relational partners can no longer speak to one another across the chasm of disappointment, heartache, and fury that separates them.

RECOVERING FROM THE TRAUMA

Finally, a word about recovery from the disaster of relational infidelity.

In our culture, most people overcome the relational, emotional, and psychological tragedies of their lives through participating in what is called the psychotherapy of everyday life. This means that they talk openly and honestly with the people who are closet to them and who love them the most about the problems they are having, and, having gotten their miseries off of their chests, feel better and move on. The people whom they select as their confidants during these times of duress and struggle are called their "wisdom community." This consultation with the wisdom community is the oldest and probably the most effective form of psychotherapy in the human repertoire.

However, when a relationship is rocked by the choice of its members to break the relationship's sexual agreement, the wisdom community may not be too helpful. Sometimes the offending mate, and even the affairee, are important figures in the wisdom community. Other times, the wisdom community may have a hard time being open and objective about sexuality. Or the wisdom community, because of its own biases and presuppositions, may be too heavily invested in keeping the offended mate in a victim position just because it needs to be needed.

Relational partners who are struggling to overcome the trauma of an extramarital affair would be wise to hire a trained couples' therapist as their wisdom community. Here are some things to look for in that therapist.

- The therapist should know how to lead the partners through the negotiation of a new sexual agreement. This means that the therapist has to have a high degree of comfort with the complexity and diversity of the partners' sexual interests and experience.

- The therapist should be clear about his or her policy regarding secrets. The best secrecy policy a therapist can have is to refuse to hold a secret for one mate and from the other mate. A good couples' therapist will tell you that he or she can hold on to a secret for a little while, but only as a preliminary step toward helping you disclose the secret to your mate.

- The therapist should be in clinical supervision. For therapists, working with couples who are trying to recover from the trauma of infidelity is emotionally demanding and laden with unconscious projections and distortions. The therapist needs a wisdom community of his or her own.

The best couples' therapists know that there is no pat answer to Rose Castorini's Moonstruck question. People break their sexual agreements for the same reasons that they make other blunders in their lives: they act on impulse, they are too nice, they trust silences and secrecy more than they should, they think that love can do more than love can do, they overinvest in what's urgent and underinvest in what's important, and so forth.

Yet, it is possible to protect a relationship from the trauma of infidelity, and, failing that, it is possible to recover from the trauma. The paths to both prevention and recovery lead through the same difficult terrain: discovering the unconscious relational premises that misgovern our closest connections and then replacing them with beliefs and behaviors that will bring satisfaction, maturity, and vitality to ourselves and our mates.

Chapter Ten

ADDICTIONS—A VAIN ATTEMPT TO MAKE US FEEL WHOLE

Daniel Hoffman

SUBSTANCE ABUSE

Addiction is a pathological attraction to any person, place, or thing. As we will see in this chapter, often, they are unconscious, vain attempts to find something outside of ourselves to make us feel whole.

If you ask the typical substance abuser why he uses a substance, you will probably get some of the following answers, which indicate that his use is a conscious process:

- I drink because it helps me unwind.
- I smoke marijuana because it helps me be creative.
- I use cocaine to enhance my sexual experience.
- I use heroin because I can escape reality.

It has been widely recognized that families can pass on the tendency toward addiction via genetic predisposition. Certainly, there is some credence to that assertion. However, when you revive the age-old nature versus nurture debate and the resulting conclusions from that debate, you see that most human behavior and personality can be attributed to a combination of nature and nurture. Nature theory holds that we are born with a complete genetic life script. We are, according to nature theory, doomed to become addicted, no matter what we experience in our lives. On the other hand, nurture theory holds that our life experiences determine whether we will become addicted or not.

For purposes of our discussion here the genes may provide the nature side of causation of addiction. It is therefore important that we also examine the nurture side. A person can be nurtured in an unconscious manner to become a substance abuser. I always inform my clients who have addictions that anyone can become an addict. If a person does not have a genetic predisposition, he still can become addicted as a result of his unique life experiences. I have certainly worked with many addictions clients who have no family members with addiction problems. Throughout the book we have discussed how families pass down various customs, modes of operation, and ways of coping via an unspoken, unconscious conduit that we are exploring in this book.

For example, in a family where there is an alcoholic father the male children are at increased risk for also developing alcoholism. According to M. A. McGue, for both men and women, genetic factors alone cannot account for their risk of alcoholism.[1] The father, by his daily activity, is training his children how to be a parent by demonstrating parenting behaviors. Most of this training is done unconsciously. For instance, when a father is consistently missing from important family events and routine family activities, the male child learns that being a father means being distant and unavailable. The child may also learn that a father should not deal with feelings or nurture positive relationships in his family.

It may be helpful to examine a case that illustrates this phenomenon. The D family comprised a mother, a father, a son, and a daughter. The father was a chronic alcoholic. In treatment as an adult, the son, Frank D, was dealing with relationship issues with his own children. He could not understand why his own son was becoming distant to him. When Frank's son was young, they spent a lot of quality time together. Lately, Frank had been missing a lot of his son's softball games because he was often late getting home from work after spending a lot of time with his work buddies at a local bar watching sports events. Frank felt he had maintained his good relationship with his son because he would always stop in his son's bedroom after a night out with the boys. Lately, his son had stopped waiting up for him.

It wasn't until Frank's son became willing, in session, to confront Dad about his behavior that Frank would realize what was wrong. The son felt repulsed by the alcohol on Dad's breath and was keenly aware that he was the only boy on his team whose dad was not around. The son had been tolerating the scenario for a while until one of his teammates asked him, "Don't you have a dad?" In individual therapy Frank came to realize that the feelings his son was expressing were the same feelings he had felt when his dad had disappointed him growing up. The shocking thing to him was that he was doing exactly what his father had done. He had learned from his father that it is okay to be unavailable to one's family members. To Frank, this was his concept of normal. Of course, this was all done unconsciously. I know that Frank's father did not consciously tell Frank, "Look, this is how you be a dad: you get yourself a couple of drinking buddies, spend little time with your family, and just do what you want." Frank learned this behavior nonetheless because just as one learns better by doing, one teaches better by demonstrating.

Similarly, Frank didn't consciously say, "I'm going to be a father like my father was." Family traditions are passed on from generation to generation. We learn how to operate within our current family system from our family of origin. When you think of family traditions, you commonly think of culturally influenced standards of operating such as holiday traditions, types of foods, and matriarchal hierarchies. Many family traditions can also be considered dysfunctional, or even detrimental. In the D family the tradition of the alcoholic, unemotionally available father was being handed down. Prior to therapy, Frank D was well on his way to handing down his father's legacy to his own son. Refer to appendix D for how alcohol affects the roles and needs of children.

Further exploration with Frank began to reveal the mechanism of Frank's unconscious malfunctioning. Unconscious thought patterns had been created in order to make sense of Frank's world. As a child, Frank needed to believe that his family was okay. Therefore witnessing the dysfunctional patterns of his father organized Frank to develop a false reality to explain or defend how his family operated. If Frank had had the capacity to reason that one typically has as an adult, he would have been better able to recognize that things were amiss. However, as a young child without the benefit of a fully developed brain, he had to find a way to make sense of his world. As time passed, Frank gradually accepted his reality on a subconscious level.

There was a struggle going on inside of Frank. Certainly, environmental cues that presented themselves regularly were in direct conflict with the reality that he was creating. Being around friends whose fathers were present and emotionally available gave incongruent information to Frank. He needed to resolve this struggle somehow. Young Frank was unable to effect a change in his family system, so he had to suppress the information that was being presented to him from his peers' environments. The result was low self-esteem, chronic depression, and an inability to discern familial expression of negative feelings.

When the counselor first asked Frank why he drank alcohol, he had answered, "To unwind." That response came from his conscious awareness. Much later in therapy, when asked the same question, Frank reported that he drank because of many hidden, unconscious motivations. He was depressed, frustrated, and scared, and he realized that he was carrying his father's legacy. This was accentuated when Frank was asked to list some adjectives to describe his father. He listed the following:

- sad
- frustrated

- fearful
- lost

UNDERSTANDING THE CYCLE OF ADDICTION
Stage One—Use

There is a cycle of addiction that addicts find themselves in. The first stage in the cycle is the abuse of a substance. The substance can be any chemical that alters ones psychic state. This cycle can also apply to the abuse of a process or behavior, such as gambling or sex. (Sexual addiction will be discussed further later in this chapter.) The difference between a chronic abuser and a minimally affected abuser is what happens when stage 3 in the cycle occurs. The minimally affected user will cease the behavior because he will make a determination that the negative consequence is not worth the payoff. The addict will continue to use the substance, such as alcohol, or continue to use an addictive process, such as gambling or sexual acting out, despite the negative consequences. In fact, the addict will be easily identified as being on the cycle of addiction by almost everyone but himself. Many times, his close family members will be the ones who are first aware of the addictive behavior.

Stage Two—Payoff

The second stage in the cycle is the payoff. The payoff may be a feeling of euphoria, relaxation, peace, excitement, and so forth. The alcoholic may report feeling more at ease with his friends. The cocaine addict will feel that he is omnipotent. The addict who abuses depressant substances, such as alcohol or downers, will report feeling more detached. The gambling addict will report feeling excited or charged up while gambling. The sexual addict will report feeling more connected or more powerful.

Stage Three—Negative Consequences

The third stage involves the negative consequences. Many addicts have difficulty identifying this stage in their cycles. Denial is a powerful mechanism by which the unconscious mind keeps the addict unaware of the negative consequences. In treatment, one of the ways we try to get addicts to acknowledge an addiction is to show the disastrous consequences that abuse brings into their lives.

Sigmund Freud identified defense mechanisms that we use to keep uncomfortable and unconscious thoughts, feelings, and beliefs from becoming conscious. Denial is not the only one of Freud's defense mechanisms that are applicable here. Addicts also use the defense mechanism of rationalization.

Rationalization is defined as creating false but plausible excuses to justify unacceptable behavior.[2] Another way to describe rationalization is justifying an action by making up a reason for it. Here are some examples of rationalization that most addictions counselors hear:

- "I am able to use and still keep a full-time job."
- "Smoking marijuana makes me creative."
- "I drink to unwind."
- "I have a better personality when I'm high."
- "Using an upper makes me work harder."

Another defense mechanism that addicts use is minimization, wherein they minimize their use or their actions. For example, in my many years of counseling addicts I have had numerous occasions when an alcoholic would report having had "a couple of beers." When questioning her further, I usually found that "a couple of beers" could mean anywhere from two beers to thirty. Other examples of minimization follow:

- "I only drink on weekends."
- "It's only beer, I don't drink the hard stuff."
- "I don't drink as much as the other guy."
- "I only play the lottery."
- "I only use cocaine every other week."

Stage Four—Negative Feelings

Subsequent to experiencing negative consequences, the addict will move through stage four of the cycle of addiction. Consequences will cause a host of different negative feelings, such as guilt, shame, anger, fear, and so forth. Some of these feelings will often be unconscious. Let's look at the similar feelings of guilt and shame. In this context, guilt is the conscious manifestation of the unconscious feeling of shame. The unconscious mind keeps these feelings out of awareness and motivates the person to take away the pain by creating urges for a return to the use stage. This is why helping the addict to get in touch with his feelings is a key ingredient to recovery.

SHAME PROVIDES POWER TO THE ADDICTIVE PROCESS

John Bradshaw asserts that shame is "the root and fuel of all compulsive/addictive behaviors." He further defines compulsive/addictive behavior as a "pathological relationship to any mood altering experience that has life damaging consequences."[3] One might be inclined to ask, Why does an addict risk losing everything he has in life for his addiction? The answer to this question lies in the examination of the very powerful intrapsychic, unconscious forces that drive any addiction. Shame is the prime example of these forces. As I related in chapter 4, Eric Berne, the founder of transactional analysis, inspired Thomas Harris to identify human beings as needing to believe that "I'm ok, you're ok."[4] We all want, on some level, to feel that we are okay. Shame simultaneously keeps us searching for a substance or an activity to hide the shame. The result is that the addict finds himself in a perpetual cycle of addiction.

To illustrate the effect of shame on addiction, consider the following case: Amy T was referred to substance abuse counseling from the state child protective services division. She was a single parent and had two children in elementary school. School staff had become concerned because the children had arrived at school late on many occasions. The children had described how they often had to cook their own dinners, which often consisted of peanut butter and jelly. They had to do this because mom was often out of the house. Not long after her divorce, Amy had begun increasing her use of alcohol. The increased use was fueled by many emotions. Shame was the most significant of these emotions. The divorce left her feeling shameful of her failed marriage. Her ex-husband had convinced her that she was not okay. When they were married, he often criticized her cooking, her appearance, and anything else of interest.

At her intake interview Amy revealed the reason that she was so willing to take on this shame from her husband—she was the scapegoat in her family of origin. "Scapegoat" is one of the terms used to describe roles that family members play when one of them is dysfunctional. The scapegoat is the family member who gets all the blame for whatever is wrong in the household. Amy reported having realized she performed this role while reading a women's magazine that discussed roles in dysfunctional families. Whenever there was chaos in her family of origin, it was always Amy's fault. She was often told by her mother, "If you weren't such a brat, your father would have stayed with the family."

As an adult, when Amy felt inadequate as a parent, she drank alcohol excessively. When she failed to take proper care of her children, the deep-rooted shame that she had developed was activated in the form of guilt. The guilt and shame led to more alcohol use and a continuing downward spiral.

How does one even begin to get off this unconscious cycle of addiction? It's sufficient to say it isn't easy. The very first thing that one needs to do is to come to the conscious realization that he is spinning on this cycle. This is usually the most difficult step in the process. The first step of Alcoholics Anonymous illustrates this awareness: "I came to believe that my life is unmanageable and that I am powerless over alcohol."

When Amy was able to see that she was on a shame-driven cycle of addiction, she was able to begin a recovery process. The prospect of losing custody of her children was enough to motivate her to examine her cycle of addiction. Unfortunately, many similar cases don't wind up that way. The various powerful, unconscious forces that drive addictions can be difficult to overcome. Shame is one of those powerful forces.

CHOOSING A POINT OF INTERVENTION ON THE CYCLE OF ADDICTION

One sure way to break a cycle of addiction is to remove one of the stages (use, payoff, negative consequences, negative feelings, use). New therapists will often ask at what point they should try to intervene in the cycle of addiction. The answer is anywhere and everywhere they can. Most current addiction treatment modalities suggest that we intervene at the use stage. AA says to newcomers, "Just don't take that first drink." That may work in the short term, but for the long term the negative-feelings stage (stage four) needs to be addressed in order to truly break the cycle of addiction. The reason for this is that you have to address the negative, unconscious forces that drive addiction. This process is addressed in the 12-step programs in step four. Step four asks that the addict take a hard look at his inner self by taking a fearless moral personal inventory.

SEXUAL ADDICTIONS

Sexual addiction exists in many forms: compulsive masturbation, compulsive sex with prostitutes, anonymous sex with multiple partners, affairs outside a committed relationship, serial sexual relationships, excessive perusal of pornography, frequent visits to strip clubs, habitual exposure of one's body parts to others, voyeurism, inappropriate sexual touching, sexual assault, sexual abuse of children, establishing affairs over the Internet, and so forth.

It's easy to see how any of these forms of sexual addiction can wreak havoc with a marriage. Unlike substance abuse, sexual addictions can remain hidden for years. In many cases of sexual addiction with which I've worked the couple had been married a number of years before it was discovered that one of the partners had been struggling with this kind of issue.

UNCONSCIOUS NEEDS THAT DRIVE SEXUAL ADDICTION

One of the primary unconscious needs that drive sexual addiction is the need for power. There are a host of childhood experiences that can make a person feel an acute lack of power. Take sexual abuse for example: "A history of child or adolescent sexual abuse is often observed in individuals with sexual addiction."[5] When a person is the victim of sexual abuse as a child, there are many adverse effects. A very significant effect is developing a sense of powerlessness over his life, his emotions, and his feelings. This lack of power creates a void that exists in the unconscious. Therefore the drive to fill that void is also unconscious.

Let's look at the case of Sally. She had presented at couples' counseling with her fiancé, Fred, for premarital counseling. She was concerned about past failures in her relationships. Sally was 13 when her live-in uncle began touching her inappropriately. By age 15, Sally's uncle had come into her bedroom at night and had sexually assaulted her on several occasions.

Sally experienced a dual reaction to the attention of her uncle. On the one hand, it was disturbing to her that she encountered such treatment from her uncle. She knew that his actions were not appropriate. On the other hand, having the attention felt good on some level. Generally, however, Sally was terrified of her uncle. In the four years that her uncle lived at her home Sally never had much other attention from him. Also, her father had moved out of the state, and she only saw him on rare occasions. Therefore she was in need of a father figure and simultaneously fearful of the one male in her life because he was abusing her. This ambivalence gave her a sense of powerlessness.

Sally became sexually promiscuous in high school and college. It was her way to have power again. She unconsciously rationalized that if she were the one to choose a male sexual partner and if she were the one to initiate the sex act, she had more power—even if it was only a temporary feeling.

As an adult in her late twenties, Sally found herself in her sixth failed romantic relationship within a period of two years. She was hoping that with Fred she would put her past failures behind her. It seems that whenever she was in a relationship, she could not control her compulsion to seek validation by dressing seductively and flirting with male strangers. This compulsion had made it very easy for her to develop new relationships with males. However, Sally desired a long-term, committed relationship. That was virtually impossible for her to do because when she was in a relationship she would continue to dress provocatively and flirt excessively with other males. One of the concerns that Fred had was that Sally would reject him and sometimes become enraged when he tried to initiate sex with her. It wasn't until she entered therapy that she was able to see the connection between her experiences with her uncle and her current behavior. She was able to discover the unconscious processes that caused her to seek power in reaction to the feeling of powerlessness she had had as a child. Patrick Carnes states, "Many of these addicts believe that if you have sex with someone, you will have that person in your power."[6] In view of that it is easy to see how sexual addiction can be a manifestation of the need for power.

SEX AS A MEANS TO REGULATE EMOTIONS

Sex is a primary tool that sex addicts use to deal with their emotions. According to Carnes, "A key point of addiction is its use to regulate emotional life."[7] Many sexual addicts will report that when they are having sex or doing a compulsive act, they are not feeling a given troublesome emotion. Let's look at the hypothetical example of Bob and Cindy. This couple came to therapy seeking help for their marriage, citing anger problems. During marital therapy the major issue that emerged was Bob's compulsive masturbation. In the third session the counselor privately asked Bob, "What do you get from masturbation?" After some thought he reported that the only time he felt any relief from the constant state of anxiety he was in was when he was masturbating or when he was making preparations to masturbate. On further discussion it was discovered that Bob was anxious for most of his adult life about his career. His father had been a perfectionist and was always prone to tell Bob that he "never gets anything right." Even as an adult, Bob felt he didn't measure up to his father's expectations. In Bob's mind he could never measure up to the son his father wanted. He could never be the great athlete or the A student. In reality Bob could never measure up to his father's expectations, just as the father never could measure up to his dad's expectations.

UNCONDITIONAL LOVE VERSUS CONDITIONAL LOVE

In an ideal marriage, both parties can expect a fair share of unconditional love. This is the kind of love that one gives just because he wants to and not as the result of some action by his partner. Unfortunately, many marriages operate with conditional love, in which one does not receive love unless he does or says something to earn it. Many times, as a child, one can learn that you have to do something or be a certain way in order to receive love. According to Carnes, "When children do not experience approval for tasks or affirmation for who they are, they have no internal way of feeling okay about themselves."[8] As reported earlier, Thomas Harris alerted us to the need for us to feel that we are okay. When a child is praised or told they are loved just because they are who they are, they tend to feel okay.

Alternatively, when a child is constantly criticized, they feel they are not okay. Subsequently, the child will try to find other ways to make himself feel he is okay. One of those ways can be sexual acting out. In successive sexual encounters, one can get temporary affirmation. This short-lived feeling of being okay necessitates the drive to compulsively act out sexually over and over. In a marriage where a sexual addict is one of the partners, love is often like a commodity to be traded for favors. There is usually a condition that has to be met before one can receive love in these relationships. In most cases, there is an unconscious bargaining process that occurs between partners. Sometimes it even becomes conscious. On more than one occasion I've heard a dialogue similar to the following go on between partners:

Wife: "If you were more romantic, I would be more sexual."
Husband: "If you were more sexual, I would be more romantic."

Looking beyond the conscious level of this type of communication, we can see that love is certainly conditional in these kinds of relationships. What has always amazed me as a couples' therapist is how much in denial couples can be about this process. A case in point is that of Rita and Harry. I had seen this couple for well over a year. They began treatment speaking of problems with communication. Early on in the process, I found that Harry was more interested in Internet pornography than in having sexual relations with his wife. It was also reported that Rita's mother had lived with the couple for several years. Rita's family was from overseas, and her dad had passed away, prompting Mom to move in with Rita and Harry. I had recognized early on that the strongest coalition in this family was between Rita and her mother. Whenever Rita was mad at Harry, Mother was also mad at him. In the evenings Rita and her mother would watch TV in the family room, while Harry would go on the Internet in the living room.

When I pointed this out in session, Harry would nod and then withdraw. Rita would change the subject. I decided to have Rita come in with her mom, Rosa. On meeting mom I recognized immediately that some of the negative things Rosa said about Harry were almost word-for-word the same as those spoken by Rita in sessions with Harry, where she would complain about his lack of caring for her. Toward the end of the session I asked Rita and her mom, "Why don't you two divorce this guy?" It was at that point that Rita took a hard look at what I had been pointing out all along.

Three weeks later, Rosa moved out of the house. The couple attended treatment for two more months, and terminated treatment in a better place than where they had started.

There were several unconscious processes going on in this family system. While growing up, Harry had three sisters and no brothers. Harry's mom was a single mom since Dad had run off right after Harry was born. Harry had once described his mom as a "man-hater." The dysfunctional relationship between Rita and her mother, both of whom had, among other things, not adequately dealt with the sudden death of Rita's dad, replicated Harry's childhood experience. In his early teens Harry had discovered pornography to be a tool that could help him escape from his feelings of isolation, and he regressed to this adolescent sanctuary whenever he felt shut out by his wife and criticized by his mother-in-law.

SO, IT'S NOT ABOUT THE SEX

Sexual encounters of the sexual addict are not about sex as much as they are about overcoming feelings of emotional deficit. According to Carnes, "It's about core feelings of loneliness and unworthiness."[9] Sexual addicts experience feelings of emptiness that are pervasive. Repetitive sex acts only serve to temporarily fill a void that really can't be filled. The only way to deal with the void is to address childhood trauma and other unresolved issues. Bessel A. Van Der Kolk reports that there are biological responses to psychic trauma.[10] Hence the sexual act is a biological solution to a psychic problem. That's why the repeated sex acts do nothing to ameliorate the underlying pain and emptiness. The only way to deal with this void is to address the unconscious psychic deficits.

To illustrate this phenomenon, let's look at a related case: a couple, Joe and Alice, entered marriage counseling with a primary complaint about their sex life. Alice reported seeing no problem with their sex life. However, Joe was concerned that Alice may have been sexually addicted. Alice would want to have sex multiple times on certain days. Yet, at other times she was not interested at all. On further inquiry it was determined that whenever there was tension in the house or the couple had a verbal disagreement, Alice would become obsessive about sex. When things were okay, she was uninterested.

After several conjoint sessions and several individual sessions with both parties it was discovered that Alice grew up in a very dysfunctional family. There were unresolved issues to be addressed. Alice's father was physically and emotionally abusive to her mother. They had many knock-down, drag-out fights. Sadly, Alice witnessed her parents having sex afterward. It seems that right after their biggest fights her parents would have sex and would make little attempt to prevent Alice from seeing and hearing their sexual encounters. Alice drew an unconscious connection between sex and crisis resolution. She had learned that fighting and family discord made for better sex and that sex resolves problems.

Addictions that a couple are confronted with are not only about compulsively seeking out a substance or a sexual act. There is always an unconscious process that underlies these behaviors. Whether trying to fill a void that exists as a result of our family of origin or reenacting some dysfunctional script that was authored by our experience as a child, there is always a past influence on present behavior.

In the counseling field, there are two basic belief systems about how mental health issues should be addressed. The behaviorist school of thought holds that counseling should only deal with what is on the surface. Treatment under behaviorism should only be designed to address the symptoms that are visible. On the other hand, the psychodynamic approach holds that the underlying causes of the symptoms should also be addressed. The latter is the premise that this test is based on. Even one of the original and influential behavioral theorists, B. F. Skinner, was cognizant of the unconscious's influence on human behavior. Skinner himself said, "All behavior is at first unconscious, but it may become conscious without becoming rational; a person may know what he is doing without knowing why he is doing it."[11] You may think a statement like this came from Sigmund Freud, who was one of the original theorists to inform us that our behavior is driven by unconscious forces. This statement highlights what I am presenting in this book. Marriages fail and marriages thrive as a direct result of unconscious processes and how we handle these processes.

Earlier in this chapter, I discussed the cycle of addiction as it pertains to substance addictions. Sexual addiction follows a similar cycle. I have been impressed by how similarly the cycles of sexual addiction and the cycles of cocaine addiction operate. The typical cocaine addict does not use cocaine on a regular, daily basis. His cocaine use runs in cycles. The cocaine addict can be drug-free for a few days or even a few weeks. However, when he uses cocaine, he goes all out. Cocaine addicts tend to spend a large block of time actively using their substance. The typical cocaine "run," as it is sometimes called, can last from several hours to several days straight. After the cocaine run is over the addict is fraught with shame and guilt for a period of time. During these brief periods of sobriety he will become very remorseful and resolve to get his act together and seem very committed to recovery. Unfortunately, that commitment is short lived. The next trigger event, such as getting a sum of money (for example, on payday), may send the addict on another run.

Similarly, the sex addict will operate in a use/shame cycle. The sexual addiction cycle looks like this: acting out–negative consequences–remorse/shame–resolve to recovery–triggers–acting out.

The pattern of the sexual addict runs very similarly to that of the cocaine addict. His use, which is called "sexual acting out," can be very similar to a cocaine run. The remorse and shame felt after a sexual acting-out episode can also be strong. Various things can also trigger sexual acting out. Seeing a seductive image on television, seeing an attractive person, or being in a store and seeing provocative magazine covers as well as feeling lonely, feeling discounted, or feeling overpowered can all be triggers to get the sexual addict thinking and planning his next encounter.

OTHER ADDICTIONS

In this chapter I have addressed two major areas of addiction that many couples deal with: substance abuse and sexual addiction. There are some other addictions that should be mentioned also. Gambling addiction, food addiction, and workaholism also wreak havoc with marriages. The cycles of these addictions and the stages that they go through are similar to those of the substance addictions and sexual addictions. The unconscious processes of shame and negative life experiences are factors in all addictions.

To illustrate, I would like to discuss the case of Betty and Ralph. Ralph was a compulsive gambler since the age of 17. Betty never discovered that until they had been married for five years. They were seeking a mortgage for the purchase of their first home. The mortgage application process required that a credit report be created for Betty and Ralph. That is how Betty found out that Ralph had exceeded the credit limit on five credit cards. As a result, they sought marriage counseling.

In one of their sessions Ralph broke down and started crying hysterically. Further inquiry revealed that Ralph had had a distant relationship with his father growing up. He had not felt important to his father. Ralph's father was a regional banking executive and spent a lot of time out of town on business. Ralph had been under the impression that money was very important to his father. Unconsciously, though, Ralph thought that if he won a large sum of money, his father would recognize him and give him the attention he was so starved for as a boy. Eventually, Ralph started increasing his gambling. Owing to his high level of gambling, he was made to feel important at the casinos he frequently visited. He reported feeling addicted to the grand sense of importance engendered by the way he was treated by casino staff. As a result, Ralph had a difficult time giving up gambling. He eventually committed to joining Gamblers Anonymous and continued couples' counseling for well over a year. He also visited an individual counselor during and after his and Betty's couples' treatment. Betty and Ralph were finally able to buy their first home several years later. The empty space that had driven Ralph to gamble compulsively was very difficult to fill.

SO, WHAT ARE SWOME HEALTHIER WAYS TO FILL THE VOIDS THAT CAUSE OUR ADDICTIVE BEHAVIORS?

First, one must become aware that she is in a cycle of addictive behavior. The first step, as in the typical 12-step program, is to help the person become aware that she has a problem. Often, that problem relates to how she is trying to fill her void. Oftentimes, she is not even aware that she has a void. The best approach is to have the subject enter into mental health counseling as well as actively participate in a 12-step recovery program. There is a 12-step program for every substance or process addiction known to man. Most of these recovery programs can be found throughout the world.

A FEW WORDS ABOUT SEEKING MENTAL HEALTH COUNSELING

As I mentioned before, there are differences of opinion in the therapy world about whether to use behavioral therapy or psychodynamic therapy. I believe both modalities have their place in mental health treatment. Behavioral therapy is most indicated if the client has the following circumstances:

- The client cannot attend therapy for the long term due to financial considerations such as a lack of funds or insurance.
- The client is not yet ready to tackle the hard issues and deal with the work it would take to accomplish that. (One of the hallmarks of ethical therapy practice is to meet the client where he is. Being ready to unveil layers of shame takes a lot of personal fortitude because many emotions and issues are likely to arise during the treatment process.)
- It's been determined that the client is dealing with an acute issue of short duration.

Psychodynamic therapy is best indicated under the following circumstances:

- The dysfunction that the client is dealing with is pervasive to the point of threatening significant life relationships or financial, physical, or spiritual well-being.
- The client has the financial resources, adequate health coverage, or public or private financial assistance to enter into long-term treatment.
- The client has attempted to rectify his issues via short-term treatment to no avail.

At the beginning of the counseling process the client should be assessed to determine how far along he is in the recovery process. There are three general stages of recovery that have been applied to planning the helping process with domestic violence victims, victims of child abuse, victims of sexual assault, victims of crime, and victims of natural disasters, to name a few. The three stages follow:

- victim;
- survivor;
- thriver.

For the purpose of this book I would like to apply these stages to the struggles of clients who are trying to fill a void that has been created by tragic experience as a child and as an adult. This relates particularly to people who are addicted to various substances and processes.

- Victim stage: In this stage the client's situation is actively affected by the negative life experiences that he has had thus far. His addictive behavior is full-blown. These behaviors are truly desperate attempts to fill the empty spaces in the client's mind and soul. At this stage the person has little or no awareness that his behavior is dysfunctional or that he is unconsciously trying to fill a void. When a client enters treatment at this stage, there are a lot of important tasks for the therapist and the client to accomplish. Included in those tasks are breaking patterns of denial, introducing the concept of personal power, helping the client to discover a point of refuge or safety in his life, assessing the level of readiness the client is setting, and the appropriate pace in the recovery process.

- Survivor stage: In this stage the client still is experiencing some of the effects of his negative life experiences. Addictive behavior is still a factor in the client's life. There is an ongoing internal dialogue where the addict alternates between admitting he has an addiction problem and regressing back into denial. In this stage the therapist needs to help the client challenge negative beliefs about addiction. The client should also be introduced to the concept of unconscious shame and conscious guilt. It is in this stage where the most significant growth can occur. During the latter part of this stage the client has made a commitment to take a hard look at the underlying pain. He also will be more ready to begin major life changes such as examining how his past experiences have affected him, getting in touch with a healthy form of spirituality, and becoming abstinent from the substance or process that has had him in its grips. This is when he will begin to make amends to those that he has affected by his addictive processes. He will begin to discover how his negative life experiences have affected him.

- Thriver stage: In this final stage the client will be functioning with minimal effect from his negative life experiences. Denial is not a large factor as in the first two stages. The client usually has a significant period of abstinence from his addiction. One of the tasks for the therapist in this stage is to help the client plan for the termination of the counseling relationship. During this stage the client can be assisted in developing a life plan. That plan could include things such as continued participation in his recovery program, firming up personal growth decisions, enhancing relationships with friends and family members, and making career enhancements. Refer to appendix D at the end of this chapter for specific recovery needs in the recovery of family members.

In closing, I would like to quote Viktor Frankl. Dr. Frankl was a renowned psychiatrist and author. He was also a survivor of the Nazi Germany concentration camps. The trauma and loss he experienced in captivity included the death of almost his entire family, including his wife, his brother, and both parents. Perhaps I should say that he was a thriver. He used his psychiatric knowledge to become a thriver. He used his strong spirit to become a thriver as well as to become an influential philosopher and accomplished psychiatrist and author. He once said, "Sometimes the patient is not only spared additional suffering, but also finds additional meaning in suffering. He may even succeed in making suffering into a triumph."[12]

APPENDIX D

Needs in Recovery of Family Members

Alcoholic Needs

1. Get out of his or her head; that is, not intellectualizing.
2. Develop awareness of how others feel.

3. Become flexible.
4. Work through problems.
5. Express anger without blaming.

Strengths: heightened awareness, gutsy, sensitivity to pain—empathy

Chief Enabler Needs

1. Let go of responsibility.
2. Get in touch with feelings.
3. Refocus on self (wants and needs).
4. Become aware of self-responsibility, and let others do the same.
5. Deal with anger without blaming or falling apart.

Strengths: nurturing, giving, loving

Family Hero Needs

1. Learn to ask for and take what he needs.
2. Learn to accept failure.
3. Let down, relax, and Be.
4. Focus on self—stop "fixing" family.

Strengths: hard workers, know how to get what they want

Family Scapegoat Needs

1. Get through anger to the hurt.
2. Learn to negotiate instead of rebel.

Strengths: can see reality, has good insight, sensitive and courageous

Lost Child Needs

1. Reach out.
2. Deal with loneliness.
3. Face pain.
4. Make new close relationships.

Strengths: patient, creative and independent

Mascot Needs

1. Take responsibility.
2. Risk being serious.
3. Assertiveness.

Strengths: humor, know how to enjoy

Chapter Eleven

OUR NERVOUS SYSTEMS AND RELATIONAL PROBLEMS

On a Saturday morning I received a frantic call from Tony, a client that I had been treating for about three months for depression. Fortunately, I was working that Saturday, and I was able to see him later that day. When I met him, he was extremely distraught and anxious to the point of being hysterical. He nervously related that on Thursday he had been at a hotel, and he had suffered from heart palpitations, had difficulty breathing, experienced disorganized thinking, and needed to get out of the hotel. Tony, for the first time in his life, had experienced a panic attack. The situation was baffling because Tony was in marketing for a major air-conditioning manufacturer, and he often traveled overnight.

After a few sessions it was revealed that, once again, hidden unconscious remembrances from the past were responsible for his panic attacks.

Another scenario that is similar to Tony's is that of Noreen. Noreen was on antianxiety medication for years before she decided to participate in counseling. Noreen, age 32, was a single, successful businesswoman. She was functional in all aspects of her life, except one: she dreaded being alone. Noreen had a roommate and was calm as long as she wasn't left alone, especially in the house. On rare occasions, when she was alone, her symptoms included dizziness, shortness of breath, a racing heartbeat, feelings of suffocation, and fainting spells.

Unknowingly, both Tony and Noreen were victims of their own visceral sensations and thought processes. Their own nervous systems were playing havoc with their lives.

Tony's main concern was that if he couldn't travel, he would lose his job. Prior to working for the air-conditioning manufacturer, he was out of work for over 14 months. His days of idleness—coupled with his drastic loss of income—caused tremendous stress on his relationship with his wife.

Noreen's phobia of being alone also stressed her relationship with her room-mate, Karl. Karl felt that Noreen was becoming too needy, and they repeatedly fought over her emotional demands.

Literally, their own states of mind were causing their problems, and via counseling, they would learn that the power to resolve these problems resided in their minds as well.

In order to understand the nature and causes of Tony's and Noreen's prob-lems, we need to briefly discuss the role and functions of our nervous system, especially the autonomic nervous system.

Our nervous system is divided into two major sections: the central nervous system, which consists of the brain and spinal cord, and the peripheral ner-vous system, which consists of the somatic nervous system and the autonomic nervous system. For our purposes we will focus on the autonomic nervous system.

The autonomic nervous system regulates all involuntary muscles and glands, including the heart, respiratory functions, gastrointestinal func-tions, sweat glands, and so forth. The sympathetic branch of the autonomic nervous system is activated under threat of danger; it prepares us for fight or flight. For example, if you leave your house, and you are attacked by a vicious dog, you have a choice of fight or flight. Refer to appendix E at the end of this chapter for a complete list of possible psychological and physical symptoms.[1]

A concept that many of my clients find intriguing is that this emergency-response system cannot distinguish between actual threats or perceived threats, the point being that if we perceive a situation as threatening, no matter how innocent, it functions as a threat, and the emergency-response system is acti-vated. In the case of Tony, when he entered a particular hotel, the emergency-response system was activated; and in the case of Noreen, it was activated when she was left alone.

The last piece of the equation that is needed to understand what happened to Tony and Noreen is a basic understanding of classical conditioning.

Classical conditioning was discovered by the famous Russian physiolo-gist, Ivan Pavlov. The original goal of Pavlov's experiments was to investi-gate the function of saliva in the digestive process in dogs.[2] However, by accident, he stumbled on the discovery of a major learning process, classi-cal conditioning. He was later to learn that classical conditioning plays a paramount role in shaping emotional responses such as phobias and panic attacks.

Pavlov's classical conditioning model is as follows:

food–salivate
UCS–UCR
bell–food–salivate
NS–UCS–UCR
bell–salivate
CS–CR

In Pavlov's scenario, the food, an unlearned or unconditioned stimulus (UCS), elicits an unlearned or unconditioned response (UCR). For example, if we are hungry, and we smell a sizzling steak, we naturally and automatically will salivate. The neutral stimulus (NS), the bell, when paired with an unconditioned stimulus, food, eventually elicits a conditioned response (CR). The dog has learned to salivate to a previously neutral stimulus, the bell; ergo learning has taken place.

An everyday example of classical conditioning that might bring the point across is that of when a small child goes to the doctor for measles or some other malady and sees a hypodermic needle. The model would look as follows:

needle–fear
UCS–UCR
doctor–needle–fear
NS–UCS–UCR
doctor–fear
CS–CR

In this example the child associates the previously neutral stimulus, the doctor, with the unconditioned stimulus, the needle, and the doctor become the conditioned stimulus (CS); Now, both the doctor and the hypodermic elicit fear.

Other examples of associations formulated by classical conditioning include pleasant memories of childhood vacations when you smell the ocean, a nauseous feeling in your stomach when you hear classical music like that heard in the dentist's office, stopping at red lights, an upset stomach when passing an elementary school, pleasant memories when seeing someone who resembles a beloved relative or friend, and so forth.

Classical conditioning affects not only behaviors, but also our physiological processes, including our immune systems. Classical conditioning processes can lead to immunosuppression, a decrease in the production of antibodies.[3] It can lower our resistance to disease and can elicit allergic reactions.[4] The learned physiological reactions eventually become automatic emotional responses and often are elicited at the unconscious level, as we'll see in the case of Tony and Noreen.

THE RELATIONSHIP OF PAVLOV'S DOG TO THE CASES OF TONY AND NOREEN

Tony's panic attack was a direct result of classical conditioning. Years ago, Tony had an affair with his secretary. However, the secretary's husband suspected his wife of having an affair, and he followed Tony and his affairee to the motel where they were meeting. During the rendezvous the husband broke down the door, and he seriously physically assaulted Tony. The hotel room had on its wall a mural with an English country setting. This setting became imprinted in Tony's unconscious mind, and it became the trigger for his recent attack. During the counseling sessions we concluded that the hotel where he recently stayed had a similar mural on the wall. The classical conditioning sequence was as follows:

beating–fear
UCS–UCR
English mural–beating–fear
NS–UCS–UCR
English mural–fear
CS–CR

The pairing or association of the English country setting with the beating elicited the conditioned emotional response of fear.

Noreen's fear of being alone also was a direct result of classical conditioning. In Noreen's case, when she was a young girl of five years, her family went on vacation with another couple. After they left the house her parents mistakenly thought that Noreen was in their friends' car. Noreen's parents were astounded when they contacted the other parents and she wasn't with them. Noreen was left alone for two hours, and when her parents found her, she was hysterical. From that point on Noreen had numerous abandonment issues. Her classical conditioning model was as follows:

abandonment–fear
UCS–UCR
being alone–abandonment–fear
NS–UCS–UCR
being alone–fear
CS–CR

Noreen had become conditioned to associate being alone with a fear of being abandoned.

ANDREW AND LINDA

Another example that illustrates the impact of this latent conditioning process is that of Andrew, age 48, and Linda, age 42. Linda was previously married for three years prior to her marriage to Andrew. Linda and Andrew were married for two years when I initially met them. Andrew and Linda had no children, and there were no children from Linda's previous marriage. During the counseling intake it appeared that the major issue between the couple was emotional abuse. I later learned that no such abuse existed between the couple—it was only perceived that way by Linda, again giving credence to the statement "we don't see things as they are, we see things as we are."

A repetitive pattern that was acted out between Andrew and Linda was when Andrew and Linda had an argument, if Andrew would raise his voice a little higher than his usual tone, Linda would have a full-blown panic attack. Her symptoms included heart palpitations, pressure on her chest, shortness of breath, and tremors. Both found themselves walking on egg shells, and they were never able to organize problem-solving conversations. The shame was that they were a lovely couple, and if they couldn't find better ways to resolve problems, their prognosis was poor. Prior to counseling they had no way of knowing that classical conditioning was the underlying unconscious factor that was playing havoc with their relationship.

After taking a case history on both Andrew and Linda it was revealed that both Linda's father and first husband physically and emotionally abused her. Both her father and first husband were alcoholics and, when drinking, would berate her and curse at her loudly. On occasion, both had physically hit her. Linda's classical conditioning schematic looked as follows:

emotional/physical abuse–withdrawal
UCS–UCR
loud voice–emotional/physical abuse–withdrawal
NS–UCS–UCR
loud voice–withdrawal
CS–CR

Linda became conditioned to withdraw from (especially) a male voice when raised. Andrew and Linda were not aware of this learned conditioned scenario that was set into action whenever an emotionally charged discussion would commence. Whenever Andrew would raise his voice, as many of us do in an attempt to get our points across, Linda would withdraw into her shell and stay there for days. During those times she would also experience gastrointestinal disturbances.

TREATMENT ISSUES

Treatment issues may vary depending on the specifics of the situation. However, as I mentioned earlier, the major problem with such cases is that the emergency-response system, that is, the sympathetic or fight/flight nervous system, is energized, and the main goal of therapy is for the client to be able to extinguish the fear. We call this "inducing a parasympathetic reaction." In the case of Noreen I utilized hypnosis, cognitive/behavioral therapy, psychotherapy, and Eye Movement Desensitization and Reprocessing (EMDR) to induce a parasympathetic reaction.

The utilization of hypnosis helps the client to relax when she is stressed or anxious. I also teach the person how to induce self-hypnosis so she can induce the relaxed state whenever it is needed. From my experience, many people, even professionals, do not understand the potential power of hypnosis as a treatment modality. I personally have found hypnosis extremely effective for treating stress, anxiety, post-traumatic stress, and even some habit disorders such as smoking cessation and overeating.

What surprises most people is that hypnosis has nothing whatsoever to do with sleep. Hypnosis is actually a heightened state of awareness. The brain waves under hypnosis are beta waves, which indicate a heightened state of alertness. However, it's a paradox that under hypnosis one is extremely relaxed.

Hypnosis is an everyday occurrence; that is, you are hypnotized every day. It is induced when you focus your attention. For example, it is induced when you focus on a book, a fire in the fireplace, or the road ahead. An example would be that you are driving to work, and landmarks are passing by without your awareness. You are hypnotized, but you are in control. If someone were to cross the street or if a traffic light turned red, you would still stop. Again, hypnosis is induced by the focusing of our attention.

Also, many people are suggestible and, when in this relaxed state of heightened awareness, tend to follow through on post-hypnotic suggestions. I often provide post-hypnotic positive suggestions to help my clients deal with stress, anxiety, and phobias.

People are also surprised to learn that all hypnosis is self-hypnosis. The hypnotist only sets the stage for the person to enter a hypnotic state. The person can also, in his own mind, learn to go to a safe place when necessary. Also, I can utilize hypnosis and mental imagery to help desensitize the fear. For example, in Noreen's case, under hypnosis, we would go to her safe place and leave that safe place to visualize her being alone, but feeling safe.

I utilized cognitive/behavioral therapy in the following manner: Noreen learned the importance of self-talk in reducing her fear of being alone. She would say a number of positive statements to herself, including, "Nothing bad has happened to me in 30 years" and "If something goes wrong, I can call 911, and they will be here in 15 minutes." The behavioral component included Noreen gradually increasing the time she was left alone.

Last, I used EMDR intervention, which recently has been found to be successful in alleviating anxiety and post-traumatic stress. When trauma occurs, it seems to get locked into the nervous system. EMDR seems to unlock traumatic pictures and allows the brain to process and let go of the traumatic experience.[5]

The purpose of EMDR is to interpret the client's behavioral set and to reduce, if not eliminate, undesirable emotional responses. The procedure involves the use of systematic eye movement, which facilitates the reprocessing of remembered traumatic or feared information or mental representations, while accessing and enhancing inner strength.

I am pleased to relate that Noreen responded well to treatment. She no longer fears being alone, and in fact, she now enjoys her solitude.

CLASSICAL CONDITIONING EXPLAINS THE RELATIONAL DESTRUCTION DUE TO SEXUAL ABUSE

Even the devastation of child sexual abuse can also be partially explained by classical conditioning. Many of the scenarios manifest as follows:

sexual abuse–fear
UCS–UCR
male–sexual abuse–fear
NS–UCS–UCR
male–fear
CS–CR

In many cases of sexual abuse the abused client learns to generalize her fear to anyone that resembles the original sexual offender. For example, if a woman was sexually abused by an uncle with a mustache, the abused woman may generalize and fear all men with mustaches or beards.

In chapter 13 we will discuss how to best find a mental health professional.

APPENDIX E

Cognitive System Malfunctions

1. Thinking Difficulties

Difficulty concentrating
Mind races, uncontrolled thoughts
Confused
Lose objectivity and perspective
Difficulty reasoning
Can't recall names, important ideas

2. Sensory-Perceptual

Self-conscious
In a daze, haze, fog, cloud
On guard

3. Conceptual

Repetition of fearful concepts   Distortion of thoughts
Frightening visual images   Fear of losing control (going crazy, being
(not hallucinations)   unable to cope, injury, death, negative
evaluation)

Affective System Malfunctions

Alarmed	Anxious	Edgy	Impatient	Fearful
Frightened	Jumpy	Jittery	Nervous	Uneasy
Wound up	Tense	Scared	Terrified	

Behavioral System Malfunctions

Immobility	Hyperventilation	Postural collapse
Flight	Speech dysfluency	Impaired coordination
Avoidance	Restlessness	Inhibition

Physiological System Malfunctions

1. Respiratory

Lump in throat	Shortness of breath	Bronchial spasms
Difficulty in getting air	Rapid breathing	Gasping
Pressure on chest	Shallow breathing	Choking sensation

2. Cardiovascular

Racing heart	Decreased/increased blood pressure	Faintness/fainting
Palpitations	Decreased pulse rate	

3. Gastrointestinal

Heartburn	Revulsion toward food	Nausea
Vomiting	Abdominal discomfort	Abdominal pain
Loss of appetite		

4. Neuromuscular

Tremors	Generalized weakness	Pacing	Spasms
Clumsy motions	Increased reflexes	Wobbly legs	Unsteady
Rigidity	Startle reaction	Strained face	Insomnia
Fidgeting/ eyelid twitching			

5. Urinary Tract

Frequent urination   Pressure to urinate

6. Skin

Pale face	Hot and cold spells	Itching
Flushed face	Generalized sweating	Sweaty palms

Chapter Twelve

EMOTIONAL DETACHMENT—THE ULTIMATE RELATIONAL DESTROYER

Tami L. Grovatt-Dawkins

In this chapter we will see how the seeds of relational failure are sown in the earliest relationships of our lives.

Michael was removed from his drug-addicted mother by his state's Child Protective Services Agency shortly after his birth. By the time he was nine years old, he had already been placed in four different foster homes. When Michael was 10 years old, he was adopted into a family that relocated frequently because of the adoptive father's job. Michael ran away from home repeatedly between ages 10 and 16, complaining about physical abuse. His complaints led the adoptive parents to give up parental rights to Michael and return him to the custody of the state until he reached maturity. When Michael was referred for counseling as an adult, he was socially isolated, fearful of commitments, and unable to sustain a relationship.

Samantha was abandoned by her mother as a newborn baby. The mother simply left her in the backseat of the car that was serving as their home and was never seen again. Samantha was adopted at three months of age by a family that had adopted several other children. In her third year with her new family Samantha began to display angry, unpredictable behaviors toward her adoptive parents and members of their extended families. By the time she began to go to preschool, Samantha was already heavily medicated. She struggled with serious academic and peer-related problems throughout her elementary and secondary school years. When she presented for counseling as an adult, her issues revolved around the way her anger and insecurity kept her from making and keeping meaningful connections with other people in her life.

WHAT WENT WRONG?

What went wrong? This question has been repeatedly asked by psychologists, educators, and social workers in attempts to evaluate and treat problem behaviors in children, adolescents, and adults. One answer postulates that broken or nonexistent bonds of attachment to at least one stable, biological, transitional caretaker often result in a variety of interpersonal problems and dilemmas later in life. Broken or nonexistent attachments in childhood frequently play themselves out in vain attempts to reattach and make first connections with another significant love.

Michael sought counseling as an adult after a long series of unsuccessful attempts to undo the abandonment that his mother had initiated with him; in addition, he never learned how to be a loving, available parent.

In my practice I have come to realize that each person reveals himself through his behavior. This "stuck" behavior repeats and refines a negative and hopeless approach to personal relationships, resulting in self-fulfilling prophecies of despair such as those experienced by Michael.

As I discussed in chapter 3, Erickson's model of childhood development defines trust as the primary developmental milestone to achieving internal stability. Forming basic trust in the world through early interactions with parents, a mother, or a primary caretaker insulates the personality of the developing child so that he is better able to cope with frustration, fear, and rejection in future interpersonal relationships. Without a set of trust-building experiences in the infant's life, a child will either give up attempting to receive positive feedback from the caretaker or will aggressively seek attention in every available opportunity. In either scenario the resulting adult personality functions in an extremely fragile and shattered way that is intolerant of deferring gratification, criticism, rejection, or conflict. Such a person grows up with distorted expectations of others, unconsciously forcing intimates into filling the internal void.

Moreover, without receiving successful parental assurance as a child, closeness and separation in later intimate relationships becomes experienced as painful. The internal concept of self is constantly insecure, uncomfortable, and looking desperately for satisfaction. In the case of Michael I saw that a series of secondary disorders (such as addictions) often emerges to fill feelings of emptiness in attempts to mitigate and suppress an internal psychological pain.

Willingness to consider counseling does not usually occur until the individual, couple, or family not only reexperiences old conflicts but also falls back on old patterns of coping. The amount of stress a family can tolerate depends on its level of development and the type of fixations its members may have learned.[1] In the initial sessions of counseling, clients who, like Michael, are manifesting this pattern of interrupted attachment begin by stating that relationships are exciting at first and then evolve into a series of disappointments that seem impossible to understand or manage.

Michael's initial conclusion was that women in general were "no good." As counseling progressed, he came to realize that this view was connected to the past and that his present life story was being shaped by the choices he was unconsciously making. He was both seeking out women who would reject him, like his mother, and unknowingly using problem-solving skills that actively, yet inadvertently, caused relationships to worsen. While he was not responsible for initiating this pattern as a child, he grew into an adult whose relationship choices continued to bring more emptiness and suffering into his own life.

Generating conscious awareness is the first and, typically, most critical step toward participating in actively making any lasting change in treatment. Clients with attachment disorders are unaware that they are looking for the therapeutic relationship to rescue them and fix their unhappiness, just as they do in their familial and romantic relationships. This expectation for outside forces or experiences to bring satisfaction into their lives is unrealistic, but it reflects the origin of their presenting issues.

While these individuals may look like adults physically, they are unconsciously being driven by the same unresolved need for parenting connections that was never met during infancy and childhood. "The more starved for appreciation the child, the less likely the adult will ever be satisfied. The reason is that the under-responded-to child does not modify the grandiose self into realistic goals and ambitions, but represses it, where it remains as an impossible standard of unconscious ambition."[2] Fortunately, this internal or intrapsychic conflict causes anxiety, which can lead to a paradigm shift in both thought and action, and which in turn leads the client along the pathways of change.

I am pleased to relate that Michael's will to change and commitment to treatment has enabled him to grow and flourish as a human being. Michael has now created more stability in his life than he ever had before by bravely processing his own negative patterns of impulsivity, drug use, and avoidance of goals, all of which were initiated by his mother's abandonment and permanent rejection. He has returned to college, is engaged after a five-year relationship, and is committed to visitation with his son on a regular basis. While the narrative of his life has been one of consistent struggle with loneliness, he is now allowing the grief to transform his identity from helpless victim to empowered survivor. Eventually, the frustration and dissatisfaction of being stuck in an unhealthy pattern drove him to change.

Nine years ago, Samantha was brought in to my office by her parents, who were desperate to understand why years of effort toward getting treatment for their adoptive daughter appeared so unsuccessful and hopeless. After gathering the family history and background information a picture of attachment disorder, combined with additional cumulative stressors that led to a childhood experienced through a cloudy lens of grief and depression, began to emerge. Like children who are threatened by physical illness, emotional damage early in life will have a negative impact on their relationships throughout their lives, if left untreated.

Samantha had so many things working against the success of her healthy development. After attachment with her biological mother was severed her father made years of false promises to reunite their relationship, until he was finally imprisoned on drug charges and never initiated contact again. As a young girl in counseling, she remained focused on this experience of double abandonment, and, in her mind, all contemporary peer and adult interactions in some way connected to her underlying feelings of inadequacy and insecurity. Since Samantha held an introjection, or image, of herself as unlovable and inferior, she perceived the outer world as just that unloving.

Her earliest interactions in life were frightening and ultimately rejecting, which she generalized and projected onto every other situation. She carried this identity with her, unconsciously anticipating rejections and then reacting negatively to all other perceived threats. What other children might momentarily be upset by, such as someone taking a toy away from them on the playground or not including them in an activity, she would quickly interpret as being hated by her peers.

Her relationships with adults were equally as fragile. If a teacher scolded or corrected her behavior, she was likely to view this as a rejection and betrayal by the transitional caretaker, sending her into a combination of rage and infantile regression. This pattern of reacting defensively in social interactions created the dynamics that she feared—adults and other children avoided contact because of her volatile behavior. The end result was a reinforced belief that life was painful and that human connection was untrustworthy. Her tainted perception of reality took her farther and farther from achieving healthy acceptance, love, and validation.

Samantha's adoptive family moved to another state during treatment. They continued to support her in altering her negative self-talk schemas by implementing skills learned in counseling. After several years she made contact with me to update her progress. Her teenage and young adult development had been a difficult battle with rapid changes, beginning and then dropping out of college, continued depression and panic attacks, migraines, drug use, and relationship instability. As anticipated, her chosen peer group often disappointed or rejected her, and she complained that she didn't have any "real friends." The primary bond that kept her peer relationships together was numbing their individual emptiness through heavy drinking and drug use on a daily basis.

In our meeting Samantha shared with me that the emotional disconnect, plus feelings of isolation she experienced during infancy, translated into such unresolved, complicated grief that she was suicidal and needed psychiatric hospitalization at age 18. Again, while some degree of trauma may help inoculate an individual to become more resilient in response to future crises, a steady accumulation of stressors overloads internal cognitive and emotional systems. The long-term effect is a fear-based, pessimistic schema about life, typically leading to depression and thoughts of suicide. While this has been her story, the last three years have shown a slow shift in her world view, including a good career choice, success in college, a long-term relationship, and a first apartment. Each step remains tenuous, but the prior stress symptoms, such as migraines and panic attacks, have diminished to the point where she can maintain an optimal level of functioning.

During our conversation Samantha stopped giving me factual information and started to cry. After a while the topic moved to the primary reason she had come in for a visit. She needed to talk about one of her former "partying" friends who had continued living the lifestyle and had died of a drug overdose a month before. She had loosely kept in touch with this girl, who usually called her "when she needed something"—a place to stay for a few days to get away from her abusive boyfriend, some money, a ride, and so forth.

In processing the events together Samantha came to several insights: (1) she saw her friend's lack of change in life as a reference point for how much she had actually improved; (2) she realized that her own guilty feelings about needing to be available for this girl during any potential crisis was an unconscious attempt to rescue herself at a previous stage of emotional development; and (3) she could identify with her friend's pain, and she was secretly longing for someone to come and rescue her. She looked at me more directly and said, "I never really thought about it, but I always did drugs with her because I didn't care if I died. I don't feel like that anymore—for the first time in my life, I want to stay alive."

TREATMENT

A more detailed outline of treatment for attachment disorders is provided in chapter 13. Briefly, for both Michael and Samantha, treatment focused on the resiliency model. Even though the resiliency model worked with Michael and Samantha, it is most effective if utilized in childhood. It attempts to prevent serious social, emotional, and academic risks, prior to the child demonstrating acting-out behaviors. Healthy physical resistance, coupled with social competency, including humor and a sense of purpose and future, are each relevant in creating a profile of a resilient individual.[3]

Just as the primary goal of infancy is to secure attachment and trust building, the final objective of healthy adulthood is to eventually secure individualization from the caretaker. There is a direct relationship between these two developmental milestones, with healthy individualization being completely dependent on successful progression through a secure attachment stage. Ironically, independence requires attachment. A young toddler cannot begin to separate from the mother and confidently venture off to explore new territory unless she has had her needs satisfactorily met during the initial trust versus mistrust stage of development.[4]

As a baby is supported by the loving interaction of a caretaker who accepts its helpless state of dependency, the child becomes emotionally inoculated to tolerate the challenges that are encountered at each developmental level. Successful parents know how to balance protection of the child against providing reasonable growth and independence.

Each event adds to the development of our psychological imprints about what to expect when interacting with the external world. When we face or overcome fearful situations, we move forward and build confidence to meet more challenges. This is a basic intropsychic operation that enhances our emotional growth, defines our self-worth, and affects our perceptions of the world.

Although some people may possess the built-in (genetic) ability to triumph in the face of bad circumstances, most others have to become resilient. Therefore children with a genetically low tolerance for stress who have early experiences where they are exposed to opportunities for learning healthy coping strategies will be more likely to have meaningful relationships and avoid negative paths that lead to relational disorder.[5]

A SECOND LOOK AT DIVORCE

Although the cases of Michael and Samantha are extreme cases of abandonment, the results of recent studies and surveys suggest that we should seriously consider the consequences that divorce has on children. I am not saying that divorce should never occur; I am saying that we should carefully consider the ramifications.

A recent professional study by E. Mavis Hetherington investigated over a thousand divorced families over 30 years and found that 20 to 25 percent of young adults from divorced families experience severe social and emotional problems as compared to 10 percent of young people from intact families. That's over a 50 percent increase in psychological problems.[6]

In another recent study Elizabeth Marquardt and Norval Glenn surveyed 1,500 young adults from divorced and intact families. They also interviewed more than 70 of the young adults at great lengths. The survey found that 52 percent of young adults from so-called good divorces felt that their lives were severely stressful and full of conflict. Of those surveyed, 33 percent that came from a so-called good divorce felt lonely. As adults, 50 percent of the participants felt lonely and between two worlds, and 50 percent of those surveyed felt like a different person in each parent's house. They apparently did not develop a strong sense of self-identity.

Children are profoundly influenced by divorce. Providing a secure home for our children requires strong, lasting marriages. Having parents who live together is not the same as having married parents. Three-quarters of cohabiting parents break up before the child's 16 birthday, so the children of cohabiting parents are in especially unstable situations.[7]

Chapter Thirteen

SO WHAT NOW?

My clients are bewildered when I mention to them that there are over 400 different kinds of therapies. Most people feel that therapy has to do with the client talking, while the therapist listens attentively. Of course, there is a place for such "talk therapy." Expressing or venting over feelings is cathartic. However, often, there is a need for more directive types of treatment.

Throughout the book I have provided self-help techniques and guidelines to help you better understand the hidden dynamics regarding relationships as well as ways to enhance relationships. In this chapter I will briefly review some of the guidelines that I outlined in the book, and I will provide you with information that will help you find good professional help, if you need it. Also, in an appendix to this chapter, I have provided a list of professional organizations and mental health agencies with toll-free numbers.

In chapter 3, "The Mixture of Unconscious Forces and Childhood Wounds Can Be Lethal to a Marriage," I discussed how family-of-origin wounds could devastate a relationship. I focused on an analysis of Erikson's psychosocial stages of development to help us uncover any potential childhood wounds that may stem from emotional needs that were not met when we were younger. Most mental health providers would agree that the first six years are critical to the formation of our personalities.

In chapter 4, "Your Family Problems May Have Started Back in Medieval Times," I discussed how dysfunctional behavior is transmitted from generation to generation without the participants being consciously aware of what is happening. One of the mechanisms that perpetuates the progression of the dysfunctional behavior over generations is the mechanism of triangulation.

Triangulation, as the name implies, is when one person allies or sides with another person against a third person.

As I discussed earlier, many family therapists feel that the triangle, a three-person system, forms the basis of all emotional systems. It is the fundamental emotional system for not only families, but all groups. A two-party system may function in a "normal fashion," but when anxiety escalates, the most vulnerable member seeks to pull in another person to form a triangle. When stress decreases, the twosome returns to their "normal" state, while the third party feels isolated and lonely.

To break the cycle of triangulation, you must first become consciously aware of the process. For example, when stress is running high between you and your partner, you need to become consciously aware of recruiting (triangulating) a child against your partner in an attempt to diffuse stress. Take a moment, and reflect on stressful moments with your spouse and how you pulled a child into your problems. Some of the stressful situations may have been financial, working too hard, in-laws, not having enough time for each other, and so forth. The goal is to make a conscious effort to discuss the issues at hand directly with your partner and not involve the children in your parenting problems.

In chapter 5, entitled "Unconscious Forces Can Destroy Not Only Relationships, but Whole Families," I hope to have enlightened the reader that acting-out behavior by children and adolescents is symptomatic of deeper family problems, and family dynamics should be evaluated. Often, the child that is acting out (for example, fighting, failing academically, displaying behavioral problems in school) is the symptom-bearer. In my opinion, if you suspect problems that we outlined in chapter 5, I highly recommend that you seek a licensed family therapist. They are quite adept at viewing and treating such problems systematically and not only focusing treatment on the symptom-bearer.

In chapter 7, entitled "Games People Play in Relationships," we discussed how such games as "if it wasn't for you," "guess what I want," and "look how hard I tried" use deception and dishonesty and have serious consequences for the relationship. The purpose of the chapter was to first help couples become consciously aware of the existence of such games in their relationship and then provide the couple with ways to terminate the power plays. Specific ways to move toward ending destructive game-playing included removing the victim utilizing Karpman's triangle and following some guidelines for dealing with power struggles.

Regarding enhancing marital and couples' relationships, in chapter 8, entitled "Organizing Problem-Solving Conversations," I discussed a number of self-help techniques and guidelines to enhance communication, including specific guidelines for effective communication, steps to form additional suggestions for constructive conflict, and the "couples' dialogue." To facilitate marital or couples' relational connections, I introduced such proven helpful techniques as "early recollections" and encouraged thinking in terms of marital best interest, positive changes to encourage getting what you want, and "caring days" to change the way couples interact.

In chapter 9, "Extramarital Affairs—Silence, Secrets, and Self-Disclosure," we discussed the powerful, unconscious forces that undermine the integrity of marriage and devastate spouses by the breaking of sexual agreements. This chapter clearly expressed the need for couples to feel okay talking between themselves about anything, including stress or everyday problems, what they won't or aren't getting from the other spouse, and even sexual agreements. The chapter outlined proven ways to construct an affair-proof relationship. One such way is to establish with your partner a clear, conscious, and communicated agreement. In summary, sexual agreements are a result of conversations regarding what the partners agree will be their sexual behaviors and limits.

Another way to help affair-proof a relationship is to observe when and why the couple stops talking about their relationship. Over and over, as therapists, we observe that when couples stop communicating about their relationship, the couple grows emotionally apart. They don't know what each other wants from the relationship, and the overt conflicts and silence only compound the problem. That's why it's imperative that couples not only take the time, but know how to effectively discuss their needs and expectations of one another.

FINDING A MARRIAGE/FAMILY THERAPIST

During the course of the book we have given you some unique ideas regarding self-analysis and analysis of your relational situation. We know that this is not easy. As therapists, we find it difficult to objectively evaluate our own personal family matters and our own closest relationships.

We don't see things as they are. We see things as we are. Even though we like to think that we are objective in our beliefs, they are formed, to a certain degree, by our upbringing. Our upbringing affects our values, morals, and perceptions of ourselves and others.

Also, as we discussed earlier in the book, we defend our egos by utilizing such defense mechanisms as denial, projection, and rationalization.

The defense mechanisms of projection and rationalization can play a part in our deception of ourselves and others. As you may recall from chapter 2, "The Unconscious Mind—Friend or Foe?" we utilize projection when we take parts of us that we don't like and project them onto others. For example, we may be tardy, and we complain that our spouse is always late. It's a lot easier for us to deal with our faults by not dealing with them in ourselves and by projecting them onto others. Again, we are taking parts of us that we want to disown and placing them onto others.

Rationalization is making illogical excuses for logical behavior. It's amazing how we can rationalize almost anything. I have seen clients rationalize affairs, sexual abuse, divorce, and worse. Rationalization allows us to live with ourselves, even though on some less conscious level we know we are distorting the truth.

So, how can we objectively analyze ourselves when so many of our behaviors occur on the unconscious level and we are barely consciously aware of our actions? To truly understand our feelings and our interactions with our partner, we may need the services of a mental health professional.

Once you realize that the relationship needs professional help, both partners must agree on counseling. Couples' counseling only works if both partners are willing to get involved in counseling. Change will only occur if you are willing to change. Since marriage or relationship counseling involves two people, it is essential that both partners not only be involved in the counseling process, but also want to make the relationship or marriage work.

As a couple, once you have decided that you would like to enhance your relationship, you need to find a professional therapist. We recommend that the professional be a licensed marriage and family therapist with extensive marriage-counseling experience.

Word of mouth is a good way of choosing a therapist. You also need to ask the right questions to the prospective therapist. The questions to be considered are his years of experience, his philosophy of marriage counseling, the length of time for the session, his fee, and how he determines the need for conjoint or separate sessions.

The therapist should know how to work with a couple as a couple. This means that the therapist should be more curious about the actual patterns of communication going on between the partners than he is about the patterns of thinking going on between the ears of either partner. Most of the talking in sessions should be between the partners and not between each partner and the therapist.

The therapist should start off on equal footing with both mates, and he should not already know one spouse better than the other. This means that the therapist should not have been one of the mates' previous individual therapist.

Couples' counseling is no one's business except yours and your partner's. By law, your counseling sessions are completely confidential. However, your counselor has the "duty to warn" if you or your spouse expresses suicidal or homicidal thoughts. Remember, too, that the right to privacy and confidentiality extends to both of you and that your therapist cannot release any information about treatment to a third person (for example, a lawyer or subsequent treatment provider) unless you both agree to waive the rights.

I give the following guidelines to new clients.

First, do not discuss your marital troubles with anyone except your spouse or your counselor. This boundary will prevent your marriage from becoming overcrowded with relatives, friends, and advisors.

Second, only attempt to talk together to solve your marital problems when *both* of you (1) are sitting down, (2) are not engaged in some other activity like chores, driving, working, tending children, and so forth, (3) are in agreement that it is a good time to talk, and (4) are not under the influence of drugs or alcohol.

Third, do not threaten separation, divorce, seeking legal advice, or other forms of marital destruction when you are angry at your spouse. These threats keep you from finding more productive ways to express anger or solve problems.

Fourth, do not waste your time trying to correct your spouse's version of your marital history. You are working on your future, not your past, in marital counseling.

Couples' therapy is a new and, for many people, an anxiety-producing experience because they are not sure what to expect. Relationship counseling is not psychoanalysis. In fact, most couples' therapies have nothing to do with psychoanalysis. Marriage counseling, generally, is not long term and usually consists of 10 to 20 sessions. For some, this may seem like a lot of sessions, but one has to remember that it takes years to get to this point, and it takes time to get in the right direction.

The content of the session will primarily revolve around organizing problem-solving conversations, promoting healthy communication skills, and analyzing family-of-origin issues.

SUBSTANCE ABUSE COUNSELING

As we discussed in chapter 10, "Addictions—A Vain Attempt to Make Us Feel Whole," addiction is a pathological attraction to any person, place, or thing. The operative word is "pathological." According to the dictionary, "pathological" means concern with or caused by disease. In my experience it is insidious. Quite often, the addict does not consciously admit that he has a problem until he "hits rock bottom" or the bottom is raised. Denial unconsciously protects the substance abuser from seeing himself as he truly is and not how others see him. Also, when we are in denial, we minimize how the addiction affects the whole family.

In chapter 10 we provided a few guidelines regarding seeking professional help, that is, the difference between utilizing a therapist with a behavioral approach or psychodynamic approach. However, in addition to seeking out such professionals, because of the insidious nature of addiction, a certified or licensed substance abuse counselor should be considered as part of the treatment plan. Certified or licensed drug and alcohol counselors are well trained in the process of addiction. Often, they are recovering themselves and are hard-nosed enough to help keep an addict on the path to recovery.

Last, as therapists, we highly recommend that the addict attends regular Alcoholics Anonymous and Narcotics Anonymous meetings and that the partner and family of the addicted person attend Al-Anon or Alateen.

FINDING A THERAPIST WHO TREATS ATTACHMENT DISORDERS

In chapter 12, "Emotional Detachment—The Ultimate Relational Destroyer," we discussed the potential devastation of such traumatic events such as separation, divorce, and lack of parental involvement, especially if they took place in early childhood and are so traumatic that they have unconsciously instilled feelings of abandonment, loneliness, and isolation. Without proper interventions, such trauma could devastate how we relate to people for a lifetime.

When seeking a therapist for abandonment issues or attachment disorders, the earlier the child is helped, the greater the likelihood of success. The therapist should be knowledgeable and skilled in the resilience mode of therapy and play therapy.

The resiliency model is a preventive model that is most effective when introduced in early childhood in an attempt to prevent serious social, emotional, and academic risk, prior to the child demonstrating acting-out behaviors.

Treatments that identify an existing pattern of behavior reflecting possible family disorganization, breakdown, or traumatic stress are defined as early intervention. For example, a child whose parents are divorcing and creates disruptions in the classroom may need early intervention to curtail disruptive behavior in school. Current understanding in the support of healthy development recommends that the earlier the intervention, the more likely the success.[1]

Further, prevention treatment is indicated when serious social, emotional, and academic risks are determined to be likely prior to exhibiting negative coping behaviors. For example, a new mother with a history of depression can receive specialized support for postpartum difficulty to help reduce the risk of attachment problems with her newborn child. This shift in perspective from taking action after behaviors are not working or a crisis exists to enhancing what is working in an individual is at the core of the resiliency model. This model also utilizes preexisting internal and environmental protective factors that contribute to and perpetuate poor coping skills that enhance risk-taking behaviors such as poor family attachment, inadequate supervision of children, difficulty forming social relationships, poor self-image, and so forth. Refer to appendix F at the end of this chapter for a more complete list.[2]

Conversely, this model focuses on enhancing such positive factors as encouraging supportive relationships with many caring people, goal setting, and finding a reinforcing, clear and internal locus of control. For a more complete list of such positive factors that enhance resiliency, refer to appendix G[3] at the end of this chapter.

Play therapy allows the therapist to interpret play behaviors and synthesize the data with existing information on our problem issues, family history, and current levels of functioning. Also, the act of play and the chosen play objects may represent intrapsychic processes that attempt to protect the child from direct awareness of conflict or provide her with a sense of control in the face of deep fear and anxiety. Without the protective support of therapeutic intervention and interpretation the child may be obsessed with and fixed on the trauma, reliving it again and again in repetitive play behaviors.[4]

THERAPISTS WHO ADDRESS ABUSE

Last, in chapter 11, entitled "Our Nervous Systems and Relational Problems," we outlined how even the devastation of sexual abuse can be partially explained by classical conditioning. I also mentioned earlier in the book how sexual abuse affects one in three girls and one in five boys. Unfortunately, it is quite common. There are innumerable resources available to the survivors of child abuse. Some are better than others. The best place to start is with your therapist, who will be able to point you to a resource best fitted to your needs.

If you feel that you need professional help, it is imperative that you find a therapist with training and experience in dealing with abuse. There are numerous issues that therapists confront, but not all therapists have the experience and expertise to deal with the trauma of sexual abuse. Trained therapists understand that you may feel uncomfortable asking questions concerning their professional expertise regarding abuse, but it's important that you get the proper help. Be assured that such inquiries will not embarrass the therapists; if it offends them, stay away.

In closing, as this book repeatedly professes, the person that each of us brings into any relationship is not self-created. Each of us is a sum total of countless messages about how we are to act and react in relationships: what we are supposed to feel and not feel in close relationships and what we are supposed to expect and not expect from others. These messages were communicated to us in childhood by people who were more powerful than we were and who were in charge of helping us to grow.

Sometimes these people knew what they were doing, and sometimes they didn't. Sometimes the messages of the past were dysfunctional; they distorted one's version of relational truth. We all need help on our interpersonal journey. Some of us—the ones that were the victims of especially cruel and pathological messages from childhood—need to take ourselves to a safe, still place to heal the psychological and emotional wounds that are keeping us stuck in unproductive, combative, self-defeating, and even dangerous patterns of relationships with the people we often most care about. Many people find this still, safe place in psychotherapy.

Contrary to popular belief and culture, psychotherapy is not something people do to cast responsibility for their lives onto someone else. It is a choice people make about taking ownership of their lives, to take charge of their relationship decisions, and to be in control of their futures. The choice to enter into counseling is a courageous choice that means saying good-bye to childhood and encountering the full meaning of adulthood.

I have seen psychotherapy create great changes for the spiritual lives of therapists and clients. Counseling enables one to find better ways to communicate oneself to others and gives a person a sense of confidence that he is indeed lovable, repairable, and resilient. Counseling enhances one's ultimate power—the power to be an adult who freely chooses the content of her character and the impact she will have on the lives of others.

APPENDIX F

The Individual

- Poor life skills, including communication, social skills, conflict resolution, assertiveness, and decision-making skills
- Early onset of dysfunctional coping skills, including aggressive behavior, hyperactivity, and shy/withdrawn behavior
- Difficulty forming social relationships
- Poor self-image
- Inappropriate expression of feelings

The Family

- Poor family attachment
- Family conflict and violence
- Poor parenting behavior
- Family drug use or favorable attitudes toward use
- Inadequate supervision of children
- Poverty

The School

- Poor school performance
- Frequent absence
- School violence

The Peer Group

- Rejection by peers
- Association with delinquent peer groups

- Pressure of peer groups regarding use of alcohol or other drugs
- Lack of positive peer group affiliation

APPENDIX G

Internal Protective Factors

- Gives of self in service to others and/or cause
- Uses life skills, including good decision making, assertiveness, impulse control, and problem solving
- Sociability; ability to be a friend to form positive relationships
- Sense of humor
- Internal locus of control
- Autonomy; independence
- Positive view of personal future
- Flexibility
- Capacity for and connection to learning
- Self-motivation
- Is "good at something"; personal competence
- Feelings of self-worth and self-confidence

Family and Social Environments

- Promotes close bonds
- Values and encourages education
- Uses high-warmth, low-criticism style of interaction
- Sets and enforces clear boundaries (rules, norms, and laws)
- Encourages supportive relationships with many caring others
- Promotes sharing of responsibilities, services to others, "required helpfulness"
- Provides access to resources for meeting basic needs of housing, employment, health care, and recreation
- Expresses high and realistic expectations of success
- Encourages goal setting and mastery
- Encourages prosocial development of values (such as altruism) and life skills (such as cooperation)

APPENDIX H

Professional Organizations

Association for the Advancement of Behavior Therapy
305 Seventh Avenue
New York, NY 10001

American Academy of Child and Adolescent Psychiatry (AACAP)
3615 Wisconsin Avenue, NW
Washington, DC 20016-3007
Voice: (202) 966-7300
Fax: (202) 966-7300
Web: www.AACAP.org
The American Academy of Child and Adolescent Psychiatry is a professional medical
organization comprising child and adolescent psychiatrists. The mission of the AACAP
is the promotion of mentally healthy children, adolescents, and families through
research, training, advocacy, prevention, comprehensive diagnosis and treatment, peer
support, and collaboration.

American Counseling Association
5999 Stevenson Avenue
Alexandria, VA 22304
Toll free: (800) 347-6647

The American Association for Marriage and Family Therapy (AAMFT)
1133 15th Street, NW, Suite 300
Washington, DC 20005-2710
Voice: (202) 452-0109
E-mail: WebMgr@aamft.org
Web: www.AAMFT.org
The American Association for Marriage and Family Therapy (AAMFT) is the
professional association for the field of marriage and family therapy, comprising marriage
and family therapists (MFTs) from the United States, Canada, and abroad.

The American Psychological Association (APA)
750 First Street, NE
Washington, DC 20002-4242
Voice: (202) 336-5500
Web: www.PsychNet.org

The American Psychiatric Association (APA)
Web: www.psych.org
The American Psychiatric Association is a national medical specialty society whose
40,500 physician members specialize in the diagnosis and treatment of mental and
emotional illnesses and substance use disorders.

The American Association of Pastoral Counselors (AAPC)
9504-A Lee Highway
Fairfax, VA 22031-2303
Voice: (703) 385-6967
Web: www.AAPC.org
AAPC was founded in 1963 as an organization that certifies pastoral counselors,
accredits pastoral counseling centers, and approves training programs. It is nonsectarian
and respects the spiritual commitments and religious traditions of those who seek
assistance without imposing counselor beliefs onto the client.

The National Association of Social Workers (NASW)
Web: www.naswdc.org
National Mental Health Association
2001 N. Beauregard Street, 12th Floor
Alexandria, VA 22311
Phone: (703) 684-7722
Fax: (703) 684-5968

Mental Health Resource Center: (800) 969-NMHA
TTY Line: (800) 433-5959

Clinical Social Work Federation (CSWF)
E-mail: nfscswlo@aol.com
Web: www.CSWF.org
The Clinical Social Work Federation is a confederation of 31 state societies for clinical social work. The state societies are formed as voluntary associations for the purpose of promoting the highest standards of professional education and clinical practice. Each society is active with legislative advocacy and lobbying efforts for adequate and appropriate mental health services and coverage at their state and national levels of government. Beyond supporting the state societies' aims, the Board of the CSWF seeks to keep clinical social work visible and understood, to generate clinical research, and to provide professional training and publications on the national level.

Mental Health Organizations

Al-Anon Family Group Headquarters
(888) 4AL-ANON (425-2666)
8:00 A.M.–6:00 P.M., Monday–Friday

Alcohol and Drug Helpline
(800) 821-4357

American Council on Alcoholism
(800) 527-5344
9:00 A.M.–5:00 P.M., Monday–Friday

CHILDHELP USA
National Child Abuse Hotline
(800) 4-A-CHILD (422-4453)
Provides multilingual crisis intervention and professional counseling on child abuse and domestic violence issues. Gives referrals to local agencies offering counseling and other services related to child abuse, adult survivor issues, and domestic violence. Provides literature on child abuse in English and Spanish. Calls are anonymous, toll-free, and counselors are paid, degreed professionals.

Covenant House Nineline
(800) 999-9999
Crisis line for youth, teens, and families. Locally based referrals throughout the United States. Help for youth and parents regarding drugs, abuse, homelessness, runaway children, and message relays.

Drug Policy Information Clearinghouse
White House Office of National Drug Policy Control
(800) 666-3332
10:00 A.M.–6:00 P.M., Monday–Friday (eastern time)

Drug-Free Workplace Helpline
(800) 967-5752
9:00 A.M.–5:30 P.M., Monday–Friday (eastern time)

Drug Help
(800) 488-DRUG (3784)
9:00 A.M.–5:00 P.M., Monday–Friday (eastern time)

ARC of the United States
(800) 433-5255

National Alliance for the Mentally Ill Helpline
(800) 950-6264

National Clearinghouse on Child Abuse and Neglect Information
(800) 394-3366
8:30 A.M.–5:30 P.M., Monday–Friday (eastern time)

National Foundation for Depressive Illness
(800) 239-1265 (recording)

National Hopeline Network
(800) SUICIDE (784-2433)

National Institute of Child Health and Human Development Information Resource
Center
(800) 370-2943
8:30 A.M.–5:00 P.M., Monday–Friday, except federal holidays (eastern time)

National Institute of Mental Health
(866) 615-6464
8:30 A.M.–5:00 P.M., Monday–Friday (eastern time)

National Mental Health Association Resource Center
(800) 969-6642
(800) 433-5959 (TTY)

National Organization on Fetal Alcohol Syndrome
(800) 66-NOFAS (666-6327)
All calls will receive a response.
Voicemail available after hours.

National Runaway Switchboard
(800) 621-4000
(800) 621-0394 (TDD)
Provides crisis intervention and travel assistance information to runaways. Gives referrals to shelters nationwide. Also relays messages to, or sets up conference calls with, parents at the request of the child. Has access to AT&T Language Line.

National Youth Crisis Hotline
(800) 448-4663
Provides counseling and referrals to local drug treatment centers, shelters, and counseling services. Responds to youths dealing with pregnancy, molestation, suicide, and child abuse.

Parents Resource Institute for Drug Education (PRIDE)
(800) 279-6361 (surveys)
(800) 668-9277 (youth program)
8:30 A.M.–4:30 P.M., Monday–Friday

Prenatal Care Hotline
(800) 311-BABY (2229) (English)
(800) 504-7081 (Spanish)

Rape, Abuse, and Incest National (RAIN) Network
(800) 656-4673
Connects caller to the nearest counseling center that provides counseling for rape, abuse, and incest victims.

SAMHSA's National Mental Health Information Center
(800) 789-2647
(866) 889-2647 (TDD)
8:30 A.M.–5:00 P.M., Monday–Friday (eastern time)

Starlight Starbright Children's Foundation
(800) 274-7827
9:00 A.M.–5:00 P.M., Monday–Friday (Pacific time)

Zero to Three: National Center for Infants, Toddlers and Families
(800) 899-4301
9:00 A.M.–5:00 P.M., Monday–Friday

NOTES

CHAPTER 2

1. Sigmund Freud, "The Interpretation of Dreams," in *Abstracts of the Standard Edition of the Complete Psychological Works of Sigmund Freud,* ed. J. Strachey (London: Hozarth, 1953).

2. Carl G. Jung, *Modern Man in Search of a Soul* (New York: Harcourt Brace and Company, 1933), p. 11.

3. National Victim Center, http://www.NAL.usda.gov/pavnetkilcjnatvic.htm.

4. Wayne Weiten, *Psychology: Themes and Variations,* 6th ed. (Belmont, Calif.: Wadsworth, 2004), p. 483.

CHAPTER 3

1. Ivan Boszormenyi-Nagy and Geraldine M. Spark, *Invisible Loyalties: Reciprocity in Intergenerational Family Therapy* (New York: Harper and Row, 1973).

2. S. J. Betchen, "Parentified Pursuers and Childhood Distancers in Marital Therapy," *The Family Journal: Counseling and Therapy for Couples and Families* 14 (1996): 99–107.

3. Harville Hendrix, *Getting the Love You Want: A Guide for Couples* (New York: Harper and Row, 1988).

4. Erik H. Erikson, *Childhood and Society* (New York: Norton, 1963).

CHAPTER 4

1. Murray Bowen, *Family Therapy in Clinical Practice* (New York: J. Aronson, 1978).

2. James C. Hansen and Luciano L'Abate, *Approaches to Family Therapy* (New York: MacMillan Publishing Company, 1982), p. 163.

3. Murray Bowen, *Family Therapy in Clinical Practice* (New York: Jason-Aronson, 1978).
4. Ibid., 1976.
5. Edward Teyber, *Helping Children Cope with Divorce: A Practical Guide for Parents* (San Francisco: Jossey-Bass, 1994).

CHAPTER 5

1. Jay Haley, *Strategies of Psychotherapy* (New York: Grune and Staton, 1963).
2. Ivan Boszormenyi-Nagy and Geraldine M. Spark, *Invisible Loyalties: Reciprocity in Intergenerational Family Therapy* (New York: Harper and Row, 1973).
3. Lawrence Metzger, *From Denial to Recovery: Counseling Problem Drinkers, Alcoholics, and Their Families* (San Francisco: Jossey-Bass, 1988), pp. 189–190.
4. Elizabeth Carter and Monica McGoldrick, *Changing Family Life Cycle: A Framework for Family Therapy* (Boston: Allyn and Bacon, 1989).
5. Jay Haley, Uncommon Therapy and the Psychiatric Techniques of Milton N Erickson, MD (New York: Norton, 1973).
6. Salvador Minuchin and H. Charles Fishman, *Family Therapy Techniques* (Cambridge, Mass.: Harvard University Press, 1981).
7. Murray Bowen, *Family Therapy in Clinical Practice* (New York: J. Aronson, 1978).
8. Taube S. Kaufman, *The Combined Family: A Guide to Creating Successful Step-Relationships* (New York: Insight Books, 1993).

CHAPTER 6

1. R. A. Sternberg, "Triangular Theory of Love," *Psychological Review* 93 (1986): 119–135.
2. Marylou Hughes, *Marriage Counseling: An Essential Guide* (New York: Continuum, 1991), p. 57.
3. L. F. Barrett and J. P. Laurenceau, "The Interpersonal Process Model of Intimacy in Marriage: A Daily-Diary and Multilevel Modeling Approach," *Journal of Family Psychology* 19 (2005): 314–323.
4. Gerald R. Weeks and Stephen Treat, *Couples in Treatment: Techniques and Approaches for Effective Practice* (New York: Brunner/Mazel, 1992), pp. 108–111.
5. American Psychiatric Association, *Quick Reference to the Diagnostic Criteria from DSM-IV* (Washington, D.C.: American Psychiatric Association, 1994), pp. 63–65.

CHAPTER 7

1. Eric Berne, *Games People Play* (New York: Grove Press, 1964).
2. Erik Erikson, *Childhood and Society* (New York: Norton, 1963).
3. Frank Pittman, *Private Lies: Infidelity and the Betrayal of Intimacy* (New York: Norton, 1989).
4. J. L. Framo, "Family of Origin as a Therapeutic Resource for Adults in Marital and Family Therapy: You Can and Should Go Home Again," *Family Process* 15 (1976): 193–210.
5. Claude Steiner, *Scripts People Live: Transactional Analysis of Life Scripts* (New York: Grove Press, 1974).

6. S. B. Karpman, "Script Drama Analysis," *Transactional Analysis Journal* 7 (1968): 26–43.

7. S. Henry, "Inside Pandora's Box: Healing the Connection Between Victimization and Perpetration," presentation, International Conference on Trauma, Attachment and Dissociation: Transforming Trauma, Critical, Controversial and Case Issues, Melbourne, Australia, September 12–14, 2003.

8. Susan M. Campbell, *Beyond the Power Struggle* (San Luis Obispo, Calif.: Impact Publishers, 1984).

CHAPTER 8

1. John M. Gottman, *Why Marriages Succeed or Fail* (New York: Simon and Schuster, 1994).

2. Lynn Blacker, "The Launching Phase of the Life Cycle," in *The Expanded Family Life Cycle: Individual, Family, and Social Perspectives,* 3rd ed., ed. Betty Carter and Monica McGoldrick (Boston: Allyn and Bacon, 1999), pp. 293–295.

3. Harville Hendrix, *Getting the Love You Want: A Guide for Couples* (New York: Harper and Row, 1988).

4. L. F. Barrett and J. P. Laurenceau, "The Interpersonal Process Model of Intimacy in Marriage: A Daily-Diary and Multilevel Modeling Approach," *Journal of Family Psychology* 19 (2005): 314–323.

5. Harville Hendrix, *Getting the Love You Want: A Guide for Couples* (New York: Harper and Row, 1988).

6. Robert Sherman and Norman Fredman, *Handbook of Structured Techniques in Marriage and Family Therapy* (New York: Brunner/Mazel, 1986), pp. 16–19.

7. Ibid., 164–165.

8. Neil S. Jacobson and Gayla Margolin, *Marital Therapy* (New York: Brunner/Mazel, 1979).

9. Dale Carnegie, *How to Win Friends and Influence People and How to Stop Worrying and Start Living* (New York: Simon and Schuster, 1936).

10. Dale Carnegie, *The Dale Carnegie Course in Effective Speaking and Human Relations* (Garden City, NY: Dale Carnegie and Associates, 1974), pp. 106–107.

11. Richard B. Stuart, *Helping Couples Change: A Social Learning Approach to Marital Therapy* (New York: Guilford Press, 1980), pp. 192–202.

12. Norman V. Peale, *The Power of Positive Thinking* (Greenwich, Conn.: Fawcett, 1956), p. 98.

13. Richard B. Stuart, *Helping Couples Change* (New York: Guilford Press, 1980).

CHAPTER 9

1. Frank Pitman, *Private Lies: Infidelity and the Betrayal of Intimacy* (New York: Norton, 1989).

2. Janis Abrahms Spring, *After the Affair: Healing the Pain and Rebuilding Trust When a Partner Has Been Unfaithful* (New York: HarperCollins, 2002).

3. Frank Pittman, *Man Enough: Fathers, Sons, and the Search for Masculinity* (New York: Norton, 1993).

4. David Schnarch, *Passionate Marriage: Love, Sex, and Intimacy in Emotionally Committed Relationships* (New York: Henry Holt and Company, 1997), 106–107.

5. Ibid, 106.

6. P. Shelton, "Recovering from Extra-Marital Affairs," 2005, http://www.CAMFT.org.

7. John M. Gottman, Why Marriages Succeed or Fail: What You Can Learn from the Breakthrough Research to Make Your Marriage Last (New York: Simon and Schuster, 1994), p. 44.

8. Janis Abrahms Spring, *How Can I Forgive You: The Courage to Forgive, the Freedom Not To* (New York: HarperCollins, 2004).

CHAPTER 10

1. M. A. McGue, Behavioral-Genetic Perspective of Children of Alcoholics, *Alcohol Health and Research World* 21 (1997): 210–217.

2. Wayne Weiten, *Psychology: Themes and Variations,* 6th ed. (Belmont, Calif.: Wadsworth, 2004), p. 483.

3. John Bradshaw, *Healing the Shame That Binds You* (Deerfield Beach, Fla: Health Communication, 1988), p. 15.

4. Thomas Harris, *I'm OK, You're OK* (New York: Avon Books, 1973).

5. Shirley P. Glass, "Couple Therapy after the Trauma of Infidelity," in *Clinical Handbook of Couple Therapy*, 3rd ed., ed. Alan S. Gurman and Neil S. Jacobson (New York: Guilford Press, 2002), p. 490.

6. Patrick Carnes, *Don't Call It Love: Recovery from Sexual Addiction* (New York: Banton Books, 1992), p. 47.

7. Ibid., p. 48.

8. Ibid., p. 99.

9. Ibid., p. 100.

10. B. Van Der Kolk and J. Saporta, "The Biological Response to Psychic Trauma: Mechanisms and Treatment of Intruism and Numbing," *Anxiety Research (UK)* 4 (1991): 199–212.

11. Burrhus F. Skinner, *About Behaviorism* (New York: Vintage Books, 1976), p. 144.

12. Viktor E. Frankl, *The Will to Meaning* (New York: New American Library, 1988), p. 131.

CHAPTER 11

1. Lynn Fossum, *Overcoming Anxiety: A Primer for Better Life Management* (Los Altos, Calif.: Crisp Publications, 1990), pp. 12–13.

2. Wayne Weiten, *Psychology: Themes and Variations,* 6th ed. (Belmont, Calif.: Wadsworth, 2004), p. 220.

3. R. Ader and N. Cohen, "Behavior and the Immune System," in W.D. Gentry, ed., *Handbook of Behavioral Medicine* (New York: Guilford, 1984), and R. Ader and N. Cohen, "Psychoneuroimmunology: Conditioning and Stress," *Annual Review of Psychology* 44 (1993): 53–58.

4. G. MacQueen, J. Marshall, M. Perdue, S. Siegel, and J. Bienenstock, "Pavlovian Conditioning of Rat Muscosal Mast Cells to Secrete Rat Mast Cell Protease II," *Science* 243 (1989): 83–86.

5. Francine Shapiro, *Eye Movement Desensitization and Reprocessing: Basic Principles, Protocols, and Procedures* (New York: Guilford Press, 1995), p. 363.

CHAPTER 12

1. Michael P. Nichols and Richard C. Schwartz, *Family Therapy: Concepts and Methods* (Boston: Allyn and Bacon, 1991), p. 33.

2. Ibid.

3. Bonnie Benard, *Fostering Resiliency in Kids: Protective Factors in the Family, School, and Community* (Portland, Oreg.: Western Center for Drug-Free Schools and Communities, 1991), pp. 1–28.

4. Erik Erickson, *Childhood and Society* (New York: Norton, 1963).

5. Robert C. Carson and James N. Butcher, *Abnormal Psychology and Modern Life* (New York: HarperCollins, 1996).

6. E. Mavis Hetherington and John Kelly, *For Better or for Worse: Divorce Reconsidered* (New York: Norton, 2002).

7. Elizabeth Marquardt, *Between Two Worlds: The Inner Lives of Children of Divorce* (New York: Crown Publishers, 2005), p. 187.

CHAPTER 13

1. Robert C. Carson and James N. Butcher, *Abnormal Psychology and Modern Life* (New York: HarperCollins, 1996).

2. Bonnie Benard, *Fostering Resiliency in Kids: Protective Factors in the Family, School, and Community* (Portland, Oreg.: Western Center for Drug-Free Schools and Communities, 1991), pp. 1–28.

3. Steven J. Wolin and Sybil Wolin, *The Resilient Self: How Survivors of Troubled Families Rise above Adversity* (New York: Villiard Books, 1993).

4. P. Wershba-Gershon, "Free Symbolic Play and Assessment of the Nature of Child Sexual Abuse," *Journal of Sexual Abuse* 5 (1994): 37–57.

INDEX

Poor self-image, 140–42
Positive change, 29, 41, 77, 137
Positive exchanges, 75
Power struggles, 2, 26, 29, 34, 63–64, 69,
    96, 136
Preconscious, 9
Premarital counseling, 110
Prenatal Care Hotline, 147
Problem child, 13
Problem solving, 3, 5, 11, 37, 41, 49, 49,
    56, 59, 65–66, 79, 80–81, 123, 129,
    136, 139, 143
Problem-solving skills, 129
Projection, 11, 37, 61, 100, 137
Protectiveness, 46
Prozac, 6
Psychodynamic therapy, 116
Psychological imprints, 1, 132
Psychological tensions, 37
Psychosocial stages, 16, 135
Psychosocial stages of
    development, 135
Psychosocial traits, 16
Psychotherapy, 10, 28, 100, 124,
    142
Punishment, 39
Pursuer, 15
Pursuer–distancer pattern, 15

Rationalization, 61, 99, 106–7, 137
Reaction formation, 10–11
Receiver, 81
Relational distance, 86–87
Relational patterns, 12
Relational problems, 91, 98, 119, 121,
    123, 125, 141
Relationship counseling, 138–39
Repressed feelings, 1–3, 19
Repressed feelings of abandonment, 3
Repressed rage, 12
Repressed sexual abuse, 60
Repression, 10
Resiliency model, 131, 140, 156
Responsibility, 12, 16, 29, 35, 41, 46,
    71, 76, 94, 97, 118, 142

Rituals, 37, 40–41, 47–48
Road maps, 40

Sabotage, 2, 4, 6, 10, 12, 14, 16, 18,
    20, 24, 26, 28, 30, 34, 36, 38, 40, 42,
    44, 46, 48, 50, 54, 56, 58, 60, 62, 64,
    66, 68, 70–72, 74, 76, 78, 80, 82, 86,
    88–90, 92, 94, 96, 98, 100, 104, 106,
    108, 110, 112, 114, 116, 118, 120,
    122, 124, 126, 128, 130, 132, 136,
    138, 140, 142, 144, 146
Scapegoat, 13, 25, 108, 118
Scapegoating, 13
Schnarch, David, 92
Scripts, 31
Self-defeating cycle, 4, 11, 18
Self-differentiation, 23, 26, 28
Self-disclosure, 45, 85, 92, 137
Self-hypnosis, 124
Self-identity, 133
Self-validating intimacy, 92
Sensitive child, 25, 37
Setting limits, 2, 39
Sexual acting-out, 106, 111, 114
Sexual addiction, 2, 106, 109, 110,
    114–15
Sexual agreements, 85, 97, 101, 137
Sexual boundaries, 89, 93, 97
Sexual exclusivity, 85
Sexual secret, 89, 90–91, 93, 96
Shame, 17, 20, 54, 93, 98–99, 107–9,
    114–17, 123
Shanley, John, 85
Sherman, Robert, 75
Silence and secrecy, 90
Single-parent families, 35, 37
Skinner, B. F., 114
Social interaction, 16, 56, 130
Speaker-listener technique, 69, 70
Spring, Janis Abrahms, 86
Stuart, Richard, 77

Three person system, 27
Transactional patterns, 16, 19, 36, 38
Traumatic experience, 10, 125

ABOUT THE AUTHOR
AND CONTRIBUTORS

WILLIAM J. MATTA is a licensed marriage and family therapist and psychotherapist who has been in private practice for over a decade. Dr. Matta has also been an adjunct professor in psychology for over 20 years. In addition to working in a consulting capacity in many school systems, he is a forerunner for the advocacy of School Based Collaboration with Families Programs, which emphasizes the importance of involving the family in the counseling process to help find solutions to children's problems. Dr. Matta has served on the New Jersey State Board of Marriage and Family Therapists. He is on the list of "America's Best Therapists" as surveyed by *Psychology Today Magazine*'s 2004 handbook of therapists. He is a certified hypnotist and has conducted many hypnotherapy seminars sponsored by hospitals, colleges, businesses, and schools. He has also been a professional guest on a number of TV and radio shows, where he has discussed such topics as improving marital and family relations and the power of the unconscious mind. He has been married for 32 years, has two children, and resides in Medford, New Jersey.

TAMI L. GROVATT-DAWKINS is a licensed professional counselor with 18 years of experience in the psychotherapeutic treatment of children, parents, and families. She has maintained 10 years of clinical out-patient practice with children and adolescents, and additionally serves as the CEO and clinical director of Project HEAL, Inc., providing specialized environmental counseling and summer programming opportunities for children. She has presented her research findings on the effectiveness of animal-assisted therapy in the treatment of childhood depression at the American Psychological Association and the Devereux Foundation. Her clinical research, presentation, and publication interests include: applied resiliency models, developmental attachment disorder, childhood grief, traumatic stress, and ecopsychology.

DANIEL HOFFMAN retired at the rank of captain from the Camden City, New Jersey Police Department. During his 25-year career in urban law enforcement, he saw firsthand the effects of addictions and family dysfunction on people from all walks of life. After retiring from the police department, he continued his education and graduated from Rutgers University with a master's degree in social work (MSW). He is a licensed clinical social worker and has private counseling practices in New Jersey and Florida. He has worked with many individuals and families who have suffered the effects of family dysfunction and addiction. He also provides training and consultation services to a variety of public and private organizations.

EDWARD IGLE is a licensed marriage and family therapist and a clinical social worker. He is a trainer on the faculty of the Philadelphia Child and Family Therapy Training Center at Friends Hospital in Philadelphia. He is a clinical member of the American Association for Marriage and Family Therapists and has been accepted as an AAMFT-approved supervisor. He is currently serving his second term as president of AAMFT-NJ's Southern Chapter. The former clinical director of Catholic Charities' Counseling Program for the Diocese of Camden, New Jersey, he now has a private practice in southern New Jersey. He has been involved in marriage and family therapy, as well as therapist training and supervision for over 30 years. He has also written numerous relationship articles that have been published in various newspapers.

YALE HISTORICAL PUBLICATIONS

JOANNA WALEY-COHEN

Exile in
Mid-Qing China

BANISHMENT TO XINJIANG,
1758–1820

YALE UNIVERSITY PRESS / NEW HAVEN & LONDON

Published under the direction
of the Department of History of Yale University
with assistance from the income of the
Frederick John Kingsbury Memorial Fund

Designed by Jill Breitbarth
Set in Sabon type by
Asco Trade Typesetting Limited, Hong Kong
Printed in the United States of America by
Vail-Ballou Press, Binghamton, New York.

Library of Congress Cataloging-in-Publication Data
Waley-Cohen, Joanna.
    Exile in Mid-Qing China : banishment to Xinjiang, 1758–1820 /
Joanna Waley-Cohen.
        p.   cm.—(Yale historical publications)
    Includes bibliographical references (p.
    Includes index.
    ISBN 0-300-04827-0
    1. Sinkiang Uighur Autonomous Region (China)—Exiles.
    2. Penal colonies—China—Sinkiang Uighur Autonomous Region—
History. I. Title. II. Series.
    DS793.S62W22   1991
    951.6—dc20   90-13005
                                                                  CIP

The paper in this book meets the guidelines for permanence and
durability of the Committee on Production Guidelines for Book
Longevity of the Council on Library Resources.

1   3   5   7   9   10   8   6   4   2

Many of the Xinjiang exiles of the late eighteenth and early nineteenth centuries were banished for their opposition to official corruption and to the Qing's repressive political authority. Others were condemned for their heterodox religious beliefs. In part, such corruption and repression led to the overthrow of the dynasty in 1911.

In June 1989, the Chinese authorities brutally suppressed peaceful demonstrations that had called for an end to bureaucratic corruption and for a minimal degree of political freedom. This book is dedicated to the courageous victims of the Tiananmen massacre and its repressive aftermath, and to all those condemned for their devotion to the new Chinese heterodoxy: democracy.

"You, cousin Herford, upon pain of life,
   Till twice five summers have enrich'd our fields,
   Shall not regreet our fair dominions
   But tread the stranger paths of banishment."

William Shakespeare, *Richard II*, I, 3

Contents

vii

Illustrations

Acknowledgments

This book, which is based on my doctoral dissertation, would never have been begun without Jonathan Spence's encouragement. I have been extraordinarily fortunate in having him as my teacher and guide throughout the project. His generous attention, astute insights, and unflagging support have been abundantly available to me over a long period of time. After I left Yale, he continued to respond to requests for advice out of a conviction that "graduate students are a life sentence." My debt to him is immeasurable.

Many others have given unsparingly of their time. Yü Ying-shih, a vital source of enlightenment and inspiration while at Yale, continued to offer advice and direction even after his departure for Princeton. Beatrice S. Bartlett offered guidance on a wide variety of matters, including in particular the intricacies of archival research. Others at Yale who have been encouraging and helpful include John E. Boswell, David B. Davis, and Hans H. Frankel.

I am most grateful to Parker Po-fei Huang, whose enthusiasm and expertise helped steer me through the law and into the more human aspects of exile, and to Monica Yu, whose patience and inexhaustible energy convinced me that understanding always comes by the fifth or sixth reading, and who helped me grasp the key to some of the most obscure passages.

Although my initiation into Chinese studies came long ago, I remain indebted to my teachers at Cambridge, in particular Denis Twitchett and

Michael Loewe, for stimulating my original interest in China and for enabling me to explore its history in greater depth.

I wish to acknowledge gratefully the hospitality and assistance given me in Taibei by Chang Pide, Zhuang Jifa, Feng Mingzhu, Wang Jinghong, and the staff of the National Palace Museum Library, and by Chang Wejen and his staff at Academia Sinica. In Beijing, Wei Qingyuan and Ju Deyuan were always ready to point my way through the maze of archival documents, and Liu Zhongying and the staff at the First Historical Archives were friendly and helpful. At Yale University, Anthony Marr and Hideo Kaneko of the East Asian Collection have provided continual and much appreciated assistance for many years. June Lawrence of the Madison, Connecticut, branch library of the Genealogical Library of the Church of Jesus Christ of Latter-Day Saints went to much trouble on my behalf.

Much of the research on which the book is based was facilitated by a grant from the American Council of Learned Societies, with practical assistance in Beijing supplied by the Committee on Scholarly Communications with the People's Republic of China. My final dissertation year was supported by a fellowship from the Mrs. Giles Whiting Foundation. A Columbia University postdoctoral fellowship in the Society of Fellows in the Humanities allowed me time to revise the manuscript.

Many others know how enormously they have helped me by offering advice, encouragement, and assistance over the years: among them are Charles Grench and his colleagues at Yale University Press, Chen Joshui, Iona Crook, Pamela Kyle Crossley, Drew Dillon, Ainslie Embree, Richard Kuhns, James Lee, Liu Yuan, Brian McKnight, Susan Naquin, Loretta Nassar, Jonathan Ocko, Lucia Pierce, William Rowe, and Robin Yates. Richard Morgan drew the maps. My son, Kit, has taught me, more effectively than anyone else could have done, the value of self-discipline. Last, but very far from least, I would like to thank my husband, Brad Gallant, for his unfailing tolerance, support, and assistance.

Archival Sources

The vast majority of the archival materials on which this study is based were gathered in Taibei and Beijing. The majority of documents consulted in Taibei are located at the National Palace Museum. I have cited the collection of secret palace memorials (*Gongzhong Dang*) as follows: collection name, abbreviation of reign-title, catalogue number in the museum archive, Chinese date—for example, *GZD* QL 40625, 47/1/18. Many of these documents from the Qianlong period have now been published under the title *Gongzhong Dang Qianlongchao Zouzhe*; however, those consulted in Taibei are cited in this study as *Gongzhong Dang*. The same method of citation is used for documents in the Palace Museum's collection of Grand Council memorial copies known as *Junji Dang*.

Portions of the Imperial Edicts Records Books (*Shangyu Dang*) are available in both Taibei and Beijing; the pagination sometimes varies, so the location in which this archive was consulted is indicated by the initial T or B. The *Shangyu Dang* exists in two forms: the *fangben*, emanating from the Grand Council, and the *changben*, emanating from the Grand Secretariat. All references are to the *fangben* unless otherwise indicated. Citation of documents in the *Shangyu Dang* is as follows: collection name, location initial, date (with reign-title abbreviation), page number—for example, *SYD* (B) QL 56/8/8, 73. A similar method of citation is used for two further collections consulted at the National Palace Museum: the Archive of Suppression and Arrest (*Jiaobu Dang*) and the Archive of Court Letters (*Jixin Dang*), although documents in the court letter collection are unpaginated.

Two other archival collections were consulted at the National Palace Museum, Taibei. *Huangchao Xingfa Zhi* (Annals of the Penal Law of Our August Dynasty) is cited as follows: collection name, fascicle number, date of entry. For example, *Huangchao Xingfa Zhi* 13, QL 44/3. Citations to documents in the biographic packets (*zhuanbao*) of the Archives of the National History Office (*Guoshi Guan Dang*) provide the name of the subject of the biography and the date of the document.

The Archives of the Three Judicial Offices, *Sanfasi*, are located at the Institute of History and Philology, Academia Sinica, Nangang, Taiwan. Citation of these documents is as follows: collection name, catalogue number in the Institute archive known as *Qingdai Fazhi Dang'an*, date— for example, *Sanfasi* Archives no. 1422, QL 49/10/26.

In Beijing, three main collections were consulted. The method of citation of the *Shangyu Dang* is explained above. The palace memorials known in Taibei as the *Gongzhong Dang* are known in Beijing as *Zhupi Zouzhe* (Palace Memorials with Vermilion Endorsement). In the First Historical Archives, this collection is divided into main categories, such as law, and into subcategories, such as exile. Documents in each category are catalogued more or less chronologically in packets covering a given period of time, although documents in a single packet are not necessarily stored in chronological order. Citation of documents in this collection is as follows: collection name, date, category, subcategory, packet (*bao*), memorialist—for example, *ZPZZ* QL 35/1/4, (law—laws, packet for QL 35–37), memorial of Bayanbi.

In Beijing the Routine Memorials of the Board of Punishments (*Xingke Tiben*) are catalogued chronologically and by category; all documents from this collection used in this study were classified at the archives in the banishment category. Citation of the *Xingke Tiben* is as follows: collection name, data, packet number, memorialist—for example, *XKTB* packet 334, QL 28/3/9, memorial of Shuhede.

The autumn assizes (*Qiushen*) category of the Routine Memorials of the Board of Punishments was unavailable for consultation when I was in Beijing because it was being microfilmed for the Genealogical Library of the Church of Jesus Christ of Latter-Day Saints. I later consulted it at a branch of this library. This collection is cited as follows: collection name, genealogical library collection and microfilm roll number, document number, date, and memorialist—for example, *XKTB Qiushen*, Chin 002A 1474290, 19, QL 22/9/19, memorial of Aibida.

Abbreviations

CHC	*The Cambridge History of China*
CSWT	*Ch'ing-Shih Wen-T'i*
DLCY	Xue Yunsheng, *Duli Cunyi*
ECCP	A. Hummel, ed., *Eminent Chinese of the Ch'ing Period*
GZD	*Gongzhong Dang*
GZDQLCZZ	*Gongzhong Dang Qianlongchao Zouzhe*
HDSL	*Qinding Daqing Huidian Shili*
HJAS	*Harvard Journal of Asiatic Studies*
JAS	*Journal of Asian Studies*
JFJL	*Qinding Pingding Jiaofei Jilüe*
JJD	*Junji Dang*
JQ	Jiaqing
LIC	*Late Imperial China*
QCWXTK	*Qingchao Wenxian Tongkao*
QCXWXTK	*Qingchao Xu Wenxian Tongkao*
QL	Qianlong
QSL	*Daqing Lichao Shilu*
SYD	*Shangyu Dang*
SZJL	*Sanzhou Jilüe*
XAHL	*Xing'an Huilan*
XJTLSL	Wu Yixian, *Xinjiang Tiaoli Shuolüe*
XKTB	*Xingke Tiben*
XKTB Qiushen	*Xingke Qiushen Tiben*
ZPZZ	*Zhupi Zouzhe*

Exile in Mid-Qing China

Chapter One

Introduction

In 1759 the Qianlong Emperor brought to a successful conclusion the northwestern campaigns initiated by his illustrious grandfather, the Kangxi Emperor. As a result, the Qing dynasty (1644–1911) annexed vast territories on China's Central Asian frontier and enormously enlarged the empire, dispelling forever the threat of nomadic invasion that had haunted its predecessors for more than fifteen hundred years. Even before the region had been completely pacified, the Qing began to explore the possibility of despatching political and criminal exiles to Xinjiang, the "new territories." Over the next decades, tens of thousands of people were exiled to this distant frontier. The Qing designed a careful system of banishment intended to combine severe punishment with both the colonization of the frontier and the rehabilitation of offenders. By combining these objectives with the removal of disruptive elements from China proper, the policy embodied the cherished principle of achieving multiple ends by a single means (*yi ju liang de*).[1]

Xinjiang lies more than three thousand miles northwest of Beijing on the old Silk Road that connected China to Western Asia and Europe (see Maps 1 and 2). Separated from China proper by the Gobi desert, it has been subject to degrees of Chinese political control at intervals for two millennia, but its heterogeneous and largely Muslim population has re-

---

1. See, e.g., *QSL* QL 599, 17b–18a, 24/10/21; *HDSL* (1899) 721, 16a–b (QL 26); *QSL* QL 716, 16a, 29/8/2.

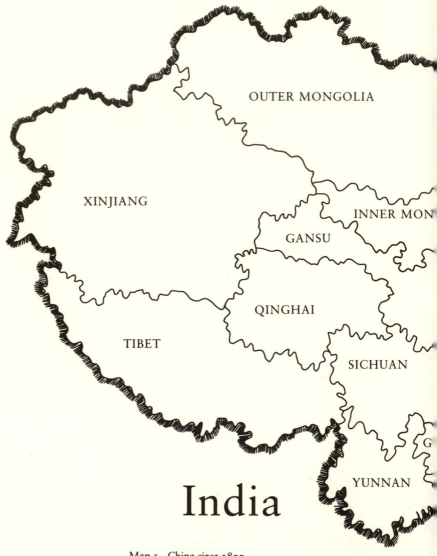

Russian Empire

OUTER MONGOLIA

XINJIANG

INNER MON

GANSU

QINGHAI

TIBET

SICHUAN

G

YUNNAN

India

Map 1. China circa 1800

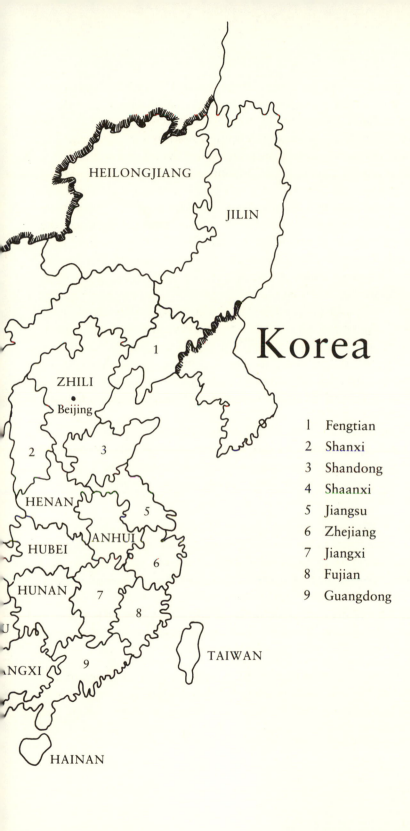

Korea

1 Fengtian
2 Shanxi
3 Shandong
4 Shaanxi
5 Jiangsu
6 Zhejiang
7 Jiangxi
8 Fujian
9 Guangdong

sisted assimilation into the Chinese cultural world. Initially governed as a military protectorate, Xinjiang was, for eighteenth-century Chinese, a largely alien land, known mainly to scholars through accounts of the "Western Regions" (*Xiyu*) found in centuries-old dynastic histories and through the occasional reports of travelers, merchants, and soldiers.

Shortly after the conquest of Xinjiang, the Qing began employing banished government officials for little or no remuneration in the lower echelons of the frontier administration. The effects of this policy were far-reaching. By exploiting these exiles' administrative experience, the Qing avoided having to match the dramatic territorial expansion of the empire with a corresponding increase in personnel expenditures. At the same time, for many exiles, including the influential geographer, poet, and population theorist Hong Liangji (1746–1809) and the well-known historians Qi Yunshi (1751–1815) and Xu Song (1781–1848), first-hand knowledge of the region brought a fascination that found expression in their scholarly work, which had a wide circulation. After their return, they fuelled a growing interest in frontier studies that laid the intellectual groundwork for granting Xinjiang provincial status in 1884, a move that confirmed the region's ultimate political integration into the Chinese state.

The personal impact of a sentence of banishment was profound. This is clear from a description written by the eminent scholar and future government minister Ji Yun (1724–1805), banished in 1768 following a serious breach of confidentiality. Shortly before his departure from Beijing, Ji wrote to his uncle:

> I have not written to my wife because I am afraid that she would come to the capital to see me off. Women are tearful, and when she saw me under restraint like a colt in harness she would not be able to help weeping and tugging at my clothes, and then she would insist on going with me to the west. If I rejected her she would not obey, and if I allowed her to go with me my children would be abandoned at home. [If she came] it would break my heart. I hope that after my departure you will explain why I did not tell her.[2]

Ji was fortunate in being recalled from Xinjiang after an exceptionally brief term of one year. His experience led him to compile a collection of notes, correspondence, and belles lettres that constitutes one of the

2. Ji, *Ji Xiaolan Jiashu*, 20.

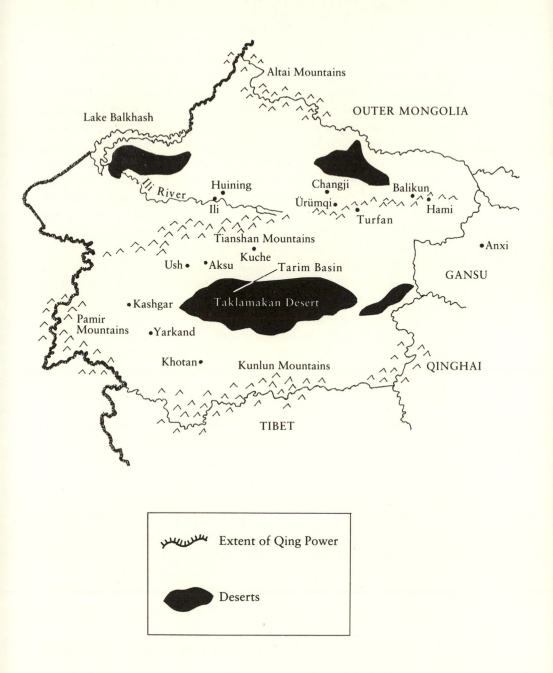

Map 2. Xinjiang circa 1800

richest known sources of information on Xinjiang exile—aside from government records that, inevitably, tend to disparage offenders against the state.[3] Ji's writings capture the emotions and experiences of many of his fellow exiled scholars and officials and, at the same time, open a rare window on the more obscure world of the far more numerous ordinary convicts banished to Xinjiang after the mid-eighteenth century.

These ordinary convicts comprised two main groups, the first mainly robbers, thieves, bandits, and the like, and the second all those peripherally involved in both peaceful and insurgent activities that threatened the state, including religious sectarians. In the second category, those banished to Xinjiang were often sentenced by virtue of their collective responsibility as relatives of the principal offenders, who were executed.

Unlike the banishment of exiled scholars and officials, the banishment of these common convicts was generally permanent. Most could achieve rehabilitation through compulsory service on public projects in Xinjiang coupled with unimpeachable behavior, but even after emancipation they were not permitted to leave the area. A deliberate practical consequence of the policy of exiling such convicts to Xinjiang was thus the provision of cheap labor and the more rapid introduction of a Han Chinese presence into the new frontier than could have been achieved with voluntary settlers alone.

For these ordinary offenders the practical effects of banishment to Xinjiang were devastating. They were most unlikely ever to see their homes again. Although a few less serious offenders took their wives and children with them into exile at government expense as the result of the colonization policy, the vast majority were never reunited with their families.[4] The exceptionally strong attachment to native place generated by the central significance of the family in Chinese culture made this hardship particularly difficult to tolerate. Traditional beliefs, moreover, included the sacred duty to worship ancestors at locally maintained altars, yet for an exile this was impossible. The system of banishment thus gave rise to a peculiar irony. State-supported Confucian beliefs promoted the idea of the family as a pivotal social force, yet the punishment of exile often

3. This consideration was also noted by the author of a recent study of exile in mediaeval and Renaissance Italy. See Starn, *Contrary Commonwealth*, xvi.

4. These women and children who accompanied their exiled husbands and fathers into exile were not themselves regarded as criminals and were treated quite differently from those banished by virtue of collective responsibility, who were regarded as serious criminals in their own right.

resulted in the permanent dispersal of families, thus subverting the very system of values it purported to protect.

In Qing law the most severe variant of the punishment of exile was banishment to Xinjiang, which involved acute uncertainty. Second only to execution, this indefinite sentence was often imposed conditionally following the commutation of a death sentence. Eligibility for emancipation or return theoretically arose after a specified term of years, but imperial approval was always required. Such approval was never automatic and depended in part on official estimation of the exile's moral regeneration, an analysis that was highly susceptible to abuse. In any event, this practice suffused the punishment of exile with a strong probationary element. For the once prominent, there was the additional fear that political enemies would permanently obstruct their return or even arrange their assassination in distant parts, although there is no hard evidence to suggest that any exile in fact died in such circumstances.

The very real dread that one might perish thousands of miles from home prompted many ordinary convicts to attempt escape. Although they risked certain execution in the event of recapture, many preferred the fragility of an outlaw's existence near home to the prospect of a permanent and distant exile. Li Erman, a convicted robber banished in 1763 from a village near Beijing, was one such escapee. He managed to give his guards the slip at the northwestern border of China proper on his way into exile in Xinjiang. One of Li's official escorts recounted the circumstances of this bid for freedom:

> At Wang Hei'er River [in Gansu, the province adjacent to Xinjiang], Li Erman said he had a bad stomach and had to empty his bowels. [The two soldiers escorting him] guarded the road in both directions; escort Xie Huan held on to the chain [around Li's neck] and escort Li Xuancai took [the convict's] trousers down. Convict Li seized the chance to roll down the cliff. Xie slipped and let go of the chain; Li wrenched off his manacles, jumped out of his red [prisoner's] garb and escaped.[5]

Li Erman was recaptured six months later and put to death in accordance with the law.

Even for those who succeeded in eluding the authorities, the extremely inhospitable Xinjiang landscape combined with the frontier's remoteness

5. *XKTB* QL 28/12/11, memorial of Changjun.

to create a formidable natural barrier that many failed to surmount. Ji Yun indirectly encountered one such fugitive:

> In the spring of 1771 on my way back from Ürümqi, my servant Xianning fell asleep in the saddle and in the thick fog became separated from the rest of the party. He mistakenly followed the tracks of a wild horse and entered a mountainous area from which he could not, in his confusion, find the way out. He thought he was sure to die when suddenly he saw a corpse lying under a cliff. It was an exile who had escaped and frozen to death while hiding. On his back he had a cotton sack with food for his journey, so Ning availed himself of it to satisfy his hunger.[6]

This book describes how the Qing developed a system of banishment to Xinjiang that exemplified both their skill in meeting new challenges and their fidelity to precedents that reached back into antiquity. It is the first book-length work on the subject of banishment to Xinjiang. Kawakubo Teirō's two articles on Qing exile and frontier policy provide a useful introduction but draw on only a limited selection of published source materials.[7] Xie Guozhen's monograph on exile to the northeast in the early Qing deals mainly with the exile of scholars and officials and does not extend beyond 1735; hence it covers both a different period and geographical area and is not concerned with the exile of common criminals.[8] Nailene Chou's chapter on the Xinjiang exile system in her unpublished work on nineteenth-century frontier studies relies mainly on laws that do not necessarily describe actual practice.[9] Zhao Tiegang's recent article on the Qing exile system is intended only as a preliminary survey.[10] Finally, Qi Qingshun's two recent articles on the Xinjiang exiles are more concerned with the exiles' impact on Xinjiang than with the exile system as such.[11]

Recent studies of the social, political, economic, and intellectual his-

---

6. Ji, *Yuewei Caotang Biji*, 6, 22b.
7. Kawakubo, "Shindai ni okeru henkyō e no zaito hairyū ni tsuite: Shinchō no ryūkei seisaku to henkyō, sono ichi"; Kawakubo, "Shindai Manshū no henkyō shakai: Shinchō no ryūkei seisaku to henkyō, sono ni."
8. Xie, *Qingchu Liuren Kaifa Dongbei Shi.*
9. Chou, "Frontier Studies and Changing Frontier Administration in Late Ch'ing China: The Case of Sinkiang 1759–1911."
10. Zhao, "Qingdai Liufang Zhidu Chutan."
11. Qi, "Qingdai Xinjiang Qianyuan Yanjiu"; Qi, "Qingdai Xinjiang Qianfan Yanjiu." Apparently neither Qi nor Zhao had access to Chinese archival sources.

tory of eighteenth-century China have replaced the old images of a stag-
nant autocracy with those of a mobile and vital society presided over by
an imperial state whose authoritarian premises were at times subtly tempered by pragmatism.[12] Likewise, the study of eighteenth-century
Chinese legal history, still barely out of its infancy, has demonstrated that
Qing law was far from being the arbitrarily unjust and gratuitously brutal system condemned by early Western accounts.[13]

In the eighteenth century, when extraordinary demographic growth
produced unprecedented problems of overcrowding, intensifying competition for limited resources, and rising crime, Chinese law and the legal
system were forced to adapt to changing social realities.[14] Qing policymakers recognized the critical need to find additional arable land, for by
midcentury acreage in outlying areas was becoming saturated with migrants who had moved from the densely occupied inner provinces in
search of a livelihood. Close government regulation was of crucial importance to maximize the benefit to the state of this trend towards internal colonization. The policymakers also recognized, obliquely perhaps,
that desperation was the driving force behind at least some crimes. As
deteriorating social and economic conditions produced sometimes widespread outbreaks of unrest, a sufficiently severe alternative to the death

12. For a sampling of recent studies of China in the eighteenth century see Bartlett,
Monarchs and Ministers; Crossley, *Orphan Warriors*; Elman, *From Philosophy to Philolo-
gy*; Guy, *The Emperor's Four Treasuries*; Huang, *The Peasant Economy and Social Change
in North China*; Lee, "State and Economy in Southwest China, 1400–1800"; Mann, *Local
Merchants and the Chinese Bureaucracy, 1750–1950*; Murray, *Pirates of the South China
Coast 1790–1810*; Naquin, *Shantung Rebellion*; Naquin and Rawski, *Chinese Society in
the Eighteenth Century*; Perdue, *Exhausting the Earth*; Rowe, *Hankow: Commerce and
Society in a Chinese City, 1796–1889*; Rowe, *Conflict and Community in a Chinese City,
1796–1885*; Will, *Bureaucratie et famine en Chine au dix-huitième siècle*; Zelin, *The
Magistrate's Tael*. This list is not intended to be exhaustive and makes no attempt to include
the many recent journal articles of relevance.

13. For a selection of recent studies of eighteenth-century legal history, see Chen, "The
Influence of Shen Chih-ch'i's *Chi-chu* Commentary upon Ch'ing Judicial Decisions"; Chen,
"Local Control of Convicted Thieves in Eighteenth-Century China"; Edwards, "Ch'ing
Legal Jurisdiction over Foreigners"; Meijer, "Homosexual Offences in Ch'ing Law"; Ng,
"Ch'ing Laws concerning the Insane"; Ng, "Ideology and Sexuality"; Ng, "Insanity and the
Law in Ch'ing China"; Ocko, "I'll Take It All the Way to Beijing". These works all build on
the pathbreaking study by Bodde and Morris, *Law in Imperial China*. Other scholars have
used legal documents to study political and economic history: see e.g., Huang, *The Peasant
Economy and Social Change in North China*; Kuhn, "Political Crime and Bureaucratic
Monarchy"; Zelin, "The Rights of Tenants in Mid-Qing Sichuan."

14. For a description of how laws changed to reflect new realities in landholding and
agriculture, see Huang, *The Peasant Economy and Social Change in North China*, 97–99.

penalty had to be invoked to avoid carrying out executions on a large scale, for a perceived absence of benevolence might raise questions of dynastic legitimacy. The development and operation of the system of banishment to Xinjiang provide one important example of the Qing adaptation of a traditional institution—punishment by exile—in response to the changing world of late eighteenth-century China.

Thus this book confirms the broad patterns of flexibility and innovative energy described by other scholars. It also explores a broad cross-section of Qing society—scholars, government officials, and ordinary people banished for widely differing reasons—by focusing on three main themes: the actual operation of Qing laws concerning the system of banishment to Xinjiang, the practical impact of Qing emphasis on the rehabilitative potential inherent in a sentence of exile, and the relationship between banishment and the project of colonizing Xinjiang. By treating the law and the functioning of the legal system both as objects of study per se and as a means of illuminating aspects of social, political, and economic life in Qing China at the time when the dynasty was unwittingly passing its zenith, it offers a fresh perspective on eighteenth-century China.

This work traces the system of banishment from its origins in 1758, the year following northern Xinjiang's fall to the Qing, until 1820. There are three reasons for choosing this period. Xinjiang became the most important exile destination for Chinese criminals almost immediately after the conquest. At the same time, banishment became a small but significant part of the new colonization policy. From the annexation of Xinjiang until the 1820s, the Qing were able to pursue their policies in the region largely free from extraneous considerations as a result of the peace that prevailed there.[15] In that decade, however, the Muslim insurgency that punctuated much of the nineteenth century in Xinjiang began with the uprising of Jahangir, a descendant of the rulers driven out by the Qing more than sixty years earlier. As a result, the then well-established system of banishment to Xinjiang gradually ceased to be the subject of continual experimentation and innovation that it had been in the early years of its existence. By the early nineteenth century, too, colonization inevitably began to take second place to growing domestic problems within China proper and to European incursions on the southeast coast. Nevertheless, exiles continued to be sent to Xinjiang until the fall of the dynasty in

15. See Fletcher, "China and Central Asia, 1368–1884," 221.

1911, with the exception of a few interruptions during the massive Muslim rebellions that engulfed the whole northwestern portion of the empire in the 1870s.

Although it would be possible to extend this study to the end of the dynasty, such an undertaking would transform it into a chronicle of the entire Xinjiang exile system. Instead, the goal of this work is to use the early years of the system of banishment to Xinjiang as a window through which to explore the organizational ability, social and political life, and economic and legal development of the Qing during this critical period of the dynasty's transition from ascendancy to decline.

Exile is an experience by no means limited to China; on the contrary, it has been and continues to be a widespread form of punishment. In the past, other states often used exile in conjunction with the establishment of colonies as the Chinese did in Xinjiang. Historians of exile will recognize similarities between the Chinese system and those of other countries, such as the well-known transportation of convicts to the American and Australian colonies of the British empire and the imperial Russian system of exile to Siberia, but they will also identify a number of differences. These differences include such significant issues as the attitude towards families, the employment of former government officials in exile, and the importance assigned to rehabilitating offenders. Although this study limits its focus to the establishment and early decades of a system of banishment on the northwestern frontier of China, it is hoped that it will contribute to an understanding of exile as an institution that remains of singular relevance in the contemporary world.

Chapter Two

Xinjiang and the Expansion of the Empire in the Eighteenth Century

By the second half of the eighteenth century, the Qing dynasty was in transition from its early greatness to the decline accentuated by the Opium War disaster of 1842. With the consolidation of Manchu control over the empire following the suppression of the Rebellion of the Three Feudatories in 1681 and the incorporation of Taiwan in 1683, the long reigns of the emperors Kangxi (1662–1722), Yongzheng (1723–1735), and Qianlong (1736–1796) provided an era of continuity and stability. The population recovered from the devastation wrought by the civil wars, natural disasters, and epidemics of the seventeenth century to surpass three hundred million by 1800. The annexation of Xinjiang in 1759 extended the empire deep into Central Asia and marked the apogee of Qing power. Yet the Qing sun was already beginning to set. Under the Qianlong Emperor, a series of cripplingly expensive border campaigns (including those in Xinjiang) and domestic rebellions undermined the fiscal stability achieved by his predecessor's economic reforms. The population explosion brought in its wake a vastly increased demand for resources, the availability of which did not expand proportionately. This led to a high rate of internal migration and to an increase in the incidence of criminal activity. By the end of the eighteenth century, a general malaise was taking hold of Chinese society.[1]

In the upper echelons of society, the traditional routes to power were

1. For a recent overview of this period, see Spence, *The Search for Modern China*, 90–116.

narrowing. Neither the quotas for the academic degrees that led to official appointment nor the size of the imperial bureaucracy expanded to take account of demographic growth, in part because it seemed impossible to raise sufficient extra revenue to pay for more government employees. Thus the relative potential for upward social mobility diminished just as competition for official position intensified. Many degree-holders spent years awaiting a government appointment.

The difficulty of obtaining an official position by legitimate means fostered a system of patronage that, in turn, led to a growth in factionalism. The effects of this development were to render a successful public life increasingly elusive, as the various power groups vied for dominance, and to create an atmosphere of continual tension in Qing political life. Another result, which was related to a commercializing trend in society at large, was the new importance of gift giving among officials and bureaucratic aspirants.[2]

The most notorious—and most successful—exponent of the new political way of life was the former imperial bodyguard Heshen (1750–1799), for more than twenty years the favorite of the Qianlong Emperor. Heshen became the emperor's most trusted adviser and took gross advantage of his position to enrich himself and his associates. Heshen's supporters were dispersed throughout officialdom both in the capital and in the provinces, and during his lifetime effectively resisted all attempts to expose or reform their practices. The origins of the decline of the Qing state are often traced to the endemic corruption that took hold during the Heshen period (1775–1799), although it may be more accurate to say that the Heshen clique elaborated an existing trend rather than initiating a new direction.

Many dark rumors circulated concerning the reason for Qianlong's apparent willingness to tolerate Heshen's activities. Yet it seems probable that the emperor hoped to bolster his own authority by keeping his bureaucracy split into highly antagonistic factions, despite the fact that it was official policy to oppose any resurgence of the factionalism generally blamed for the demise of the Ming.

Heshen's opponents, a group committed to radical revitalization of the government, enjoyed the support of such key figures as the senior Grand Councillor Agui (1717–1797) and the fraternal scholars Zhu Gui (1731–1807) and Zhu Yun (1729–1781), but they proved unable to dis-

---

2. See Mann Jones and Kuhn, "Dynastic Decline and the Roots of Rebellion," 113–116.

lodge the favorite as long as the Qianlong Emperor lived. Yet following his death in 1799, Heshen's removal from power was one of the first independent acts of Qianlong's successor, the Jiaqing Emperor (1796–1820). The new emperor introduced measures to curb corruption and reform the bureaucracy but chose to avoid the massive disruption to the mechanism of government that a wholesale purge of Heshen's supporters would have caused. This policy also denied Heshen's opposition the moral triumph and vindication that such a purge would have brought. Instead, the court's restrained actions were intended to encourage the Heshen clique to reform themselves after their leader had fallen. Yet in part as a result of this decision, the wavering of bureaucratic integrity, sensed by many contemporaries as auguring a general dynastic decline, was merely checked rather than halted as the nineteenth century began.[3]

One result of the volatility of late eighteenth-century public life was a change in the causes underlying political success or failure. Scholars and officials were now more likely to lose favor as the result of power struggles at court than as the result of opposition to the dynasty itself. In the seventeenth and early eighteenth centuries, Manchu consciousness of the tenuous nature of the Qing dynasty's claim to legitimacy had meant that sedition and armed resistance were among the most serious crimes. Ringleaders of these movements were generally executed, and their families and cohorts exiled. But perceptions of political opposition had evolved since the early years of dynastic consolidation; the attitudes of both rulers and ruled had changed. The fierce attachment to native Ming rule and hostility to the Manchu invaders that had marked the earlier period had become muted and, at the same time, the ensuing long period of relative peace and stability had reduced Qing sensitivities concerning perceived slurs against the dynasty and its alien origins. In addition, by the end of the eighteenth century, the geographic and demographic expansion of the empire had diluted the imperial capacity for direct personal control of public affairs, and this in turn had tended to alter the notion of what constituted a political threat.

Yet at the lower levels of society, outbreaks of opposition to Qing authority continued through the eighteenth century and into the nineteenth. Across the empire Muslim minorities and indigenous folk Buddhist sects were stirring with dissatisfaction. Sometimes these groups were peaceful, albeit implicitly threatening to the Confucian-oriented

---

3. Mann Jones and Kuhn, "Dynastic Decline and the Roots of Rebellion," 108. See also Yao, "Jiu Wen Sui Bi," 2, 3a.

state orthodoxy, but on several occasions, beginning in the 1770s, their activities erupted into rebellions tinged with millenarian and antidynastic overtones. The resulting campaigns of suppression were sometimes so harsh that they provoked further resistance, creating unsettling cycles that produced considerable instability among the population at large. This state of affairs was exacerbated by the well-organized piracy that plagued inland rivers and coastal waters, disrupting law and order and interfering with the flow of state revenues from the rich southern provinces to the capital.

The unprecedented population growth that was in part responsible for these developments also gave rise to a more general restlessness in Chinese society. Geographic mobility increased sharply because of the acute pressure on the land. Impoverished segments of the rural population began to abandon their native villages in favor of the underpopulated territories on the imperial peripheries. Such movements were given impetus by the introduction of New World crops such as maize and sweet potatoes that could grow in marginal land. Other migrants found work in the cities, where the rapidly commercializing economy offered a broad range of new opportunities.

One result of land reclamation and urban construction was severe deforestation that led to a dire increase in the silting-up of rivers. This situation both obstructed important transportation networks and caused floods that often brought devastating famine in their wake, prompting many to flee their homes in search of food.

Frontier expansion during the eighteenth century resulted not only from spontaneous migration but also from the conscious efforts of the Qing government to encourage and in some cases to compel migration with a view to relieving the effects of demographic pressure in the heartland. From the government's point of view, the urgent practical necessity of increasing the food supply for the burgeoning population was enhanced by its particularly powerful need as an alien dynasty to win and keep popular support. Conspicuous concern for public welfare, manifested in part by territorial expansion, was also critical to the Qianlong Emperor's ambition to surpass the achievements of the most glorious rulers of Chinese history.[4]

4. On the conscious efforts of the Qianlong Emperor to emulate his Han and Tang predecessors, see Kahn, *Monarchy in the Emperor's Eyes*, esp. 127. On the connections between political legitimacy and economic expansion in classical Chinese thought, see chapter 3.

The steady settlement of the frontiers altered the empire in several ways. It both extended imperial control and, at the same time, created commercial and other unofficial networks that strengthened links between the interior and the periphery. An increasing number of ethnic minorities came under Qing sway, and the empire became truly heterogeneous in composition.[5]

In addition, under the Qing the demarcation of China proper (*neidi*), long an important aspect of Chinese self-definition, became extremely fluid.[6] The boundaries initially corresponded roughly to those of the eighteen provinces of the Chinese heartland, where settled agriculture was the norm. However, as demographic pressure forced the steady spread of this traditional form of livelihood in all directions, the old definitions began to lose their significance. To the north, the Great Wall represented at least an emotional boundary between China proper and the frontier zone, but it did not always run precisely along provincial boundaries. Gansu province, for example, extends well beyond the western extremity of the Wall at Jiayuguan. Certain regions located beyond the Great Wall, for example Liaodong in southern Manchuria, belonged to an intermediate zone between the heartland and the frontier. The sense of shifting boundaries undoubtedly resulted from the complex new dimensions that traditional notions of heartland and frontiers assumed under the alien Qing.[7]

The Qing followed ancient tradition in exiling offenders to various imperial frontiers. Thus no understanding of banishment under the Qing is possible without reference to some of the principal aspects of general Qing frontier policy in the eighteenth century.

SICHUAN

One of the best-known migrations of the early Qing is the movement into the once prosperous western province of Sichuan. When the Qing came to power, Sichuan's population had been greatly reduced, leaving substantial tracts of land available for resettlement. This attracted large-scale migration, encouraged by government offers of tax exemptions and

---

5. See Naquin and Rawski, *Chinese Society in the Eighteenth Century*, 130–133.
6. For a discussion of the traditional Chinese conception of the world, see chapter 3.
7. On the Great Wall as frontier, see, generally, Waldron, "The Great Wall Myth."

material aid, and from 1667 to 1707 more than 1.5 million people moved there, mainly from Hunan, Hubei, and Shaanxi provinces. The goal of colonization led the Qing to discourage single males from migrating to Sichuan.[8]

The province suffered from considerable unrest between unruly settlers and the native tribes on whose lands they began to encroach.[9] In addition, attempts to bring aboriginal territory in western Sichuan under central authority during the eighteenth century were met with open rebellion in 1742 and 1771. These uprisings were suppressed only with considerable difficulty. Following the second rebellion, aborigines who submitted to Qing authority were settled on military agricultural colonies (*tun*) both as a means of incorporating their territory into the regular administrative framework and in the hope of securing native loyalty.[10] A similar policy was applied to the Miao tribes in the central China province of Hunan following suppression of their uprising in the late eighteenth century.[11]

SOUTHWEST CHINA

The Rebellion of the Three Feudatories (1673–1681) in the southwestern provinces of Yunnan and Guizhou had generated profound imperial distrust of the entire region. In the early part of the dynasty, much of the southwest was inhabited by a complex mixture of largely self-governing ethnic minorities with hereditary chieftains over whom the central government did not exercise firm control. The Qing's general desire to consolidate imperial authority in the southwest was strengthened by the availability of land ripe both for cultivation and for the extraction of rich mineral deposits that offered a solution to the monetary crisis threatened by the sharp decline in Japanese copper exports after 1715.

The government's colonization policy in the southwest consisted of two interconnected strategies: the acculturation of the indigenous population and the promotion of intensive migration from the crowded Chinese heartland. Thus in the Yongzheng reign the government initiated

8. Entenmann, "Migration and Settlement in Sichuan," 122.

9. Ibid., 107, 122–124.

10. Shepherd, "Plains Aborigines and Chinese Settlers on the Taiwan Frontier in the Seventeenth and Eighteenth Centuries," 345.

11. See Mann Jones and Kuhn, "Dynastic Decline and the Roots of Rebellion," 133.

a policy of "returning the native tribes to regular administration" (*gaitu guiliu*) in addition to establishing schools for the tribespeople in the hope of inculcating Chinese language and values. The reallocation of extra troops to the most recalcitrant areas helped to reinforce the imposition of central government control. This policy, and the officials charged with its implementation, showed little concern for aboriginal land rights, and during the 1720s and 1730s resistance erupted into outright rebellion against the Qing government's attempt to undermine the tribal chiefs' hereditary power base.[12]

At the same time the government induced massive migration to the southwest by gilding the prospect of empty land with the offer of substantial cash incentives. By 1850 the balance between native population and immigrants in the southwest had shifted in favor of the immigrants, whose overwhelming presence helped to bring about the acculturation of the tribal peoples.[13]

TAIWAN

The island of Taiwan was another area of settlement during the eighteenth century. Throughout the early part of the dynasty, Taiwan's offshore location facilitated its use as a base for dynastic resistance by supporters of the deposed Ming, so that the Qing regarded it, like the southwest, as unreliable and volatile. After the resistance was crushed in 1683, the Qing governed Taiwan as a prefecture of Fujian province, under a civil administration backed by a strong military presence. The desire to prevent the island's continued use as a rebel base, combined with an awareness of its rich potential as a source of revenue, were the principal determinants of Qing policy towards Taiwan.

This policy differed from Qing attitudes towards the southwest in a number of ways. For much of the early and middle Qing, migration to Taiwan was nominally subject to severe restrictions that reflected the official view that partial isolation was the best means of preventing a resurgence of rebel activity on the island. Written permission was required for mainland residents to cross the Taiwan straits; wives and

---

12. Smith, "Ch'ing Policy and the Development of Southwest China," 274.
13. Lee, "State and Economy in Southwest China, 1400–1800," 63–73. See also, generally, Lombard-Salmon, *Un Exemple d'acculturation chinoise.*

families were generally allowed neither to accompany migrants nor to join them at a later date. These regulations were intended to discourage permanent settlement and to preserve order by fostering migrant dependence on the government, even though policy debates deplored the deliberate separation of families. In practice, however, it proved extremely difficult to limit the growth of the immigrant population, especially after the restrictive policy was temporarily relaxed in the Yongzheng and Qianlong periods. Moreover, the curious expectation that limiting migration to single males would encourage law-abiding behavior proved vain. In the absence of their families migrants tended to be more unruly.[14]

The policies of aboriginal assimilation adopted for the southwest were inappropriate to Taiwan, where much aboriginal territory was not farmed but reserved for deer hunting. Frequent disputes arose between aborigines and settlers wishing to convert these hunting grounds to agriculture. By the mid-eighteenth century, settlement was spreading and the supply of deer was dwindling; colonists from the mainland were allowed to occupy aboriginal lands but only as tenants of the native tribespeople.[15] Aboriginal revolts against government authority, although rare, were not unknown, but the main source of unrest on the island was strife among settlers from different communities on the mainland, notably Zhangzhou and Quanzhou, just inland from the Fujian coast. After detachments of native troops helped suppress the late-eighteenth-century immigrant-led rebellions, aboriginal military agricultural colonies were established on the model of those in Sichuan, with the distinction that in Taiwan the aborigines' military service had already proved their loyalty to the dynasty, unlike their counterparts whose allegiance the Qing sought to ensure.[16]

THE INNER ASIAN FRONTIER

Along China's northern borders lay vast areas in which the sparse population offered a striking contrast to the bursting heartland. Much of

14. Shepherd, "Plains Aborigines," 162–175.

15. Shepherd, "Plains Aborigines," 245–320 covers in detail the evolution of aboriginal land rights. On the early settlement of Taiwan by Chinese from the mainland, see also Meskill, *A Chinese Pioneer Family*, chapter 3.

16. Shepherd, "Plains Aborigines," 345.

the Inner Asian frontier was steppe traditionally used for pasturage, but the possibility existed of converting it to agricultural use. To adventurers prepared to risk flouting Qing economic laws and government monopolies, this area also offered the potent attraction of such valuable commodities as ginseng root, furs, and gold. Until foreign encroachment in the nineteenth century forced a belated change in policy, however, the Qing were reluctant to relax restrictions on Han Chinese immigration to their northern frontiers, preferring to keep separate from the rest of their empire Mongolia, Manchuria, and at least part of Xinjiang.[17] In Tibet, the fourth region of Qing China's Inner Asian territory, inaccessibility was a more effective exclusionary device than any laws could have been. However, in the late eighteenth century the Qing established a military protectorate there as a means of securing the imperial borders.[18]

MONGOLIA

In Mongolia the Manchus had established dominance by the end of the seventeenth century through a combination of military and diplomatic means. Their administration of Mongolia was overseen by a centrally appointed military governor (*jiangjun*) who, consistent with the Qing policy of closely restricting Han Chinese access to positions of power on any frontier, was either a Manchu or, occasionally, a Mongol; no Han Chinese were appointed to senior administrative positions in Mongolia. The Mongolian people were organized into banner units unique to Mongolia and distinct from the Manchu, Mongol, and Chinese-martial banners that formed part of the basic Qing military and administrative structure in the rest of the empire. These banner units were assigned to strictly defined areas of land, a move intended to "divide and rule" tribes that had traditionally roamed freely. The Mongolian banner units further combined to form leagues whose power was closely controlled; they were ruled by hereditary princes from whom the Qing extracted quasi-feudal personal oaths of loyalty in exchange for the land grants and the recognition of their position. To strengthen ties to the central government, the Qing primarily applied Chinese rather than Mongolian laws and prece-

17. Fletcher, "Ch'ing Inner Asia," 36.
18. For an account of Qing policy towards and government of Tibet, see Fletcher, "Ch'ing Inner Asia," 90–106.

dents and conferred Qing titles upon members of the Mongol nobility. A strong military presence served as a constant reminder of the Mongolian lack of autonomy.[19]

Qing policy was designed to keep the Mongols in thrall yet to maintain them as a potential source of military support. For most of the dynasty the first ambition was largely realized. To discourage the dilution of traditional Mongol martial values—already threatened by the attractions of monastic life within the ascendant lamaist Buddhist church—the government tried to limit Han Chinese immigration to specific agricultural colonies that supported Qing garrisons and the imperial postal system. Yet infiltration was unremitting, spearheaded by merchants who, despite government opposition, quickly made themselves indispensable purveyors of Chinese commodities in Mongolia. At the same time, a steady flow of settlers from north China gradually began to reclaim traditional pasturelands for settled agriculture. By the end of the eighteenth century, the extension into Mongolia of civil authority with responsibility for the immigrant population acknowledged the failure of immigration restrictions, and in 1860 the Qing bowed to reality and lifted the official ban on Han Chinese settlement in some parts of Mongolia.[20]

MANCHURIA

For cultural, strategic, and economic reasons, the Qing desire to exclude Han Chinese influence from Manchuria was at least as strong as it was in Mongolia; the wish to preserve traditional values in the face of the insidious effects of Chinese culture was all the more fervent in the ruling dynasty's own homeland.[21] This concern reflected both the wish to keep an unadulterated Manchu army at the ready in case of Chinese insurgency, and the hope of leaving available a place of retreat in the event that the Manchus might one day be driven out of China—although by the late eighteenth century these fears had receded substantially. Also contribut-

19. See Farquhar, "The Ch'ing Administration of Mongolia up to the Nineteenth Century," 315–317; see also Fletcher, "Ch'ing Inner Asia," 48–58.

20. Fletcher, "The Heyday of the Ch'ing Order in Mongolia, Sinkiang and Tibet," 356–357.

21. On Qing efforts to preserve and legitimize Manchu culture during the eighteenth century, see Crossley, "*Manzhou Yuanliu Kao* and the Formalization of the Manchu Heritage."

ing to the desire for exclusivity on the northeast frontier was the hope of preserving lucrative government monopolies in ginseng, pearls, and furs—precisely the lures that attracted illicit settlement.

The administration of the Three Eastern Provinces (*Dong San Sheng*) of Manchuria—Liaodong, the true Manchu homeland, and Jilin and Heilongjiang farther to the north—was unique to that region. Yet much of the Qing experience on the Manchurian frontier, for instance varying the form of administration in different zones, later influenced the approach adopted in Xinjiang and the specifics are thus relevant to this study.

Theoretically, overall control of each of the northeastern provinces was in the hands of a military governor, usually a Manchu or, occasionally, a Mongol. In the two northern provinces, where proximity to the Russian frontier made military affairs a priority, these governors exercised supreme civil and military jurisdiction. In Liaodong the situation was more complicated, for the Qing maintained a secondary capital at Shengjing (modern Shenyang), and civil administration operated through Boards of Revenue, Rites, Punishments, War, and Works that paralleled those at Beijing. By no later than 1727 local government in Liaodong was structured into departments (*zhou*) and counties (*xian*) on the model of local administration in the interior.

The division of authority in the northeast proved a fertile breeding ground for jurisdictional disputes, and this in turn facilitated the growth of corruption in government. At the same time, continued dependence on the central government for financial subsidies served to inhibit the power of senior frontier officials and to erode their autonomy.[22]

For much of the early and middle Qing, official policy aimed at preventing Han Chinese colonization in the far northeast. Nevertheless, immigration restrictions had little significant impact on the long-standing Han Chinese infiltration of Liaodong, and even in Jilin and Heilongjiang further to the north, Han inroads, although gradual, were steady. The difficulty of enforcing restrictions in the face of the shortage of land in north China was compounded by the tendency of local authorities in Manchuria to turn a blind eye to the flow of settlers. This disregard was mainly due to officials' correctly perceiving that Chinese settlers were a promising source of additional revenue because they were far more adept than the native inhabitants at exploiting the untapped agricultural potential of the northeast.[23]

22. Lee, *Manchurian Frontier*, 59–77.
23. Fletcher, "Ch'ing Inner Asia," 40.

Further undermining the anti-immigration policy in the northeast was the introduction of tens of thousands of exiles, both political offenders and common criminals, some of whom were accompanied by their wives and families. They and their descendants soon came to constitute a significant proportion of the Han Chinese population in the northeast; an early eighteenth-century scholar living in exile in Qiqihar, Heilongjiang, commented that exiles outnumbered the troops stationed there by the government.[24] The lives and experiences of some of these exiles are discussed in chapter 4.

XINJIANG

With the annexation of Xinjiang in the mid-eighteenth century, "the dimensions of the Middle Kingdom's effective sovereignty were greater than at any [other] time in her history."[25] The vast Central Asian lands conquered by the Qing armies were geographically, ethnically, culturally, and economically diverse.[26] They extended from Gansu province west to the Tarim Basin and to the borders of Afghanistan and Kashmir, north to Mongolia and the fringes of the Russian empire, and south to the frontier with Tibet. Edged by the Pamir, Kunlun, and Altai mountain ranges to the west, south, and north, respectively, they were bisected into distinct regions by a fourth range, the Tianshan.

The Qing designated the two regions of Xinjiang thus created the northern and southern circuits of the Tianshan (*Tianshan Beilu, Nanlu*). The northern circuit consisted of primarily pastoral Zungharia, with its principal centers in the fertile Ili valley and in the Ürümqi area; the southern circuit comprised both Uighuristan, essentially the princely states of Hami and Turfan located relatively near China proper, and Altishahr, including the formidable Taklamakan desert, in the heart of Central Asia. In Altishahr the principal centers of agriculture and of trade—with China proper and with their neighbors to the west—were the oases of Kashgar, Aksu, Ush, and Yarkand.

The climate and topography of Xinjiang sharply differentiated it from China proper. The summer heat was as fierce as the winters were bitterly

24. Liu, "Qingdai Dong San Sheng Yimin Yu Kaiku," 68, citing Fang Shiqi, "Longsha Jilüe."
25. Fletcher, "Ch'ing Inner Asia," 35.
26. See Borei, "Images of the Northwest Frontier."

cold, and the low level of precipitation did not support intensive cultivation. The ice and snow from the mountains provided the main source of irrigation, and for the oasis agriculture of southern Xinjiang this runoff was the sole source. In the north, however, the runoff flowed into the Ili and other rivers, providing scope for irrigating the vast tracts of pastoral land that the Qing sought to convert to settled agriculture.[27]

To most Chinese, the native population of Xinjiang was as unfamiliar as the land. At the time of the Qing conquest, this population consisted of a number of different ethnic groups. Some, such as the Ölöds, were of Mongol origin. They were generally organized along the lines of the tribes in Mongolia; many belonged to the Tibetan lamaist branch of Buddhism. Others, such as the oasis-dwelling Uighurs and the nomadic Kazakhs and Kirghiz, were Turkic rather than Chinese in origin and adhered to Islam. These Turkic groups had more in common with their Western Asian neighbors than with the Chinese, whose language and culture were alien to them, and who in some instances treated them as foreign tributaries subject to the authority of the Court of Colonial Affairs (*Lifan Yuan*).[28]

The vast area that the Qing designated Xinjiang was thus far from uniform; the diverse forms of administration that the Qing established to govern their new territories acknowledged the area's complexities. Overall Xinjiang was under the control of a military governor stationed at the newly built city of Huiyuan in the Ili area and responsible for both the civilian and military sectors. He was assisted by lieutenant governors (*dutong*) and councillors (*canzan dachen*) stationed in the major cities and administrative centers. Garrison troops reinforced his authority throughout the region. By the 1770s, with the influx of settlers from China proper, Ürümqi and other centers to the east of northern Xinjiang were brought under a local administration modeled on that of China proper, with departments and counties. This region thereby became an administratively transitional area between the interior and the frontier.[29]

In the south, in Uighuristan, the hereditary princes of Hami and Turfan—members of the Qing nobility like the Mongol banner princes— were technically subject to the authority of the Ürümqi lieutenant governor but in practice ruled with a fair degree of autonomy. In Altishahr the Qing replaced the hereditary elite, long the leaders of revolts

27. Lattimore, *Inner Asian Frontiers of China*, 152–153.
28. See Fletcher, "Ch'ing Inner Asia," 62–64.
29. Lin, "Qingdai Xinjiang Zhouxian Zhidu zhi Yanjiu," 29–39.

against Qing authority, with indigenous local officials, known as begs (*bo ke*). These were appointed and removed at the pleasure of the central government in Beijing, where they fell under the jurisdiction of the Court of Colonial Affairs. Their corruption and oppression of the people they governed became legendary. Throughout the south, a strong Islamic religious establishment retained some political power and, particularly in Altishahr, considerable local influence.[30]

Consistent with Qing policy on other frontiers, Han Chinese were excluded from all senior positions in Xinjiang. However, with the sinicization of the local administration in eastern Xinjiang, the Qing found it advisable to appoint a few Chinese to low-level posts such as magistracies in that region, since these positions involved a certain amount of contact with ordinary people, including immigrants from China proper.[31]

Even before the military conquest of Xinjiang was completed, the Qing introduced colonists in order to gain control over these strategically located regions that had been subject to Chinese authority intermittently during the preceding two millennia. Through colonization, they sought to achieve a number of interrelated goals. The first was to make Xinjiang self-sufficient to prevent it from becoming a burden on the already over-taxed Chinese heartland.[32] Indeed, with its rich natural resources and still untapped expanses of arable land, Xinjiang seemed to offer the Qing a means of addressing some of the problems caused by demographic pressures within China proper. The Qing government's second goal was to subjugate the native peoples of the Central Asian periphery to maintain the region as a buffer zone. The Qing were particularly concerned about the expansionist tendencies of the Russians and Kazakhs on the northern steppes and the various Central Asian states such as Kokand to the west. The third goal of the colonization policy was to establish a Han Chinese presence in the newly annexed territories to counterbalance the multiethnic indigenous population, denying ascendancy to any single group and thereby permitting the Qing to rule them all.[33]

For the first seven decades following the annexation of Xinjiang in

30. See Fletcher, "Ch'ing Inner Asia," 73–74.

31. The only other Han Chinese employed in the frontier administration were banished officials. The Qing took advantage of their experience both to keep the exiles beneficially occupied and to save money; see chapter 7.

32. The need for self-sufficiency in Xinjiang was recognized from the outset. See, e.g., ZPZZ QL 24/8/4 (agriculture—opening new lands, packet 31), memorial of Fan Shishou.

33. Chu, *The Moslem Rebellion in Northwest China*, 4.

1758–59, the Qing concentrated their settlement efforts in the area north of the Tianshan because of the abundance of arable land and, thanks to the predominance of nomadism and the devastation wrought by the long Qing campaigns, the relative shortage of a sedentary native population.[34] The main centers of settlement were at Ili, Ürümqi, and Balikun (Barkul). In southern Xinjiang, the Qing severely restricted contact between the native population and Han Chinese and, sensitive to their unpopularity as conquerors, also limited their military occupation of the region. Until the 1830s they discouraged Chinese settlers, particularly in the distant and heavily Muslim region of Altishahr. They especially feared the consequences of economic infiltration, for this was already giving rise to resentment in Mongolia and Manchuria.[35]

The Qing government undertook a wide range of projects to develop the new frontier and realize the important goal of self-sufficiency, particularly in northern Xinjiang. The construction of the new city of Huiyuan, intended to serve as the administrative capital of the entire region, formed a part of this general pattern and, together with the construction of a number of other cities, contributed greatly to altering the nomadic character of the indigenous peoples of northern Xinjiang. The Qing further encouraged the traditional sedentary life-style of the Chinese by initiating large-scale land reclamation projects and creating widespread irrigation networks. To support their various projects, the Qing developed mines, extracting gold and copper as sources of revenue and iron and lead for farming implements and bullets. In several places they operated smelting yards at the pitheads. They built a boatyard that produced a small fleet of boats to transport grain and other commodities on the Ili River.

As on other imperial frontiers, the Qing both encouraged and compelled controlled immigration from China proper into northern Xinjiang to implement their settlement schemes, as well as transferring Muslims from the oases of the south.[36] The colonists who came to northern Xinjiang from China proper consisted of five main groups: soldiers, mer-

---

34. Zeng, *Zhongguo Jingying Xiyu Shi*, 279. At least hundreds of thousands of Zunghars died in the Qing campaigns. See Borei, "Economic Implications of Empire-Building," 16, n. 28.

35. On the beginnings of government-sanctioned civilian immigration into Altishahr in the 1830s, see Fletcher, "The Heyday of the Ch'ing Order in Mongolia, Sinkiang and Tibet," 374.

36. On the transfer of Muslims to agricultural colonies (*huitun*) at Ili, where they constituted an important source of support for the garrison troops, see Wu, "Qing Qianlong Nianjian Ili Tuntian Shulüe," 93.

chants, civilian immigrants, troublemakers moved to Xinjiang by the government, and exiles.

The varied composition of the garrison forces enriched the already complex ethnic mixture of the region. In Xinjiang were Manchu and Mongol banner troops transferred from China proper; Ölöds from Rehe and Chahars from Mongolia; Chinese Green Standard soldiers and tribesmen, such as the Sibos, Solons, and Daghurs transferred from the northeast.[37]

Initially the Green Standard forces were seconded from Shaanxi and Gansu for tours of duty lasting three (later five) years to serve on newly established military agricultural colonies (*bingtun*), whose primary purpose was to supply food for the army of occupation. However, the limited duration of their terms of service in Xinjiang proved both inefficient from the point of view of defense and agriculture and expensive because of the high cost of constant transfers from China proper. After 1762 Green Standard soldiers were encouraged to settle permanently with their families in colonies throughout northern Xinjiang. After 1802 the government also established agricultural colonies for the banner and tribal forces (*qitun*) to supplement the inadequate food production of the bingtun.[38]

On the bingtun the government allocated each family about three acres (twenty *mu*) of land, issued seed, livestock, and farm implements to them, and assisted in arranging for the construction of accommodations.[39] The families paid the government an annual tax of 12 to 18 *sheng* (approximately 80 to 120 kilograms) of grain per mu, depending on the quality of the land. The children of these soldiers were allotted additional land upon reaching adulthood and were registered as civilian settlers.[40] On the qitun the land allotment was four to six acres (thirty to forty mu) and no land tax was payable.[41] In southern Xinjiang, there were few government farms other than at the garrison at Hami. In Altishahr some six thousand banner and Green Standard troops served on rotating tours of duty, unaccompanied by their families in order to

37. Fletcher, "Ch'ing Inner Asia," 59–60; Zeng, *Zhongguo Jingying Xiyu Shi*, 266–267.

38. Wang, "Qingdai Shibian Xinjiang Shulüe," 67. Cf. Fletcher, "Ch'ing Inner Asia," 65, which states that the tribal soldiers were in the bingtun system, not the qitun system.

39. *HDSL* (1899) 178, 13a–b. See also, e.g., *Qinding Huangyu Xiyu Tuzhi* 34, 5b–6a.

40. Xu, "Qingdai Qianqi Xinjiang Dichu de Mintun," 86.

41. Borei, "Economic Implications," citing Luo, *Qing Gaozong Tongzhi Xinjiang Zhengce de Tantao*, 215.

deter permanent settlement. Food supplies for the army in the south were produced by native farmers who leased land from the government.[42]

The second group of settlers consisted of merchants from China proper who found the Xinjiang market so profitable that they were reluctant to return home. Some merchants settled their families in northern Xinjiang, where they were allocated four and a half acres (thirty mu) of land in much the same way as other civilian immigrants.[43] From China they brought such goods as silk and tea. Xinjiang yielded such commodities as jade and cattle. Their prosperity was further enhanced by Qing taxation policies that discriminated in their favor and against indigenous Xinjiang merchants and by the considerable scope for illegal trading in restricted goods. Government officials throughout Xinjiang also occasionally indulged in illegal trading, as illustrated by a major scandal of the 1770s involving jade smuggling between Xinjiang and the lower Yangzi region of China proper.[44] Merchant settlers were liable for repatriation to the heartland if they committed any serious infringement of the law while in Xinjiang.[45]

The third, and most substantial, group of immigrants to northern Xinjiang consisted of civilians who migrated from China proper. These included both Han Chinese from Gansu and Shaanxi provinces and Chinese Muslims, who were well placed to bridge the cultural gulf between the Chinese and the indigenous peoples of Xinjiang.[46] The government encouraged these settlers to migrate, initially even providing subsidies to those who could not afford traveling expenses, and, as on other frontiers such as Sichuan and the southwest, offering incentives in the form of land (four and a half acres or thirty mu per family), loans for seed, livestock, and housing, and temporary tax exemptions during periods of reclamation. The relatively low cost of living on the frontier provided a further inducement to immigration.[47]

---

42. Fletcher, "Ch'ing Inner Asia," 76.

43. Wang, "Qingdai Shibian Xinjiang Shulüe," 67; Ji, "Wulumuqi Zashi," 9b, 12b.

44. On trade, see Fletcher, "Ch'ing Inner Asia," 81–83; on the jade scandal, see *Shiliao Xunkan*, nos. 19–29; McElderry, "Frontier Commerce: An Incident of Smuggling."

45. *DLCY* 45–34. References to this work are to numbered laws (*lü* and *li*) and not to chapters (*juan*).

46. Fletcher, "Ch'ing Inner Asia," 66–68.

47. For a comment on cheap grain prices at Ürümqi in 1770, see Ji, "Wulumuqi Zashi," 16a. In 1794 in Shuntian prefecture (the capital area), maize cost between 1.4 and 2.1 taels per *shi*, 0.6 to 1.3 taels more than at Ürümqi. (The imperial shi was equal to between 175 and 195 pounds; see Ch'üan and Kraus, *Mid-Ch'ing Rice Markets and Trade*, 84, 92–98).

The Qing established civilian colonies (*mintun* or *hutun*) throughout northern Xinjiang, attracting at least two hundred thousand colonists by the end of the eighteenth century. These settlers brought to Xinjiang not only farming techniques from China proper but also a variety of crafts and skills that contributed to Qing sinicization efforts. As the second generation of civilian (and presumably merchant) settlers reached adulthood, they were allocated additional land to farm; as in the case of soldier-colonists, civilian families were not expected to divide the original grants of land into ever-decreasing shares.[48]

A fourth category of colonists consisted of trouble-makers (*weifei*) compulsorily transferred from the Chinese heartland for resettlement (*ancha*) in Xinjiang. Such, for instance, was the fate of twenty-three households of the Wu clan of Hubei between 1763 and 1765. Members of this clan had long been ensconced in the Majiling area of Wuchang, where they were known as local troublemakers. The government resettled them in three different locations in Xinjiang and gave them the same resources allocated to ordinary civilian settlers. However, their first few years in their new homes were regarded as probationary, and they were sometimes referred to as criminals (*fan*).[49]

Another such group consisted of almost one thousand people, many of whom were migrants from other parts of China, relocated from Yunnan to Xinjiang in 1775–76. They had worked in the silver mines in Vietnam but were repatriated following a series of disturbances that did nothing to alleviate the shakiness of Sino-Vietnamese relations.[50] These

---

Wheat cost 1.5 to 2.7 taels per shi in Shuntian prefecture, 0.05 to 1.7 taels more than at Ürümqi. Sorghum varied more—in Shuntian prefecture it cost from 0.08 to 1.8 taels per shi; at Ürümqi it might cost the same or it might be twice as expensive. Peas (*wandou*), though not grown in Shuntian, cost from 0.9 to 1.3 taels in Gansu province, 0.2 to 0.6 taels more than at Ürümqi. *Qingke* barley (a type grown in west and northwest China and in Xinjiang but not in Beijing) cost from 0.76 to 1.8 taels in Sichuan province, 0.2 to 1.3 taels more than at Ürümqi. *SYD* (B) 59/1/18, 81–82.

48. Wang, "Qingdai Shibian Xinjiang Shulüe," 64–65, citing *SZJL* and *Xinjiang Tuzhi*; see also 67.

49. ZPZZ QL 32/4/11 (agriculture—opening new lands, packet 32) memorial of Wudashan. For some other examples of the compulsory resettlement in Xinjiang of "bad elements" from the heartland, see Wang, "Qingdai Shibian Xinjiang Shulüe," 68. On groups of soldiers sent to Xinjiang with semi-criminal status, see Waley-Cohen, "The Stranger Paths of Banishment," 84–85.

50. "Annan Tuohui Changtu An," *Shiliao Xunkan* 21, *tian* 740a–744b. Another approximately eight hundred were resettled in Jiangsu, Anhui, Zhejiang, and Henan or sent home.

troublemakers were escorted in groups across China. Some died en route and others escaped; like convicts, those who escaped were subject to execution upon recapture.[51] Those who arrived in Xinjiang were resettled in widely separated colonies.[52]

The fifth source of immigrants to Xinjiang was the exile population, the vast majority of whom were convicts sent to northern Xinjiang to serve under the soldiers either on the military agricultural colonies or on separate colonies established specifically for them (*fantun* or *qiantun*).[53] The emperor first approved the banishment to Xinjiang of a group of more than 100 criminals in 1758, as soon as the government had gained sufficient control over Xinjiang to turn its attention to large-scale settlement there. In the 1760s the annual flow of convicts to Xinjiang was never less than six or seven hundred and in some years it surpassed one thousand.[54] The numbers Xinjiang had to absorb thus mounted rapidly: by the end of the decade an unofficial observer (castigated by some later scholars for his reckless inaccuracy) referred to several thousand convicts in the Ürümqi area and more than two thousand in the Ili area and claimed that in some locations exiles outnumbered civilian settlers, as they did in Manchuria.[55] In 1775 there were more than seventeen hundred convicts at Ili (possibly excluding convict slaves) and another thousand at Ürümqi;[56] in 1783 government sources recorded more than three thousand convicts in Ili.[57] Five years later, the military governor in Ili made the possibly inflated assertion that the convict population exceeded six thousand in Ili alone.[58] In 1790 officials reported almost two

51. *QSL* QL 1010, 9b–10b, 41/6/6.

52. *ZPZZ* QL 40/10/29, (agriculture—opening new lands, packet 34) memorial of Suonuomuceling. Their families were later sent to join them. *QSL* QL 1010, 8b–9b, 41/6/6.

53. On these colonies, see also chapter 8.

54. *QSL* QL 782, 32/4/12; *XKTB* QL 27/11/24, packet 285, memorial of Changjun; *XKTB* QL 31/4/25, packet 286, memorial of Shuhede.

55. Qi, *Xiyu Ji*, 1, 6a, 8a; see also Qi, *Xichui Yaolüe*, preface.

56. Qi, *Xi Yu Wen Jian Lu*, 1, cited by Qi, "Qingdai Xinjiang Qianfan Yanjiu," 86. Cf. *Qinding Huangyu Xiyu Tuzhi* 32, and Wu, "Qing Qianlong Nianjian Ili Tuntian Shulüe," 96, which give a much lower figure, presumably because the authors are concerned only with convicts engaged in farming.

57. *QSL* QL 1195, 14b–15a, 48/12/25.

58. This figure may be exaggerated because it was offered to justify a claim to be unable to recall the precise details of a particular case. *SYD* (T) QL 53/2/9, 153. Cf. Fletcher, "Ch'ing Inner Asia," 65, which gives the maximum number of criminal exiles in northern Xinjiang as two thousand.

thousand convict slaves at Ili and Ürümqi combined; this figure did not include convicts not subject to enslavement.[59] Convicts formed a small but not insignificant minority in Xinjiang; excluding their families and emancipists, they constituted at most 5 percent of the immigrant population.

Criminal exiles were eventually emancipated but were not allowed to leave Xinjiang. They and their descendants formed part of the permanent population of northern Xinjiang, and by the early twentieth century they were one of the principal groups of Han Chinese in the region.[60]

The use of criminal exiles to colonize Xinjiang declined in the nineteenth century, for the influx of civilian immigrants had been so large that the Han Chinese population was deemed sufficient. After 1799 convicts were no longer used expressly for this purpose, although the banishment of certain types of common criminals to the region continued to the end of the dynasty.[61]

Despite the restrictions on colonization in southern Xinjiang, a few convicts were exiled there starting in the mid-eighteenth century. A maximum of 180 worked in the military agricultural colonies at Hami.[62] Some of the most serious offenders were banished to Altishahr, but in those cases the main purpose of exile was isolation rather than colonization. Such exiles were not settled on farms but were enslaved to the begs, in payment for services rendered to the Qing and as a reward for past or an inducement to future loyalty. Because these offenders were not permitted to return home, they also constituted a de facto immigrant population, albeit a small one. Although few overall figures are available, in 1797 more than 600 convicts were enslaved to begs in that region.[63]

In addition to the convicts, a few hundred disgraced government officials were also in exile in Xinjiang. In 1794, one of the few years for which a figure is available, 455 former officials were serving sentences there, a small percentage of the perhaps 20,000 in the empire who could

---

59. *QSL* QL 1353, 40b, 55/4/29.

60. Forbes, *Warlords and Muslims in Chinese Central Asia*, 9.

61. See *Cheng'an Suojian Ji* 2, 48a; Fletcher, "Ch'ing Inner Asia," 65.

62. Convicts initially assigned to Hami might be transferred later to northern Xinjiang for resettlement. See chapter 6.

63. ZPZZ JQ 2/1/21 (law—exile, packet for JQ 1–9), memorial of Changlin and Tuolun.

lay claim to the title of official.[64] These exiles almost invariably returned to China proper after a few years in exile and thus cannot strictly be described as colonists. They did, however, make an important contribution to the colonization process both through their service in the frontier bureaucracy and, after their return, through their stimulation of intellectual interest in Xinjiang's importance to China.

In the early nineteenth century, as the emphasis on the exile of ordinary convicts declined, there was a marked increase in the number of officials subject to frontier banishment. This resulted from the growing complexity of political life as state power began to wane, as well as the campaign of the Jiaqing Emperor to curb rising bureaucratic corruption. As a consequence, more disgraced officials began to be sent to the northeast frontier in Manchuria than had previously been the case. Yet although the reluctant, gradual relaxation of colonization restrictions in the northeast was beginning to bring a larger Han population to that region and was giving rise to a concomitant need for more experienced officials, those exiled to the northeast were still not employed there by the government. This underscores what was perhaps the principal difference between exile to Manchuria and exile to Xinjiang: only in Xinjiang did the government take advantage of the punishment by turning it specifically and consciously to serve the broader purposes of imperial expansion.

The presence of exiles on the newly conquered Xinjiang frontier continued a characteristic Chinese practice of two thousand years' standing, thereby reproducing a traditional paradox: reliance on offenders against the state to promote state policies in sensitive areas. What distinguished the Qing exile and employment of ordinary and elite offenders was the institutionalization and systematization of the ancient practice, processes that led to greater efficiency. These characteristics help to explain the extraordinary range of Qing power at the very moment when "the culmination of the empire also meant the beginning of its downfall."[65]

---

64. *SYD* (B) QL 59/4/27, 188. An early nineteenth-century text, *SZJL*, compiled by a senior Mongol official then stationed in Xinjiang, lists 385 exiled officials banished to Ürümqi between 1760 and 1807, but these figures are not absolutely accurate. Archival sources show that some of those he lists were at Ili, not Ürümqi; thus one cannot be certain that some Ürümqi exiles were not omitted from his list. For estimates of the total number of officials, see Chang, *The Chinese Gentry*, 71–141.

65. Perdue, "The West Route Army and the Silk Road," 29.

Chapter Three

Exile and Expansion
prior to the Qing

Traditionally the Chinese conceived of a universe composed of a series of concentric circles centered on their own world and culture. They designated the heartland of China proper—the precise boundaries of which varied over the centuries—as the "inner territories" (*neidi*) and the periphery as the areas "beyond the borders" (*bianwai*). Throughout Chinese history a vibrant and mutually transformative tension characterized the relationship between the interior and exterior regions. On the one hand, the outward spread of Chinese influence tended to promote the acculturation of the uncivilized peoples of the borderlands; on the other hand, the peripheral territories and their inhabitants helped furnish the Chinese with a self-definition that reached beyond the purely geographical into the realms of politics and culture in general.[1]

The classification into inner and outer zones carried over in complex ways to the banishment of offenders. As a general rule, the greater one's disgrace, the more remote was one's place of exile. The *Shujing*, the classic historical work of antiquity, postulated three areas to which criminals might be banished, differentiated by their distance from the center of the then-known world.[2] The outermost region consisted of the barbarian

1. For a discussion of traditional conceptions of the world, see Yü, "Han Foreign Relations," 377–383; for a view of the relationship of heartland and periphery in the late imperial period, see Lipman, "The Border World of Gansu, 1895–1935," 2–4.
2. Karlgren, "The Book of Documents," 7. Although the authenticity of the texts of the classical canon, including the *Shujing*, has long been the subject of scholarly debate,

lands beyond the pale of Chinese civilization; next came the outer dependencies where the Chinese state exercised somewhat tenuous control; and third were the outlying regions of what then constituted China proper.

The ancient, graduated system casts some light on the mentality underlying the traditional practice of exile in China. From the cultural perspective, it implied progressive degrees of unfitness to participate in the benefits derived from residence within the orbit of Chinese civilization. From the political perspective, it added further possible refinements to the removal of the disfavored from the center. From the social perspective, it offered a variant on the "inner and outer" theme, for the degraded status of convicts distinguished them from respectable members of society (*liangmin*), however humble, and turned them into outcasts unworthy to participate in regular society. Thus the punishment of exile placed offenders on the fringes of society figuratively as well as physically.[3]

At least since the beginning of the imperial period (221 B.C.–1911), banishment in China, even at its most severe, entailed removal only to the borders of the state and not beyond the limits of Chinese political control.[4] With the gradual expansion of Chinese hegemony over the centuries, it became possible to banish offenders to increasingly distant locations. The most remote frontier to which Chinese exiles were ever sent was Xinjiang, parts of which were subject to degrees of Chinese control under the Han (206 B.C.–A.D. 220) and the Tang (618–906) dynasties as well as under the Qing.

Banishment to the outer boundaries of Chinese-controlled territory was often associated with ambitious expansion policies. These stemmed in part from the relentless need for new sources of revenue and the need to secure the border against hostile tribes and states, but territorial expansion was important for ideological reasons as well. In addition to broadening the fiscal base of the state and enhancing its prestige, it promoted public welfare by creating the conditions necessary for absorbing

---

nonetheless their authority as evidence of ancient practice has always been highly influential.

3. See, generally, Yates, "Slavery in Ancient China in Comparative and Historical Perspective."

4. In this respect the Chinese system resembled that of imperial Russia but differed from the practice in ancient Greece. This point has been noted by Hulsewé, "Ch'in and Han Law," 535.

the demographic growth generally regarded as an indication of good government.[5]

According to classical ideals, a ruler's concern with public welfare generated the popular support that was essential to the political legitimacy that each dynasty repeatedly sought to assert and to reconfirm.[6] Furthermore, the punishment of exile is said to have originated when Shun, one of the sage kings of high antiquity, decided that the finality of capital punishment was intolerable.[7] Throughout Chinese history the reversibility of exile frequently led rulers to favor its imposition in mitigation of a death sentence.[8] By these associations, therefore, exile offered an opportunity to display the benevolence integral to good rulership.

The aura of clemency that often surrounded a sentence of banishment was tempered, however, by the conditional nature of such a reprieve. Second chances were rare; recidivists and fugitives could expect to be treated with the utmost severity. There was, moreover, another side to the conditional nature of commutation: the pervasive belief in man's potential for validation through effort, a potential that was assumed to be universal and in no way connected to social status or education. This belief later became an important aspect of the Neo-Confucian advocacy of moral self-cultivation and public-spirited activism as means to the achievement of human perfection or sagehood. In jurisprudential terms, this belief ultimately crystallized in the possibility of achieving moral self-renewal (*zixin*) through disgrace and punishment leading eventually to rehabilitation and the restoration of one's former status, although this process was deeply susceptible to the risk of political manipulation. These notions produced a dialectical tendency to counterbalance the imperial quest for benevolence by keeping alive the uncertainty that underlay the authoritarian rule generally favored by the traditional Chinese state.

5. There were, of course, diverse reasons for state expansion, but detailed analysis lies beyond the scope of this work.

6. For a discussion of the connections between economic expansion and political legitimacy in classical Chinese political thought, see Lee, "State and Economy in Southwest China, 1400–1800," 14–16.

7. See subcommentary to article 4 of the Tang Code, translated in Johnson, *The T'ang Code*, 59.

8. The reality that technically less severe punishments, such as beatings, in practice often resulted in the prisoner's death did not detract from the symbolic value of the commutation of the death penalty.

Moral, legal, and political issues thus all played their parts in the imperial Chinese system of banishment, a system that reached its height with the exile of offenders to Xinjiang in the middle of the eighteenth century, but whose roots can be traced back to the Qin system of banishment, which was in operation at the inception of the Chinese empire in the third century B.C.

THE QIN DYNASTY (221–206 B.C.)

The association of exile with policies of territorial expansion began no later than under the short-lived Qin dynasty that inaugurated the imperial era of Chinese history by unifying the country. Only sketchy information exists on the crimes that led to a sentence of exile under the Qin, but these often involved abuse of power or corruption on the part of government officials. In such cases the sentence normally did not stipulate penal servitude and lasted for a specified period only. Usually those sentenced to exile under the Qin were sent to the outer limits of the empire; this generally meant that they were sent to newly conquered territory, such as the state of Shu (present-day Sichuan) to the southwest of the Qin homelands.[9]

It was not only those formally sentenced to exile who found themselves deported to the frontiers under the Qin. After the unification in 221 B.C., the emperor (Qin Shi Huang Di, 221–210 B.C.) embarked on a program of expansion both to the north and to the south of his newly created empire. He deported considerable numbers to colonize his new lands and to labor on such public works projects as the construction of a great defensive wall along his northern boundaries.[10] Those transferred to the frontiers in this way included convicts and other socially inferior groups, as well as certain disgraced members of the nascent imperial bureaucracy. Many had not necessarily been sentenced to exile as such but rather to

9. Hulsewé, *Remnants of Ch'in Law*, 17, and 195, n. 5. Exiles were probably sent to Shu even before the unification of 221 B.C., since Shu was conquered by the Qin state at the end of the fourth century B.C. For examples of crimes punished by banishment, see ibid., 105, 115.

10. *Shiji* 110, translated by Watson, *Records of the Grand Historian of China*, 2, 160. On the relationship of the Qin wall to the Great Wall, see, generally, Waldron, "The Great Wall Myth."

some form of penal servitude; they were sent to the edges of the empire because there the most pressing need for manpower was to be found.[11] Yet whatever the stipulated sentence, removal to the frontiers undoubtedly often amounted to a de facto sentence of exile, thus firmly establishing the concept of using offenders, among others, to populate the frontier and work there.

THE HAN DYNASTY (206 B.C.–A.D. 220)

Beginning with the Han Dynasty, traditional Chinese historiography, under rising Confucian influence, took the view that the rapid demise of the Qin was largely attributable to the cruelty of their system of government. Under the influence of the Legalist school of thought, the Qin had favored universal application of a written code of harsh laws, on the assumption that deterrence was the most effective method of ruling. This approach contrasted with the practices that came to be associated with the Confucian school of thought, which emphasized moral precepts over written laws as the cornerstone of government and recognized social distinctions by differential application of the law depending on the status of the offender and on his relationship to his victim.

Despite the Han's propagandizing efforts, they did not break cleanly with the Qin legal tradition in founding their own régime. Harsh penalties continued to be a characteristic feature of Chinese law during the Han and subsequent dynasties, although their application was often moderated through humanitarian interpretation that drew its inspiration from Confucian ideals.[12] Yet the differences between the two schools of thought are sometimes less clearly defined than Confucians would have one believe. For example, although the origin of the often vilified doctrine of collective responsibility, through which relatives of major criminals were also subject to punishment, was attributed to the Legalists from the Han, the practice clearly reflects the family-oriented ideology central to Confucian thought as well as the authoritarian influence

11. See Bodde, "The State and Empire of Ch'in," 64–66. This type of penal servitude should of course be distinguished from corvée labor, which it sometimes superficially resembled; moreover, it is not intended to suggest that forced migration in Chinese history invariably involved criminal elements.
12. See Bünger, "Genesis and Change of Law in China," 77.

of Legalism.[13] The application of this important doctrine in the context of exile is discussed below.

The effort to expand the dimensions of Chinese political control, initiated under the Qin, continued under the Han dynasty. The great Han emperor Wudi (141–87 B.C.) sent exploratory missions, followed by well-disciplined armies, deep into Central Asia, which the Han called the "Western Regions" (*Xiyu*). During Wudi's reign the northwestern limits of the empire were extended to Dunhuang in Gansu province; the radius of Chinese influence reached much further west, even beyond Kashgar into distant Ferghana. Despite the extraordinary logistical difficulties involved in the subjugation of territories thousands of miles from the Chinese heartland, military force and diplomatic alliances enabled the incorporation of vast areas of the Western Regions into a system of Han tributary states under the supervision of a resident protector-general (*xiyu duhu*).

At this time the system of military agricultural colonies (*tuntian*) was also established. Initially these colonies were intended to resupply Han embassies bound for the Western Regions, but later they were more commonly used to provision troops engaged in distant frontier campaigns. Some of the earliest colonies were located at Hami, the gateway to the Western Regions; others were at the oasis of Turfan. Over the centuries the establishment of such colonies became an important part of imperial frontier policy. They frequently served as the vanguard of territorial expansion, and as such they often made use of convict labor.[14]

Chinese expansion under emperor Han Wudi was not confined to the northwest. Once these borderlands had been at least temporarily pacified, imperial armies made possible the establishment of Han administrative units in Sichuan to the West, in Yunnan, Hainan island, and parts of Vietnam to the south and southwest, and in parts of Korea to the northeast.[15] The conquest and retention of all these new frontiers required the injection of sizeable numbers of people. Exiles and other convicts were among those involved in these ambitious projects.

Exile as such was not a major punishment during the Han, but it was

13. See Yates, "Social Status in the Ch'in," 219–231; Yates, "Slavery in Ancient China in Comparative and Historical Perspective, 9. On collective responsibility, see appendix 1.

14. Yü, "Han Foreign Relations," 411–420.

15. Except as otherwise noted, geographical references employ modern versions of place-names.

not uncommon. It was imposed principally on the beneficiaries of commuted death sentences, in a reprise of the ancient practice of treating
exile as a mitigation of the death penalty. Those exiled also included the
family members of those executed for such heinous crimes as rebellion.

Sometimes the relatives of executed criminals were enslaved during the
Han, continuing what was then widely believed to have been an earlier
practice. The issue of the enslavement of convicts in the early imperial
period is a vexed one that has long divided scholars. Under the Qin,
slaves ranked even lower on the social scale than convicts and hence were
distinguished from them. Yet the precise circumstances under which Qin
and Han period exiles might be enslaved, and the extent to which their
punishment amounted to enslavement even when not formally so designated, remain unclear.[16]

Frontier exile sites during the Han ranged from Kurla and Turfan in
Xinjiang to Dunhuang and other locations in Gansu province in the
northwest, Sichuan in the west, and the Guangdong area in the far
south.[17] There are also scattered instances of banishment to locations in
Vietnam, northeast China, and southern Korea.

Exile sometimes took the form of relocation not necessarily involving
the frontiers. A number of members of the royal house, dispossessed for
various reasons from their domains and reduced to commoner status,
were compelled to take up residence away from their bases of power, in
locations where they could be kept under strict control but still within
China proper.[18]

A term of labor was sometimes added to a sentence of exile under the
Han. Especially in the northwest, exiles might be sent to serve in the
armies or on the military agricultural colonies servicing them.[19] As under
the Qin, a sentence of hard labor, probably the commonest of all Han
punishments, frequently involved relocation. Some of those sentenced to
hard labor were sent to the frontiers to fight in campaigns or to serve in a
border garrison; others served their term within China proper, although

16. See Yates, "Social Status in the Ch'in," 201; Yates, "Slavery in Ancient China in
Comparative and Historical Perspective," 9, 52; Wilbur, *Slavery in China during the Former Han Dynasty*, 73–79.

17. See Qi, "Qingdai Xinjiang Qianfan Yanjiu," 83 for references to banishment to
present-day Xinjiang during the Han dynasty.

18. Hulsewé, "Ch'in and Han Law," 535.

19. Shen, "Chongjun Kao," 1, 1b.

sometimes at considerable distances from their native place.[20] Thus under the Han, exile could include penal servitude, and penal servitude often involved some form of exile.

THE PERIOD OF DIVISION (220–580)

For almost four centuries after the fall of the Han, China was divided between partly "barbarian" northern and more "nativist" southern dynasties. For these insecure régimes, survival was a more realistic goal than expansion. Inevitably during this unsettled time (220–580), the boundaries of Chinese-controlled territories receded.

During much of this period, exile as a punishment appears to have been used inconsistently, and among southern dynasties it was formally reintroduced only in the early sixth century, under the Liang (502–556), in a case resulting in exile to the far south for lack of filiality. Several of the northern dynasties during the latter part of this period included some form of exile in their statutes, for instance stipulating the despatch of collectively responsible relatives of executed criminals into army service on the frontiers.[21] During the Northern Qi dynasty (550–589), offenders themselves again began to be banished to the frontiers for military service, but such exile was not necessarily for life. Some scholars perceive in the use of criminals in frontier military service at this time the origins of the formal punishment of military exile imposed under the Yuan, Ming, and Qing dynasties.[22]

20. See Hulsewé, *Remnants of Han Law*, 131–133, 147–149, 176; Loewe, "The Structure and Practice of Government," 479. See also Lee, "Migration and Expansion in Chinese History," 43, n. 33, for a reference to convicts transferred almost a thousand kilometers from their native place to labor at the capital at Luoyang during the Later Han (A.D. 25–220).

21. On the punishment of criminals' relatives during the northern dynasties, see Wang, "Slaves and Other Comparable Groups during the Northern Dynasties (386–618)," 308–310; on the existence (but not the implementation) of a law stipulating exile to a distance of 500 *li* (167 miles), see ibid., 324; on what appears to be a form of exile with penal servitude, see ibid., 346.

22. See Shen, "Xingfa Fenkao," 10, 3b; "Chongjun Kao," 1, 1b; see also Balazs, *Traité juridique du "Souei-Chou"* 173, n. 270. Balazs, whose work remains the most useful western-language source on the law of the period of division, disagrees with Shen's suggestion that this practice somehow differed from the regular form of exile. For an analysis of the early terminology of exile, see also ibid., 113, n. 78.

THE SUI (581–617) AND TANG (618–906) DYNASTIES

The Kaihuang Code of the Sui (581–617), the first dynasty of a reunified China, was promulgated in 581–583. It became the model for all the subsequent legal codes of the imperial era. Largely a rationalized synthesis of the diverse legal traditions of the preceding centuries, it enumerated five principal types of punishment: the death penalty (*si*); life exile (*liu*), now for the first time actually intended to be lifelong and routinely including a period of penal servitude;[23] penal servitude without exile (*tu*); and beatings of two different degrees of severity (*zhang* and *chi*).[24] Although little is known concerning the implementation of specific provisions of the Kaihuang Code, life exile had clearly become an integral part of the legal tradition and remained so into the twentieth century.

Thus the fourth article of the (still extant) Tang Code, first promulgated in 653, provided for three degrees of life exile (*liu*), to be served at progressively remoter locations up to a maximum of one thousand miles (three thousand *li*) from the offender's native place. The extent to which these stipulated distances were treated more symbolically than literally is uncertain. Each degree of life exile also carried a limited term of penal servitude. A further variant was added by article eleven, which provided expressly for "life exile with added labor" (*jia yi liu*), the latter to endure for a maximum of four years.[25] Upon the expiration of the stipulated term of servitude, the convict, whose family often accompanied him into exile, was entered in the population register at his place of banishment; he could not normally return home.[26]

After the fall of the Han, the goal of reestablishing China's position as a great power in East Asia remained hopelessly out of reach. Only after the Sui reunification was it again feasible to consider military ventures beyond the Chinese heartland. The Sui's repeated attempts to reconquer parts of Korea eventually destroyed that dynasty, but the Tang were far more successful in extending Chinese dominion. Political changes after the third century, involving the rise of powerful new adversaries in Korea and in Yunnan province, meant that in those areas Chinese influence

23. An amnesty might mitigate a life sentence but frequently the threat of permanent exile became a reality. See McKnight, *The Quality of Mercy*, 66–69.

24. Wright, *The Sui Dynasty*, 104–106.

25. Johnson, *The T'ang Code* 59, 94.

26. Shen, "Xingfa Fenkao," 10, 6a; Twitchett, "Hsüan-tsung," 362.

remained more cultural than political. Elsewhere, however, the Tang devoted much of the first century of the dynasty to reestablishing Chinese hegemony. They focused in particular on Central Asia, for during this highly cosmopolitan period commercial, intellectual, artistic, and technical influences flowed in both directions along the Silk Road, and it was as important to keep open the lines of communication as it was to protect against foreign incursions.

The defeat or collapse of the principal powers threatening the northwest frontier in the early seventh century allowed the Tang to establish a series of protectorates stretching westward from Gansu province. These consisted of a Chinese civil administration backed by a significant military presence. At their most extensive, these protectorates reached into Transoxiana in the heart of Central Asia. Thus the westward span of the Tang empire surpassed its own model, the Han, and set the standard that the Qing empire sought to emulate in the eighteenth century.

Large standing armies were crucial to maintaining Tang power in these remote locations. Until the end of the eighth century, these armies were generally composed of varying combinations of professional soldiers, militiamen, and convicts. With the punishment of exile newly institutionalized, it seems probable that in the seventh and early eighth centuries criminals deported to serve in the border armies and in the revived garrison colonies at Hami and Turfan had been formally sentenced to exile, unlike some of their Qin and Han predecessors.

Regional governors controlled the frontier zones of Tang China, and their military power came in due course to threaten the central government. One regional governor, An Lushan, led a rebellion (755–763) that almost destroyed the dynasty and irrevocably altered Tang ability to maintain so far-flung an empire. The withdrawal of armies from remote outposts to fight the rebels within China proper amounted to a virtual abandonment of much of the Central Asian territories, and it became clear that the consolidation of the overextended borders was critical.[27]

This imperative led to increasing military professionalization, which reduced the demand for exiles in the frontier armies. The new situation was reflected in an early ninth-century decision to limit exiles' service on the frontiers to six years, since many of them had not committed very serious crimes and their presence served little purpose.[28] This develop-

27. See Twitchett, "Hsüan-tsung," 453–461.
28. See Shen, "Xingfa Fenkao," 10, 6a–b.

ment testifies to the growing instability of Tang military power and to the consequent revision of dynastic priorities to focus on defense rather than expansion.

Under the Tang the banishment of politically disfavored officials to remote border locations paralleled that of ordinary criminals and was of similarly ancient origin.[29] In antiquity these often distinguished exiles were simply sent away from court, as in the case of the great third-century B.C. poet Qu Yuan who, banished to the south (that is, to present-day Hunan province) as the result of his loyal opposition to the ruling faction at court, is said to have drowned himself in despair. Qu's action became enshrined in the tradition surrounding the duty of the truly loyal minister to express criticism of the ruler without regard to personal risk; it was often evoked explicitly by later exiles. Indeed, the theme of exile in general gave rise to an important genre of Chinese literature.[30]

By no later than the Han dynasty, the banishment of a disgraced official was often combined with his appointment to some inferior position at the place of exile, thereby enabling the government to take advantage of his experience while consigning him to an unpopular and distant location. Such, for example, was the fate of one of the most famous statesmen and literati of the Han dynasty, Jia Yi (201–169 B.C.), whose career in some ways echoed that of Qu Yuan. When Jia lost the emperor's confidence, he was sent away from court and appointed tutor to the king of Changsha, near Qu's place of exile. There Jia committed suicide at the age of thirty-three.[31]

Under the Tang the combination of factional disputes at court and the dramatically increased extent of the empire—which engendered a need for qualified administrators—resulted more and more often in state employment of exiled officials in their place of banishment. The regularization of this practice under the Tang, like the use of ordinary exiles' labor on the frontier, added a new dimension to the punishment of exile in that now, for disgraced officials as well as for ordinary criminals, the adaptation of exile to serve larger policies of imperial expansion and colonization became standard. Many of the great politicians and literati of the

---

29. See *Shujing*, "Shundian" 12.
30. See, generally, Schneider, *A Madman of Ch'u.*
31. For Han period biographies identifying the fate of Jia Yi with that of Qu Yuan, see *Shiji* 84, translated by Watson, *Records of the Grand Historian of China*, 1, 499–516.

Tang—including Han Yu (768–824), Liu Zongyuan (773–819), Li Bai (701–762), and Bai Juyi (772–846), to mention but a few of the best known—were banished in this way. Some suffered exile more than once, interrupted by intervals of renewed imperial favor.[32]

Exiled Tang officials were usually sent to hot, unhealthy destinations on the southern peripheries of the empire, including Guangdong, northern Vietnam, and Hainan Island, where many died of such tropical diseases as malaria. The practice of banishing officials to serve in low-level administrative positions in the south became so commonplace that some lived in constant dread of it. This fear is vividly illustrated in the description of the exiled statesman Wei Zhiyi, written by the great Tang figure Han Yu, who was himself twice a victim of banishment:

> Even in the days of [Wei's] early obscurity he was obsessed by the idea that his career would end in banishment, and he had a horror of mentioning the name of any place south of the mountains. Later on it was noticed that when he and his fellow secretaries were looking at maps of China, so soon as they came to a map of the south, Wei shut his eyes and would not look. When he became Prime Minister and took over his new official quarters, he noticed at once that there was a map on the wall. For a week he could not bring himself to examine it. When at last he screwed up his courage and looked, he found it was a map of Yai-chou [on Hainan Island]. And sure enough, it was to Yai-chou that he was banished in the end, and at Yai-chou that he died when not much over forty.[33]

THE SONG DYNASTY (960–1276)

The final overthrow of the Tang in 906 was followed by more than half a century of political division culminating in the establishment of the Song dynasty (960–1276). Although this dynasty endured until the late thirteenth century, incursions by the Jurchen state of Jin in 1127 forced the Song to shift their capital southward from Kaifeng in modern Henan province to Hangzhou in Zhejiang province. This move inevitably reduced the geographical scope of exile.

32. The best account in English of Tang official exiles is Schafer, *The Vermilion Bird*, 37–44.
33. Waley, "China's Greatest Writer," 167, translating Han Yu, "The Record of Shun Tsung's Reign." This passage is also cited by Schafer, *The Vermilion Bird*, 39.

Although during the early years of the dynasty the principal concern and greatest expenditure of governmental funds focused on securing the state against aggression by powerful neighbors to the north and northwest, the urgent need to defend the realm combined with a revolution in transportation and commerce to bring the question of frontier settlement to the forefront of official attention. From the latter part of the eleventh century until the collapse of the northern capital in 1127, policymakers attached great importance to frontier expansion as an instrument of economic growth, and Song military power backed a steady movement into frontier regions. Initially, state-sponsored efforts to settle border areas concentrated on the threatened northwest, leaving the southwest open to private settlement. However, in time the state intervened on all frontiers to protect the interests of Han Chinese migrants, and with increased foreign encroachment into northern China, expansion southwards steadily gained in importance.[34]

This political situation was reflected in changes in the Song system of exile, which, with some embellishments, such as the addition of tattooing and beating, generally followed the Tang practice of combining exile with hard labor. Many exiles were conscripted into the Song armies, but the military instability of the Song meant that attempts to banish common criminals to such service in the northwest were not entirely successful. Some exiles absconded westward; others engaged in banditry. Ultimately it proved expedient to transfer exiles to southern destinations such as Guangdong and Guangxi provinces, where Song control was still relatively firm. After 1127 the southern Song had no alternative but to adjust the range of exile destinations to reflect their loss of control over northern China, although practice did not always correspond exactly to policy.[35]

During much of the Song, the punishment of life exile was in fact rarely for life because of frequent amnesties, which seem to have provided greater leniency at this time than formerly. Amnesties applied to both ordinary criminals and disgraced officials, although the most serious

---

34. von Glahn, *The Country of Streams and Grottoes,* 5–6, 203–212.

35. See Sogabe, "Sōdai no shihai ni tsuite," esp. 12–16. Convicts registered for military service did not necessarily see action as soldiers, but might merely become workers attached to the army. I am grateful to Brian McKnight for pointing out this possibility, which probably holds true for other periods of Chinese history. For a note on banishment under the northern barbarian dynasties of Liao (916–1125) and Jin (1115–1234), see Shen, "Xingfa Fenkao," 10, 8b–9a; Shen, "Zongkao," 4, 7a, 10a–b.

offenders in either category were always excluded. Amnesties theoretically involved the transfer of eligible exiles to a less remote jurisdiction, and it was possible to undergo several such transfers and gradually return to the center; eventually the "average" exile could even hope for release. In spite of these amnesties, however, exigency probably demanded the permanent retention in their place of banishment of certain exiles, such as those serving in the army.[36]

The bitter factionalism that characterized much of Song politics resulted in the banishment of considerable numbers of bureaucrats, as successively dominant groups sought revenge on their predecessors in the imperial favor. Thus, for instance, in the final decade of the eleventh century, scores of officials were deprived of their positions and banished to the south. Among the most famous of these was the statesman and man of letters Su Dongpo (1037–1101), who at an earlier stage in his career had served a term of exile in Hunan. Initially exiled to Guangdong province and appointed to a magistracy, Su was later demoted further to a merely nominal rank. After three years in Guangdong, he was transferred again, this time to that most insalubrious of southern exile destinations, Hainan Island. There he held no official position and to a large extent had to rely on the goodwill that his literary and political renown brought him.[37] Su's misfortunes and his poetic stature placed him squarely within the tradition of Qu Yuan—a fact that did not escape his Qing dynasty admirers almost seven centuries later, including the eminent scholar and editor of Su's poetry, the exile Ji Yun.[38]

THE YUAN DYNASTY (1272–1368)

The Southern Song eventually collapsed under pressure from the Mongols, whose troops completed their conquest of southern China in 1279, seven years after Khubilai Khan had proclaimed the Yuan dynasty from his capital at Beijing.

The Yuan, the first alien dynasty of a united China, added to the indigenous Chinese legal system they inherited elements drawn from their own legal principles. Many of these were subsequently absorbed into the

36. McKnight, *The Quality of Mercy*, 80–82. On amnesties in the Qing, see chapter 9.
37. See Lin, *The Gay Genius*, 340, 369–383.
38. Ji, *Su Wenzhong Gong Shi Ji*, preface.

Chinese legal tradition. Exile was one context in which this blend of traditional and new principles occurred.

Instead of adopting the old Chinese practice of dividing life exile into a number of degrees on the basis of distance, the Yuan system of exile reflected the Mongol segregation of the inhabitants of their new dominions into geopolitical and ethnic categories. At the top of the hierarchy were Mongols and other non-Chinese; southern Chinese were at the lowest point on the social scale. Mongols and other northerners, including Chinese who had formerly lived under the Jin dynasty, were banished to "the south," Hunan or Hubei, whereas southern Chinese were sent to Liaodong (Manchuria) in the northeast, "ten thousand li" from their homes. These exiles worked on agricultural colonies or at postal stations.[39]

The Yuan also institutionalized the earlier ad hoc system of requiring military service of exiles by establishing an additional formal variant of exile known as *chujun*—banishment for army service. This punishment applied in particular to salt smugglers and to violent robbers, probably including those who received commuted death penalties. The place of exile for an offender subjected to chujun was generally determined on the same basis as it was in the case of those condemned to life exile, with the addition of Yunnan province (well-known as the object of major colonization efforts by Khubilai Khan) and Hainan island for those banished from the north.[40]

THE MING DYNASTY (1368–1644)

The replacement of the Yuan dynasty by that of the native Ming in the mid-fourteenth century involved a bloody civil war and the concomitant militarization of substantial portions of society. The first Ming emperor, Hongwu (1368–1398), having consolidated his position, faced the choice of demobilizing his vast armed forces or maintaining a standing army irrespective of military need. Either solution risked considerable

---

39. Shen, "Xingfa Fenkao," 10, 9b; Chen, *Chinese Legal Tradition under the Mongols*, 47.

40. Shen, "Xingfa Fenkao," 10, 12b–13a; Chen, *Chinese Legal Tradition under the Mongols*, 48. A further form of exile employed in the Yuan, *qianxi*, echoed an earlier Tang practice of removing disruptive elements a short distance from their native place. See Shen, "Zongkao," 4, 13a. *Qianxi* lasted into the Qing but by then was only rarely imposed.

social and economic instability at a time when the country gravely needed order to be restored. He resolved the problem by greatly extending the Yuan system of agricultural garrisons, creating new colonies (*weisuo*) throughout the empire instead of solely along the frontiers.[41]

The weisuo created a national system of military settlement; that they were intended, among other things, to promote colonization was made clear by the requirement that military settlers be accompanied by their families. Unmarried soldiers were required to marry before their transfer or, in the event they could not find a wife, to marry a woman chosen by the state from the female criminal population.[42]

The establishment of the weisuo system facilitated the major Ming refinement of the system of exile. This was the elaboration of the Yuan punishment of chujun into a new form, known as military exile (*chongjun*). As a supplement to the Ming code's three degrees of life exile (*liu*) differentiated on the basis of distance, it created an important addition to the range of available punishments. Although the military use of exiles and other convicts was of ancient origin, only under the Ming did military exile become a statutorily recognized and widely used variant of the punishment of life exile.

Initially intended to punish errant officers or soldiers by sending them to serve at some distant garrison, military exile gradually expanded to include civilian offenders, such as illicit sellers of government salt and miscreant eunuchs. In the early Ming, military exile endured either for the rest of the offender's life or, in a more severe variant applicable in particular to those with commuted death penalties, "in perpetuity," reaching beyond the offender himself to include his descendants. However, this hereditary aspect of the punishment was later abolished as unduly onerous.[43]

Early Ming military exile destinations followed the general Yuan principle of sending northerners to the south and southerners to the north, although the class system imposed by the Mongols had been abandoned.

41. Dreyer, *Early Ming China*, 79–80; the general rule was that 70% of colonists farmed the land and the remaining 30% manned the garrisons or went out on campaigns. See also Taylor, "Yuan Origins of the *Wei-so* System."

42. Lee, "State and Economy in Southwest China, 1400–1800," 79, n. 37. For a Qing echo of this policy, see Entenmann, "Migration and Settlement in Sichuan, 1644–1796," 122, noting that single males were discouraged from migrating to Sichuan in the early Qing.

43. Except as noted, this discussion of Ming military exile is based on the following sources: *Ming Shi*, "Xingfa Zhi," 1, and Shen, "Chongjun Kao." See Bodde and Morris, *Law in Imperial China*, 87–91, for summaries of these texts.

In effect this meant that Chinese from northern and eastern China were sent to Yunnan or Sichuan, whereas those from the south and west were sent to Shanxi or to the Liaodong peninsula in the northeast. In time, destinations for military exiles were specified by a number of descriptive categories, ranging from "very near" (*fujin*) to "furthest frontier" (*jibian*) and even "beyond the passes" (*kouwai*). The precise distances involved remained vague until shortly before the end of the Ming when a specific distance was established for each category, ranging from 666 miles (2,000 li) to a maximum of 1,330 miles (4,000 li).

Military exiles engaged in a variety of activities as well as actually serving in the army. A recent study of Ming exiles in Liaodong drawn from local archival and archaeological materials casts considerable further light on their activities. Exiles (and their families) made important contributions in a number of areas, including land reclamation and related economic development, defense and fortification, and the social and cultural arenas. These social and cultural advances came about in part indirectly as the result of the inevitable sinicization caused by the influx of exiles from China proper and in part as the direct result of teaching undertaken by educated exiles, some of whom also wrote the earliest known accounts of the region.[44] The descendants of these exiles were among the first Han Chinese to be incorporated into the Manchu administrative structure as Han bannermen (*Hanjun*) in the early seventeenth century.[45]

In addition to establishing the weisuo, the Hongwu Emperor, deeply suspicious of any potential opposition to his rule, also uprooted considerable numbers of gentry families from their bases of power, mainly in the lower Yangzi region, and sent them into what amounted to permanent exile. Many of these families were transferred to frontier regions such as the developing southwest, where they imparted the distinctive flavor of their "alien" origins to their adoptive communities.[46] Others were ordered to live in the capital, in a move somewhat reminiscent of the Han dynasty's relocation within China proper of suspect members of the royal house.

The familiar employment of banished officials in their place of exile continued during the Ming. Perhaps most notable in a distinguished line

44. Yang and Sun, "Mingdai Liuren Zai Dongbei," esp. 14–19.

45. On the Han bannermen, see Crossley, "The Qianlong Retrospect on the Chinese-Martial Banners."

46. See Lee, "State and Economy in Southwest China, 1400–1800," 62.

of such exiles was the great philosopher Wang Yangming (1472–1529), banished in 1507 to head a postal station in the southwestern province of Guizhou after he defended officials who had dared to criticize a powerful eunuch. Wang forms an intellectual link between the illustrious exiles of the past and those of the Qing studied in this book, for his close sense of identification with the Qu Yuan tradition of unjustly banished loyal ministers helped guide him toward a reformulation of Confucian ideas of self-cultivation even as he endured the isolation of exile.[47]

Wang's exile experience, including his awareness of the need to reconcile himself to his fate, led to his realization that the capacity for moral perfection was subjective and internal, rather than dependent on exclusively objective factors. Thus the cultivation of one's inner strength, as manifested, for instance, in contemplation and in scholarship, was at least as important as external political success in offering a potential path to sagehood.[48] As Wang himself later wrote:

> In the past during my exile in Kweichow, not a month passed without my suffering tribulation [at the hands of others]. Yet, when I think of it now, it was there that I could have made the most progress in all that relates to the stimulation of the mind, the strengthening of human nature, the practice of polishing and perfecting oneself. At that time, however, I only stopped at an imperfect accomplishment of my duties in order to pass time, and so I wasted the precious opportunity.[49]

Wang's ideas and attitudes were absorbed into the Neo-Confucian tradition, of which they became a highly influential constituent. In the specific context of exile, these attitudes confirmed and enhanced the belief that, among other things, the punishment offered its victims a formidable opportunity for self-cultivation as a means of achieving moral goals.

These, then, were the antecedents of the Qing system of exile. The second most severe of all punishments, often applied in commutation of the death penalty, exile in its various transformations served for succes-

---

47. For a discussion of Wang's identification, in common with some of his predecessors, with the Qu Yuan tradition, see Schneider, *A Madman of Ch'u*, 68–69. On the significance of Qu Yuan for Wang's thought, see also Tu, *Neo-Confucian Thought in Action*, 118.

48. Tu, *Neo-Confucian Thought in Action*, 120–122.

49. Ching, *The Philosophical Letters of Wang Yang-ming*, 51.

sive dynasties the dual purposes of law enforcement and labor supply. The reluctance to execute any but the most serious offenders reflected both a concern for the benevolent rule that had been a vital component of political legitimacy since antiquity and a pragmatic recognition that China's people were a highly valuable resource. Moreover—although there seems to be a notable dearth of scholarly debate on this issue—the empirical experience of centuries of conditional commutation from capital punishment to exile must have led to the conclusion that the threat of death could be as effective a deterrent as death itself.

Chapter Four

The Law and Policy of
Exile under the Qing

Prior to conquering China the Manchus had little experience in managing the large-scale bureaucracy that their new empire required. Certainly the Qing dynasty was not prepared, and could not attempt, to replace the existing Chinese governmental infrastructure with an exclusively Manchu one, although Manchu officials initially occupied all senior positions. To an even greater extent than the earlier Mongol dynasty of the Yuan, the Qing accepted the codified Chinese law existing at the time of their conquest as the basis for their own legal code (*Da Qing Lü Li*). Although relatively little is yet known about traditional Manchu law, it is reasonable to suppose that, as was true with other administrative practices, the Qing retained those aspects of their own legal tradition that they regarded either as essential or as particularly well suited to ruling China.[1]

The first Qing code, promulgated in 1646, only two years after the fall of Beijing and the establishment of the new dynasty, necessarily drew heavily on its Ming predecessor.[2] Although the code was later revised a number of times, its general format and the majority of the principal statutes (*lü*) remained much the same throughout the dynasty.

The continuing vitality and contemporary relevance of the code was

1. On the Manchu adaptation of Chinese legal concepts prior to the Qing conquest, see Roth, "The Manchu-Chinese Relationship, 1618–1636," 24.
2. See Zhang, "Qing Lü Chu Tan."

assured through both the amendment of existing substatutes (*li*) and the enactment of additional ones to address new exigencies.[3] The Qing laws governing exile illustrate the code's dynamism. Entitled "Places of Exile" (*Tu Liu Qianxi Difang*), the principal statute was practically unchanged during the course of the dynasty, yet no fewer than forty-nine substatutes were enacted to supplement this basic law.[4]

Under the Qing, the statutory system of exile came to have three tiers: regular life exile (*liu*), military life exile (*jun* or *chongjun*), and banishment to the frontier (*fapei* or, sometimes, *waiqian*). The codification of frontier banishment as a new variant of exile constituted a major legal innovation. In part as a result of this new diversification of exile, by the end of the dynasty more laws called for some form of exile than for any other punishment except the relatively "mild" one of beating with the heavy stick (*zhang*).[5]

EXILE WITHIN CHINA PROPER

During the Qing, as in the Tang, Song, and Ming dynasties, regular exile, in an echo of the practices of antiquity, consisted of three degrees of severity. All endured for life, but they were differentiated by reference to the distance of the destination from the offender's native place, the most severe punishment involving the greatest distance. These distances, possibly more symbolic than literal, ranged from 666 miles to 1,000 miles (2,000 to 3,000 li).[6] Officials determined the prefecture of exile by consulting a detailed compendium (*San Liu Dao Li Biao*) that listed the three appropriate destinations—one for each degree—for criminals from every prefecture in the country.[7]

The second tier of exile under the Qing, military exile, was derived from Ming practice and used the same terminology. It differed, however, in that there was no longer a requirement of military (or military-related)

---

3. For a concise history of the development of the Qing code, see Metzger, *The Internal Organization of Ch'ing Bureaucracy*, 86–88.

4. DLCY 45.

5. See *Huidian* (1899) 54, 1a–b.

6. On the issue of the symbolism of the stipulated distances, see Bodde and Morris, *Law in Imperial China*, 85–86.

7. On the exile of criminals residing away from their native place, see *DLCY* 45-09.

service; under the Qing some of the attributes of Ming military exile were absorbed by the new frontier banishment.[8] Qing military exile consisted of five degrees, each of which was known by a descriptive name and corresponded to a specific distance from the offender's native place. The first three degrees all involved distances identical to those required for the three degrees of regular exile. In ascending order of severity, these were: "very near" (*fujin*—2,000 li or 666 miles), "to a nearby frontier" (*jinbian*—2,500 li or 833 miles), and "to a distant frontier" (*bianyuan*—3,000 li or 1,000 miles). The last two degrees of military exile each involved a maximum distance of 4,000 li (1,333 miles). One was "to the furthest frontiers" (*jibian*) and the other was "to an insalubrious region (*yanzhang*) in Yunnan, Guizhou, Guangdong, or Guangxi."[9] The specific destinations for military exiles were governed by a second compendium (*Wu Jun Dao Li Biao*) that listed alternate places of exile for each of the five degrees.[10]

The system set out in the compendia did not necessarily function reciprocally. Zhili province and, after 1751, Fengtian prefecture, for instance, received no regular or military exiles because of those areas' proximity to Beijing and to the auxiliary capital at Shengjing.[11] Taiwan, which as part of Fujian province was eligible in theory to receive some exiles, appears, in fact, to have received few or none, to judge from the paucity of references to the resettlement of exiles on the island. This de facto exemption was no doubt due to Taiwan's long history as a rebel base. On the other hand, Yunnan province received a disproportionate number of exiles because of its remoteness and its classification as an unhealthy place that nurtured malaria and other diseases.[12] A further potential imbalance arose from the dependence of a criminal's prospects on the chance circumstance of his native place. Those from outlying areas might be exiled to some more desirable interior province, whereas those from the

8. See Shen, "Chongjun Kao," 3, 1a–2a. See also *Qing Shi Gao Xingfa Zhi Zhujie*, 52–53. The continued use of antiquated terminology long after the metamorphosis or even disappearance of the corresponding practice, not unknown in other legal systems, is a characteristic of traditional Chinese law; see, e.g., Hulsewé, "Ch'in and Han Law," 533.

9. *QCXWXTK* 250, p. 9955.

10. Both compendia were first published during the Qianlong reign. See Bodde and Morris, *Law in Imperial China*, 85–90.

11. *DLCY* 46–02.

12. In the late eighteenth century, Yunnan experienced a major outbreak of bubonic plague. See Benedict, "Bubonic Plague in Nineteenth-Century China," 112–118.

prosperous heartland were more likely to find themselves exiled to the outer periphery.

The formal goal was to achieve an even distribution and to avoid creating new problems in a given locality through the excessive introduction of criminals. Officials were allowed some latitude in applying the system of destinations set out in the compendia as long as they abided by a guideline that required the stipulated distances to vary by no more than 100 li (33 miles).[13] Moreover the choice of destination had to be tempered by common sense. For example, the government did not wish to banish salt smugglers to salt-producing centers or counterfeiters to areas rich in copper deposits, and it sought to avoid flooding sensitive areas such as aboriginal homelands with unwelcome exiles.[14]

Under the Qing, regular and military exile shared a number of features. First, because both forms were inherited directly from the Ming, neither involved banishment to the remote frontiers of Inner Asia since these regions were added to the empire only after the Manchu conquest. Second, both forms normally endured for life unless some exceptional circumstance, such as an amnesty, intervened. Third, although both forms theoretically involved close surveillance and labor in public works at the place of banishment, the reality was often markedly less restrictive. The individual exile tended to be left alone as long as he did not commit further crimes or attempt to escape, with the result that the boundaries between these convicts and other local residents were somewhat blurred.[15] Fourth, the law required that both regular and military exiles receive a set number of blows after their arrival in exile; only degree-holders and officials were exempted by virtue of their status.[16] That the exile's ensuing, at least temporary, disability for work seems not to have been a concern suggests that despite the statutory requirement, no actual labor was expected of these exiles. Thus the principal goals of the system of exile within China proper were, simply, the imposition of punishment and the permanent removal of offenders from their native areas.

13. *Huidian* (1818) 41, 4b. It is difficult to reconcile Professor Bodde's view that the distances were "symbolic" (see n. 6) with the precise language of the *Huidian* unless the 100 li either were themselves symbolic or were merely a guideline and not a requirement.

14. See, e.g., *Huidian* (1818) 41, 3b; *HDSL* (1899) 721, 10b–11b.

15. For an example of the sometimes disastrous consequences of this relaxed attitude, see *Shiliao Xunkan* 13, *tian* 467–471.

16. Bodde and Morris, *Law in Imperial China*, 77–78; Chen, "Local Control of Convicted Thieves," 125, n. 18.

BANISHMENT TO THE FRONTIER

Banishment to the frontier (fapei), the third tier of exile established under the Qing, involved the greatest distances and was reserved for the worst offenders. It shared few of the characteristics of the first two forms of exile. First, those sentenced to fapei were sent to Manchuria, on China's northeastern frontier, and later, after its conquest in the mid-eighteenth century, to Xinjiang in the northwest.[17] Both these regions were located beyond the frontiers of China proper, considerably farther than the maximum four thousand li stipulated for regular or military exile. The traditional principle of sending the worst offenders to the most distant locations continued in force. Thus as a general rule, the most serious offenders went to Xinjiang, for its estrangement from Chinese cultural norms increased, for many, the sense of its geographical remoteness. In this way banishment to Xinjiang became the gravest punishment in Qing law other than death.

A second distinction lay in the fact that frontier banishment was not necessarily for life. After serving a number of years in exile, former government officials banished to the frontiers were eligible to return home, and even ordinary convicts, although not normally permitted to leave the area, were often eligible to shed their criminal status and become formally emancipated. This distinction underscored a moral component of the system of frontier banishment that was far less significant and rarely specifically invoked in the system of exile within China proper: in other words, especially for those in Xinjiang, the punishment carried with it the potential for self-renewal (zixin).

A third difference lay in the fact that, unlike their counterparts in China proper, frontier exiles were actually subject to close supervision, particularly in Xinjiang where their work formed an integral part of the government colonization project and their performance affected their prospects for formal emancipation. Last, the beatings that formed part of the punishment of those exiled within China proper were not required for offenders banished to the frontier. This was precisely because the government wished to exploit these exiles' labor, except in a limited number of cases in the northeast, and, hence, wished to avoid disabling them.

17. Certain parts of eastern Xinjiang were for a time listed as exile destinations for military exiles, but no evidence has come to light to suggest that any exiles were in fact sent there. See HDSL (1899) 721, 11b.

BANISHMENT TO MANCHURIA

The banishment of offenders to the northeast was not entirely without precedent. Liaodong, in southern Manchuria, had received some military exiles (*junfan*) under the Ming, as noted in the previous chapter. The Manchus themselves had also used the remoter parts of Manchuria as a repository for criminals since at least 1633, even before they established the Qing dynasty in 1644.[18]

By 1655 the Qing legal code provided explicitly for the exile of certain criminals to specific destinations in the northeast, using the fapei terminology. Initially the Qing designated Shangyangbao, in the southern Manchurian prefecture of Fengtian, an exile destination.[19] Soon afterwards, exiles began to be sent to the remoter destinations of Ninguta, in modern Jilin province, and to Heilongjiang in the far north, and these became the principal sites of exile in the northeast.[20] No destination tables, such as those used for exile within China proper, were used for offenders banished to the northeast.

Until the conquest of Xinjiang, all those sentenced to frontier banishment were sent to Manchuria. They and their families numbered at least in the tens of thousands and came to play a significant part in the long-term sinicization of that region.[21]

The majority of early Qing exiles to Manchuria were common criminals such as robbers, counterfeiters, and smugglers. Traditionally such crimes ranked among the most serious, other than rebellion and treason, and many of these exiles had originally been sentenced to death but had had their sentences commuted. However, one important group of early exiles to the northeast consisted of those banished in the wake of the Rebellion of the Three Feudatories (1673–1681), which had posed a major threat to Qing hegemony. Since this revolt originated in the southwest, the despatch to the northeast of those implicated recalled the Yuan practice of sending exiles to the opposite ends of the empire.

Under the Qing, convicts exiled to the northeast became a valuable source of labor as had their predecessors in Liaodong under the Ming.

18. Yang, *Liubian Jilüe*, 3a.
19. For an example of an early Qing exile sent to Shengjing in southern Manchuria (in 1653, prior to the first Qing codification of fapei), see Wakeman, *The Great Enterprise*, 953–954.
20. *QCWXTK* 203, p. 6677; *HDSL* (1899) 721, 16a.
21. See Lee, *Manchurian Frontier*, 101–102.

These exiles worked on military agricultural colonies (*tuntian*), in postal stations, on river patrol, or in the dockyards building boats for defense against Russian incursions across the Siberian border. However, the convicts' work does not appear to have been subject to systematic central planning, and in Manchuria exile was not, after the first few years of the dynasty, connected with a state colonization project as it was later to be in Xinjiang.

The more serious offenders exiled to the northeast were enslaved and were often awarded to bannermen to relieve the government of the expense of their upkeep. However, since the numbers involved proved greater than the banner population was capable of supporting, some exiles were set free illicitly and others were transferred to officials better able to maintain them. The less serious convicts were not enslaved. Some took up respectable occupations as farmers, craftsmen, or small traders, but others formed the nucleus of a growing lawless population on the frontier. A lack of rigorous surveillance allowed many to escape, prompting the establishment of checkpoints in 1690.[22]

The other principal group of exiles in the northeast, most of whom had also benefitted from commuted death sentences, consisted of disgraced scholars and former officials and their families. Best known among these early exiles were those condemned for various political offences such as supporting the Ming, particularly through the circulation of seditious material.[23] Many were implicated peripherally in "literary cases" (*wenzi yu an*), in which allegedly anti-Manchu writings led to the execution of the ringleaders and to the banishment of their associates, either for direct involvement or, in the case of their relatives, for guilt by virtue of collective responsibility.[24] Other officials exiled to the northeast were banished for failing to perform their duties in a satisfactory manner.

The government did not find employment for scholars exiled to Manchuria, as it was to do for those banished to Xinjiang, nor did it seek to exercise close control over them. In Manchuria most exiled scholars took up new occupations such as trade, medicine, and teaching Chinese language and culture. Not surprisingly, they often sought each other out. In the 1640s and 1650s, for instance, a Buddhist monk formed a poetry

22. Lee, *Manchurian Frontier*, 78–81; Fletcher, "Ch'ing Inner Asia," 46–47.
23. Xie, *Qingchu Liuren Kaifa Dongbei Shi*, 7–9.
24. See, e.g., "Shuci Kuangbei Bizhao Dani Yuanzuo Renfan Qingdan."

club with fellow exiles, later preaching sermons that strongly attracted still others.[25]

Among the banished scholars' pupils were Manchu officials anxious to acquire the Chinese literary and cultural attributes indispensable to elite status in the heartland. The intimate familiarity of many political exiles with these emblems of civilization meant that those charged with their surveillance admired and aspired to emulate their accomplishments, despite the exiles' profound political disgrace and their distance from the cultural centers of China.

Thus the presence of banished scholars as well as of other convicts militated in different ways against the policy of preserving Manchuria for the Manchus. Paradoxically, it proved difficult, if not impossible, to enforce the cultural policies of the central government in the distant reaches of the empire. Chinese civilization exercised an irresistible attraction even over the representatives of those who sought to contain its influence.

The persecution of the descendants of Lü Liuliang, initiated by the Yongzheng Emperor, was one of the most famous early Qing literary cases involving banishment to the northeast. This case resulted in the exile of more than one hundred members of Lü households to Ninguta in Jilin province. There they were enrolled in the banners and forever forbidden to sit for the civil service examinations or to purchase a degree that could lead to official position. When, some forty years later, it transpired that two of the exiled Lü family members had nonetheless succeeded in purchasing degrees through intermediaries, all those involved were sent into slavery in even remoter regions of the far northeast frontier, in Heilongjiang.[26] Yet despite their double disgrace—first as the relatives of a traitor and second as lawbreakers in their own right—some of the Lüs were able to establish a position of respect for themselves on the frontier. According to information given to an early twentieth-century scholar visiting the northeast, the Lüs, together with the descendants of another famous exile family, became the most highly valued teachers in the area.[27]

25. See Wakeman, *The Great Enterprise*, 763, n. 131

26. Chen Yuan, "Ji Lü Wancun Zisun." On the original Lü case, see Fisher, "Lü Liuliang (1629–1683) and the Tseng Ching Case (1728–1733)."

27. Xie, *Qingchu Liuren Kaifa Dongbei Shi*, 78. For a detailed account of this case, see appendix 2. The other famous exile family was the Fangs, descendants of the scholars Fang Shiqi and Fang Dengyi, exiled in the early Qing. On some of the Fang descendants who returned to China proper, see chapter 9.

The Lü incident and, in general, the influx of exiles into Manchuria prompted concern about potentially detrimental influences on frontier society and on Manchu morals. But until the conquest of Xinjiang, sufficiently remote frontiers were in short supply. Provisional remedial strategies included sending Han Chinese criminals, who would normally have gone to the northeast, to the insalubrious areas of southwest China instead, and sending only Manchus to the northeast, but in the long term these measures failed to prevent the gradual sinification of Manchuria.[28]

The rate of exile to the northeast appears to have slowed considerably once the Xinjiang frontier became available as an alternative destination in 1758. For instance, in contrast to the thousands of convicts sent to Manchuria in the early Qing, in 1765 only sixty-seven were sent to six different northeastern destinations.[29] Yet the "overcrowding" of the Manchurian frontier with criminals remained a problem. In the early nineteenth century, more than six thousand convict slaves lived in Heilongjiang and another twenty-seven hundred lived in Jilin;[30] in 1813 an order suspended banishment to the northeast after the suppression of a riotous assembly of exiles in Heilongjiang.[31]

BANISHMENT TO MONGOLIA

The Mongolian frontier, to the north of China, theoretically offered an alternative location for a convict colony. However, there is no evidence that it was ever extensively used for this purpose.[32] Nonetheless, from 1741 certain officials were banished to Mongolia to serve in military postal stations (*juntai*).[33] The juntai punishment, in effect a form of exile, was a special, supplementary sanction intended to prevent corrupt officials from reverting to their old habits. It later extended beyond those convicted of corruption to cover officials convicted of crimes for which a commoner would have been sentenced to penal servitude (*tu*). Penal ser-

---

28. See edict of 1736 cited by Xie, *Qingchu Liuren Kaifa Dongbei Shi*, 3.
29. *XKTB* QL 30/5/14, packet 327, memorial of Liu Tongxun.
30. *HDSL* (1899) 721, 25b.
31. On this episode, see numerous documents in *SYD* (T) JQ 18, 2d through 4th months.
32. A few laws called for banishment to Khobdo in Mongolia but it never became a major exile destination.
33. On the juntai, see *Huidian* (1899) 51, 1b–2a.

vitude normally involved working for a specified period, up to a maximum of three years, in a postal station within the offender's native province.[34] The subjection of officials to the juntai punishment—regarded as more severe than ordinary penal servitude because of the distances involved—was based on the principle that officials were undoubtedly familiar with the law and by virtue of their privileged position should be more rigorously punished for infractions than commoners.

Officials banished to serve at juntai were obliged to make contributions to the expenses of these postal stations; while assisting in the cost of operating the juntai they were also repaying the funds they had acquired through their corruption. If after three years an official had not completely repaid the stipulated amounts, he might be retained for a further term until the full amount was received. Severe punishment awaited those who tried to avoid payment by falsely pleading poverty.[35]

BANISHMENT TO XINJIANG

Among the initial Xinjiang exiles, the vast majority had their original sentences either decreased or increased. In 1756, for instance, seven former officials whose death sentences had been repeatedly deferred were ordered into exile at Balikun in eastern Xinjiang.[36] The first law stipulating the banishment to Xinjiang of ordinary convicts was passed in 1758; it covered counterfeiters and explicitly followed an earlier precedent of commuting to banishment to Manchuria the death sentences of those who had committed robberies involving violence.[37] The first proposal to send common convicts to Xinjiang was made in the same year and involved 114 criminals, mostly robbers, who had originally been

34. The specific location depended on labor requirements. *Huidian* (1818) 41, 3b.

35. *DLCY* 45–37; see note following this substatute for a discussion of some of the inequities in the application of the juntai law. The capacity of the juntai to absorb corrupt bureaucrats sentenced to banishment was not infinite. Thus in 1794, in addition to twenty-seven disgraced officials whose original sentences of penal servitude had been increased to banishment to a juntai there were twenty-eight others, originally sentenced to penal servitude for virtually indistinguishable crimes, serving sentences in Xinjiang. *SYD* (B) QL 59/4/27, 195–297.

36. *SYD* (T) *changben* QL 21/10/13, 162.

37. *QCWXTK* 199, p. 6639.

sentenced to death. In each case execution had been deferred at the annual assizes for at least three years.[38]

A brief explanation of Qing sentencing procedures is essential to understanding the system of banishment to Xinjiang. Traditional Chinese legal codes imposed specific punishments for specific crimes. However, in practice many sentences were either increased or decreased from those stipulated by the law. This system of modification resulted from the need for flexibility inherent in a system characterized by differential treatment based on status. Under the Qing, the government used the modifications to fulfil such policies as the colonization of Xinjiang without awaiting formal changes in the legal code. In fact, Qing statutes often merely formalized existing practice.[39]

Most sentences were subject to an intricate system of review before implementation. After a sentencing recommendation was received from the local magistrate, it was evaluated at both the prefectural and the provincial judicial levels and was then subject to further review by the provincial governor.[40] For banishment, the governor's confirmation took place only after consultation with senior officials in the capital. At each stage the matter might be remanded for reconsideration at a lower level.[41] In capital cases, the emperor's approval was normally required, except in dangerous situations such as rebellion, when ex post facto ratification was usually sufficient.[42]

Under Qing law the death sentence, the only punishment more severe than exile, involved either immediate execution or execution "after the

38. For some of the many laws involved, see, e.g., *DLCY* 266; 268; 269 (all involving various forms of robbery); 276 (desecration of graves); 359 (counterfeiting). For the proposal, involving 114 cases (i.e., at least that many criminals, because a single case could and often did involve more than one person) see *SYD* (T) *changben*, QL 23/5/24, 27–32.

39. See, e.g., *DLCY* 287–17.

40. The magistrate had final jurisdiction when the punishment was restricted to beating or confinement in the wooden frame known as the cangue, which was similar to the wooden stocks used in England.

41. See Shiga, "Criminal Procedure in the Ch'ing Dynasty," 14–16. The highest level of review (short of the emperor) was not necessarily limited to the Board of Punishments as suggested by Shiga. The top judicial organs were the Three Judicial Offices (*Sanfasi*), which included the Board of Punishments (*Xingbu*), the Censorate (*Duchayuan*), and the Court of Judicature (*Dalisi*). They sometimes acted in conjunction with such other organs of the central government as the Board of War or the Grand Secretariat. In addition, certain political cases, including rebellion, were reviewed by the Grand Council, by Manchu princes, or other specially selected officials. Chang, "The Grand Secretariat Archive," 114.

42. However, the emperor's involvement in the judicial process was not limited to capital cases. See Chang, "The Grand Secretariat Archive," 114–115.

assizes." Offenders who were to be executed after the assizes were initially imprisoned, normally in their native province. At the annual assizes, their cases were placed in one of several categories. The two most important categories were *qingshi*, meaning that the criminal deserved execution, and *huanjue*, deferring decision until the assizes of the following year.[43]

The emperor did not necessarily sanction the execution of all those placed in the qingshi category; perhaps no more than 20 percent of those condemned were actually put to death each year.[44] Thus criminals might survive several assizes in the qingshi category and obtain an eventual reduction to huanjue status.[45] Usually a criminal had to survive ten assizes before being eligible for downgrading from qingshi to huanjue, but sometimes this reclassification occurred more quickly. In 1772, for instance, the cases of those who had survived five assizes in the qingshi category were reconsidered, and in 1793 the cases of those who had survived only three assizes were reevaluated.[46]

It became common for capital offenders to spend many years in the huanjue category. For example, in 1757, the year before the introduction of Xinjiang banishment, 50 of 103 cases reported from Xi'an (48.5 percent) involved from three to twenty years' incarceration in this category, and 165 of 281 cases reported from Suzhou (58.7 percent) involved from three to twenty-one years' such incarceration.[47] In time, overall numbers of prisoners subject to continuing postponements of execution became very substantial. In the three years from 1790 to 1792, some 8,000 criminals were placed in the huanjue category three or more times.[48] From late 1800 to the assizes of 1803, more than 10,000 were so classified and from 1809 to 1812, nearly 13,000 were so classified.[49]

43. On the assizes, see Meijer, "The Autumn Assizes in Ch'ing Law."

44. According to Shen Jiaben, cited by Bodde and Morris, *Law in Imperial China*, 142, perhaps no more than 10% of those "sentenced to death after the assizes" were in fact executed. My research in archival assizes records (*XKTB Qiushen*) confirms this view.

45. See *DLCY* 411–16 (regulation dating from 1774).

46. *SYD* (T) QL 37/11/7, 119a; *SYD* (B) QL 58/11/27, 177. It was possible to have one's classification upgraded from huanjue to qingshi and to undergo more than one reclassification. See, e.g., *XKTB Qiushen* Chin 002A, 1474291, 2, QL 22/10/10, memorial of Emida.

47. *XKTB Qiushen* Chin 002A, 1474290, 19, QL 22/9/13, memorial of Chen Hongmou, and QL 22/9/19, memorial of Aibida.

48. *SYD* (B) QL 57/11/4. Prior to this, more than 6,000 criminals had been placed in the huanjue category 3 or more times in each of 2 two-year periods. *QSL* QL 1218, 25a–b, 49/11/14; *QSL* QL 1272, 12a, 52/1/7.

49. See, respectively, *QSL* JQ 122, 23a–b, 8/10/31; *SYD* (T) JQ 17/11/8, 89.

As a result of the enormous numbers involved, the government sought an alternative to execution, both because large-scale killing deviated from the Confucian ideal of benevolent rule and because of the unmanageable logistical problems. Eventually the majority of those whose executions were deferred at three or more successive assizes received commutation of their sentence to, inter alia, frontier banishment.[50] Reduction was not guaranteed, however, as illustrated by an 1812 case in which six criminals (three of them women) who had survived twenty or more assizes were not granted a reduction of sentence; it may be assumed that many such people died in prison before the final resolution of their cases.[51]

As had long been the practice, the commutation of the death penalty in such cases was conditional on the exile's good behavior, and any lapse, such as further criminal activity or an escape attempt, served to reinstate the original death sentence. To make this quite clear, official language differentiated the commutee exiles from others by referring to them as "criminals a fraction away from death" (*qusi yi jian zhi feitu*).

In 1759 the Qianlong Emperor affirmed that the purpose of sending convicts to Xinjiang was to clear the crowded heartland, to settle the new frontier and, through punishment, to offer criminals a means of redeeming themselves (zixin).[52] Developing this theme again a few years later, government officials declared that after a term of years commoner convicts who had manifested an appropriate degree of repentance would be allocated their own land in Xinjiang and registered as civilians.[53]

The punishment of banished officials was explicitly associated with the idea of self-renewal. Banished officials were ordered to "expiate their crimes by putting forth effort" (*xiaoli shuzui*), following the accomplishment of which at least partial recovery from political disgrace could be expected. Successful expiation depended on the nature of the original

---

50. See, e.g., *SYD* (T) QL 41/10/27, 178; *QSL* JQ 76, 15a–b, 5/11/13; *QSL* JQ 263, 13b–14a, 17/11/8. For one of several examples of review and reduction of sentence after twenty assizes, see *QSL* JQ 79, 8b, 6/4/2.

51. *QSL* JQ 264, 7b–8a, 17/12/7. The death of long-term prison inmates of course obviated the need to decide their fate. The increase in the number of those imprisoned as the result of repeated deferrals of execution may reflect a certain indecision, symptomatic of impending dynastic decline, on the part of Qing authorities, as well as the growing crime rate.

52. *QSL* QL 599, 16a–19a, 24/10/21.

53. *QSL* QL 759, 12a–13b, 31/4/21.

offense and on imperial acknowledgment of the achievement of self-renewal through the suitably penitent performance of assigned tasks; the more serious the offense, the more effort was required.[54]

Although the exile of officials was framed as a form of moral and political probation whose success depended on the exile's behavior and attitude, this was somewhat misleading.[55] The Qianlong Emperor often observed that his action in imposing a sentence of banishment to Xinjiang set the offender on "the path to self-renewal" (*zixin zhi lu*), thereby suggesting that within the conducive milieu provided by the imposition of punishment the exile nonetheless retained a degree of autonomy.[56] Yet ultimately the assessment of the successful (or otherwise) accomplishment of self-renewal depended exclusively on the judgment of the emperor, through his officials, and this removed the whole process of self-renewal from the exclusively self-determining moral sphere it theoretically occupied. It also introduced unbounded scope for unscrupulous manipulation.

Whether or not this was an articulated policy is an issue that must for now remain open to question, for there appears to be no documentary evidence on the subject. However, by clothing an important means of political and social control in language that for any educated person recalled the idealized notions of internally focused self-cultivation associated with the influential school of the Ming philosopher Wang Yang-ming, the Qing undoubtedly believed there was a political advantage to be achieved.

In addition to the commutees, certain of the more serious offenders among those ordinarily due for exile within China proper had their sentences increased to frontier banishment and were sent to Xinjiang.[57] In the case of common convicts, they were probably regarded as "more serious" precisely because they, too, had had their original death sentences commuted to exile within China proper; the emperor frequently observed that all the Xinjiang convicts had originally been sentenced to

54. See also chapter 9.

55. For a discussion of the "probationary ethic" inherent in the public life of Qing intellectuals, see Metzger, *Internal Organization*, 263–266; see also Metzger, *Escape from Predicament*, 170–176.

56. See, e.g., *QSL* QL 875, 10b, 35/12/23; *SYD* (B) QL 59/4/27, 191; *QSL* JQ 156, 11a, 11/1/9.

57. See, e.g., *QSL* QL 556, 17b–18a, 23/2/18.

death.[58] The sentences of disgraced officials ordinarily due for exile within China proper also began to be increased routinely to banishment to Xinjiang, on the grounds of greater responsibility and privilege. In 1794, for instance, 149 out of 260 such exiles—more than half—had had their sentences increased in this way.[59]

Exiles whose sentences had been subject to increase were generally more leniently treated than commutees. For instance, the former group was not normally sent to the remotest parts of Xinjiang, and the minimum term of banishment prior to emancipation or return was briefer than for commutees.[60] When in due course the code was amended to stipulate exile to Xinjiang directly, those banished under the new laws were usually treated like the commutees.[61]

EXILE ALLOCATION POLICY IN XINJIANG

Many of the convicts who now began to be banished to Xinjiang had committed the same types of crimes as those who had previously been sent to the northeast. As noted above, however, banishment to Manchuria did not end abruptly in 1758, and there seem to have been no fixed rules determining which criminals were sent to which frontier. In general terms, Xinjiang became the more important exile destination because convicts were needed as laborers on this new frontier.

The effort to distribute exiles evenly and in accordance with local needs prompted the development of a far more coherent policy concerning exile allocation within Xinjiang than ever prevailed in Manchuria. In 1758 the government established guidelines for assigning common convicts to Xinjiang. Initially these exiles were sent to areas where Qing authority had been established for some time. Since such regions were located relatively near the northwestern borders of China proper, this limited the cost and inconvenience of transportation. The first convicts were sent only as far as Anxi, near the Gansu-Xinjiang border. When

58. See, e.g., *SYD* (B) QL 23/5/2, 175; *SYD* (B) QL 24/5/18, 102–103; *HDSL* (1818), 582, 12b–13a.

59. *SYD* (B) QL 59/4/27, 195–284.

60. Qing approaches to the duration of banishment are discussed in the context of the end of exile. See chapter 9.

61. For a list of early laws stipulating banishment to Xinjiang, see Qi, "Qingdai Xinjiang Qianfan Yanjiu," 85. See also *XJTLSL*.

Anxi had as much convict labor as it could use, the next arrivals were sent to Hami, further to the west. When Hami's needs were filled, the next batch was sent to Balikun, and the next to Ürümqi.[62]

The first reports of saturation surfaced in 1761. In that year, the governor of Gansu, whose office was responsible for assigning convicts within Xinjiang, reported that Anxi, Hami, and Balikun already had 507, 340, and 622 convicts respectively, and that they could not absorb any more.[63]

Thereafter quotas were established for convicts at Balikun and Hami, limiting the number of convicts at each location to 350 and 180 respectively; Anxi ceased to be a major center for convict resettlement after this time.[64] If the numbers of working convicts at either location dropped below the full quota due to emancipation, illness, or death, replacements were drawn from new batches of transient convicts bound for Ürümqi and beyond.[65]

The goal was to select convicts whose crimes were relatively mild for retention at Hami or Balikun, since distance was equated with severity and these convict colonies were nearest to China proper. Sometimes, however, the only convicts available for retention were major criminals (*zhongfan*), a category that included those whose death sentences had been commuted and those sentenced by statute to Xinjiang banishment. Such convicts remained at Hami or Balikun only until less serious convicts arrived to replace them and then continued to their original exile destinations, usually Ili or Ürümqi, for Qing officials were anxious not to lessen fortuitously the severity of these convicts' punishment.[66]

No other exile destination in Xinjiang had a convict quota, and the

62. *SYD* (B) QL 23/5/22, 246. A proposal from officials in situ to send five hundred convicts to Toksun and Kalashar, to the south and west of Turfan, appears not to have been implemented. See *SYD* (B) QL 23/6/9, 359–363.

63. *HDSL* (1899) 744, 19a–b (1761). Cf. *Qinding Pingding Zhunke'er Fanglüe Xubian* 13, 7a–9a, QL 26/8/15 which states that at Balikun there were approximately 480 convicts in 1761. No other figures are available for the number of convicts then at Anxi or Hami. After 1764 convict allocation was the responsibility of the office of the governor-general of Shaanxi and Gansu. *QSL* QL 633, 10a–11a, 26/3/22.

64. *QSL* QL 635, 28a, 26/4/29. Cf. *SYD* (T) QL 44/9/1, 326, which implies that the Balikun quota was established in 1762. On the Hami quota, see *Qinding Huangyu Xiyu Tuzhi* 32, 1b–3a. In the Hami area, 130 convicts were located at Tarnaqinq and 50 at Caibashihu.

65. *ZPZZ* QL 38/i3/27 (agriculture—opening new lands, packet 32).

66. *ZPZZ* JQ 1/10/28 (law—exile, packet for JQ 1–9), memorial of Sengbaozhu. See also *QSL* QL 1414, 5a–b, 57/10/2.

allocation procedure continued to be somewhat flexible, as indicated by a memorial submitted in 1766 by Shuhede, acting governor-general of Shaanxi and Gansu:

> Convicts bound for Xinjiang all come to the governor-general's office for onward transmission. Some have documents saying "Ili"; some have documents saying "Ürümqi"; and some say "Ili and Ürümqi." So we assign convicts according to which place is listed first in the document; there is no regulation requiring even distribution. Now Ili is vast and they need people for reclamation work, so probably we should send more convicts there than to Ürümqi. In future may we send three convicts to Ili for every one that we send to Ürümqi . . . unless their documents specify where they are to go?[67]

The proposal was approved.

The loose terminology used in the convicts' documents to which Shuhede referred suggests a considerable degree of ignorance about Xinjiang geography on the part of officials in China proper. Ili and Ürümqi are six hundred miles apart—a journey of a month or more. Yet the two destinations were frequently referred to in early statutes, and hence in convict transmission documents, as though they were virtually contiguous. By the 1780s, some twenty years after the conquest of Xinjiang, this type of confusion, not found in statutes concerning the more familiar Manchuria, had become less common, and it became general policy to send the more serious offenders to Ili. This was both because officials equated Ili's greater remoteness with greater severity of punishment and because Ili had more substantial labor requirements.[68]

Some convicts were sentenced to banishment to "the Muslim cities," a term that designated Kashgar, Aksu, Yarkand, and Ush in southern Xinjiang.[69] In keeping with the general goal of not creating new problems, Chinese Muslims ordinarily liable for banishment to Xinjiang were sent instead to the unhealthy provinces of China's southwest; perennial Qing fears about the subversive effects of Islam gave rise to a sense among officials that it was too risky to resettle criminal Muslims in such

67. *QSL* QL 762, 5a–b, 31/6/7.
68. *SYD* (T) QL 49/4/15, 126.
69. See, e.g., *DLCY* 162–01. When allocating convicts to be enslaved to the begs, the governor-general of Shaanxi and Gansu and the imperial agent (*banshi dachen*) stationed at Hami obtained their information on local conditions from officials in those cities. Those enslaved to "government soldiers in southern Xinjiang" were allocated by the imperial agent stationed at Aksu. *Huijiang Tongzhi* 7, 18a.

heavily Muslim areas, and, moreover, that Xinjiang was insufficiently alien an exile destination for Muslim criminals from China proper.[70]

The continuing attempt to balance labor needs in Xinjiang against the threat posed by too great an accumulation of criminals prompted a policy of switching exile destinations between points in Manchuria and in Xinjiang, as convenient. Yet this produced unsatisfactory results.[71] In the first place, increasing the number of exiles sent to Manchuria contradicted the unabated, if unrequited, desire to preserve what still remained of the ethnic integrity of the northeast. On the other hand, unless criminals continued to be sent to Manchuria, more would arrive in Xinjiang than could be absorbed easily into the already potentially volatile society of that new frontier.

Officials became conscious of this problem within a few years after the arrival of the first exiles in Xinjiang. In 1767, those sentenced to Xinjiang banishment under sixteen substatutes covering various types of robbery were exiled instead to the remoter parts of China proper, in particular the four "insalubrious" provinces of the south. These convicts were known as "Xinjiang changees" (*Xinjiang gaifa neidi qianfan*) to distinguish them from other criminals exiled (*liu* or *jun*) at first instance within China proper.[72] The effect of this distinction was that although the "changees" in fact never reached Xinjiang, they were treated like Xinjiang exiles in certain respects, such as receiving more severe punishment for subsequent misdeeds. Later, when Qing economic development of Xinjiang intensified and more labor was needed, some of those who committed crimes covered by the sixteen "changee" substatutes were then sent to work in Xinjiang.[73]

The allocation of disgraced officials to exile destinations was based on different considerations since they did not present a threat to frontier security. Their destination, normally specified in the sentence of banishment, was known before their arrival in Xinjiang, although occasionally such exiles were subsequently reallocated to meet particular administrative needs.

The vast majority were sent to the northern part of the region. As with

70. *DLCY* 45–27, 45–38. These laws, passed in 1787 and 1806 respectively, formalized existing practice. For this period, the sole instance of banishment to Hainan Island, a common exile destination in the Tang dynasty, involved Muslims from Gansu province. *SYD* (T) QL 49/13/8, 607–608.

71. *Huidian* (1818) 41, 5b; see also *QCWXTK* 204, p. 6687.

72. *QCWXTK* 205, p. 6694.

73. See *Huidian* (1818) 41, 5b.

ordinary convicts, the general rule was that the more serious offenders were sent to Ili and the less serious to Ürümqi.[74] An additional reason involved Ili's status as the principal seat of government in Xinjiang; exiled officials could be employed in the extensive local bureaucracy. Furthermore, the greater convict labor requirements in the Ili area gave rise to a concomitant need for more supervisors, and such positions were often assigned to banished officials. Thus of 260 banished officials in Xinjiang in 1794, 151—more than half—were at Ili and 101—nearly 40 percent—were at Ürümqi. The remaining 8 were in southern Xinjiang: 2 at Yarkand, 2 at Kashgar, 2 at Ush, 1 at Kuche, and 1 at an unidentified "Muslim city."[75]

A few disgraced officials continued to be sent to the northeast after the conquest of Xinjiang but this practice did not continue in any systematic way. In 1794 there were only 44 such exiles in Manchuria, 30 of whom had been banished in a single corruption case some ten years previously.[76] One reason for banishing some disgraced officials to Manchuria may have been the authorities' desire to avoid the regrouping of political cliques in Xinjiang. Only occasionally did the ethnic background of such exiles appear to have affected the government's choice of frontier destination, for instance when Manchus were sent to the southwest and Han Chinese to Manchuria in the corruption case just mentioned. In general, however, such considerations were not given much prominence.

THE BANISHMENT OF EXILES' FAMILIES

The attempt to achieve simultaneously the two goals of punishment and colonization raised the issue of the treatment of convicts' families.[77] Should they be required, or at least permitted, to accompany the convict, and, if so, at whose expense? The question was irrelevant for banished officials since it was not intended that they should remain in Xinjiang as

74. See *SYD* (T) JQ 15/5/n.d., 63.
75. *SYD* (B) QL 59/4/27, 195–284.
76. *SYD* (B) QL 59/4/27, 190.
77. The members of a major criminal's family held guilty by virtue of collective responsibility were treated as criminals in their own right and hence their banishment was at government expense. In such cases, the principal offender, in whose crime these family members were implicated, was executed. Such cases should be distinguished from those under discussion here, where the family members who accompanied a convict were not personally treated as criminals. On banishment by virtue of collective responsibility, see appendix 1.

colonists. The government discouraged exiled officials from taking their families with them to Xinjiang and provided no subsidies, and their families rarely accompanied them.[78]

In the early days of Xinjiang banishment, the wives of convicts whose sentences were the result of commutation or were required by statute were generally compelled to join in the exile; children could accompany their parents if the convict wished. The wife and children of a convict whose sentence had been increased to Xinjiang banishment could accompany him, but this was not mandatory. In either case the government paid traveling expenses for all family members.[79]

In 1759—because continuing military activities in Gansu made it difficult to cope with large numbers of exiles—these rules were temporarily modified so that only family members banished by virtue of collective responsibility were subsidized by the government.[80] A convict might still take his family into exile, but the government would pay only the expenses of the actual offender.[81]

In 1766, however, the old system was reinstated at the suggestion of the future ranking Grand Councillor Agui, then an imperial agent working on colonial affairs in Xinjiang. Arguing that convicts would work harder and be less tempted to escape if their families were with them, Agui noted that without government subsidies most convicts could not afford to bring their families. He proposed that if a convict regretted not having brought his family with him into exile, the government should make arrangements for reunification in Xinjiang.[82]

Thereafter most convicts were banished to Xinjiang with their wives and children accompanying them at government expense, and this practice continued for the next several decades. Exceptions included convicts

78. *QSL JQ* 373, 19a–b, 25/7/15. In 1842 Lin Zexu took one or possibly two of his three sons into exile, but his case appears to have been unique and to have resulted from Lin's extraordinary prestige. See Lin, *Lin Zexu Jiashu* 65–66, 232.

79. *XJTLSL*, 2, 20a–b. See also *DLCY* 15–08. The husband of a woman banished in her own right would probably not have accompanied her into exile. In any event the husbands of exiled women were often already dead.

80. *HDSL* (1899) 721, 6a–b.

81. *XKTB* QL 27/11/24, packet 285, memorial of Changjun. Those who had begun their journey before this order took effect were subsidized for the balance, provided they had already reached Gansu. What happened to the families of those who had departed but had not yet reached Gansu is unclear.

82. *QSL QL* 759, 12a–13b, 31/4/21; see also *Cheng'an Suojian Ji*, 2, 48a–b. On the shortage of women in Xinjiang in the 1760s, see Ji, "Wulumuqi Zashi," 15b.

banished in connection with religious sects, and other serious offenders banished to southern Xinjiang, because these convicts were to be punished by isolation not used as colonists. Furthermore, women more than sixty years old or in poor health were not encouraged to accompany their husbands into exile since their contribution to the colonization of Xinjiang (if they survived the journey) would have been minimal. By the turn of the century, there was no shortage of Han settlers in Xinjiang. After 1799 a convict was still permitted to bring his family into exile if he wished, but the government again ceased to subsidize the expenses of the journey.[83]

The removal of whole families to Xinjiang is a striking feature of the Chinese system. In imperial Russia, exile to Siberia normally involved the permanent separation of families, marked by the annulment of the exile's marriage, although the exile's wife and children might, if they wished, accompany him at government expense.[84] The English system of transportation to Australia, which began in the late eighteenth century, did not generally allow convicts' families to accompany them into exile at any price.[85] The Qing practice in Xinjiang suggests that they had learned from their experience on other frontiers. In Taiwan, for instance, separating settlers from their families had proved subversive to law and order, while in Sichuan the shortage of immigrant women had led to disputes between settlers and natives.[86]

The Xinjiang policy on convicts' families reaffirms that colonization was as important a goal of the system of banishment to Xinjiang as was punishment. Previously the primary purpose of exile had been to isolate the offender not only from his native community but also from his family.[87] In Xinjiang this goal was partially defeated by the procedure

---

83. See *Cheng'an Suojian Ji* 2, 48a.

84. Kennan, *Siberia and the Exile System*, 1:81–84. Kennan's figures for 1885 show that the largest single group of "exiles" consisted of women and children who voluntarily accompanied their husbands and fathers. At first glance these figures would seem to suggest that the practice was a common one at that time, but the disproportion can also be explained by the large size of families. See also Mazour, *The First Russian Revolution*, 222–260; Campion, *Etude sur la colonisation par les transportés anglais, russes et français*, 35.

85. See, generally, Hughes, *The Fatal Shore*.

86. Shepherd, "Plains Aborigines," 162–175; Entenmann, "Migration and Settlement in Sichuan," 123.

87. Banishment to Xinjiang did remove the criminal from his ancestral home so that he was unable to care for family tombs and otherwise perform his formal filial duties. However, the Qing sometimes permitted the return for burial at home of the corpse of a deceased exile.

recommended by Agui, who was prompted by an overriding interest in importing able-bodied Han Chinese, criminal or otherwise, to populate and cultivate Xinjiang.

MONETARY REDEMPTION OF A SENTENCE OF BANISHMENT

In part as a result of the policy of using convicts as colonists, the law permitted certain categories of criminals to avoid their fate by monetary redemption.[88] Availability was governed mainly by laws relating to the status, age, or physical condition of the offender, and in some instances monetary redemption was also available on the ground of family need.[89] The option of monetary redemption applied to a number of other punishments as well as to Xinjiang banishment, but in all cases the perpetrators of serious crimes were excluded.

Monetary redemption involved paying a small sum to reduce or even eliminate a criminal sentence. The amount payable was determined by the severity of the punishment and ranged from a few hundredths of a tael for a beating to fewer than 1.5 taels for a death sentence.[90] The extraordinarily small sums involved symbolized the function of monetary redemption as an expression of Confucian humanitarianism permitting flexibility in the application of harsh laws. Hence the sums bore no relation to the criminal's financial means.

Theoretically women were entitled to avoid punishment by paying such a fine unless this was expressly excluded by the law they had contravened. In practice, however, they seem never to have been permitted to avoid banishment to Xinjiang by this means.[91] Moreover, the majority of banished women were convicted by virtue of collective responsibility, and as such were guilty of crimes too serious to be avoided by monetary redemption.[92]

88. The principle of monetary redemption had its origins in classical antiquity. See *Shujing*, "Shundian," 11, cited in *GZD* QL 51476, 52/8/6.

89. See in particular *DLCY* 1–08; 2; 6; 18; 20; 22.

90. *DLCY* 1–08. Different types of redemption—*nashu, shoushu or shuzui* applied—depending on the basis of availability.

91. For an example in which a woman was specifically denied permission to avoid any part of her punishment by means of monetary redemption, see Fu, *Documentary Chronicle*, 353.

92. See *XJTLSL* 2, 7b. The same appears to have been true for very young children.

Monetary redemption was available to the aged and the physically infirm on humanitarian grounds, although it was denied even to these individuals if convicted of the most serious crimes.[93] The rules were more restrictive for those sentenced to Xinjiang banishment than for those sentenced to exile within China proper, where the minimum age required to avoid punishment was seventy. Few criminals more than fifty years old or in poor health were actually exiled to Xinjiang, for they would have been unable to work satisfactorily. Instead, such offenders were despatched to distant and insalubrious places within China proper; they were permitted to avoid this less severe form of exile through monetary redemption only if they were more than seventy years old at the time of sentencing.[94]

The relevant moment at which age or physical condition determined a criminal's fate was not the time of the crime's commission but that of sentencing. Thus a criminal who committed a crime at the age of forty-nine but whose case was not concluded until he was fifty was exiled within China proper rather than to Xinjiang. Monetary redemption was available only prior to exile; it could not be invoked by an offender who had grown old in exile.[95] A criminal who developed a physical disability after committing a crime but prior to exile was also entitled to monetary redemption; nevertheless there is no evidence to suggest that criminals maimed themselves to avoid exile.[96]

The rules concerning older exiles recognized that one of the original purposes of Xinjiang banishment was to provide a source of labor. Thus the rules concerning age and infirmity did not generally extend to officials. Indeed, the age of banished officials was rarely mentioned, suggesting that it was not regarded as significant in this context.[97]

As noted above, a criminal sentence was sometimes redeemable on the grounds of family need. Such a plea usually asserted that the criminal was the only child of elderly parents who would be deprived of support if the

---

93. "Infirmity" included those with impaired vision or speech as well as those who had lost or seriously injured a limb. See Bodde, "Age, Youth and Infirmity," 150–151.

94. See *XJTLSL* 2, 1b–2a.

95. *XAHL* 4, 20a.

96. *DLCY* 23; *XJTLSL* 2, 6b–7a. Physical disabilities caused by imprisonment prior to sentencing were sometimes sufficient to permit redemption. See Bodde, "Age, Youth and Infirmity," 154.

97. For a rare example of a case in which the disgraced official's age was mentioned, see *GZD* QL 29682, 39/8/25 (former subprefect sentenced to Xinjiang banishment was aged 68).

criminal were banished. After verifying his claim, officials might reduce the criminal's sentence to a beating if he paid the specified amount.[98]

Many convicts were automatically excluded from the scope of the monetary redemption laws because their crimes appeared in a list of "non-amnestiable" offences.[99] In addition, there were lists of criminals specifically excluded from the right to avoid punishment" by asserting family need. These included many convicts subject to Xinjiang banishment, for example, ginseng thieves originally exiled within China proper who had subsequently escaped and criminals whose original death sentences had first been commuted to life terms in the cangue and then modified to banishment to Xinjiang.[100]

In rare cases the exclusions might be overruled on compassionate grounds. Huang Wenfu, for instance, had masterminded the robbery of goods and money worth a total of 260 taels, but he had neither participated in the actual crime nor shared in the robbers' haul. Although his crime appeared on the list of exclusions, as the only son of elderly parents he was allowed to remain at home.[101] His case was truly exceptional, however, and a plea of family need in an excluded case was unlikely to succeed.[102]

Officials sentenced to banishment were sometimes entitled to use monetary redemption to avoid punishment because of their privileged status.[103] However, the rules were complicated. Although officials were

98. *DLCY* 18. The amount of monetary redemption payable in cases of family need was the same as that applicable to the elderly and infirm.

99. *DLCY* 16. See chapter 9.

100. For a 1799 list of twenty-five crimes whose perpetrators were not normally entitled to avoid Xinjiang banishment on the ground of family need, see *Cheng'an Suojian Ji* 2, 13b–16a. Some of these were included in the list of non-amnestiable crimes. A second list of twenty-two types of criminals allowed to invoke family need indicates that Xinjiang banishment was not necessarily incompatible with permission to redeem on such grounds. Fourteen of the twenty-two were "changees" who in fact would have been banished within China proper, but the remaining eight would have been sent to Xinjiang. If criminals in this group committed further crimes, they were not allowed to invoke family need again. Ibid., 16a–17b.

101. *Cheng'an Suojian Ji*, 2, 10a–13b.

102. Even when a criminal could not avoid Xinjiang banishment on the ground of family need, his wife may sometimes have been able to do so. See *QCWXTK* 205, p. 6693, for a ruling dating from 1766.

103. Official status seems to have carried more weight than age or infirmity in determining whether monetary redemption of a sentence of banishment to Xinjiang was permissible. For examples of monetary redemption of less serious punishments granted to disgraced officials on the ground of infirmity, see Bodde, "Age, Youth and Infirmity," 150–154. The

often protected by virtue of their status, at the same time they were held to a higher standard of conduct. Thus those convicted of crimes punishable by anything more than a beating, and in particular those convicted of corruption, were prohibited precisely by virtue of their status from using monetary redemption to avoid punishment. Corruption in this context generally involved criminal intent; thus officials responsible for "juggling" state funds (that is, using them for unauthorized state purposes) were distinguished from those who embezzled for private purposes. Generally, only the embezzlers were banished.[104]

Derk Bodde, one of the great scholars of Chinese legal history, has suggested that the purpose of the laws on monetary redemption was "to provide fixed guidelines" rather than to establish inflexible rules.[105] That approach was exemplified in the application of those laws to the system of banishment to Xinjiang, whose introduction they long preceded, and, indeed, in the Qing development of that entire system.

The law of exile expanded under the Qing in proportion and in response to the expansion of imperial territory. In Xinjiang the close attention the Qing paid to their evolving system of banishment demonstrated their ability to learn from experience. The heyday of exile to Manchuria had coincided with the century of dynastic consolidation, when it was expedient to clear bad elements from the heartland without especially careful regard for the long-term consequences for the frontier. By the time of the annexation of Xinjiang, by contrast, there was a growing awareness that no region was so remote or so limitless that it could safely be left to its own devices. As a result, the Qing paid much closer attention to such issues as the even distribution of convicts and the most effective use of their labor. The higher level of central government planning for the system of banishment to Xinjiang also reflected Qing awareness that their control in Xinjiang—imposed by occupying forces—was never as secure as it was in their native Manchuria, even in the late eighteenth and

---

law on entitlement to monetary redemption for family need in cases involving officials was unclear, and such entitlement generally depended on the gravity of their crime, see *XAHL* 3, 35b–38b.

104. See Zelin, *The Magistrate's Tael*, 319, n. 35. For a history of Qing policy on the redemption of crimes by officials, see Metzger, "*Internal Organization*," 303–307.

105. Bodde, "Age, Youth and Infirmity," 158.

early nineteenth centuries, in the relatively peaceful decades following the conquest.

The frequency with which exile was imposed in commutation of execution indicates a powerful reluctance to take the irreversible step of destroying human life. Yet the frequent grant of only conditional commutation suggests an equally strong reluctance to abandon life-threatening control over the exiles. Although a ruler might bestow the opportunity for self-renewal, and in so doing display the benevolence appropriate to his position, this opportunity was purely discretionary and was never regarded by the Qing as a right. The inference was always that the capacity for self-renewal depended on the exile, yet this was belied by the requirement that no convict be emancipated and no banished official be released without specific imperial authorization. With its built-in uncertainties, conditionally commuting the death sentence provided broader possibilities for social and political control than capital punishment could ever offer.

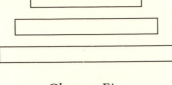

Chapter Five

Who Were the
Xinjiang Exiles?

The Xinjiang exiles were as diverse as the crimes they had committed. Scholars, sectarians, bureaucrats, eunuchs, imperial clansmen, bannermen, soldiers, pirates, merchants, actors, farmers, slaves and others, men, women, and children—all suffered this punishment, although for different reasons and in different forms.

Some of the Xinjiang exiles were banished for a common crime, such as fraud or robbery; others were condemned for a political offense. In late eighteenth- and early nineteenth-century China "political offense" meant one of two things: conduct that constituted "a transgression against the values or institutional foundations of the polity, as distinct from ordinary crime such as corruption, which merely eroded its effectiveness"[1] or involvement in the factional struggles that tainted much of public life at the time. Often the boundaries between activities that were purely criminal and those that were primarily political were loosely drawn, as continues to be true in China today.[2]

In many cases abundant evidence supported the charges such as negligence, corruption, or incompetence that led to a sentence of banishment, but some exiles undoubtedly fell victim to the vagaries of political life. As

---

1. Kuhn, "Political Crime and Bureaucratic Monarchy," 85.
2. See, e.g., *DLCY* 62—disobeying imperial orders (*zhi shu you wei*); *DLCY* 386—doing what ought not to be done (*bu ying wei*) two catchall statutes that foreshadow the provisions against "counterrevolutionary activity" invoked in contemporary China.

one official, who suspected that the true cause of his exile was the favor shown him by the emperor, put it: "One knows that at its height the sun begins to set and that waters at their fullest must recede. So heaven punished me, putting me in a position to excite people's hostility."[3]

Many of the Xinjiang exiles were banished in large groups, often due to the ancient doctrine of collective responsibility, through which the relatives of such major criminals as rebels and mass murderers were subject to punishment. In such cases, the principal offenders were executed.[4] Large-scale banishment also occurred when the death penalty was commuted to avoid the appearance of tyranny invoked by mass executions. This pragmatic clemency policy was invoked, for instance, in cases involving heterodox religious sects, which by their very nature generally involved considerable numbers of people.

Reinforcing a fundamental principle of traditional law that accorded differential treatment to offenders based on their status, the Qing applied separate standards and, sometimes, separate laws to government officials and common criminals in imposing a sentence of banishment to Xinjiang. This chapter follows Qing practice and treats the two groups separately.

GOVERNMENT OFFICIALS

In late imperial China, government officials enjoyed a multitude of privileges unavailable to ordinary people, but these very advantages exposed them to a much broader range of potential punishments. Not only were they held to a higher standard of conduct than commoners, but they were also governed by various administrative regulations (*chufen zeli*) that applied to all civil and military officials.[5]

The most common forms of administrative punishments were salary fines (*fafeng*); demotion with retention of duties (*jiangji liuren*); demotion and transfer (*tiaoyong*); dismissal with retention of duties (*gezhi liuren*); and outright dismissal (*gezhi*), sometimes with a lifelong prohibi-

---

3. Ji, *Ji Xiaolan Jiashu*, 18, 21.

4. See appendix 1 on collective responsibility.

5. Each of the Six Boards (*Liu Bu*) had its own regulations (e.g., the Board of War's *Zhongshu Zhengkao*), and in addition there were the "Administrative Regulations of the Six Boards" (*Liubu Chufen Zeli*). Regulations of this kind were frequently amended and reissued.

tion against reappointment.[6] Administrative punishments could not be imposed without imperial approval.

Officials were also governed, as were all subjects of the Chinese empire, by the penal code (*lüli*). Thus their more serious infringements could lead to a criminal sentence, including, after 1758, banishment to Xinjiang. As explained in the preceding chapter, such a sentence might be imposed either by modification of a previous sentence or by direct statutory provision. The administrative regulations also provided for punishment in accordance with that code, and administrative punishments could be increased to criminal ones. However, prior to the imposition of any criminal sanction, an official had to be dismissed from office.[7]

The period of acute political tension (1775–1799) dominated by the corrupt minister Heshen was marked by frequent impeachments and accusations, and many of its victims were sentenced to frontier banishment. In some cases the sons and political affiliates of those whose fall from power culminated in their own execution were exiled. The vast majority of these were sent to Xinjiang. For example, in 1789 the four sons of the military leader Chai Daji, vilified and executed for political reasons following the campaign to suppress Lin Shuangwen's rebellion in Taiwan, were sentenced to Xinjiang banishment. Chai's younger brother was banished there in the same year, ostensibly for bribery and extortion and for meddling in public affairs under his elder brother's protection. Twenty-one other officials were banished to Xinjiang "in Chai Daji's case."[8]

Heshen's associates were sometimes able to shelter under his protection; such has generally been assumed to be the case for Yunnan governor Sun Shiyi. Sun was sentenced to banishment in Xinjiang in 1779 for having failed to expose disgraced governor-general Li Shiyao, but Sun's sentence was unexpectedly revoked by special edict. The attack on Li is generally considered to represent an early attempt by Heshen to intimidate the provincial bureaucracy. Sun's impeachment and subse-

6. Metzger, *Internal Organization*, 300–302.

7. The meshing of the administrative regulations and the penal code is an immensely complex topic beyond the scope of this study. For some discussion of the issues involved, see Watt, *The District Magistrate in Late Imperial China*, 18–19, and 294–295, n. 12. See also Metzger, *Internal Organization*, 311–313.

8. On the sons of Chai Daji see *SYD* (B) 54/6/28, 681; on Chai's younger brother, see *SYD* (B) 59/4/27, 264; on the twenty-one other officials, see *SYD* (B) 57/9/19, 137.

quent release were thus almost certainly the result of political maneuvers. Sun later became notorious as Heshen's close associate.[9]

Banishment sometimes occurred when Heshen's enemies targeted his associates in an attempt to undermine his power. The case of Sichuan governor-general Wenshou, whose son Guotai was closely connected with Heshen, probably illustrates this situation. Wenshou was first exiled to Ili in 1772, before the rise of Heshen, for allegedly screening his predecessor's son from accusations of extortion. The emperor rejected Guotai's offer to take his father's place in exile, but nonetheless Wenshou was recalled after only a year.[10] Wenshou was banished again in 1781 for failing to suppress the banditry (*guoluzi*) that had spread throughout Sichuan and into the neighboring provinces of Hunan, Hubei, and Guizhou.[11] This time Guotai, by then himself the target of impeachment charges that formed part of an unsuccessful bid to discredit Heshen, was permitted to contribute part of his own stipend as governor to the imperial treasury to "redeem" his father's crime.[12] Wenshou returned home in 1783 even though Guotai had been condemned for massive embezzlement and allowed to commit suicide in prison. The father's relatively rapid release from his second exile probably represented some form of quid pro quo for the disgrace and death of the son, which even Heshen had been unable to prevent.

The Heshen era gave rise to a trend towards banishing increased numbers of officials. Even after the favorite's disgrace and death in 1799, this trend did not subside. Most of Heshen's former associates remained in office, due to the new emperor's policy of avoiding a wholesale purge, and thus many of those in senior positions were already entrenched in corrupt ways. Moreover, there were undoubtedly old scores to be settled, and by then political infighting had become an integral part of the established order.[13]

After 1799 an official might be penalized simply for having been associated with Heshen. In that year, for example, Taifeiyin, a senior

---

9. See *ECCP* 481.

10. *Qing Shi Gao* 339, p. 11077.

11. Ibid. 332, p. 10959.

12. Guotai's payment was a "self-imposed fine"; on these, see chapter 9.

13. See Nivison, "Ho-shen and His Accusers: Ideology and Political Behavior in the Eighteenth Century"; Polachek, "Literati Groups and Literati Politics in Early Nineteenth-Century China."

official in the capital, was banished to Ili because he had tried to conceal his former association with the deceased minister, even claiming to have been a protégé of Heshen's opponent, Agui. Although such guilt was often extremely difficult to prove, Taifeiyin's link to Heshen was established because he had given Heshen some land in southern Manchuria when stationed there as a brigade general (*fudutong*).[14]

The case of the famous scholar Hong Liangji, a member of the group of officials most resolutely opposed to Heshen, illustrates the complex maneuvering that continued after the fall of the imperial favorite. Hong, a court scholar and royal tutor, was dismissed from office in 1799 after writing a letter to one of the imperial princes in which he criticized the emperor personally and attributed the White Lotus rebellion (1796–1803) to corruption on the part of local officials. He also leveled serious accusations against several dozen named senior officials, active and retired, thereby presenting a direct challenge to those who blamed the empire's ills on the religious fervor and unruliness of the rebels and brushed aside suggestions that these were largely caused by official malpractice. Hong was sentenced to immediate decapitation for "great lack of respect" (*da bu jing*); shortly thereafter the sentence was commuted, probably due to the influence of Hong's powerful friends, such as the imperial tutor and Board President Zhu Gui. Hong was banished to Xinjiang, only to be granted an imperial pardon within a few months.[15]

Factionalism alone did not account for the increased number of government officials who fell into disgrace from the late eighteenth century onward. Other factors were related to trends in society in general. The commercialization of the economy, for instance, combined with escalating pressures on official budgets caused by demographic growth to make it increasingly difficult for bureaucrats to avoid some form of financial misfeasance in order to meet all their obligations. In particular when this involved corrupt intent, banishment often followed.

Thus corruption was one of the prime reasons for which Qing officials were banished to Xinjiang. The well-known scholar Xu Song, for instance, was educational commissioner of Hubei province when he was exiled in 1811 for trying to force the purchase of books he himself

14. *QSL JQ* 46, 4a–5b, 4/6/2; *Guochao Qixian Leizheng Chubian* 298, 34a–36a. On Taifeiyin's subsequent career, see chapter 9.
15. Hong, "Ili Riji," 1a. On Hong's pardon, see chapter 9.

had printed and for not assigning traditional essay topics.[16] He was one of several punished for corruption relating to examinations.[17] Similarly, Jiangxi governor Chen Huai and Nanchang magistrate Xu Wu were impeached together in 1796, partly on the basis of a popular ditty on the cost of vacancies they controlled, to the effect that high positions cost ten thousand taels whereas medium-level ones cost only eight thousand. Investigators could trace no specific act of malpractice to Chen Huai beyond responsibility for his subordinate's "overbearing behavior"; the two were banished to Ili and Ürümqi respectively, on loosely framed charges of corruption and a "lack of regard for morality." Although exile was usually regarded as sufficient punishment in itself, a heavy fine was also imposed upon Chen, which suggests that such evidence as did come to light strongly implied the presence of corrupt intent.[18]

The financial duties of officials, in particular the tax collection that was one of the principal responsibilities of county magistrates, provided ample scope for corruption and other forms of economic crime. A substantial proportion of those banished to Xinjiang had misappropriated public funds—for example, failing to remit taxes that had been collected, embezzling from a local treasury or from military supplies, or stealing valuable items on which the government wished to retain a monopoly, such as ginseng or furs.[19] Moreover, quite apart from actual official duties, the aura of power that surrounded any government position lent convincing force to threats issued in support of demands for money. Thus other banished officials were guilty of extortion, ranging from thousands of taels demanded from salt merchants by Fujian and Zhejiang governor-general Yade, to small amounts demanded from boatmen by escorts of government goods.[20] Some had committed fraud or forgery,

16. *QSL* JQ 252, 23b–24b, 16/12/28; on this case see Chen, "Ji Xu Song Qianshu Shi." The prominence of Xu's connections raises the possibility that his exile was politically motivated.

17. *SYD* (B) QL 59/4/27, 206–207.

18. See *Qingshi Liezhuan* 27, 39b.

19. *SYD* (B) QL 59/4/27, 248; 251–252, 256–259, 265, 275–276; 283; *GZD* JQ 15621, 19/6/5.

20. *QSL* QL 1486, 34b–35a, 60/9/9. Yade, who seems to have been associated with Heshen, had a chequered career. In 1786, under sentence of death on charges of corruption, he was pardoned and sent to a post in Ush (in Xinjiang). In that year a "self-imposed fine" (see chapter 9) amounting to 60,000 taels was paid on his behalf. In 1788 he was again sentenced to death for having failed, as governor-general, to supervise Chai Daji properly; after paying a further "fine" of 50,000 taels, he was again pardoned. A later impeachment

for example, allowing unauthorized parties to use the official seal (to certify land contracts); others were guilty of such offenses as accepting bribes, swindling, smuggling, and price-fixing.[21]

Corruption, ordinarily not a threat to the polity, took on a political hue when it was conducted on so large a scale that it threatened the flow of national revenues. Large-scale corruption could involve execution for the principal culprits and the banishment of their sons by virtue of collective responsibility. The case that established the precedent for banishment in such circumstances occurred in 1781 when evidence of massive corruption in Gansu was uncovered.

Misappropriations from military supplies intended for the suppression of a Muslim uprising and the embezzlement of emergency funds advanced to relieve a nonexistent famine combined to produce a serious depletion in the coffers of the Gansu provincial treasury. The discovery resulted in the execution of fifty-six ringleaders, and the conditional banishment through commutation of the death sentence of forty-six less culpable officials.[22] These forty-six banished officials were given a three-year grace period to repay the money (almost thirty thousand taels) they had misappropriated. Failing repayment they were to be executed, although ultimately they all escaped that fate.[23]

---

resulted in a sentence of banishment to Ili, but he was permitted to stay in Beijing on grounds of age. In 1791 he was given rank and employed at Kashgar, but two years later he had to return at his own expense to present himself for punishment in a case relating to the sensitive issue of Muslims. *SYD* (B) 59/6/n.d., 289. Subsequently he returned to take up various posts in Xinjiang and was working at Yarkand in 1795 when the discovery that he had extorted money from the salt merchants led to his banishment to Ili. On small-scale extortion, see *GZDQLCZZ* vol. 29, 852–853, QL 33/3/4, *SYD* (B) QL 59/4/27, 253.

21. *SYD* (B) QL 59/4/27, 244–248; 263; 266.

22. For the law under which sentence was passed, see *DLCY* 264–06. This involved theft from the government of at least 1,000 taels. When the sum involved exceeded 10,000 taels, as in this case, the offender was ineligible for amnesty. *DLCY* 16–10.

23. *SYD* (T) QL 48/1/9, 137–153. When some of the banished officials complained that the time limit was too short owing to the difficulty of communicating with their homes from the frontier, their requests to their families were ordered transmitted under Grand Council auspices. The governors of their respective native provinces were to attempt to secure a written guarantee of repayment from the officials' families (*SYD* [T] QL 48/10/1, 363–364). Yet shortly before the time limit expired, all the money had been neither repaid nor guaranteed (*SYD* [T] QL 50/10/n.d., 15–16); it is unclear whether the entire amount was ever repaid. These exiles were allowed home in 1794 (*SYD* [B] JQ 11/11/20, 261–263). The existence of monuments at Qiqihar, Heilongjiang, to some of these exiles was noted by a Manchu official stationed there in the Jiaqing reign (Xiqing, "Heilongjiang Waiji," 31b), indicating that they did not sink into obscurity.

The sons of the executed ringleaders in the Gansu case were held collectively responsible for their father's crimes. Of the eleven sons of the principal culprit, Wang Danwang, three were banished to Xinjiang,[24] together with the sons of at least eleven of the other main offenders.[25] The remaining eight sons of Wang Danwang, all of whom were less than five years old, were ordered imprisoned at the Board of Punishments in Beijing until they were eleven years of age, which was regarded as old enough for them to follow their brothers. Initially the eight children were detained in the yamen of the judicial commissioner of Shanxi, Wang Danwang's native province. However, the problems caused by their presence and the influx of female relatives and nursemaids soon prompted a plea for their removal to some other place of detention, and as a result they were transferred to Beijing.[26] The under-age sons of at least twelve other officials executed in the Gansu case were treated in the same way as Wang Danwang's sons; the absence of statutory provision for collective responsibility in such cases suggests that the ancient doctrine was invoked on a case-by-case basis, a practice that offered tremendous scope for abuse.[27]

This case alone led to twenty little boys being incarcerated at the Board of Punishments for several years preparatory to their banishment. In addition, in particular during the late Qianlong period, numerous other sons of disgraced officials whose fall from grace was due to corruption or political misfortune—or a combination—were punished in accordance with the precedent established in the Gansu case.[28] The precedent

24. *SYD* (T) 46/8/8, 644; *QSL* 1138, 17b, 46/8/8. Collectively responsible sons and grandsons were normally enslaved, but those banished in the Gansu case were not, presumably because of their fathers' erstwhile position.

25. *QSL* QL 1141, 20a, 46/9/27; *GZD* QL 40625, 47/1/18. The sons of the ringleaders in a contemporaneous (and possibly connected) corruption case that took place at Ürümqi were ordered punished in the same way as the sons of the officials in the Gansu case. See *SYD* (T) QL 47/7/4, 47.

26. *SYD* (T) QL 46/8/25, 138–139; *GZD* 39177, 46/9/6; *QSL* QL 46/9/18, 1141, 8a–9a.

27. *SYD* (T) QL 46/11/3, 376–377; *GZD* QL 40625, 47/1/18. For the law, see *DLCY* 264–06.

28. See, e.g., *QSL* QL 1316, 16a, 53/11/7. In 1789 two of the sons of Chai Daji (see text accompanying n. 8), aged two and four, were imprisoned in Beijing pending their majority. *SYD* (T) 54/6/28, 681. An unknown number of other boys, the sons of rebellious, corrupt, or murderous fathers, also were imprisoned at the Board of Punishments until they attained the legal age for castration or banishment. Although the prison at the Board of Punishments included separate quarters for women prisoners, there is no evidence of a children's prison.

appears to have lapsed into desuetude in the nineteenth century, although it continued to be invoked from time to time.[29]

The general downturn in dynastic fortunes, a development clearly connected to court politics, also affected the fate of individuals. For instance, as the impotence of Qing military forces led to a series of setbacks in the national and regional campaigns of the late eighteenth century, culminating in the drawn-out debacle of the White Lotus Rebellion, those in need of plausible scapegoats found that officials charged with the suppression of "bandits," a term that included sectarian rebels, were the most obvious candidates. Thus social unrest helped increase the number of officials sentenced to banishment.[30]

Another factor in the growth of official banishment was the increasingly tenacious attempts by Western powers to open contacts with China in the late eighteenth and early nineteenth centuries. Unsatisfactory management of foreigners was clearly a political offense in that it exposed the state to great peril.

One of the earliest Chinese officials to be exiled for this reason was Wu Xiongguang, then governor-general of Guangdong and Guangxi provinces. Wu was banished to Ili in 1808 after a confrontation with the British. Thirteen British warships landed several hundred soldiers at Macao and occupied a fort on the pretext of protecting Portuguese colonists from the French navy.[31] Wu refused to permit British merchants at Guangzhou to release their cargoes until these troops departed, which in due course they did. He was punished for not dealing with the British sternly enough to preclude a recurrence.[32]

Wu's banishment may have been connected to his earlier unfriendly relationship with the Heshen clique.[33] His case foreshadowed that of one of the most famous Qing officials, Lin Zexu (1785–1850), the imperial commissioner charged with solving the opium problem on the southeast

---

29. QSL JQ 319, 10a–b, 22/4/9.

30. SYD (B) 59/4/27, 211, 221, 224, 227, 264; Hong, "Wanli Hege Ji," 3a; QSL JQ 55, 19a–20a, 4/11/24; QSL JQ 66, 17b–19a, 5/i4/29; QSL JQ 125, 19a–20a, 9/1/19; JFJL 15, 9b, JQ 18/10/29.

31. England and France were then engaged in the Napoleonic Wars.

32. See the documents on this case translated by Fu, A Documentary Chronicle of Sino-Western Relations, 1644–1820, 369–374, and Wu's biography in Qing Shi Gao 357, pp. 11323–11324. ECCP 684 gives the date of Wu's exile as 1809.

33. See Mann Jones and Kuhn, "Dynastic Decline and the Roots of Rebellion," 117.

coast in the 1830s and 1840s. Lin was exiled to Xinjiang in 1842 for his failure to deal effectively with the British opium traders.[34]

Others exiled for their unsatisfactory dealings with foreigners included at least five of the merchants authorized to act as exclusive agents for foreign trade at Canton, the so-called Hong merchants. They were punished following their bankruptcies that resulted from their commerce with British merchants.[35] The law under which they were sentenced penalized commercial relations with foreigners that risked inspiring unruliness and thus potentially endangering the state; after 1760 this law was extended to apply specifically to Hong merchants indebted to foreigners. Thus the nature of their offense bordered, at least, on political territory.[36]

There was a certain irony in banishing men guilty of inadequacy in their dealings with "barbarians" on one frontier—the southeast coast—to another frontier—Xinjiang—where as part of their punishment they frequently had to cope with other "barbarians," in the form of ethnic minorities resistant to absorption into Chinese civilization. Apparently Qing policy makers were oblivious to this irony.

The general decline in bureaucratic morale and integrity that marked late eighteenth-century China produced another substantial group among the exiled officials in Xinjiang: all those banished for various types of misfeasance and malfeasance in office. Many were banished for mishandling judicial matters—for example, failing to make adequate investigations, failing to make arrests, failing to prevent prisoners from escaping or dying in custody, delaying trials, refusing to hear cases, con-

---

34. *QSL* Daoguang 352, 9a–10a, 21/3/10.

35. *QSL* QL 41/11/25, 1021, 8b–10a, translated by Fu, *Documentary Chronicle,* 276–277 (Ni Hongwen, known to the British as Wayqua); *Yuehaiguan Zhi* 26, 8b–9a, QL 45/6/n.d. (Fu, 291–292): Yan Shiying and Zhang Tianqiu, known to the British as Yngshaw and Kewshaw; *QSL* QL 56/4/29, 1377, 25a–26b, (Fu, 317–318): Wu Zhaoping, known as Eegua. "Wyequa," the brother of the bankrupt Hong merchant "Shy Kinqua" (identified as Shi Zhonghe), set off for banishment in Ili on QL 60/12/1; See Morse *The Chronicles of the East India Company Trading to China 1635–1834* 2:271. Citing Morse, Fu states that Shi Zhonghe died in jail before his departure (Fu, 586). See, however, *ZPZZ* JQ 9/12/23 (law—exile, packet for JQ 1–9), memorial of Weishibu, requesting permission for "banished Hong merchant Shi Zhonghe" to return home.

36. *DLCY* 224–01; *Yuehaiguan Zhi* 26, 8b–9a; Morse, *The East India Company* 2:53–54. To a later British observer, the Chinese government's virtual guarantee of the Hong merchants' debts to foreigners seemed a quid pro quo for the restrictions imposed by the Canton system. Edwards, "Ch'ing Legal Jurisdiction over Foreigners," 238.

ducting hearings in a prejudicial manner, permitting illegal private settlement of cases,[37] and forcing false confessions through excessive torture.[38] Most of those banished for these crimes were county magistrates (*zhixian*); a few were jail wardens (*dianshi*).

Frequently, officials were banished because they failed to prevent their subordinates from breaking the law; in many cases the crimes of the subordinates paralleled the crimes for which other officials themselves were banished, for instance extortion, embezzlement and accepting bribes.[39] Others failed to report illegal activities of which they knew or should have known.[40] In such cases punishment constituted a form of collective responsibility; the exiles were held responsible for the acts of others.

Still others were punished because of deficits that they had either caused directly or had neglected to rectify; the amount of the missing funds was not always as important as the mere existence of a shortfall. The scholar Qi Yunshi was banished in 1805 because of discrepancies in the coinage office where he worked;[41] Zhili governor-general Yan Jian was banished in 1806 after huge treasury deficits were uncovered there.[42] A few officials were banished simply because they were lazy or incompetent.[43]

A final group of officials were banished for cases involving personal

37. *SYD* (B) QL 59/4/27, 207, 224, 227, 240–241, 248–249, 252, 255, and 256. See also *GZDQLCZZ* vol. 20, 456–457, 29/2/1. Officials were responsible for the death of a prisoner in custody whether the death resulted from mistreatment, lack of medical care, or suicide.

38. *SYD* (B) QL 59/4/27, 273. See also *SYD* (B) JQ 11/8/14, 195–196; *GZD* JQ 18029, 20/3/4; *GZD* JQ 19265, 20/7/6. The size and weight of instruments of torture were closely regulated by law.

39. For a sampling of such cases, see *SYD* (B) QL 59/4/27, 214 (clerk made false real estate contracts with a forged seal); 224 (clerk practiced extortion in connection with relief work); 242–243 (soldiers discovered in league with gang of robbers). See also *QSL* JQ 75, 18b–19a, 5/10/15 (magistrate's servants and clerks caused such trouble they provoked rebellion by local sectarians).

40. *SYD* (B) QL 59/4/27, 231 (failure to report a predecessor's corruption, which had resulted in a suicide; predecessor sentenced to strangulation). See also *GZD* JQ 10067, 13/2/25 (concealing the escape from prison of major criminal who then joined a robber gang); *SYD* (B) JQ 16/7/18, 213 (failure to report mass sect activity).

41. *ECCP* 134.

42. *QSL* JQ 166, 19b–24a, 11/9/9. Several other senior provincial officials were banished in the same case.

43. *SYD* (B) QL 59/4/27, 236–237; *SYD* (B) JQ 12/7/24, 270–272 (laziness or incompetence); *SYD* (B) QL 59/4/27, 206, 213 (delays in copper transport), and 197 (procrastination leading to spoilage of sacrificial silk).

injury, both injury they inflicted and injury resulting from actions taken under their orders.[44] Into this category, for example, come suicides induced by such harassment as extortionate demands made by subordinates with the official's knowledge or overzealous interrogation of a witness.[45]

The range of crimes that could lead to the banishment of disgraced government officials to Xinjiang shows that this punishment touched the lives of officials at every level of the administration, from the high-ranking governors-general (*zongdu*) whose jurisdiction covered one or more provinces to unranked county jail wardens. The Qing referred to all such exiles, irrespective of their former positions, as "criminal officials" (*guanfan*) or "discarded officers" (*feiyuan*).

Among the most senior provincial officials, at least 12 governors-general out of the 118 who served in the office between 1758 and 1820 (more than 10 percent) were banished to Xinjiang.[46] The post of provincial governor was also a perilous one: at least 14 of the more than 250 persons holding that office during this period (between 5 and 6 percent) were banished to Xinjiang.[47] Six of the 15 governors and 1 of the 8 governors-general in office when Heshen fell from power were among those banished within the next few years, in some cases after having first been promoted.[48]

The combination of different circumstances that could lead to a sentence of banishment was beyond the control of many officials, and the

44. *SYD* (T) QL 41/2/12, 131 (eunuch killed a gardener).
45. *SYD* (B) QL 59/4/27 251, 260, 268, 269, 280, *SYD* (B) JQ 12/7/24, 270.
46. These were Aibida, Wenshou, Fulehun, Muhelin, Yade, Yude, Qingbao, Yan Jian, Wu Xiongguang, Nayancheng, Tiebao, and Yimian; all had attained the governor-generalship before their exile. Others attained it subsequent to a period of frontier banishment, e.g., Fang Shouchou.
47. These were Asiha, Zhou Wan, Wu Shigong, Changjun, Chen Huai, Qin Cheng'en, Yijiang'a, Hening, Weishibu, Gaoqi, Zhang Chengji, Changling, Jing'an, and Wenning. All these named officials were banished from the governorship; others who held this post had served sentences of banishment prior to their promotion. Examples include Li Luanxuan and Taifeiyin. A fifteenth, Kang Jitian, was sentenced to frontier banishment in 1790 for inaccurate memorializing. Perhaps as the result of his political connections, he was permitted to redeem his crime and was demoted to a junior position in water conservancy. See *Qing Shi Gao* 360, p. 11369.
48. The governors were Yijiang'a, Weishibu, Qin Cheng'en, Gaoqi, Zhang Chengji, and Yude, who was promoted to a governor-generalship before being disgraced. Yimian had been governor-general of Shaanxi and Gansu provinces. A seventh governor, Jiang Sheng, was promoted to a governor-generalship but dismissed two years later and sent to work on a water conservancy project.

more junior a bureaucrat, the less likely he was to be able to invoke political influence to save himself. Thus it is not surprising that by far the largest single group of officials to be banished to Xinjiang consisted of county magistrates, among the most junior of centrally appointed civil officials.[49] The disproportionately high number of magistrates banished reflected the inherent difficulty of meeting the complex demands of a post that became more and more unmanageable with the population growth of the late eighteenth century, as well as their relative lack of political influence.

Most exiled magistrates were Han Chinese, in part because of a deliberate policy of using Han Chinese for that position because such officials came into contact with ordinary people to a far greater extent than did most of their superiors. By contrast, the majority of provincial governors-general and governors banished to Xinjiang were Manchus, a statistic that is hardly surprising given that at this time Manchus held more than half these senior positions.[50] Since more junior than senior officials were banished, Han Chinese constituted the majority among Xinjiang feiyuan, as they did nationally. Unfortunately, available information is insufficient for a precise breakdown of the ethnic composition of officials banished to Xinjiang.

It was not only civilian officials who were banished to Xinjiang. During the Qianlong reign, considerably more military than civilian officials were banished, a statistic that reflects the growing challenge to the forces of law and order in the late eighteenth century. An early nineteenth-century gazetteer of the Ürümqi area that lists exiles sent there from 1760 to 1807 suggests that this trend may have been reversed in the early Jiaqing reign, presumably due to the ever-growing volatility of political life.[51]

Senior military officials were banished to Xinjiang less often than their senior civilian counterparts, perhaps because military positions tended to carry less prestige and less power and hence tended to be less vulnerable to politically motivated attack. They were not immune, however. In 1795 the great strategist Mingliang, then the ranking official in Xinjiang—Ili

---

49. This statistic contradicts a recent suggestion that the administrative regulations were effective tools of control in part because they correlated severity of punishment only to the seriousness of offence and not to the status of the offender, in contrast to other traditional Chinese law. Metzger, *Internal Organization*, 337.

50. See Kessler, "Ethnic Composition of Provincial Leadership during the Qing period."

51. *SZJL* 220–233; on this text see chapter 2, n. 63.

military governor (*jiangjun*)—was demoted and transferred as an exile to the regional center at Ürümqi for forcing troops to sell him goods at favorable prices. However, the hard-pressed imperial military forces found Mingliang's services indispensable, and he was shortly reinstated to military office to assist in the suppression of a Miao uprising.[52]

As with civilian officials, the most frequently banished military officials held a low bureaucratic rank that belied their responsibilities. Many were lieutenants in the Chinese Green Standard army (*qianzong*). The majority of banished military officials were officers in that army rather than of the Manchu banner troops. This difference arose from the fact that the Green Standard troops were often charged with tricky local peacekeeping duties for which they were inadequately equipped, whereas the banners' military presence in the provinces tended to have more symbolic than actual force.[53]

Tables 1 and 2 list the positions that officials banished to Xinjiang held prior to their banishment. The information in these tables is drawn from a study of several hundred cases that occurred between 1758 and 1820 and is confirmed by figures drawn from a single document dating from 1794. In that year the Grand Council, in response to an edict ordering a general review of the cases of officials serving sentences of banishment in Xinjiang, made proposals regarding the fate of 260 such exiles.[54] These officials, exiled for a variety of reasons over the preceding three decades, can be taken as typical of those banished to Xinjiang during the course of the sixty-odd years from 1758 to 1820.

The vast majority of banished officials was employed in provincial posts. Some provinces were more troublesome than others and hence were particularly well represented among banished officials. Indeed, by a substantial margin, more officials were banished from Fujian, including Taiwan, than from any other province, even if one discounts a single group of forty-seven low-ranking military officers banished in 1789 in the wake of a Taiwan customs scandal. Table 3 lists the provinces from which officials serving their terms in Xinjiang in 1794 had been banished.

Many of the men included in the "unknown" category in table 2 were probably natives of Fujian, for many were lower-level military officials employed in that province, and unlike most civilian officials whose em-

---

52. *Qing Shi Gao* 330, p. 10931.
53. See Luo, *Lüyingbing Zhi*, 6; Murray, *Pirates of the South China Coast*, 100.
54. SYD (B) QL 59/4/27, 195–284.

Table 1. Positions Formerly Held by Civilian Officials in Exile
in Xinjiang in 1794

Chinese Term	No. in exile	English Equivalent	Rank
Zhixian	44	County Magistrate	7B
Dianshi	6	County Jailwarden	0
Tongpan	6	Second-class Subprefect	6A
Tongzhi	5	First-class Subprefect	5A
Xiancheng	5	Asst. Magistrate	8A
Xunjian	5	Subcounty Magistrate	9B
Bitieshi	4	Clerk	7–9
Zhizhou	4	Departmental Magistrate	5B
Zhifu	3	Prefect	4B
Xundao	2	Subdirector of Schools	8B
Zhaomo	2	Correspondence Secretary	8B
Bagong	1	First-class Senior Licentiate	0
Beg	1	(Xinjiang Muslim official)	6
Buzhengshi	1	Financial Commissioner	2B
Dianda	1	Palace Official	(?)
Jiaoxi	1	Teacher	0
Jiaoyu	1	Schools Director	8A
Langzhong	1	Departmental Director	5A
Yandashi	1	Tea/Salt Official Examiner	0
Zhongshu	1	Grand Secretariat Clerk	7B
Zhoutong	1	First-class Asst. Dept. Magistrate	6B
Others[a]	5		

[a] The five others were one imperial family member (*zongshi*), one imperial clan member (*Gioro*) employed in the Banqueting Department, one recidivist *feiyuan*, one merchant (*zongshang*), and Chai Dajing, brother of Chai Daji.

ployment was governed by the law of avoidance, such soldiers usually worked close to home.[55]

The predominance of Fujian as a source of banished officials primarily reflects the high level of unrest on Taiwan in the late eighteenth century. For the most part, this took the form of feuding between settlers who had moved to Taiwan from Zhangzhou and Quanzhou on the mainland; the

55. Shepherd, "Plains Aborigines," 192–193, notes that Green Standard troops deployed in Taiwan were, unusually, not Taiwan natives but came from mainland Fujian on a rotating basis because of the court's distrust of Taiwanese settlers and their rebel past, for "stricter control could be exercised over mainland soldiers who left their families behind to serve temporarily in Taiwan."

Table 2. Positions Formerly Held by Military Officials in Exile
in Xinjiang in 1794

Chinese Term	No. in exile	English Equivalent	Rank
Qianzong	39	Green Standard Lieutenant	6A
Bazong	17	Green Standard Sub-lieutenant	7A
Waiwei	17	Green Standard Corporal (?)	8/9(?)
Youji	16	Green Standard Major	3B
Shoubei	13	Green Standard Second Captain	5B
Zongbing	10	Green Standard Brigade General	2A
Canjiang	8	Green Standard Lieutenant Colonel	3A
Fujiang	8	Green Standard Colonel	2B
Xiefujiang	4	Green Standard Assistant Colonel (?)	
Dusi	3	Green Standard First Captain	4A
Junxiao	3	Banner Adjutant (?)	(?)
Xiaoqixiao	3	Banner Lieutenant	6A
Qianzongwaiwei	2	Green Standard Ensign	8A
Xieling	2	Regimental Colonel, Provincial Banner Garrison	3B
Canling	1	Banner Regimental Commander	3A
Ewaiwaiwei	1	Green Standard Sergeant	9B
Fangyu	1	Banner Platoon Captain	5A
Fudutong	1	Banner Brigade General	2A
Jiduwei	1	Cavalry Commandant; Nobleman	7
Tidu	1	Green Standard Provincial Commander-in-Chief	1B
Xiaoqi	1	First-class Banner Private	
Zhanyuan	1	Postal Station Inspector	

Table 3. Provinces from which Disgraced Officials in Xinjiang
in 1794 Had Been Banished

Fujian	85	Beijing	4
Zhejiang	22	Shanxi	3
Jiangsu	16	Anhui	3
Hubei	13	Henan	3
Guangdong	8	Sichuan	3
Xinjiang	7	Guangxi	3
Fengtian	6	Hunan	2
Shandong	6	Mongolia	2
Zhili	5	Northeast	1
Gansu	5	Shaanxi	0
Yunnan	5	No Post	2
Jiangxi	5	Unknown	47
Guizhou	4		

Source: SYD (B) 59/4/27, 195–284.

rebellion of Lin Shuangwen on Taiwan in 1786–87 also resulted in the banishment of a considerable number of officials.

The second most prolific source of exiled officials was the southeastern coastal province of Zhejiang with twenty-two, followed by Jiangsu, with sixteen. This was attributable in large measure to the growth of coastal and river piracy, a problem whose suppression was primarily the responsibility of Green Standard troops. Officials formerly employed in these two coastal provinces and in neighboring Fujian accounted for almost half the total number of banished officials; perhaps their transfer from the southeastern coast to the desert terrain of the northwest frontier had its own peculiar logic. Other than Hubei province, from which thirteen officials had been banished, no other province was represented by more than eight banished officials.[56]

ORDINARY CONVICTS

The convict population in Xinjiang came from all over China. Although there is no consistent and complete source giving the numbers annually sent from each province, annual provincial reports detailing convicts' escapes, many of which still survive, sometimes included this information. Among those banished in 1763, for instance, were fourteen from Zhejiang, eight each from Henan and Yunnan, eight (plus four family members) from Guangdong, seven from Shandong, six each from Guizhou and Sichuan, five each from Anhui and Jiangxi, three from Hunan, and none from Fujian.[57] In 1788 Jiangxi reported thirty-two criminals banished to Xinjiang not only from Jiangxi but also from

56. *SYD* (B) QL 59/4/27, 195–284.
57. These reports are in *GZDQLCZZ* vol. 20, 86, 28/12/15 (Guizhou); 280, 29/1/10 (Fujian); 382, 29/1/21 (Zhejiang); 453, 29/1/30 (Guangdong); 456–457, 29/2/1 (Yunnan); 532–533, 29/2/10 (Hunan); 619–620, 29/2/20 (Shandong); 661, 29/2/24 (Henan); 669, 29/2/25, (Jiangxi); vol. 21, 13, 29/3/25, (Anhui). Most reports do not give details of family members who accompanied criminals into exile. Given the fact that the annual number of convicts sent to Xinjiang at this time was at least several hundred, presumably many more were sent that year from other provinces. Among those banished in 1788 were 217 people from Henan banished "to Xinjiang" but this figure included "changees"—convicts whose crimes were serious enough to make them liable for Xinjiang banishment but who for policy reasons were exiled elsewhere. *GZD* QL 56266, 54/1/15. Zhejiang (58), Guangdong (65), and Guangxi (16) gave similarly undifferentiated figures for that year. *GZD* QL 56378, 54/1/26 (Zhejiang); 56424, 54/1/29 (Guangdong); 56208, 54/1/6 (Guangxi).

Fujian and Guangdong; convicts from the latter two provinces passed through Jiangxi on their way into exile.[58] Yunnan banished sixteen criminals to Xinjiang, Hubei banished fifteen, Hunan nine, and Shandong two in 1788.[59]

The largest single group of Xinjiang convicts were banished in the wake of the many rebellions of the late eighteenth and early nineteenth centuries. Thus, for instance, ninety-seven collectively responsible relatives of Suonuomu, one of the leaders of the aboriginal Jinchuan rebellion, were exiled to Ili in 1776. Fifty-two of these were enslaved to the Ölöds and the other forty-five to the Solon troops.[60] In the following year, the wives and children of forty-one accessories in a Muslim uprising in Gansu province were exiled to Ürümqi, despite the general reluctance to banish Muslims to Xinjiang.[61]

Many of the late eighteenth- and early nineteenth-century uprisings expressed the millenarian aspirations of heterodox religious sects (*xie jiao*), one expression of the spreading disillusion of the times. The rebellion laws applied to these uprisings, but even peaceful sect activity was banned by separate laws directed primarily against indigenous sects based on a mixture of folk Buddhism and Daoism.[62] The latter provisions stipulated the execution of principals and the banishment of secondary offenders but did not mention collective responsibility. That doctrine therefore applied to sect participants only when rebellion was involved.

A few examples give some sense of the waves of sect offenders

58. *GZD* QL 56346, 54/1/22.

59. *GZD* QL 56358, 54/1/25 (Yunnan); 56307 54/1/19 (Hubei); 56304, 54/1/19 (Hunan); 56431, 54/2/2 (Shandong). None of these figures includes ordinary *jun* or *liu* criminals sentenced to exile within China proper.

60. *QSL* QL 1008, 10a–11b, 41/5/2. Thirty-four others involved in the Jinchuan rebellion directly or by virtue of collective responsibility were banished to the northeast; fifty-eight more were enslaved to the families of meritorious officials and fifteen lamas were sent to a lamasery in Jiangning. Sixteen others were imprisoned for life for involvement in the rebellion. Those executed included Suonuomu's mother; his daughter was sentenced to life imprisonment at the Board of Punishments in Beijing. *QSL* QL 1007, 10b–11a, 41/4/22. The principal offenders were of course executed.

61. *GZDQLCZZ* vol. 41, 426–428, 42/12/15. The reluctance was later made into law: see *DLCY* 45–27, passed in 1787; *DLCY* 45–38, passed in 1806, and see chapter 4.

62. *DLCY* 162. Chinese law did not treat Islam as a heterodox sect but more or less tolerated it unless it gave rise to overt disruption, in which case the rebellion laws applied. However, some laws were specifically directed against antisocial Muslim behavior. See, e.g., on Muslim robber gangs, *DLCY* 268–17.

banished in the late eighteenth and early nineteenth centuries. The vast majority was sent to Xinjiang; the despatch of some sect exiles to other destinations reflected the wish to prevent undue accumulations of like-minded people in a single location. Thus in 1774, after the suppression of Wang Lun's uprising in Shandong, nearly two thousand of his followers were sentenced either to execution or to banishment, variously to the northeast, to Ili, or to the far south of China proper.[63] In 1782 more than a thousand people were exiled to Ili and Heilongjiang from Shandong and Henan provinces in several cases involving religious sects.[64] Six years later, more than fifty additional sect followers in Henan were sentenced to slavery in the southern Xinjiang cities of Aksu, Yarkand, and Kashgar.[65] They were sent to southern Xinjiang in part from a general desire to isolate them and in part as a means of using one religion to control another; the hope was that placing them in a predominantly Muslim setting would discourage them from continuing their practices.[66] Other sectarian exiles included more than one hundred people involved in sect activities in Shaanxi province in 1794, during the preamble to the great White Lotus Rebellion. Many more were probably banished to Xinjiang and other destinations in the wake of this protracted disturbance.[67] The last great sectarian outbreak of this period, the Eight Trigrams uprising of 1813, swelled the ranks of such convicts in Xinjiang by at least another one hundred.[68]

---

63. One group of 544 was banished "as appropriate" (*fenbie*)—some were probably sent to Xinjiang, some to the northeast, and some to the south. *Qinding Jiaobu Linqing Nifei Jilüe* 11, 5a, cited by Naquin, *Shantung Rebellion*, 204. Another group (conceivably involving some overlap with the first) of 1,372 was sentenced to execution and banishment to the three destinations. *QSL* QL 968, 24a–b, 39/10/4.

64. *SYD* (T) QL 461, 47/5/22 (1,000 people); *QSL* QL 1159, 24a–b, 47/6/29 (72 people).

65. *QSL* QL 1306, 34b–35b, 53/6/13. Some of the dozen or more sect members discovered practicing their religion in these places of exile a few years later may well have been in this group. See chapter 8.

66. *QSL* QL 1382, 26a, 56/7/13.

67. *QSL* QL 1461, at 15b, 59/9/20. See QSL JQ 39, 19a–b, 4/2/6, where a detailed ruling affecting the banishment of the collectively responsible wives and children of sect rebels (*jiaofei*) suggests a high incidence of such cases within the preceding few years.

68. For some of their sentences, see *JFJL* 7, 34b (JQ 18/9/30: 3 banished because of collective responsibility); 12, 17b–18a (JQ 18/10/18: 27 members of a Red Sun sect, together with 3 other sect followers); 22, 25a–b (JQ 18/11/27: 8 men and women sect followers and 2 collectively responsible people); 27, 42a–b (JQ 18/12/20: 5 more sent to Xinjiang for the same reason, and 5 others who had quit the sect but had not "shown repentance by turning themselves in"); 33, 16b (JQ 19/1/27: 8 sect followers); 36, 2a (JQ

From the 1770s, the law proscribing religious sects was invoked against Catholicism as well as the indigenous religious groups.[69] This development reflected both the rise of increasingly militant native sects, a situation that tended to activate the government's worst apprehensions, and the Qing's failure to distinguish Catholicism from Islam, then increasingly unruly, and from other forms of heterodoxy. Thus in 1770 a bannerman convert discovered actively practicing Catholicism in the capital was banished to Ili.[70] This incident was followed by a number of others. In 1805, for instance, after the discovery of a map prepared for the Pope, showing the distribution of Catholic converts in China, thirteen people were banished to Xinjiang. Two were distant cousins of the emperor; their names were excised from the imperial genealogy. The names of two other bannermen involved in the same case were removed from their banner register. All four were condemned to wear the wooden frame known as the cangue (*jia hao*) for several months prior to their exile and were forever banned from returning home.[71] The other nine, converts and confederates in Guangzhou of Adeodato, the Italian missionary in whose possession the map was found, were sentenced to slavery in Ili after spending three months in the cangue.[72] Adeodato was

---

19/2/12: 8 more); 36, 7b (JQ 19/2/14: a person introduced into the sect by a deceased relative); 41, 27b (JQ 19/11/15: 1 person who had hidden a rebel's son); 42, 3a–b (JQ 20/2/6: 4 women, both collectively responsible and sect followers in their own right); 42, 4a–b (JQ 20/2/29: 2 harborers of rebels). Another source records 25 more, including 2 palace gatekeepers and a eunuch, sentenced under various statutes: "Linqing Jiao'an," in *Gugong Zhoukan* 223, 3, JQ 18/10/17. Some of these sentences are cited by Naquin, *Millenarian Rebellion in China*, 341, and by de Groot, *Sectarianism and Religious Persecution in China*, 427–428.

69. Chinese acquaintance with Christianity was more or less limited to Catholicism until Robert Morrison, the first Protestant missionary in China, arrived in 1807. Until the Taipings in the mid-nineteenth century, no Chinese rebellion drew its inspiration from Christianity. A substatute directed specifically against Christianity (*DLCY* 162–08) was passed only in 1860.

70. Fu, *Documentary Chronicle*, 252.

71. *QSL* JQ 146, 21b–22a, 10/16/19, translated by Fu, *Documentary Chronicle*, 357–358. Of the four, three died in exile; a hesitant request to allow home the fourth was rejected in late 1814. Earlier the Board of Punishments had refused to submit to the emperor a similar request made on the exile's behalf, because of the original prohibition. The Board agreed to forward the request in 1814 because the exile's aged mother had no one else to support her. *GZD* JQ 16928, 19/11/17; *QSL* JQ 19/12/14, 300, 23b–24a.

72. *QSL* JQ 10/4/30, 142, 33b–36a, translated by Fu, *Documentary Chronicle*, 352–354.

ordered confined in Rehe under Ölöd supervision; he remained there for four years.[73]

Piracy (*haidao*) and to a lesser extent communal feuding (*xiedou*), both of which were increasingly widespread in south and southeast China during this period, were the other principal crimes that gave rise to the banishment of large groups of convicts to Xinjiang. The Qing response to these types of outlawry depended on such circumstances as the number of people involved, the weapons used and the extent of injuries inflicted. In the most serious cases, offenders were put to death and their relatives punished as collectively responsible, probably because large-scale piracy seemed to the authorities to be verging on insurrection. In less serious cases, only the principal offenders themselves were banished.[74]

Thus in two cases resolved within a period of two months in 1780, a total of 227 pirates operating off the coast of Guangzhou were executed and their relatives ordered into slavery in the northeast and Xinjiang.[75] The emperor noted that the sentence imposed in one of these cases was extraordinarily severe because of the exceptionally large number of people involved (about 150). These exiles were sent to different destinations because, as in the case of sectarian believers, officials were unwilling to banish so great a number of them to the same place for fear of a resurgence of lawbreaking. In 1794, however, almost as many actual pirates (145) were banished to Muslim cities in Xinjiang after spending three years in prison.[76] The somewhat inconsistent treatment of pirates illus-

73. *Qingdai Jiaqing Waijiao Shiliao*, 3, 20a. See also de Groot, *Sectarianism*, 394–395, citing the account of another missionary who encountered Adeodato in Manila in 1818. Adeodato had previously served as interpreter to members of Lord Macartney's mission to the Qianlong Emperor. Cranmer-Byng, *An Embassy to China*, 358, n. 9. For another example of Catholics banished to Xinjiang, see *QSL*, JQ 20/3/26, 304, 21b–22b, translated by Fu, *Documentary Chronicle*, 396–397; see also Entenmann, "Migration and Settlement in Sichuan, 1644–1796," 194–196.

74. The precise laws under which banishment was ordered were not always specified. When piracy or communal feuding were treated as a political threat and collective responsibility applied, the sentence was sometimes imposed by reference to the treason laws: see, e.g., *Mingqing Shiliao si* 10, 954–956, QL 48/4/21. In less serious cases, other laws, including those involving robbery, robbery with violence, plundering, or resisting the authorities (*DLCY* 266, 268, 269, 388) might apply, and then the doctrine of collective responsibility was not invoked.

75. See *SYD* (T) QL 45/6/19, 461; *SYD* (T) QL 45/8/16, 206.

76. Sixty-seven were from Zhejiang, sixty from Jiangsu, twelve from Fujian, and six from Guangdong. Thirty-nine had originally been imprisoned for life. *SYD* (B) 59/2/5, 45–46. For the law see *DLCY* 266, esp. 266–49. No record concerning punishment of the relatives of these exiled pirates has been found; when offenders were exiled rather than put to death, their relatives were not usually subject to punishment.

trated by these cases suggests that at the highest policy-making levels there was a degree of uncertainty concerning the appropriate handling of these particular offenders.[77]

Communal feuders seem to have been treated with a similar ambivalence.[78] In 1783, when a sublieutenant (*bazong*) investigating a communal feud was murdered in Taiwan, the principals were executed and their relatives held collectively responsible under the treason laws. Four peripherally involved people were banished to Ili by special order because they had done nothing to prevent the crime.[79] In the following year, however, almost three hundred communal feuders from Taiwan were themselves banished to Xinjiang.[80]

The banishment of criminals' families to Xinjiang through the application of collective responsibility also occurred in the case of massacre, particularly when the victims were members of a single family. This crime was considered political because it violated the cosmic order in traditional China and constituted an attack on the family, a central institution within the Chinese social structure.[81]

Punishment in massacre cases often reflected the important role of law as an instrument of requital. Thus in 1779 the three elder sons of the killer of four members of a family were sentenced to death. His wife and youngest son were banished to Ili as slaves to the Ölöds. The boy was spared in order that the number of those executed would not exceed the number of murder victims.[82]

In another massacre case concluded a few years later, a Xinjiang con-

---

77. For a study of piracy at this time, see Murray, *Pirates of the South China Coast, 1790–1910*.

78. See Lamley, "Subethnic Rivalry in the Ch'ing Period."

79. *Mingqing Shiliao, ji* 10, 954–956, QL 48/4/21. Some of the collectively responsible relatives in this case were probably banished to Xinjiang.

80. *SYD* (T) QL 49/2/18, 275. Ili military governor Yiletu's request that these feuders be sent to the insalubrious areas of the far south, because Xinjiang was already saturated with undesirables, was rejected. *SYD* (T) QL 49/8/20, 329–330. It may well have been their descendants whose presence west of Ürümqi was observed by Lin Zexu in 1842. Lin, "Hege Jicheng," 9b.

81. On concepts of cosmic order and the law, see Bodde and Morris, *Law in Imperial China*, 43–48; for another view, see Hsu, "Crime and Cosmic Order."

82. *HDSL* (1899) 803, 11b. In a 1783 case where six members of a single family had been murdered, the killer had also seduced the wife of his own eldest son. Because the son was regarded as having been wronged, his life was spared, though he was still condemned to castration, to be followed one hundred days later by banishment to Ürümqi. *SYD* (T) QL 48/3/9, 525–526. On the idea of law as requital, see Bodde and Morris, *Law in Imperial China*, 182–183.

vict slave testified (before he was slowly cut to death) that he had killed five members of his master's family because of their cruelty, and that he had one son who lived in his native province of Zhili. The emperor ordered a thorough search of that area in the belief that the killer had attempted to conceal the existence of other sons to shield them from punishment by virtue of collective responsibility.[83] The results of the search are unknown.

Although those banished in rebellion and sect cases, including those banished by virtue of collective responsibility, numerically constituted the largest group of convicts in Xinjiang, robbery and theft accounted for much the largest number of individual cases during this period when land shortages made the struggle for subsistence increasingly difficult. The crimes of these convicts were covered by several laws whose frequent and detailed amplification and amendment were indicative of their constant usage. The punishments stipulated by these laws varied by reference to a number of factors including, for instance, the value of the objects stolen and the degree of violence involved.[84]

Another substantial group of convicts was banished because they deserted from the army, a significant problem in the many military campaigns of the late eighteenth century. The major defeat of Qing forces in 1773 at the battle of Muguomu in Sichuan during the second Jinchuan campaign was blamed on deserters; the hundreds of troops who fled were ordered executed upon recapture. Not long afterwards this was modified because of the number involved (more than seven hundred were still at large in 1781)[85] and any deserter who voluntarily surrendered was banished to Xinjiang in lieu of execution. Two years later about one hundred had taken advantage of this offer of clemency, with a further

83. *SYD* (T) QL 53/3/27, 517–518. The convict slave had been banished because he had falsely accused someone of being a follower of Wang Lun. Punishment for false accusation reflected the punishment the falsely accused person had or would have received. *DLCY* 336.

84. The laws most frequently invoked were *DLCY* 266, robbery with violence (*qiangdao*); 268, plundering (*baizhou qiangduo*); and 269, stealing (*qiedao*)—all of these contained scores of substatutes. Cf. Chen, "Local Control of Convicted Thieves," 122, citing *HDSL* (1899), noting that banishment of thieves was said to have been infrequent. This may be true insofar as the total number of thieves eligible for banishment was concerned, nonetheless a high proportion of the Xinjiang convicts were thieves.

85. *SYD* (T) QL 46/2/27, 357. The order seems to date from earlier; see *Huangchao Xingfa Zhi* 13, QL 44/3. Certain deserters who turned themselves in had been banished to Xinjiang in 1773, but at that time this was apparently exceptional: see *QSL* QL 942, 20a–b, 38/9/9.

eighty-two following suit within the next twenty months.[86] Some other deserters, from, for instance, the Burmese campaign of 1766–1770, were resettled in Yunnan, Hunan, Sichuan, and Shaanxi and treated as criminals.[87]

Other commoners who were banished to Xinjiang in considerable numbers included counterfeiters who had supplied their illegal mint with metals stolen from government mines.[88] This crime was by no means a new one in China; counterfeiting had been punishable by banishment at least since the Han dynasty (221 B.C.–A.D. 220). Yet it experienced a resurgence from the late eighteenth century in response to such problems as the failure of copper production to match silver imports; the effort to monopolize coin production was an important part of Qing attempts to control price fluctuations.[89]

Some convicts were banished because they committed crimes while already serving a sentence of exile within China proper, or because they had escaped from such exile.[90] Others were exiled to Xinjiang after spending considerable time wearing the cangue; in 1768 three such people were banished.[91] A few convicts, particularly women, were banished for their involvement in murders. Thus in a matchmaking dispute, old Mrs. Zhao instigated a servant to kill his master.[92] Mrs. Bao Yang's lover killed her son,[93] and Mrs. Wang Li killed her son at her lover's urging.[94] All three women were banished to Xinjiang.

86. *QSL* QL 1173, 1b–2b, 48/1/16: "more than one hundred from Sichuan but very few from other provinces"; *SYD* (T) QL 49/9/15, 499–501. Deadlines for surrender were repeatedly extended.

87. See, e.g., *GZD* QL 28061, 39/2/4.

88. *SYD* (B) QL 59/9/10, 107–111. Not all those banished in this case were sent to Xinjiang, first because they were so numerous (200 or 300) and second because many White Lotus sect members were due to be banished at the same time. *QSL* QL 1460, 19a–23a, 59/9/9. Some were sent to "areas that do not produce copper" within China proper, including Fujian, Gansu, Guangdong, and Shaanxi provinces. *SYD* (B) QL 59/10/ n.d., 239.

89. See Vogel, "Ch'ing Central Monetary Policy, 1644–1800."

90. *GZDQLCZZ* vol. 20, 456–457, 29/2/1; vol. 23, 424, 29/12/7.

91. *Sanfasi* Archives no. 309, QL 33/12/16. At that time fifty-three others were then under a life sentence in the cangue; in addition, two had escaped, and three had died from illness during that year. For another example of banishment after ten years in the cangue, see *QSL* QL 1271, 20a–b, 51/12/26. For a law passed in 1786 that appears to have clarified this practice, see *DLCY* 45–36.

92. *QSL* QL 862, 1a–2b, 35/6/1. For the law, see *DLCY* 282.

93. *GZDQLCZZ* vol. 20, 669–670, 29/2/25.

94. *QSL* QL 916, 2a–3a, 37/9/1. The reason Mrs. Wang Li, a killer, received the same punishment as Mrs. Bao Yang, a collaborator in murder, was that traditional law assigned

The Xinjiang exiles spanned the entire spectrum of Qing society, reflecting the fact that the new availability of Xinjiang coincided with changing social and political conditions that were producing more offenders liable to banishment than there had ever been in the past. This development may also have been due in part to the possibility that Qing authorities, uncertain how best to deal with the crime wave, sometimes tended to resort to exile as a panacea.

Political offenses in Qing China often corresponded to of a group of particularly heinous crimes known as the ten great evils (*shi e*), although not all the ten great evils were necessarily political.[95] These crimes were rebellion (*mou fan*), treason (*mou dani*), disloyalty (*mou pan*), parricide (*e'ni*), massacre or murder by magical means (*bu dao*), great lack of respect (*da bu jing*), lack of filial piety (*bu xiao*), acute family discord (*bu mu*), incest (*bu yi*), and insurrection (*nei luan*). Moreover, each of the crimes to which collective responsibility applied was included in this list, with the exception of massive corruption, which was a political crime in another sense.

Some of the exiles had consciously and undeniably broken the law; others, matched in numbers perhaps by those who were never punished because they were protected by their political influence, were guilty of the more nebulous crime of political opposition in an environment intolerant of dissidence. Thus among the exiles banished for political reasons, some were simply on the wrong side of a factional dispute, and some peacefully adhered to beliefs and values incompatible with state orthodoxy. Others, however, had resorted to open criticism of the existing order, and a significant group had attempted armed uprisings, inspired on some occasions by heretical religious fervor.

Once in Xinjiang, the exiles seemed to replicate in microcosm Chinese society in the heartland, with the difference that they shared one general characteristic: they were all the objects of Qing disfavor.

---

to instigators the role of principal; in other words, Mrs. Wang Li's crime was considered secondary to that of her lover who urged her to commit it.

95. *DLCY* 2. For the sake of clarity, the English names given here for the ten great evils are not exact translations of the romanized terms but are descriptive titles based on the explanatory notes in the code.

Chapter Six

The Journey into Exile

On February 15, 1766, two prisoners arrived under escort in Nanping, Fujian, from the neighboring county of Gutian. One, Li Dangui, was an official (*guanfan*) traveling to Beijing to be tried on charges of embezzling state funds. The other, Yang Xiang, was a gangster from Taiwan, traveling into banishment in Xinjiang. On the next day, the two continued their journey: first Li, in a sedan chair, and later Yang, on foot.

Li's transmission papers included instructions to move him with all due speed. Thus Wang Tingxi, one of Li's escorts, who had accompanied him the entire journey, was anxious to leave Nanping as soon as possible. He persuaded the Nanping jail warden, to whom the magistrate, absent on other business, had delegated responsibility for the safe conduct of both prisoners, and a local color-sergeant, to travel with him in Li's party. Two local runners and two soldiers accompanied them. As a result Yang and his four escorts were left without direct supervision; on February 17, Yang escaped.

During the ensuing investigation, officials at first suspected that two of Yang's four escorts were illicit substitutes because their names were not included on his documents. It transpired that, because those whose names were on the documents were on river patrol, the head runner had assigned these two as replacements. A clerk in the yamen's justice section (*xingfang*) explained that he had not altered the documents to reflect this arrangement because any change would have required the magistrate's seal. To have obtained this would have run the risk of delaying transmission of the convict.

Yang's other assigned escorts were soldiers. One of these paid a bribe of 120 copper cash to another man to take his place; later the soldier testified that he had been too ill to go. However, the hired substitute was a servant of the color-sergeant accompanying Li Dangui and had departed with his master in the advance party. The other soldier developed stomach pains within twenty-four hours of leaving Nanping and was unable to proceed apace.

At nightfall on February 17, Yang and his two remaining escorts had reached neither the next yamen nor a government postal station. The escorts explained that the party advanced only thirteen miles that day because Yang had claimed to be too unwell to walk quickly. They found lodgings at a restaurant, although it did not normally provide accommodation. The escorts chained Yang to a post beside the bed; after the innkeeper bolted the doors, they went to sleep. The escorts awoke in the small hours to discover that Yang had escaped and raised a general alarm. Despite a long search, Yang was never found.[1]

Moving criminals across China was not a novel undertaking for the Qing government in the mid-eighteenth century. However, the unprecedented use of exiles as tools in the colonization of Xinjiang meant that their transfer involved special requirements. Although the chief concern was the exiles' arrival at their destination, it was almost as important to maintain them in reasonably good physical condition so that they could work effectively once in Xinjiang.

Consistent with the differential treatment they received in all aspects of life in Qing China, banished government officials were treated with much less harshness than common convicts bound for Xinjiang, on the assumption that their sense of honor made them relatively trustworthy. Nonetheless some of the same general problems faced the Qing as they conducted both groups of criminals in custody across China to Xinjiang.

THE ROUTE TO XINJIANG

Exiles were sent to Xinjiang from all over China. They did not necessarily travel by way of the capital, but their routes all converged in Gansu province, which forms a northwest corridor separating China proper

1. *XKTB* QL 31/6/23, packet 288, memorial of Suchang. See also text accompanying n. 118.

from Xinjiang.[2] Since, for security reasons, officials along the route into exile had to confirm the convict's safe arrival and onward transmission, there could be little flexibility in the travel arrangements. For this reason the exiles traveled via yamens located in administrative centers such as county towns, and not necessarily via the sometimes more direct government postal route.[3]

There were two main points of entry into Gansu, as map 3 shows. Most exiles crossed the border at the hill town of Changwu, on the Shaanxi border. From Changwu their route took them to Lanzhou, the provincial capital, by way of Jingzhou, Pingliang, Longde, Jingning, Huining, Anding, and Jinxian counties. Others entered Gansu by way of Qingshui, farther to the south. They crossed Qinzhou, Fuqiang, Ningyuan, Longxi, Weiyuan, and Didao counties on their way to Lanzhou.[4]

From Lanzhou the route to Xinjiang turned sharply north-northwest. The exiles crossed Pingfan, Gulang, Wuwei, Yongchang, Shandan, Zhangye, Fuyi, and Gaotai counties before reaching Suzhou, the last major center in China proper, which functioned as a border post where ordinary travelers bound for Xinjiang obtained travel passes for their journey beyond China proper.[5] Thence they proceeded through the pass at Jiayuguan, the western end of the Great Wall, which for many marked the boundary of civilization. As the scholar Ji Yun, journeying into exile in 1769, wrote to his wife, the territory beyond Jiayuguan was "another world."[6] This attitude lingered on seventy-three years later, when the lands beyond China proper still offered the exile a forbidding and alien prospect. Imperial commissioner Lin Zexu observed in his exile journal: "Everywhere I looked there was desert. There was no water or vegetation, not a tree in sight. In the distance there were mountains."[7]

From Jiayuguan the exiles proceeded by way of Anxi, near the Gansu-Xinjiang border, to Hami, the last principal oasis of their journey. From

2. During the Qing dynasty, Gansu included present-day Ningxia and part of present-day Qinghai.

3. Hong, "Ili Riji," 2b. On postal routes, see Cheng Ying-wan, *Postal Communication in China*, 12.

4. *XKTB* QL 31/4/25, packet 286, memorial of Shuhede.

5. Qi, "Wanli Xingcheng Ji," 12b. See also *SYD* (B) QL 56/8/8, 51–2. Outside China proper, passes had to be obtained for each stage of the journey. In the early nineteenth century, the cost of such a pass from Hami to Balikun or Turfan was seven *qian*. The cost of a pass to reenter China proper from Hami was four *qian*. *Hami Zhi* 21, 1a.

6. Ji, *Ji Xiaolan Jiashu*, 20.

7. Lin, "Hege Jicheng," 5b.

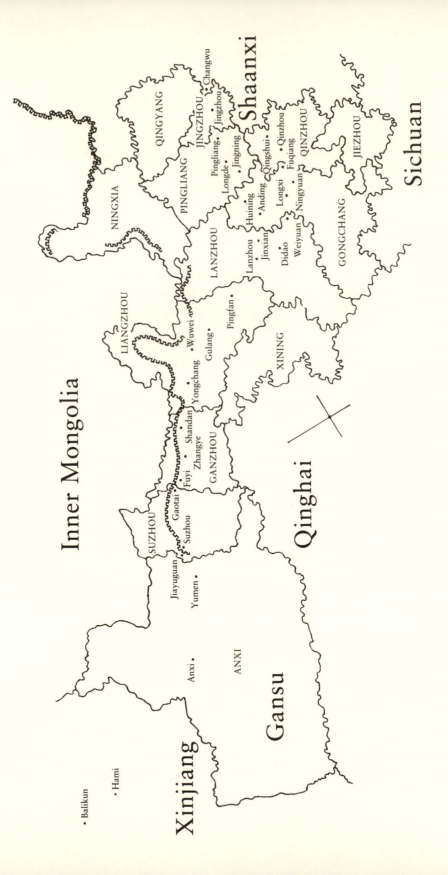

Map 3. The Route to Xinjiang

there to Ürümqi and Ili, the major exile destinations in northern Xin-jiang, there were two possible routes. The northern one, via Balikun, was the more direct, but it was difficult to negotiate in winter. The southern route took the traveler about ninety miles towards Turfan before turning north.[8] Those whose exile destination lay even farther west, at Ili or one of the Muslim cities in southern Xinjiang, still faced several weeks' uncomfortable journey.[9]

ESCORTS

Escorts were the lynchpin of the convict transmission system. Unless they properly performed their duties, some convicts most likely would never reach Xinjiang. In theory the required minimum number of escorts for each convict was four: two yamen runners, assigned on a rotating basis by the head runner, and two soldiers assigned from the local garrison. In addition, one low-ranking civilian official (*zuoza*), such as an assistant magistrate or jail warden, and one low-level military officer (*fangbian*), such as a sergeant, were required to accompany the exile and his escorts.[10] The Qing practice of "escorting the escorts" suggests a singular lack of faith in the escort personnel.

There were both long-distance and local escorts. In the case of ordinary convicts exiled to Xinjiang, most escorts were responsible only for the safe delivery of their charges to the next county. For banished officials, there was no clear rule concerning whether the escorts should accompany the offender for his entire journey or only as far as the next county. In 1794 when Zhejiang province requested permission to use only local escorts for disgraced officials traveling to Xinjiang, as was the practice in Fujian and Jiangxi, the Board of Punishments recommended allowing the provinces flexibility on this question.[11] It is unclear whether escorts ever traveled the whole way to Xinjiang even with disgraced

8. Qi, "Wanli Xingcheng Ji," 15b; Lin, "Hege Jicheng," 7b.

9. Exiles traveling to destinations in southern Xinjiang took the road to Turfan. No record of the route they took from there on has come to light.

10. See *GZDQLCZZ* vol. 20, 636, 29/2/23. See also *XKTB* QL 28/3/9, packet 334, memorial of Shuhede; *XKTB* QL 31/6/23, packet 288, memorial of Suchang. On the need for escorts, see *QSL* QL 585, 19b–20a, 24/4/28. See also Ch'ü, *Local Government*, 250.

11. *XAHL* 58, 65b–66a. For an example of an escort who held the rank of assistant magistrate and escorted an official all the way to trial in Beijing from Fujian, see *XKTB* QL 31/6/23, packet 288, memorial of Suchang.

officials, but in view of the distance involved this must have been very rare.

Escorts carried the convict's identification papers as well as their own identification tags (*bingpai*).[12] They guarded the convict at all times (except when he was in prison overnight), tried to assure that he proceeded with all due despatch, and delivered him to prison at the next yamen. There they received a return certificate, stamped with the magistrate's seal, confirming the safe arrival of the convict. They submitted the certificate to their own yamen upon their return.[13]

It was not unusual for a convoy to contain fewer than the required number of escorts, since county yamens could not spare an unlimited portion of their manpower. Escorts were not always able to return home before a new batch of convicts arrived because of the considerable distances between administrative centers; time constraints meant that the new arrivals could not always await the return of the escorts.[14] The distances local escorts had to cover were particularly great outside China proper; escorts from Hami, for instance, might be absent for as much as four weeks at a time.[15] Escapes were, of course, much more likely when there were too few escorts, and it was usually following an escape that an insufficiency of escorts came to light.[16]

If an exile escaped en route to Xinjiang, his escorts were normally subject to imprisonment with a deferred death sentence for the duration of the investigation.[17] The severity of their eventual treatment depended to some extent on whether there was evidence of bribery. If so, their sentence was the same as that of the escapee. Also relevant was the degree of negligence attributed to the escorts, and whether the convict was

12. *Bingpai* were used by soldiers passing though an area on escort duty. These credentials entitled the holders to obtain supplies and transportation facilities at postal stations. Sun, *Ch'ing Administrative Terms*, 246–247.

13. See "Gongmen Yaolüe," in Cai, *Qingdai Zhouxian Gushi*, 52, cited by Ch'ü, *Local Government*, 251.

14. *GZDQLCZZ* vol. 23, 140–141, 29/11/8.

15. *Hami Zhi* 20, 2b.

16. See, e.g., *QSL* QL 659, 10b–11a, 27/4/23 (two escorts accompanying five criminals); *SYD* (T) JQ 8/3/17, 189 (two runners and one soldier escorting three criminals). For a detailed description of the escape of three out of five inadequately escorted Muslims in Hubei, en route from Gansu into exile in Guizhou as changees, see *GZDQLCZZ* vol. 31, 513–515, 33/8/6.

17. Escorts sometimes joined in the search for the escaped convict. See, e.g., the case of Li Erman.

recaptured.[18] If at the end of a year the criminal was still at large, the escorts themselves were subject to banishment.[19] Even if the escort safely delivered his charge, he could theoretically still be punished for mistreatment, such as unduly tightening the convicts's irons or otherwise injuring him, rifling the convict's possessions, or stealing his clothes. The existence of these laws illustrates, again, official fears about the unreliability of the escort system—fears that were perhaps the product of experience.[20]

After the escape of convict Mi Tianxi in late 1765, one of his three escorts described their progress: "One went ahead pulling the chain around his neck while the two of us followed behind. At night the other two took turns watching him." Mi Tianxi was recaptured a few months later.[21]

The inherent risks of escort duty, combined with a lack of a uniform system of recompense, prompted many to try to avoid it.[22] One common ploy was to hire a substitute, which, although strictly forbidden, was by no means unknown.[23] Some offered convincing reasons for their reluctance to act as escorts. One substitute testified that he had taken the place of the assigned runner because the latter's wife was about to give birth and had no other relatives to help her.[24] Yang Xiang's escort, the soldier who paid 120 copper cash to a substitute, claimed to have been unwell.[25] Yet in another substitution case dating from 1766, the assigned escort

18. *DLCY* 392–04.

19. See *QSL* QL 753, 23a–b, 31/1/29; *SYD* (T) QL 32/4/12, 56b–57b; *QSL* QL 782, 18a–19b, 32/4/12.

20. For the law, see *DLCY* 398–01. For some examples of cases involving brutal escorts, see *XAHL* 59, 13a–17b; none of these relate to Xinjiang convicts.

21. *XKTB* QL 30/12/19, packet 325, memorial of Liu Tongxun; *XKTB* QL 31/9/26, packet 286.

22. See *SYD* (T) JQ 15/9/19, 157–158, for a case in which the relatives of convicts in transit from Anhui attacked the escorts in Shandong, enabling some convicts to escape. Shanxi province set aside extra funds each year to pay escorts, partly in order to discourage substitution. *GZD* QL 35603, 43/16/23. In 1846 soldiers escorting convicts from Hami were issued one *jin* of white flour (approximately 1.3 lbs) and three *fen* "salt vegetable money" (*yancaiqian*) per diem. *Hami Zhi* 20, 2b. No information from other provinces on this point has come to light.

23. *DLCY* 392–04 includes substitution in the list of punishable acts by convicts' escorts. See *XKTB* QL 28/12/11, memorial of Changjun, for a case in which a substitute was to receive a punishment one degree less severe than that of the escorts.

24. *XKTB* QL 28/12/11, memorial of Changjun.

25. *XKTB* QL 31/4/26, packet 288, memorial of Suchang.

offered no excuse for his failure to carry out his duties. His hired substitute had himself sent a fifteen-year-old boy in his stead. The only other escort was also an illegal replacement.[26] Since most known cases of substitution came to light only after a convict escaped, there is no way to determine just how common the practice was.

The bribe of 120 copper cash—perhaps not even one-tenth the amount required to buy an ounce of silver—paid for substitution appears extremely paltry.[27] This suggests that either such illegal activity was so common that only a nominal fee had to be paid or that people were desperate enough for money that they would take substantial risks for a mere pittance.[28] The similarity in the amount of the bribe admitted in several different cases also raises the possibility that the confessions were made in response to a standard question posed by Qing interrogators, as sometimes occurred in mediaeval Europe, even though the bribery may in fact have involved more substantial sums.[29]

The escort system's acknowledged shortcomings make the inadequate allocation of supporting funds seem irrational at best. This skimping was, however, consistent with the Qing's general reluctance to commit additional money for new needs without having available a corresponding new source of revenue. This reluctance was in turn attributable partly to the cupidity of local officials anxious about the possible erosion of their own traditional sources of income and partly to a growing unwillingness on the part of the imperial bureaucracy to attack fresh problems at their foundations.[30]

GROUP SIZE

Security was balanced against economy in determining the number of criminals to be grouped together for the journey into exile. Several crim-

---

26. *QSL* QL 775, 12a–13a, 31/12/21; 18a–19a, 31/12/26. See also *SYD* (T) QL 31/12/26, 112–113.

27. The same amount was reportedly paid as a bribe to a coroner in a tattooing fraud; see text accompanying n. 57.

28. On the cost of living in the 1810s—slightly higher than that in the late eighteenth century—see Naquin, *Millenarian Rebellion in China*, 281–282. A string of cash was formally made up of one thousand cash coins but in reality it often took much more. See Vogel, "Ch'ing Central Monetary Policy 1644–1800."

29. See, generally, Naquin, "True Confessions."

30. See Zelin, *The Magistrate's Tael*.

inals might be banished from one county at different times during the course of a single year. However, time requirements for their despatch into exile meant that the issue of maximum group size usually arose only when several criminals in the same case were banished, for normally all were sentenced simultaneously.

In 1762, as the number of convicts banished to Xinjiang increased, the size of groups for the journey into exile was set at ten to twenty convicts. This figure was based on the following considerations. On the one hand, it was thought that escorts might be tempted to mistreat convicts in transit if they traveled individually or in a very small group, in which case the convicts might either die, which was clearly a miscarriage of justice, or be too debilitated to work when they reached Xinjiang. On the other hand, very large groups obviously presented a security risk and could place too great a strain on the ability of local authorities to provide food and lodging en route. In practice, in determining the precise size of each group, officials took into account such factors as the attempt to comply with time limits and the degree of urgency indicated by the sentences of those awaiting banishment.[31]

After 1764 groups of five became the standard for convict transmission.[32] When the numbers of convicts were such that they had to travel in several batches, these groups departed on successive days. In practice, however, many convicts traveled individually because time restrictions precluded waiting for others to arrive to complete a group of five.[33]

With rare exceptions, disgraced officials did not make their journey into exile in groups but traveled on their own with their servants and government escorts. Nevertheless, some exceptions occurred through chance circumstances. At Pingfan, northwest of Lanzhou, for instance, the scholar Hong Liangji encountered his former colleague Wei Peijin, a

31. *QSL* QL 633, 10a–11a, 26/3/22. In this document the expression *huanji*, which I have taken to mean "the degree of urgency," could also imply that convicts should be grouped according to the speed at which they were able to travel.

32. Whether accompanying family members were included in these numbers was never made explicit, but it seems unlikely, although most convict families were probably kept together both for the sake of convenience and as a matter of public policy.

33. *HDSL* (1899) 721, 18a–b. In 1775 when more than nine hundred miners from Yunnan were forcibly resettled in Xinjiang, they traveled in eleven groups, with about eighty people in each group. "Annan Tuohui Changtu An," *tian* 795–801, QL 40/10/16. Apparently they were not accompanied by their families, who joined them later. See *QSL* QL 1010, 8b–9b, 41/6/6. However, this group was not necessarily treated as convicts were.

magistrate who was also traveling into exile, and arranged to travel with him for part of the remainder of the journey.[34]

CONVICT IDENTIFICATION

A reliable means of convict identification was needed both as a matter of routine and in the event of escape.[35] Every exile had identification papers that listed his crime, native place, age, any scars or other distinguishing marks,[36] and described the shape of his fingerprints, which the Chinese classified as *dou*, denoting whorls, or *qi*, denoting open wavy lines.[37] In addition, most ordinary convicts were tattooed on the temple, in black characters whose size was set by law at just under two inches (one and one-half Chinese inches) square, with strokes not more than about one-fifth of an inch (0.15 of a Chinese inch) wide.[38] Both Chinese characters and their Manchu equivalents were used.[39]

Across the seal of the convict's transmission papers a brief notation

34. Hong, "Ili Riji," 4b. Wei, a *jinshi* of 1778, (and hence a classmate of Qi Yunshi, exiled in 1805, two years after Wei's recall) had been banished from his post as a magistrate in Guangxi for causing delays in a military campaign.

35. The provision of clear identification was the responsibility of the office that despatched the criminal on his journey into exile. In Beijing this was the Board of War (*Bingbu*); in the provinces the governor had overall responsibility, although the district magistrate normally made the actual arrangements. Provincial governors reported to the Board of War. Within the magistrate's yamen, the office of military affairs (*bingfang*) was responsible for feiyuan, whereas the office of justice (*xingfang*) was responsible for ordinary criminals. *XKTB* QL 31/6/23, packet 288, memorial of Suchang. For an example of an exile's transfer after sentence from the Board of Punishments to the Board of War, see Hong, "Ili Riji," 1a.

36. The possibility that a criminal had changed his name or lied about his native place sometimes caused concern. See, e.g., *SYD* (T) QL 51/2/20, 265.

37. *DLCY* 390–15; *Qinding Liubu Chufen Zeli* 46, 6a. The Chinese use of fingerprints to identify prisoners began relatively early. In Western countries it was only in the 1880s that fingerprinting came to be used for this purpose. See Glaser, ed., *Handbook of Criminology*, 342.

38. *Huidian* (1899) 53, 7a. One traditional Chinese inch was almost exactly one and one-quarter English inches. Ch'üan and Kraus, *Mid-Ch'ing Rice Markets and Trade*, 84, citing *Huidian* (1764) 11, 1–6. Less serious criminals were tattooed on the arm, above the elbow, but for the Xinjiang convicts this was not conspicuous enough. See Chen, "Local Control of Convicted Thieves," 129.

39. In 1767 when the Xinjiang changee system was introduced, the changees banished within China proper were tattooed "*gaiqian*" if no tattoo was stipulated in the statute under which they were sentenced, to distinguish them from other exiles banished within China proper. The Manchu equivalent was not required for changees. *HDSL* (1899) 799, 12a.

was added in large characters that read "Under banishment to Ili and Ürümqi" (*difa Ili Wulumuqi dengchu*). Although the despatching official did not know the exile's precise destination, these words alerted those along the way to the fact that the convict was bound for Xinjiang and hence was a serious criminal, to be handled with special caution.[40]

Thus in the event of an escape, a detailed description was immediately available, and if the escapee was recaptured, his tattoos, if he had them, and the description of his fingerprints—for it was impossible to make accurate copies of fingerprints from a convict's documents for general circulation after a convict excaped—served as an instant identification.[41]

The exile's transmission documents were entrusted to the convict's escorts, whose identification tags bore the same information.[42] Every magistrate at whose yamen the exile halted on the route to Xinjiang checked that the criminal corresponded to the information in his documents and his fingerprints and tattoos, to make certain there had been no error or substitution since the convict began his journey.[43]

These methods of identification were fairly efficacious. In 1788, for instance, a substitute was exposed because his fingerprints did not match those on the documents. In that case an exile bribed a former jail night-watchman, who had hired himself out to the criminal as a porter, to take his place. The exile paid his substitute the substantial figure of ten "yuan" (sic) and gave him some civilian clothes, also paying the assigned escorts a bribe of one yuan and two hundred copper cash.[44]

However, even such detailed information about an escapee did not lead inevitably to recapture. Thus Wu Yasan, a native of Guangdong, escaped in Henan province while en route to Xinjiang. Wu had been banished to Xinjiang after seven years in prison for participating in a

40. In the case of changees sent to China proper instead of Xinjiang, the notation across the seal informed the reader that the criminal had been sentenced under a particular substatute and that he was a changee; it also identified his destination in China proper. *XJTLSL* 2, 35a.

41. Sketches of convicts in transit were not used, their principal function being to supplement descriptions of other wanted criminals such as known rebels. Naquin, "True Confessions," 12; *QSL* QL 755, 25a, 31/2/27.

42. *XJTLSL* 2, 35b–36a.

43. The status of a convict's wife and children traveling with him—that is, whether they accompanied him compulsorily or not—was also noted in his transmission documents to ensure appropriate treatment. *XJTLSL* 2, 35b. On procedures in the event of a discrepancy, see *XJTLSL* 2, 36a; conceivably substitution sometimes occurred as a result of human error.

44. *GZD* QL 53164, 53/1/29, a case involving exile within China proper.

homicide. The memorial reporting his escape provided a description taken from the information in his identification documents:

> He is thirty-two *sui*, average size, with a reddish complexion and no beard. Previously he had been tattooed with the characters *xiong-fan*; he now has the same information tattooed on the left of his face in Manchu. In his upper jaw a front tooth is missing and one tooth is crooked on the left-hand side. On his left hand the fingerprints on the thumb and the second and third fingers are *dou* but on the fourth and fifth fingers the prints are *qi*; on his right hand all five fingerprints are *qi*. He is from Heping county in Huizhou prefecture and is wearing a red coat and red trousers.[45]

Yet Wu was never found, and his ultimate fate is unknown.

Changes were made a number of times before a satisfactory, uniform type of tattoo was established for the Xinjiang exiles. At first the despatching county tattooed the convict either with up to four characters summarizing his crime, if the statute under which the convict had been sentenced so stipulated, or with his exile destination, which similarly consisted of at most four characters. However, this system soon proved impractical, because the actual exile destination was determined only when the convict reached Gansu province. The arrival of a convict with his exile destination already tattooed on his temple severely hampered Gansu's flexibility in this respect. To resolve this problem, the despatching province stopped tattooing a convict after 1759 except with the crime where this was stipulated. The exile's destination, once decided, was added in Gansu.[46]

In 1763 Jiangxi judicial commissioner Qianqi identified the shortcomings of this practice:

> If the statute [under which a criminal was sentenced] contains no provision for tattooing, there is no tattoo that the despatching province can apply. The convict is sent to Gansu and there tattooed with

---

45. *XKTB* QL 28/3/9, packet 334, memorial of Shuhede. Prisoners were required to wear government-issue reddish-brown (*chi*) clothing; *DLCY* 401–08. This particular color of cloth was not used for any other purpose, so prisoners thus clad were always identifiable as such. The description of Wu's clothing at the time of his escape as "red" (*hong*) may mean he was not dressed in regulation garb. However, it is possible that bureaucratic usage did not distinguish between chi and hong; see, e.g., *XKTB* QL 28/12/11, memorial of Changjun concerning Li Erman.

46. *XJTLSL* 2, 9a.

his destination. The distance from the provinces to Gansu is a thousand or several thousand li and the time involved in transferring the criminal is considerable. If the convict has no tattoo mark on his face then [if he should hire a substitute or escape] he is indistinguishable from ordinary people.[47]

Qianqi's proposal, to reduce the risk of letting convicts travel unmarked for the first part of their journey by having the despatching province tattoo every convict with two characters—*waiqian*—identifying him as an "exile beyond the borders" of China proper, was adopted. In appropriate cases this was combined with two characters summarizing the crime. As before, the tattoo mark showing the exile destination was added once the convict reached Gansu.[48]

By the time a convict arrived in exile, he had tattoos on both temples. On the right-hand side he was marked with a summary of his crime or with the two characters *waiqian*, or with a four-character combination of these two, and on the left-hand side he was marked with his destination.[49] See Figure 1 for a 1788 list of tattoos of crimes and exile destinations.[50]

Those banished into slavery, a category that included the majority of ordinary convicts, were almost always tattooed. Other convicts, however, were not normally tattooed to avoid a stigma that might prejudice their later reintegration into society.[51] Officials and members of their families who were exiled were not enslaved except in highly excep-

47. *GZDQLCZZ* vol. 19, 636–637, 28/11/19.

48. *Sanfasi* Archives no. 351, QL 28/12/17. The use of the waiqian mark was abolished in the early Jiaqing reign when comprehensive changes in the laws made it irrelevant. See *DLCY* 281–05, and discussion following the text of the law (*juan* 31, pages 767–768).

49. *Huidian* (1899) 53, 7a–b; *XJTLSL* 2, 9a–11b. After the waiqian tattoo was introduced, it was used for all convicts regardless of whether the sentencing statute stipulated tattooing. Where convicts were marked with a combination of a crime summary and waiqian, the first two characters of their crime were followed by "waiqian". See, e.g., *GZD* QL 29407, 39/7/25. First tattoos were almost always on the right-hand side. See *Daqing Lüli Huitong Xinzuan* 24, 2b, p. 2322. A recidivist was tattooed on the left temple if his right temple already had a tattoo; if the second crime was the same as the first, duplication was not required. *DLCY* 281–06; *XJTLSL*, 2, 9b. However, a criminal whose first crime had been punished by less than Xinjiang banishment and whose second crime (i.e., the one for which he was banished) was identical to the first, might have a second tattoo added in Manchu, as in the case of Wu Yasan.

50. This list of tattoos includes one for Muslim robbers: *huizei*. From 1772 to 1801, Muslim robbers were marked *qiezei* (*DLCY* 281–08), but since this form of tattoo was used exclusively for Muslims, it was no less discriminatory than the actual *hui* character.

51. *XJTLSL* 2, 10b.

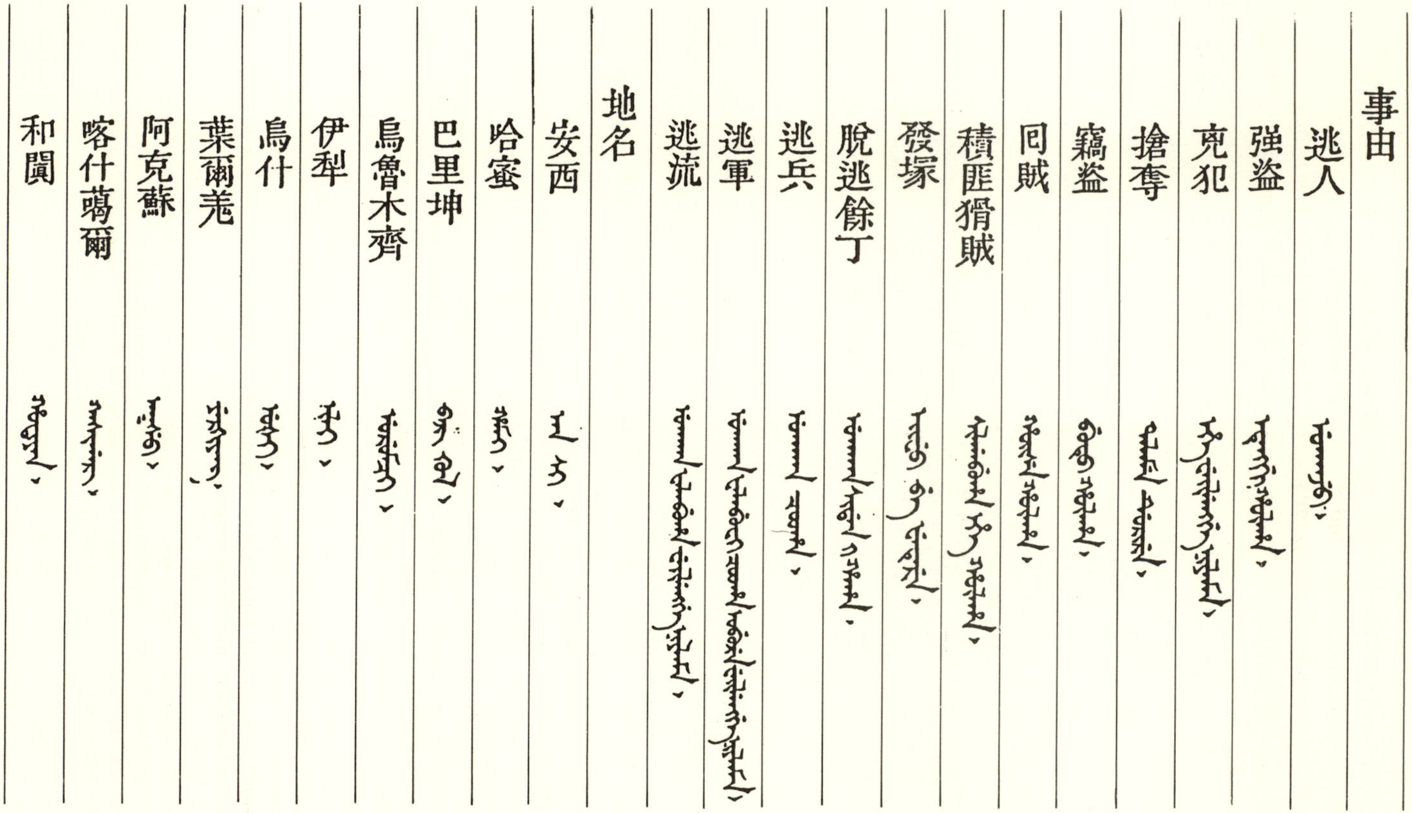

事由	
逃人	
强盗	
窎犯	
搶奪	
竊盜	
回賊	
積匪猾賊	
發塚	
脫逃餘丁	
逃兵	
逃軍	
逃流	

地名	
安西	
哈密	
巴里坤	
烏魯木齊	
伊犁	
烏什	
葉爾羌	
阿克蘇	
喀什噶爾	
和闐	

Figure 1. Tattoos Used on Convicts

tional circumstances, and hence were usually spared tattooing.[52]
Degree-holders above the *juren* level were also usually exempt, as were
bannermen, women, children, and those over seventy.[53]

Xinjiang convicts were by no means the only criminals to be tattooed
in Qing China, but in their case the marks carried special significance.[54]
Unlike other escaped exiles, the Xinjiang convict who escaped was subject to execution upon recapture, in keeping with the more severe nature
of this punishment and its originally conditional character. Thus his tattoos sealed his fate.[55] However, the absence of a tattoo did not necessarily guarantee clemency. For instance, four women (one more than eighty
years old) and a four-year-old child who had been enslaved to high officials after Wang Lun's 1774 rebellion escaped together. The three who
were recaptured were apparently put to death.[56]

The removal of tattoo marks was unauthorized unless a convict was
restored to civilian status, but because of the marks' fatal significance,
attempts to remove them illegally were common. Sometimes this was
facilitated by the official charged with applying them, normally the
coroner. Convict Wang Erlou bribed a coroner with 120 copper cash to

52. *QCWXTK* 204, p. 6688. Cf. *DLCY* 264–00.

53. *DLCY* 45–16; *XJTLSL* 2, 10b. The removal of a bannerman's name from the register of his banner was prerequisite to his enslavement, but enslavement did not invariably
follow such removal. For example, those involved with the missionary Adeodato (see chapter 5) were not enslaved, despite the heinous nature of their crime. Those more than seventy
or less than fifteen were not normally tattooed because they were permitted to redeem a
sentence of banishment on the ground of their age. Exiles between fifty and seventy who
were banished to the insalubrious areas of the southwest rather than to Xinjiang because of
their age and unsuitability as colonists (see chapter 4, text accompanying n. 93) were tattooed with the crime summary when this was stipulated but not with the characters *gaiqian*.
XJTLSL 2, 15a.

54. On the Song reintroduction and Yuan codification of tattooing as a supplemental
penalty, see Chen, *Chinese Legal Tradition under the Mongols*, 63. Tattooing was one of
the five mutilating punishments of antiquity theoretically abolished in 167 B.C.; see Hulsewé, *Remnants of Han Law*, 124–125. It seems never to have died out completely in the
imperial period.

55. The law requiring the execution of all escaped Xinjiang convicts upon recapture,
regardless of the gravity of their original offence, was modified in 1799. Thereafter it generally applied only to convicts with commuted death sentences. See *DLCY juan* 26, p. 605,
note following 266–26. The stipulation of execution upon recapture also applied to Xinjiang changees banished within China proper.

56. *QSL* QL 978, 18a–19a, 40/3/12; *QSL* QL 983, 15a–16b, 40/5/22. On the tattooing
exemption for women, see *HDSL* (1899) 734, 2a. Children banished by virtue of collective
responsibility were not normally tattooed. See discussion following *DLCY* 281–12, *juan*
31, p. 770; for examples, see *XJTLSL* 2, 11a–b and 25b–26a. For a later example of
compassion shown to young exiles in the context of tattooing, see *HDSL* (1899) 799, 16a.

make only a shallow incision and to blacken the mark with a mixture of charcoal mixed with water. Later Wang washed off his tattoo, leaving no discernible scar. Two others involved in the same case testified that the coroner had proposed the bribes through the medium of a fourth prisoner in the local jail. The coroner had used "the side of a slipper" (*xie bangzi*) to soften and blur the incision and then rubbed in the charcoal mixture to simulate the appearance of a properly executed tattoo mark. This fraud was discovered after the three had safely arrived in exile. All those involved were punished including the coroner and the magistrates who had failed to notice the absence of tattoo marks on the three criminals.[57] Officials frequently observed that the Xinjiang convicts' tattoos made them relatively easy to identify. Yet many escaped convicts testifed upon recapture that they had obliterated the marks by applying ointment or burning their skin.[58]

FOOD

The daily ration of food issued to convicts in transit was the same as that issued to prison inmates.[59] Each convict and each member of his family received one pint (*sheng*) of grain (approximately 840 grams) and a supplement valued at 5 copper cash for other food. The type of grain issued varied from province to province and could include rice, millet, wheat, soy, and other cereals. Most provided approximately twenty-eight hundred calories per sheng, except the more nutritious soy.[60]

57. *GZD QL* 29407, 39/7/25. *QSL QL* 965, 16a–17a, 39/8/28. *GZD QL* 29765, 39/9/5. The three criminals were changees banished within China proper. Their tattoo marks identified their crimes and their status as changees. They testified that they feared the pain of the tattoo but denied that they planned to escape. For comments on the amount of bribes, see text accompanying nn. 27–29.

58. See, e.g., *GZD JQ* 16244, 19/8/8; *GZD JQ* 16709, 19/10/26; *GZD QL* 34347, 43/3/8. The absence of tattoo marks could be a point of honor even among thieves, at least in eighteenth-century Sichuan province, where one robber gang declined to accept members with tattoos. Chen, "Local Control," 130.

59. See *HDSL* (1899) 270, 4a–12b.

60. *XKTB QL* 27/11/24, packet 285, memorial of Changjun. Will, *Bureaucratie et famine en Chine*, 120–121, notes that the expression "grain" (*mi*) refers to cereals that have been husked and polished and are ready to be eaten. The supplement may have been issued in kind and not in cash. Although regulations designated the supplement as "salt vegetable money" (*yancaiqian*), the same amount was often described in other official documents as "allowance for lamp oil [in prison] and *yancai.*"

Half a sheng was regarded as a subsistence ration; it was the amount of famine relief issued to adult males (children under fifteen received half that amount). For a time the food issue to exiles in transit was reduced to half a sheng for adults and to a quarter of a sheng for children, but this proved inadequate; the undernourished travelers were unable to proceed at the required pace of sixteen miles per day, and in due course the full ration was restored. In 1775, however, the ration was reduced permanently, in part to prevent convicts' receiving more than soldiers. The new ration was 0.83 sheng, with half that quantity for children.[61]

Officials traveling into exile generally purchased food as required. The scholar Hong Liangji, whose considerable interest in food makes him a valuable source on this subject, sometimes described particular meals in his diary. On one occasion he particularly enjoyed a meal of congee and dried meat; once he had only plain rice, and on another occasion he lamented that he had nothing to eat all day.[62]

The treatment Hong received as he traveled towards his Xinjiang exile reflected the popularity among many contemporaries of his ill-fated criticism of imperial policy. At different times during his journey he was the guest of local officials, scholars, and gentry (including some who had been his fellow students) and of friends whose sojourn in a particular area coincided with Hong's arrival.[63] Sometimes Hong's friends made arrangements for his meals even when they did not join him. For example, the prefect at Binzhou, Shaanxi, was an old friend of Hong's and was married to Hong's cousin. When Hong reached the outskirts of Binzhou he discovered that the prefect had sent someone to prepare a meal for him. In addition, Hong often received gifts of food while he was traveling. These included fruit, dried food, tea, "spring cakes," glutinous rice balls, and southern-style vegetables. Even after he entered Xinjiang, Hong was regaled with Jiangsu delicacies by a fellow countryman in exile

61. *XKTB* QL 27/11/24, packet 285, memorial of Changjun. A temporary restoration of the full ration occurred in 1766, four years later. On the subsequent reduction, see *HDSL* (1899) 270, 10b–11a.

62. Hong, "Ili Riji," 8a.

63. See, e.g., Hong, "Ili Riji," 2b (local degree-holder); 3a (friend); 5a (magistrate); 6a (prefect); 6b (fellow countryman). Hong met several scholars whom he described as his fellow students (*tongnian*) although not all received degrees when Hong did. His apparently loose usage of this expression may be due to his having failed the *juren* examination three times and the *jinshi* examination four times; possibly he referred to all his fellow students as tongnian regardless of the date of their examination success.

shortly before his arrival in Ili.[64] Hong was not, however, typical of all banished officials, many of whom were far less well connected and consequently less well provided for.

Before crossing the desert it was necessary to obtain supplies at Anxi. There were few places where food could be purchased, and the water was often brackish.[65] Ji Yun encountered some soldiers on guard duty at Tianshengdun fort. They made tea and told him: "It is very difficult to get drinking water here. In winter we save the snow and ice; in summer we collect rainwater, and that is how we allay our thirst." Ji suggested that they dig for water at the foot of the mound. The soldiers were not enthusiastic. They told him that General Yue (presumably Yue Zhongqi [1686–1754], who had conducted the campaigns in the northwest a few decades earlier) had made the same suggestion. Several dozen men had dug to a considerable depth when the sandy ground caved in and the men were buried. Only six or seven had survived.[66] Ji, who had read that there was no water at Ürümqi, was horrified at the prospect of serving his term of exile in such conditions and was much relieved to find he had been misinformed.[67]

TRANSPORT

The remount department of the Board of War (*chejiasi*) provided carts for the journey into exile.[68] For ordinary convicts the quota was one cart for every six people. This number included members of a convict's family. It compared unfavorably with the quota for soldiers and their families moving from Gansu to Ili, who were allotted one cart for every three people, and one luggage cart per household. However, in the event that a member of a convict group was unwell, the quota was two or three to a cart.[69]

64. Hong, "Ili Riji," 3a–b, 6b–7a, 8a.
65. Qi, "Wanli Xingcheng Ji," 14a. Qi found the water, and hence the tea, unpalatable even in his native Shanxi province. Ibid., 1b.
66. Ji, *Ji Xiaolan Jiashu*, 20.
67. Ibid., 24.
68. In 1762, instituting changes in the system of providing government carts for official business, the emperor gave priority to the transport of prisoners and expressly excluded carts used for that purpose from the cutbacks he made. SYD (T) QL 27/12/17, 114.
69. XKTB QL 31/4/25, packet 286, memorial of Shuhede. On soldiers, see GZDQLCZZ vol. 20, 319–320, 29/1/15. HDSL (1899) 721, 1b–2a; the provision of carts

A cash allowance for cart rental provided for the possibility that government carts might be unavailable in some locations. This allowance was 0.45 taels for each hundred li (about thirty-three miles) traveled by cart within China proper. Outside China proper the allowance was just under 2 taels per hundred li to allow for the poor condition of many roads.[70]

A special type of cart was sometimes used for the desert crossing. It was wide and had high wheels and a curved shaft to increase stability.[71] The exiled historian Qi Yunshi noted that water had frequently to be applied to the wheels in the desert to prevent them from cracking, although even this precaution was not always effective.[72]

Banished officials normally traveled by sedan chair within China proper. If road conditions were particularly bad, they sometimes had to walk short distances.[73] Outside China proper sedan-chair travel was rarer. Some traveled by cart or even, for the desert crossing, had to ride a camel.[74] They also often had a separate cart, presumably for their luggage, which sometimes traveled more slowly, arriving much later than they did at the nightly halt.[75] In 1766 the Board of War issued an order requiring each county to supply transport to disgraced officials whenever it was needed, thereby adding to the burdens of the counties through which exiles passed on their way to Xinjiang.[76]

---

for soldiers proved burdensome and expensive. There is no evidence that Xinjiang convicts were ever transported in the cage-carts of earlier periods (see Goodrich, "The Ancient Chinese Prisoner's Van"), although these were still used in the Qing for some major criminals. See, e.g., Naquin, "True Confessions," 8.

70. *XKTB* QL 27/11/24, packet 285, memorial of Changjun. Cf. *Hami Zhi* 20, 2b, which gives the rate as only 1.2 taels per cart per hundred li (i. e., outside China proper); possibly the allowance had been reduced by 1846.

71. See, e.g., Qi, "Wanli Xingcheng Ji," 14a; Lin, "Hege Jicheng," 5b. It is unclear whether this type of cart was used by ordinary convicts for the desert crossing, or only by those formerly of high rank.

72. Qi, "Wanli Xingcheng Ji," 14a.

73. See, e.g., Hong, "Ili Riji," 8a.

74. Ji, *Ji Xiaolan Jiashu*, 20, mentions riding a camel. Descriptions of the carts used by Hong Liangji, Qi Yunshi, and Lin Zexu in Xinjiang suggest that they were drawn by animals, not carried by men. See, e.g., Hong, "Ili Riji," 6b; Qi, "Wanli Xingcheng Ji," 14a; Lin, "Hege Jicheng," 5b. However, Hong mentions a sedan chair in which he rode west of Ürümqi. "Ili Riji," 7b.

75. Hong, "Ili Riji," 1b, 6b. At Ganzhou, Gansu, the assistant magistrate gave Hong a mule, but Hong never mentions it; perhaps he used it for his luggage. Ibid., 5a.

76. See *XKTB* QL 31/4/25, packet 286, memorial of Shuhede.

ACCOMMODATION

Convicts en route to Xinjiang were kept in prison overnight whenever possible. In China proper most counties had a prison within the magistrate's yamen. Regulations required the division of the prison compound into an inner and an outer jail for male prisoners, with separate quarters for women.[77] In practice, however, there were often four levels within the prison: the "soft jail" for minor prisoners in the temple to the prison god and, in increasingly secure order, the outer jail, the inner jail, and the dark or black jail.[78] Exiles in transit normally occupied the outer jail, where they were kept in irons.

An influx of convicts could cause serious overcrowding in prisons, aggravating conditions that were already notoriously bad.[79] An epidemic that raged through prisons in two counties of Gansu in 1784 resulted in the death of hundreds of inmates bound for Xinjiang. More than 540 were reported dead at Jingning; some 200 more died at Longde. Many of these were the wives and children of Muslim rebels, banished by virtue of collective responsibility.

One reason for the high number of deaths in this case may have been the authorities' reluctance to release any prisoners in case they should infect the local population. The authorities implied that they feared "spiritual pollution" almost as much as the infectiousness of the disease.[80] This was a common reaction where Muslims were involved and was understandable given the recent spread of rebellion among Muslim communities in the northwest. Earlier in the same year when a group of Muslims involved in the Hezhou uprising in Gansu had crossed China en route to banishment on Hainan island, the emperor had particularly ordered that they were to be allowed no contact whatsoever with local Muslims en route, for fear of further disturbances.[81]

In county capitals, if the local prison was full, exiles sometimes stayed

77. *Huidian* (1899) 56, 1a.

78. Huang, *A Complete Book concerning Happiness and Benevolence*, 311.

79. For a description of the prison of the Board of Punishments in Beijing in 1711, see Bodde, "Prison Life in Eighteenth-Century Peking." On early nineteenth-century prison conditions, see Li, "Sihuan Zashi." Both these accounts were written by disgraced officials, Fang Bao and Li Luanxuan.

80. *Sanfasi* Archives 1422, QL 49/10/26.

81. *SYD* (T) QL 49/i3/8, 607–608; *GZD* QL 47670, 49/i3/14.

overnight in a more informal type of jail (*banfang*).[82] In the absence of any secure custodial facilities, convicts and their escorts lodged at an inn, where local reinforcements (soldiers and runners) helped the escorts to mount a close guard.[83] On one occasion a magistrate ordered a local policeman to provide overnight accomodation for two prisoners at his home; this breach of proper procedure enabled one of the desperate prisoners to commit suicide.[84]

At the many overnight stops between county capitals, and in particular in Xinjiang where these were far apart, ad hoc arrangements were necessary. The convict and his escorts might stay at a postal station with facilities for securing prisoners.[85] Failing this they found lodging wherever they could, including at local hostelries not regularly used to accommodate prisoners. Since such substitute jails were usually outside county centers and thus local reinforcements were not necessarily available to help guard the prisoners, this practice tended to facilitate escapes, particularly given the various temptations that such places presented to the escorts.

Disgraced officials were often imprisoned before their departure into exile, but once they set off they were not normally locked up overnight, nor did they wear irons.[86] They usually stayed in a guesthouse or at a postal station en route. Hong Liangji, for one, noted in his diary that the presence of offenders serving time at a postal station in Gansu made him nervous, and for the rest of his journey he rarely used such accommodation.[87]

Occasionally an incumbent official invited a former colleague traveling into exile to stay at a yamen; this was particularly true in the case of

82. A prison (*jianyu*) usually denoted a high-walled, well-guarded structure within the yamen compound, constructed for the express purpose of imprisonment. See Tao, *Qingdai Zhouxian Yamen Xingshi Shenpan Zhidu ji Chengxu*, 13. The term *banfang* denoted a place of detention that was normally outside the yamen compound, including granaries and postal stations. Many such buildings that were used as prisons were not necessarily designed as such and hence were less secure. Niida, *Chūgoku Hōsei-shi Kenkyū*, 653.

83. *DLCY* 395–05. Inns were sometimes referred to as *banfang*.

84. *XKTB* QL 41/1/27, packet 344, memorial of Yu Wenyi.

85. On the use of postal stations as jails, see Lü, *Shizheng Lu*, 7, 15a–20b.

86. See Ji, *Ji Xiaolan Jiashu*, 18–19 for a description of Ji Yun's sojourn in prison prior to exile. Hong Liangji was handcuffed while he was in the Board of Punishments prison, but the handcuffs were removed before he set off on his journey. Hong, "Ili Riji," 1a. See also *GZD* QL 42488, 47/9/14.

87. Hong, "Ili Riji," 3b.

well-known officials such as Hong Liangji. At Huozhou, relatively near Beijing, Hong refused such hospitality on the ground that it was inappropriate for a person of criminal status. Ten days later, at Huazhou, he accepted, possibly in part because the magistrate had been his fellow student. At Jinxian, near Lanzhou, there was no inn and Hong much enjoyed spending the night in a private home, even a simple one: "I saw all the crops stacked up and the spinning wheel at the side. I felt the warmth of a home and slept extremely well."[88] Once, Hong stayed in a temple; he also spent several uncomfortable nights in his cart for lack of anywhere else to sleep.[89]

These experiences, and the unfamiliar landscape of the journey to Xinjiang, combined to emphasize the strangeness of the entire exile experience even before arrival at the final destination.

COSTS

It was impossible to determine in advance the annual provincial cost for convict transmission because the numbers of criminals constantly fluctuated. Instead each province advanced money and supplies for this purpose; at the end of the year it reported all such expenditures to the Boards of Punishments and Revenue and requested authorization to make up any shortfall from specified funds. Most provinces used meltage fees (*haoxian*) to meet these expenses.[90]

In 1761 the various counties of Gansu provided for the thirty-five convicts who crossed the province out of local granary stores and public funds in the local treasuries; Hami used some of its military reserves.[91] The total cost to Gansu and Hami of providing for these convicts, including funds spent for grain, cash supplements, and transport, was 484.76 taels, as shown in table 4.[92]

88. Ibid., 2b–4a.
89. Hong, "Tianshan Kehua," 5a. Other disgraced officials, including Qi Yunshi, in 1805, and Lin Zexu, in 1842, passed some nights in their carts. See, e.g., Qi, "Wanli Xingcheng Ji," 8a; Lin, "Hege Jicheng," 4b, 7a.
90. *HDSL* (1899) 270, 7a–11a. In Yunnan copper revenues were used for this purpose. *HDSL* (1899) 270, 10b. On meltage fees, see, generally, Zelin, *The Magistrate's Tael*.
91. *XKTB* QL 27/11/24, packet 285, memorial of Changjun. In addition to the thirty-five convicts, twenty-two members of the convicts' families journeyed across Gansu. At that time their expenses were not paid by the government.
92. *XKTB* QL 27/11/24, packet 285, memorial of Changjun.

Table 4. Cost of Convict Transmission in Gansu and Hami, 1761

Area	No. of Xian	No. of Convicts	Amount of Grain in shi[a]	Total Cost of Grain in Taels	Cash Supplement	Transport[b]	Total
Pingliang	4	35	3.85	8.48	1.92	17.64	28.05
Gongchang	2	35	1.75	2.98	0.87	8.50	12.36
Lanzhou	2	34	4.75	10.42	2.37	no hire	12.80
Liangzhou	2	34	4.42	10.22	2.21	no hire	12.43
Ganzhou	3	34	1.70	3.31	0.85	no hire	4.16
Suzhou and Gaotai[c]	n/a	34	4.80	9.47	2.04	51.63	63.14
Anxi	3	34	7.82	43.96	3.91	163.97	211.84
Hami[d]	n/a	34	(6.46)	n/a	3.23	136.75	139.98
						Total	484.76

Source: XKTB QL 27/11/24, packet 285, memorial of Changjun.

[a] The imperial shi was equivalent to between 175 and 195 pounds, see Ch'üan and Kraus, Mid-Ch'ing Rice Markets, 84, 92–98; on the tael as a unit of account, see ibid, 12–13. Totals in these documents were reported in cangshi, the standard imperial granary measure; see Perdue, "The Qing State and the Gansu Grain Market," 29, n. 20.

[b] "No hire" means that government carts were available.

[c] Suzhou was an independent department.

[d] Hami was a subprefecture (ting) without subordinate xian. It supplied grain from its military reserves and hence had no outlay for grain.

The nearer the convicts came to Xinjiang, the more it cost the government to feed and transport them. There were several reasons for the increased cost, the first of which was the greater distances between county capitals outside China proper and the consequent higher allowance for transport.[93] Second were the regional and seasonal discrepancies in grain prices, and variations in the amount of cash that constituted one tael, due to local differences in the ratio of copper to silver.[94] Other reasons for the greater cost outside China proper included the relative unavailability of government carts—private carts were hired only where government carts were not available—and local taxes.[95]

By 1765—after only four years—the number of convicts—and the overall expenditure—had increased dramatically. During that year, slightly more than one thousand convicts bound for Xinjiang crossed Gansu and Hami. Some of these died; others, commencing their journey in Gansu, replaced them. The total combined cost of providing food and transport for these convicts in 1765 amounted to 12,589.14 taels, as shown in table 5.

The cost per convict did not increase in every area between 1761 and 1765, and overall it decreased by almost 2 taels. At Lanzhou, Liangzhou, Ganzhou, and Hami the per convict cost rose, but it fell at Pingliang, Gongchang, Suzhou and Gaotai, and Anxi. The cost of a shi of grain (which weighed between 175 and 195 pounds) rose except in Pingliang, where it fell slightly, and Anxi, where it fell sharply. The cost of the supplementary issue varied little between 1761 and 1765. The cost of

93. The convicts spent approximately the same amount of time in each prefecture in both 1761 and 1765, with the unexplained exception of Suzhou and Gaotai. They averaged eleven days in Pingliang, eight days in Qingshui (in 1765), five days in Gongchang, fourteen days in Lanzhou, twelve to thirteen days in Liangzhou, five days in Ganzhou, fourteen days in Suzhou and Gaotai in 1761 but only ten days in 1765, twenty-two to twenty-three days in Anxi, and nineteen days in Hami.

94. The exchange rate in Gansu in 1761 was in the 800s; that is, it took eight hundred and some copper cash to constitute one silver tael. Vogel, "Ch'ing Central Monetary Policy, 1644–1800," 27. Efforts to standardize the rate indicate it was not uniform. See Perdue, "The Qing State and the Gansu Grain Market, 1739–1864," 13. On variations in rice prices within a single province (Hunan), see Ch'üan and Kraus, *Mid-Ch'ing Rice Markets and Trade*, 5.

95. An 1846 gazetteer recorded an annual road tax of two taels per cart between Hami and Turfan or Balikun; in addition there was a tax on carts amounting to two or three taels for carts with iron or wooden wheels respectively. Although convict carts do not appear to have been subject to these taxes—the revenue was applied to the cost of convict transmission—there may have been other taxes to which they were subject. *Hami Zhi*, 21, 1a.

Table 5. Cost of Convict Transmission in Gansu and Hami, 1765

Area	No. of Xian	No. of Convicts	Amount of Grain in shi	Total Cost of Grain in Taels	Cash Supplement	Transport	Total
Pingliang	4	896	97.98	191.26	48.99	no hire	240.25
Qinzhou and Qingshui	n/a	160	6.56	16.61	3.28	30.73	50.63
Gongchang	2	1063	54.61	237.54	27.31	38.11	302.96
Lanzhou	4	1023	147.95	454.65	73.98	42.12	570.74
Liangzhou	4	1024	122.60	413.20	61.30	no hire	474.50
Ganzhou	3	1022	50.97	123.61	25.49	no hire	149.10
Suzhou and Gaotai	n/a	1022	101.94	243.14	50.97	923.06	1217.18
Anxi	3	1022	224.29	746.52	112.14	3880.29	4738.95
Hami	n/a	1026	194.08	1397.41	97.04	3350.38	4844.83

Total 12,589.14

Source: XKTB QL 31/4/25, packet 286, memorial of Shuhede.

Table 6. Comparison of Transmission Costs per Convict in Gansu
and Hami, 1761 and 1765

	1761	1765
Pingliang	0.80	0.27
Gongchang	0.35	0.28
Lanzhou	0.38	0.56
Liangzhou	0.37	0.46
Ganzhou	0.12	0.15
Suzhou and Gaotai	1.86	1.19
Anxi	6.23	4.64
Hami	4.12	4.72
Total	14.23	12.27

Note: Costs are given in taels.

transport was uniformly lower in 1765 than it had been in 1761. This reduction may partly be attributable to the possibility that in 1761 there were smaller groups of convicts traveling into exile, for example with only one or two to a cart; by 1765, with greater overall numbers traveling into exile, the transmission system had become more efficient in this respect. At least as important was the fact that the end of the Xinjiang military campaigns in 1759 had brought Gansu some economic relief, as agricultural production intensified after the war and the province recovered from a severe drought in 1759–60.[96] Table 6 compares the costs of convict transmission in 1761 and 1765, the two years for which figures are available.

In China proper only Gansu, acting as a funnel for the convicts traveling to Xinjiang, can consistently have incurred high costs, although for most other provinces no such detailed information is available.[97] Yet

96. See, generally, Perdue, "The Qing State and the Gansu Grain Market, 1739–1864." In 1761 grain cost much more at Anxi than elsewhere: almost 9.5 taels per shi, whereas in the other areas in Gansu it ranged from 1.7 to 2.3 taels. The high price in Anxi reflected a combination of poor harvests, lingering war expenses, and its location as the last center in Gansu on the way to Xinjiang. In 1765 grain cost 3.33 taels per shi at Anxi, well within the range of prices in the other areas. The limited increase in the transmission cost per convict at Hami (see table 5) is noteworthy because in 1765 there were no military reserves available to supply the convicts' needs; presumably these had been used up. Because Hami used its military reserves of grain in 1761 but not in 1765, there is no evidence on the change in the cost of grain there.

97. Some provinces included in their reports annual expenses attributable to stationary prison inmates as well as convicts in transit; others combined the costs for all the different

Gansu was a poor province with a low level of grain production, granary reserves that regularly failed to meet the targets set by the state, and a record of tax arrears. Already unusually burdened with military expenses by virtue of its strategic location en route to the heavily garrisoned Xinjiang frontier, it was ill placed to absorb any additional costs such as those occasioned by the passage of exiles.

One of the few other provinces for which information is available is Shanxi, which because of its relatively isolated location to the north of China proper—it was a thoroughfare on the way to Xinjiang only for those traveling from the capital area, Shandong province, and the northeast—provides an interesting contrast with Gansu. In 1776, for example, Shanxi spent 43.8 taels on food for convicts banished to Xinjiang. In 1777, it spent 22.8 taels for this purpose, and in 1779 it spent 16.09 taels. In 1787 Shanxi spent 25.5 taels on supplies for convicts. These figures do not include transportation costs, which accounted for a considerable proportion of Gansu's transmission expenses; no record of Shanxi's expenditures in that category has come to light.[98]

Within Xinjiang itself the funds required for convict transmission were an important part of the annual budget. In 1784 Ürümqi lieutenant governor Hailu cited such costs as one among many heavy expenses, noting that in 1782 convict transmission expenditure had amounted to more than eight thousand taels.[99] In comparison with the several million taels annually expended to support the Qing occupation of Xinjiang, this amount seems relatively insignificant.

Provincial provision of funds to defray the cost of convict transmission did not need to take into account any disgraced officials passing through on their way into exile. Banished officials were expected to pay their own traveling expenses. However, in certain instances the government issued a lump sum equivalent to one year's salary; this was intended to be used for the purchase of clothing for the journey and was provided only to those upon whom new rank was conferred after dismissal from office but prior to departure into exile.[100]

---

kinds of exiles rather than isolating the costs associated with exiles traveling to Xinjiang. See, e.g., *GZD* QL 38037, 44/3/18.

98. *GZD* QL 30988, 42/3/18; *GZD* QL 34338, 43/3/6; *JJD* QL 26443, 45/2/10; *GZD* QL 53535, 53/3/20.

99. *SYD* (T) QL 49/3/17, 499.

100. *HDSL* (1899) 251, 23a–24b; *Hubu Zeli* 64, 9b–10b. On the practice of awarding new rank prior to departure, see chapter 7.

TIME LIMITS

Time limits for departure and arrirval were established to discourage any delay in departure on the journey and the risk of dawdling en route. In addition, a term of banishment did not begin to run until the convict arrived at his exile destination.

The maximum period of time allowed before departure was two months from the day the exile received confirmation of the sentence. However, in 1819 this was reduced to one month on the curious ground that many of those sentenced to frontier banishment had disregarded the rule.[101] In the event of illness, departure could be postponed for an additional month but such a plea was subject to official verification to ensure that the illness was not a mere pretext for delay.[102] Thus former subprefect Xu Mingbiao was imprisoned in Yunnan when he was too ill from malaria to set off on his journey; he died there.[103] A former magistrate who contracted dysentery on the journey to Xinjiang spent three months in Gaolan, Gansu, regaining his strength. He, too, was confined to jail during his convalescence.[104]

On rare occasions a woman could postpone departure into exile to nurse a newborn child. In 1784, for instance, the collectively responsible wife of the killer of several members of a family gave birth in prison where she was awaiting despatch to Xinjiang. The child was subject to life imprisonment with a deferred death sentence; the woman was

---

101. *HDSL* (1899) 835, 3a–b; *DLCY* 391–03, which gives the time limit as one month; *Qinding Liubu Chufen Zeli* 46, 5b, which gives the time limit as two months. This discrepancy arose from the lack of coordination among the several separate legislative offices involved in drafting regulations. As long as the Commission of Laws (*Lüli Guan*) drafted regulations for all six Boards, there was uniformity, but once each Board became responsible for drafting its own regulations, this uniformity was lost. See discussion following *DLCY* 391–03, *juan* 46, pp. 1164–1165. Thus apparently contradictory regulations were simultaneously in force; it is unclear which normally prevailed, but obviously there was scope for abuse.

102. *DLCY* 391–03; *Qinding Liubu Chufen Zeli* allowed a maximum delay before departure of one hundred days for those too ill to travel. Annual reports on convict transmission included information on any such delays. *DLCY* 391–01.

103. *GZD QL* 29682, 39/8/25.

104. *GZD QL* 42488, 47/9/14. See *GZDQLCZZ* vol. 17, 54, 28/2/24 for a reference to delays of several years by convicts who fell ill en route into exile in the northeast. Such protracted delays apparently never occurred during this period in the case of Xinjiang exiles, who seem to have been more closely monitored. See, however, Cohen, *China and Christianity*, 121–122, on the delay of at least two years achieved by an official exiled in 1865 for flouting the foreign treaties. The popularity of this official's actions among some of his colleagues may have made it possible for him to avoid proceeding directly to Xinjiang.

granted a deferral of banishment for two years to enable her to nurse the incarcerated infant. The child was not exiled with his mother.[105] This case is striking both because of the concern that the child, although doomed from birth to spend a life in prison at government expense, should not simply be allowed to die and because of the contrast with contemporaneous British practice, where women bound for Botany Bay were sometimes wrenched from their suckling infants to be sent into exile.[106]

The journey into exile invariably took several months, for the distance to even the nearest Xinjiang destination was enormous. Qing records show that Hami, closest to China proper, was almost 2,400 miles (7,180 li) from Beijing. Ürümqi was almost 3,000 miles (9,000 li) away, and Ili was more than 3,500 miles (10,600 li) from the capital.[107] A journey that originated in the southeastern provinces would have been even longer, although criminals were not required to travel by way of Beijing.

The rule was that exiles should cover an average of fifty li—approximately sixteen miles—per day. Thus the journey from Beijing to Hami might take six months, to Ürümqi it might take seven months, and to Ili it might take eight or nine months.[108] As was so often true of this type of regulation in Qing China, these were general guidelines rather than absolute requirements, because it was possible to check progress only at county yamens, which were usually more than fifty li apart. In keeping with the general policy of minimizing costs, there is no evidence that the Qing ever considered incurring the expense of establishing intermediate checkpoints.

In the event that a criminal failed to arrive at his exile destination more or less punctually, officials were alerted to the possibility that something was amiss and were required to report the problem to the emperor. Thus Chai Jijia, the second son of the executed military commander Chai Daji, was said to have left Zhejiang "in the winter" of 1788; he traveled from Jiangsu to Henan across Anhui province during the fourth month of 1789 but by the ninth month he had still not reached Xinjiang.[109] Chai Jijia may never have arrived in Xinjiang; a number of edicts inquiring into his whereabouts exist, but no satisfactory answer appears to have been given. How could Chai have disappeared despite the network of

---

105. *Daqing Lüli Huitong Xinzuan* 25, 7b, p. 2462.
106. Hughes, *The Fatal Shore*, 143.
107. *Huidian* (1899) 218, 220.
108. *QCWXTK* 203, p. 6678.
109. GZD QL 58217, 54/9/11.

officials charged with his safe conduct across the country? Was he secretly killed on Heshen's orders since that minister had been instrumental in Chai's father's disgrace? Did he quietly disappear with the help of some provincial official opposed to Heshen? There is at present no answer to these intriguing questions, but Chai's case demonstrates that even the most elaborate surveillance mechanisms such as those found in Qing China sometimes proved ineffectual.[110]

As a general rule, unjustified delays en route were forbidden, and there were few acceptable reasons for prolonging the journey into exile. Proof of genuine obstruction was required. For instance, one official bound for exile in Xinjiang claimed he had to wait two days for the high winds to drop to be able to make a crossing by ferry. However, aware of the time constraints, he sent a subordinate ahead with a message. The messenger safely made the crossing in a small boat. Further investigation was ordered: how was it that the messenger could make the crossing but the official had to wait?[111]

Unsettled conditions were an acceptable reason for delay. These could affect ordinary convicts as well as disgraced officials. In 1784 a group of some two hundred communal feuders from Taiwan was detained in Zhejiang until a Muslim uprising in Gansu was suppressed. There is no indication that the government was concerned about their potential involvement on behalf of the rebels; the purpose of the delay was merely to avoid placing an additional burden on Gansu's already strained resources.[112]

Convicts exiled within China proper were not normally required to travel in the height of the midsummer heat, that is, during the sixth lunar month, nor in winter from the tenth to the first month. They were imprisoned during these seasonal interruptions of their journey.[113] The extension of this ruling to those exiled to the northeast resulted from the Kangxi Emperor's view that the extreme hardship of travel in adverse weather conditions would have rendered the journey virtually an additional punishment.[114] Xinjiang exiles, however, were normally required to continue their journey once they had reached Shaanxi province whatever the

110. See *QSL* QL 1337, 18a–b, 54/8/21; *GZD* QL 58374, 54/10/1; *QSL* QL 1339, 11a–b, 54/9/22; *SYD* (T) QL 54/11/6.
111. *QSL* QL 1337, 30b–31b, 54/8/29.
112. *SYD* (T) QL 49/8/20, 329.
113. See *DLCY* 45–01, 401–01. On the cost (166.88 taels) of extra supplies of clothing and hats for 150 criminals kept in prison during the winter, see *XKTB* QL 28/4/15, packet 334, memorial of Shuhede. These criminals apparently did not include any Xinjiang exiles.
114. *HDSL* (1899) 744, 1b.

time of year, notwithstanding the extreme temperatures of the northwest reported by government officials. Gansu, for instance, was unusually susceptible to "floods and droughts, hail, wind, sandstorms, insect plagues, frost, and snow." [115] In Xinjiang itself the winters were among the worst in the empire and accumulations of snow could make the journey extremely difficult; in the summer, the heat in the Gobi desert was sometimes so intense that traveling was bearable only at night. [116]

ESCAPES

Preventing escape was a key concern in the transfer of convicts to Xinjiang. When a convict did escape, everyone involved received severe punishment. Those stipulated for careless or unlucky escorts have already been described. The magistrate of the district in which the convict escaped was usually subject to dismissal and his superiors fined. [117]

Thus when the investigation of the escape of Yang Xiang, described in the opening section of this chapter, revealed that magistrate Wei had not personally checked the convicts before despatching them and that he had misreported the date of Yang's arrival and escape in the hope that Yang would be recaptured quickly, Wei was dismissed and ordered to help in the search. Two years later Wei was still in Fujian, the scene of the escape; he had not yet received any additional punishment. The jail warden who had left his post to travel with the party of the disgraced official was dismissed, and the escorts were sentenced to deferred execution for their part in the chain of events that led to Yang's escape. Their ultimate fate is unknown. [118]

Li Erman, the exile who fled from his escorts while pretending to re-

115. Memorial of 1742 submitted by Huang Tinggui, cited by Perdue, "The Qing State and the Gansu Grain Market," 3.

116. Many officials and exiles commented on the traveling conditions en route to Xinjiang. See, e.g., Hong, "Ili Riji," 6b–7a; Bi, "Qiuyue Yinjiaji," 9b–10a; Li, "Kou Zhan Liang Duan Ju"; Qi, "Wanli Xingcheng Ji," 14a. Ji Yun, returning from exile during the winter of 1770–71, sometimes traveled by night after the ground froze because mud and melting snow made daytime travel impossible. Ji, "Wulumuqi Zashi," preface.

117. *XJTLSL* 2, 27a–b.

118. *XKTB* QL 31/6/23, packet 288, memorial of Suchang. The jail warden had checked the prisoners on behalf of magistrate Wei, who had been absent investigating a murder. Wei thus committed the offence of not personally fulfilling his responsibilities. Wei had previously served a sentence of exile at a military postal station on the Mongolian border. He was, by his own admission, particularly anxious to avoid further punishment. *GZDQLCZZ* vol. 29, 546, 33/2/6.

lieve himself, did not long remain at liberty. A native of Anping district, near Beijing, Li was recaptured six months later in Ansu county, not far from his home. His captors were two runners, one from Longde, the district in Gansu from which he had escaped, and one from Ansu. Before his execution, Li told his interrogators: "[After I escaped] I begged for food and slept in empty temples. I had no fixed abode and I did not dare return home. On the twenty-second of the first month, I unexpectedly met my son, Li Erxiao, and we went together to Moushan village in Ansu. We supported ourselves by selling baked wheatcakes." [119]

When a convict escaped, an immediate report was made to the central government, which then alerted the convict's native place and all provinces between there and the place of escape; it was assumed that the convict would attempt to return home. This procedure was normally straightforward but might become more complicated if migrants were involved. For instance, convict Rao Yuxiang had been banished from Sichuan but was not necessarily a native of that province, for members of the Rao clan had moved to Sichuan from Jiangxi and Guangdong provinces. All three provinces were notified of Rao's escape. [120]

After a convict was recaptured, officials through whose jurisdictions he had passed undiscovered might be demoted. The extent of punishment depended on the length of time the convict had remained undetected in a particular place. [121] At the convict's native place, local officials questioned his family, neighbors, and mutual surveillance groups, all of whom were punished if they concealed information. [122] It thus was extremely difficult for a fugitive to elude the authorities for long, but some nonetheless managed to remain in hiding indefinitely.

As we have seen, the system of convict transmission depended heavily on the cooperation of both officials and escorts. Considerable numbers of people, including convicts and their escorts, traveled between adjacent counties in the course of the journey to Xinjiang. Each district received notice of the impending arrival of a convict and returned confirmation of his safe arrival to the previous district. Thus a degree of cooperation was

119. *GZDQLCZZ* vol. 20, 584–585, 29/2/17. For other memorials on Li's case, see also *GZDQLCZZ* vol. 94, 28/12/16; 414–415, 29/1/24; 650, 29/2/24.

120. See *QSL* QL 782, 12a–b, 32/4/8.

121. *XJTLSL* 33a–34a. For edicts on the punishment of officials in connection with convict escapes, see *QSL* QL 716, 10b–11a, 29/8/7; *QSL* QL 775, 7a–b, 31/12/19; *QSL* QL 945, 19a–b, 38/10/24.

122. *QSL* QL 685, 5a–b, 28/4/18.

necessary even when all went smoothly. In the event of an escape, however, the fate of those responsible depended to a large extent on the convict's recapture wherever he might be, thus making cooperation among
personnel in different parts of the country crucially important.

After 1763 each province submitted an annual report of the number of
criminals despatched to Xinjiang.[123] The reports included the following
information: how many of those despatched were known to have arrived
safely in exile, how many had escaped, and how many of the escapees
had been recaptured. Later the reports also listed the escapes of which
notice had been received from other provinces. The same data on the
Xinjiang "changees" was sometimes included in these reports.[124]

The possibility that those responsible for convict escapes might suppress such information because of the risk of punishment is suggested by
the relatively low numbers of reported escapes, although it may be that
the system was in fact highly efficient.[125] In 1767 2 of the 17 criminals
banished to Xinjiang from Shandong province escaped; both were recaptured. Zhejiang province sent 84 convicts to Xinjiang in the same year.
One escaped in Shaanxi; he was recaptured and executed. In 1776 2 of
the 137 criminals banished to Xinjiang from Guangdong province
escaped; both were recaptured.[126] In 1779 Jiangxi reported that none of
the 61 convicts sent to Xinjiang during the previous year had escaped.[127]
In 1787, Hunan province had a similar success with the 11 convicts it
sent to Xinjiang. In the same year, Hunan was notified of 225 convicts
from other provinces who had escaped over the years and were still at
large. As a proportion of the total number of exiles, this figure was small,
but in absolute terms it was not insignificant.[128]

It was inevitable that some convicts would escape during their long
journey to Xinjiang; the often well documented efforts to recapture them
indicate the government's reluctance to recognize or acquiesce in a necessary degree of slippage. Security improved somewhat in the course of

123. *QSL* QL 690, 8b–9b, 28/7/5.

124. See, e.g., *JJD* QL 25312, 45/2/20; *JJD* QL 26234, 45/1/27.

125. See GZD QL 34347, 43/3/8.

126. GZDQLCZZ vol. 30, 19, 33/3/8; GZDQLCZZ vol. 29, 700–701, 33/2/19; GZD
QL 30505, 42/1/9.

127. *JJD* QL 26154, 45/1/28. This figure included criminals from Jiangxi and Guangdong.

128. GZD QL 53073, 53/1/20. This figure included those who had escaped in previous
years and were still at large, as well as new escapees.

time. Recaptured convicts interrogated prior to their execution rarely admitted to having bribed their way to liberty, although in reality this doubtless occurred. The convicts' continuing attempts to escape clearly reflected the horror with which many ordinary Chinese viewed the prospect of permanent detachment from their native place and a lifetime in Xinjiang.

DEATH IN TRANSIT

The annual provincial escape reports included information on the death of convicts. For example, the report submitted for Guangdong province in early 1768 reported that of fifty-three criminals despatched to Xinjiang during the previous year, fifteen (almost 30 percent) had died en route. The rest had arrived safely.[129] The report from Guangdong submitted in early 1774 noted that four of the six criminals sentenced to Xinjiang banishment in the previous year had died before arriving in exile. One had died of illness, one had drowned, and one had committed suicide en route. The fourth had killed himself in the local jail before departure.[130] This high mortality rate was not necessarily typical of all provinces. Guangdong was the only one that consistently reported the death of its convicts en route to Xinjiang; other provinces occasionally reported one or two such deaths in the course of a year.

If the convict's family were not far from the exile destination at his death, or if the convict's sons were robust enough to work, they were permitted to proceed if they wished. In Xinjiang they were registered as civilians even if the deceased convict would have been enslaved. They could return home if they preferred.[131] These rules gave the deceased's family remarkable latitude; the dearth of evidence concerning their implementation suggests that few chose to return in such circumstances, no doubt in part because the government did not defray the expenses of such journeys.[132]

Some convicts resorted to suicide rather than submitting to exile. In 1768 a woman poisoned herself en route to Xinjiang, leaving a note writ-

129. *GZDQLCZZ* vol. 29, 395, 33/1/18.
130. *GZD* QL 27880, 39/1/22.
131. *DLCY* 15–09.
132. See *QCWXTK* 205, p. 6693 (ruling of 1767).

ten in Manchu that the local officials could not understand.[133] In 1782, the banished magistrate Yin Changlin was authorized to delay his journey at Gaolan, Gansu, for three months while he recovered from dysentery contracted on the journey. By the time he was well enough to travel (the latter part of the eighth month) the weather had turned cold. Yin was granted a further delay of a few days to acquire a coat. He killed himself in Gaolan while his servant and escorts slept.[134]

The large influx of criminals and escorts undoubtedly placed heavy pressures on local resources.[135] The need to supply food, transport, accommodation, and escorts affected every province, but the burden was particularly heavy in Gansu province, through which all Xinjiang exiles passed. Not only was it one of the poorest provinces in the empire, but Gansu was also frequently subject to other demands because of its strategic location as a conduit to the northwest.[136] For local officials throughout China maintaining a close watch over convicts in transit was crucial, both because of the perceived risk to local social stability and because of the risk of severe punishment in the event of an escape.

The transportation of exiles across China to Xinjiang thus required a high level of efficiency. It called for careful practical and economic coordination both between individual provinces, prefectures, and counties and between the central government and the provincial administrations temporarily responsible for the safe passage of the exiles. That the complicated logistics on the whole operated successfully is testimony to the continuing overall strength, despite its many shortcomings, of the Chinese governmental infrastructure in the late eighteenth and early nineteenth centuries.

133. *GZDQLCZZ* vol. 30, 4–5, 33/3/6.

134. *GZD* QL 42488, 47/9/14. According to the testimony of Yin's servant, Yin requested the delay to enable himself to obtain some money, possibly from a government source, to defray his expenses. For other examples of the suicide of officials sentenced to banishment in Xinjiang, see *SYD* (T) QL 41/3/3, 281; *SYD* (B) QL 57/6/12, 91–2, 121.

135. Such pressure was a continuing problem of convict transmission. See, e.g., *QSL* QL 737, 26b–27a, 30/5/30.

136. See Perdue, "The Qing State and the Gansu Grain Market," 2–5.

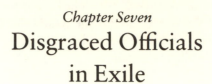

Chapter Seven
Disgraced Officials
in Exile

The difficult and unpredictable journey into exile was but a taste of things to come. Banished scholars and officials, accustomed to the privileges of their elevated social position, and conscious, too, of a weighty intellectual tradition of exile, perhaps had some grounds for optimism, but for common criminals there was little hope. For every exile a measure of uncertainty lay in store. None really knew or could even imagine fully what their life in exile would hold nor for how long it would endure.

The two groups of exiles, disgraced officials and ordinary convicts, were not isolated from each other in Xinjiang; indeed, their paths often crossed in the relatively limited society of the new frontier. Contact was also to be expected at work, where former officials might be assigned to supervise convict laborers in the iron mines or to direct convicts serving as copyists in a yamen. On a different level, a common native place might create certain links, although perhaps not often overcoming the barriers of social class and education. Similarly, shared dialects doubtless facilitated contacts between certain exiles in the two groups, while creating corresponding barriers among others.

Two principal aspects of the exile experience affected both officials and commoners banished to Xinjiang. The first was the ambiguity of their relationship with the government. These exiles' presence in Xinjiang and the work they performed were essential components of the colonization process, yet the state's reliance on the loyalty and honesty of these "criminals" involved an element of calculated risk. The second common experience was the intensification of the insecurity and uncertainty that pervaded all life in late eighteenth- and early nineteenth-century China.

This and the following chapter present extracts of a mosaic composed of the diverse experiences of the men and women exiled to Xinjiang. In keeping with the differential treatment accorded disgraced officials and common convicts, these chapters describe their lives in exile separately. The description begins with officials, who had some hope of returning home after serving a term of years in exile, and whose lives in the meantime were far less circumscribed and far less brutal than those of the ordinary convicts.

WORK IN EXILE

The work required of banished government officials formed an integral part of their punishment, not least because it was one of the principal vehicles for self-renewal (*zixin*) in exile. Thus some sentences of banishment to Xinjiang explicitly ordered the exile to expiate his crime through exertion (*xiaoli shuzui*); others did so implicitly, directing the exile to perform government service (*dangchai*), hard labor (*kuchai*) or, occasionally, grindingly hard labor (*zhemo chaishi*). Other sentences did not involve expiation through labor in any of these specific categories, as in the case of an official banished to Ürümqi to "exert himself farming" (*chongdi xiaoli*), yet expiation was clearly the purpose of the sentence.[1]

Officials were dismissed from their positions before being sentenced to banishment. However, some were awarded a new rank or title before being sent to Xinjiang, and others, already serving sentences of banishment, received such awards when they were seconded to perform particular duties within Xinjiang.[2] Thus former governor Asiha, originally sentenced to death for corruption, had his sentence commuted; the emperor conferred an official button of the third rank before banishing him to Ürümqi.[3] Former judicial commissioner Detai, banished to Ili for corruption, was awarded the rank of a secretary (*zhushi*) and seconded to work as a subprefect (*tongzhi*).[4] While in exile disgraced officials usually re-

1. *QSL* QL 864, 27b–29a, 35/7/12.
2. See *SYD* (B) QL 59/4/27, 187; *SZJL* 4, 131–132.
3. *Qing Shi Gao* 337, pp. 11050–11051. After his recall, Asiha rose to a governor-generalship.
4. *SYD* (T) JQ 6/2/16, 133. See also *SYD* (T) JQ 7/6/11, 69. The rank of a secretary was 6A; that of a subprefect was 5A. Brunnert and Hagelstrom, *Present Day Political Organization of China*, nos. 292, 849.

ceived no salary; even rank or title did not necessarily carry the entitlement to a salary or "integrity-nourishing" supplement (*yanglian*).[5]

The rationale behind conferring ranks or titles on some disgraced officials is unclear, possibly because there was no firm system. In any event,
the simultaneous award of official status, albeit reduced, and punishment
conformed to the treatment of bureaucrats in mid-Qing China. It was a
method of control that at once raised hopes and crushed aspirations.[6]

The employment of banished officials in the frontier bureaucracy
served the central government in several important ways. The availability
of these educated and experienced men to work without remuneration in
Xinjiang enabled the Qing to administer the frontier without significantly
enlarging the imperial bureaucracy for this purpose. This went some way
towards achieving the goal of self-sufficiency and hence towards satisfying the critics of the huge expense involved in garrisoning and governing the new frontier.[7] An additional advantage was that positions in
China proper vacated by banished officials became available for new
candidates from the growing pool of qualified men awaiting official
appointment. Thus, through a process of juggling, it became possible to
find positions for a larger number of candidates than would otherwise
have been available.

In Xinjiang during the Qianlong and Jiaqing periods the balance of
prestige and power between civil and military officials gradually shifted
in favor of the former. Certainly in the early years after the conquest the
indigenous population esteemed military success over scholarly achievement as a measure of status at Ürümqi.[8] As Xinjiang became more settled, the manifestation of military strength became less important and
civilian accomplishments, including education, gained in prestige.

In the initial years of Xinjiang banishment no precise regulations gov-

5. See *SZJL* 4, 131. Some partially disgraced officials sent to Xinjiang and ordered to
defray their own expenses were entitled to receive half the amount of the *yanglian* salary
supplement once they had arrived at their exile destination. After 1807 such officials were
no longer entitled to any *yanglian* payment until they were transferred. After one transfer
they received half their *yanglian* and after two transfers they received the full amount.
Members of their family employed in Beijing were not permitted to remit any part of their
own salaries to Xinjiang. *HDSL* (1899) 252, 6a. In some cases such officials, although
otherwise unpaid, were entitled to receive a food allowance. See *QSL* QL 634, 24a, 26/4/
15; *HDSL* (1899) 263, 9a–b.

6. See, generally, Metzger, *Internal Organization*, 236–417, (on the administrative
punishment of civil officials).

7. The soldiers' annual pay alone amounted to approximately three million taels. See
Fletcher, "Ch'ing Inner Asia," 60.

8. Ji, "Wulumuqi Zashi," 11b.

erned the employment of banished officials. The first proposal to use such exiles for specific positions in the frontier administration was made in 1766, although at the time it represented an ad hoc arrangement rather than the establishment of a new system.[9] In the late 1760s the scholar-official Ji Yun was chiefly employed drafting documents, such as memorials and military orders, at Ürümqi, where he was serving his term of exile. (See figure 2 for a picture of Ji Yun). In 1770 when Ürümqi lieutenant governor Bayanbi proposed to emancipate certain ordinary convicts who had served several years in exile, for instance, Ji drafted the memorial on Bayanbi's behalf.[10] Ji also assisted the Ili military governor in a pacification campaign.[11]

By the turn of the century, the employment of banished officials had become more or less regularized, although there was considerable scope for flexibility to meet pressing needs. Thus in 1800 at Ili disgraced officials performed much of the work within the yamen of the military governor, where certain positions were specifically reserved for them.[12] The organization of the yamen was modeled on that of the central government, as was the case with local administration in China proper. There were separate offices in charge of personnel, revenue, rites, military affairs, justice (where Manchus and Chinese were handled separately), and public works, an office of merits and demerits that corresponded to the Beijing censorate, and offices for handling the drafting and despatch of documents.[13] The exiled scholar Hong Liangji, for instance, worked first in the office of document despatch and then, with banished magistrate Wei Peijin, in the office of document storage.[14]

High-ranking civilian exiles such as former governors or provincial judicial commissioners were normally assigned to work on revenue matters, whereas their military counterparts were assigned to work in the office of military affairs.[15] In practice it was often possible to adapt the

9. See *QSL* QL 753, 11b–12b, 31/1/20, for an early proposal to use officials expiating their crimes at Ili to fill certain yamen vacancies.

10. See Ji's biography: *Guochao Hanxue Shicheng Ji* 6, 1b.

11. Ji, *Yuewei Caotang Biji* 1, 23a–b, and 16, 33b; Ji, *Ji Xiaolan Jiashu*, 36.

12. *Huidian* (1818) 3, 5a–b. Seven positions were reserved for disgraced officials at Ili; three at Ürümqi, and one each at Kalashar, Kuche, Aksu, Yarkand, Kashgar, and Ush.

13. Hong, "Tianshan Kehua," 4a–b. See also Xu, "Xinjiang Fu," 17b.

14. Hong, "Wanli Hege Ji," 11a.

15. Hong, "Tianshan Kehua," 4b. In 1800 some seventy exiles joined the military governor in attending an archery contest. On army service by disgraced military officials, see, e.g., ZPZZ JQ 18/1/15, (law—exile, packet for JQ 10–18), memorial of Jinchang; *GZD* JQ 19696, 20/8/25.

紀
昀

Figure 2. Ji Yun

assignment of disgraced officials to current needs.[16] Attempts were made to give available personnel the type of work best suited to their skills. For instance, the former Hong merchants from Canton, banished following the bankruptcy to which their dealings with foreigners had brought them, put their skills to use by serving as bookkeepers at the boatyards.[17]

Disgraced officials were particularly useful for drafting and handling Chinese documents in Xinjiang; there were very few Han Chinese (other than those in disgrace) employed in Xinjiang during the Qianlong and Jiaqing periods except at the lowest levels of the bureaucracy.[18] Disgraced officials serving sentences of exile at Ili were sometimes transferred to fill vacancies at other locations within Xinjiang when skill in written Chinese was needed.[19] Drafting, checking, and transmitting documents involved considerable responsibility and as a safeguard, many of the most important communications between Xinjiang and the capital were written in Manchu, which the majority of Chinese officials were unable to understand.

A number of banished officials were assigned to supervisory work in Xinjiang. Supervisory work was much needed on the farms and, at least in the early days of the frontier colony, on construction sites. A 1767 document described the work of four disgraced officials who had been serving sentences of banishment at Balikun for more than three years. They had directed land reclamation, helped extend an irrigation channel, assisted in construction work, and raised money to purchase horses for use in the imperial postal service.[20] Some disgraced officials were assigned to work at the arsenal, an undemanding position that, according to one exile, involved only a monthly trip to the yamen and was reserved for elderly or impoverished exiles.[21]

Part of the colonization process involved establishing quotas in Xinjiang for the examination degrees that led to appointment in the imperial

16. The assignment of former regimental colonel Jilehang'a to revenue work exemplified this lack of rigidity. *GZD* JQ 15621, 19/6/5.

17. *SYD* (B) QL 60/8/9, 97.

18. Lin, "Qingdai Xinjiang Zhouxian Zhidu zhi Yanjiu," 29–39.

19. See, e.g., *SYD* (B) JQ 11/1/20, 195, on a former magistrate who spent eighteen years in exile handling Chinese documents at Tarbagatai, northwest of Ürümqi. See also *SYD* (B) JQ 11/12/20, 295; *GZD* JQ 13846, 14/4/11.

20. *ZPZZ* QL 32/3/21 (law—exile, packet for QL 32–50), memorial of Wudashan.

21. Hong, "Tianshan Kehua," 4b. Other employment, such as mine work, often involved contributions by the disgraced officials. On the use of locally mined lead at the Ili arsenal, see *Xichui Zongtong Shilüe* 8, 2b–3a.

bureaucracy. At Ürümqi, in a move that seemed to reconfirm the area's status as an administrative and cultural bridge between China proper and the world beyond, such quotas were established in 1767. In addition, at Ürümqi the Qing followed their general policy of establishing schools on the imperial frontiers to educate local inhabitants in the ways of Chinese civilization.

The highly educated exiles were a vital resource for this purpose. Thus banished civil officials were sent to teach in the charity schools founded in 1767 by Ürümqi lieutenant governor Wenfu.[22] In the 1760s Ji Yun recorded the existence of four academies (*shuyuan*) in that area, as well as local schools in the agricultural colonies and charity schools for teaching the soldiers' children.[23] The Hufeng academy at Ürümqi was directed by former Baxian magistrate Chen Zhili and later by former Wuyuan magistrate Yang Fengyuan.[24]

At Ili, however, no examination degree quota existed prior to 1884, when Xinjiang was given provincial status. An 1803 proposal to establish schools, with disgraced officials responsible for teaching and examinations, was rejected, in a move that seemed to express imperial ambivalence towards the sinicization of the whole of Xinjiang. The Jiaqing period exile Xu Song noted the existence of some schools at Ili, but these taught mainly Manchu and instilled respect for imperial pronouncements, rather than teaching the curriculum for the examinations.[25] Disgraced officials were not formally employed as teachers at Ili during this period, although some exiles offered informal instruction on Chinese history and the classics[26] and some low-ranking banished military officials were employed teaching skills such as archery.[27]

The access to power afforded disgraced officials by their work certainly offered considerable scope for corruption or sabotage, especially since their exile often resulted from malfeasance of some kind. However, there is little evidence to suggest that they took advantage of such opportuni-

22. *SZJL* 6, 219.

23. Ji, "Wulumuqi Zashi," 17a.

24. Ji, *Yuewei Caotang Biji*, 4, 13b–14a. Others whose exile involved teaching included Hong Liangji's contemporary Wang Liyuan, who taught in the military governor's yamen at Ili (Hong, "Wanli Hege Ji," 11b), and Song Yu, a Chinese bannerman who had received his *jinshi* degree in 1761 (*Yutianxian Zhi* 18, 11a).

25. See Xu, "Xinjiang Fu," 22b.

26. Hong, "Wanli Hege Ji," 6b; 15a. Hong Liangji punctuated the classics for someone while in exile and was paid with a sheep.

27. See *SZJL* 6, 219; Hong, "Wanli Hege Ji," 12a.

ties. Some may have been committed, sincerely or superficially, to the idea that their exile involved a process of self-renewal; others were simply too intimidated by the punishment they had already received to risk flouting the law again.

Wu Yulin's involvement in a major corruption case uncovered at Ürümqi in 1781 was an exception to the general level of honesty found among feiyuan. Wu, a bannerman exiled in the early 1760s for attempting to change his name to avoid paying debts, spent almost twenty years in Xinjiang. He served for a decade in the Green Standard army and was then emancipated, attaining civilian status but remaining at Ürümqi.[28] He used his subsequent appointment to a post in the lieutenant governor's yamen to extort bribes from local officials and was eventually executed.[29]

Military governor Songyun (in office 1802–1809), employed several disgraced officials in the compilation of a Xinjiang gazetteer. This represented something of a departure from the practice in China proper, for local histories, elevated in the eighteenth century to a new level of respect through the writings of the historian Zhang Xuecheng (1738–1801), were normally compiled by scholars, usually native sons, completely familiar with their subject through long residence.

Songyun's original proposal for a local history project was rejected by the emperor, partly on the ground there were not enough qualified people in Xinjiang to undertake such a task.[30] To the extent that there were no suitably qualified Xinjiang natives, this claim was true; moreover, most officials employed in the frontier bureaucracy were not especially noted for their scholarly accomplishments. Yet some exiles were extremely well qualified to do the work. For example, Qi Yunshi, in Xinjiang from 1805 to 1809, had earlier participated in the compilation of an officially sponsored study of the frontier regions and had used the information he acquired to write his own history of the same areas.[31]

The emperor also opposed the proposed compilation of a gazetteer of

28. *SYD* (T) QL 41/n.d. (late first month or early second month), 81–83. Wu thus no longer had feiyuan status by 1781. His treatment—military service followed by civilian registration—was admittedly unusual, apparently because his long service in Xinjiang made him extremely familiar with local conditions.

29. *QSL* QL 1160, 7b–10a, 47/7/3. For another example of recidivism, see *SYD* (T) JQ 6/9/6, 55.

30. *SYD* (B) JQ 11/12/14, 211.

31. *ECCP* 134.

Xinjiang on other grounds. In a further affirmation of the region's status as a military protectorate, he stressed that, on the new frontier, agriculture and defense were far more important than education. Any continuation of the official history compiled soon after the conquest of Xinjiang should be undertaken in due course by the Fanglüe Guan, the office in Beijing responsible for compiling the official records of military campaigns. Nonetheless, only a few months later, an edict declared (in another context) that "Xinjiang is no different from China proper."[32]

In any event, under Songyun's sponsorship the compilation of a history of Xinjiang was eventually begun by former magistrate Wang Tingkai, continued by Qi Yunshi, and completed by former education commissioner Xu Song.[33] All worked on the project while serving sentences of banishment in Xinjiang, gathering information as they compiled an authorized continuation of an earlier work on the languages of the frontier regions (*Xiyu Tongwen Zhi*).[34] The resulting work in twelve chapters was entitled *Xinjiang Shilüe*. It was presented to the emperor by Songyun and published in 1821 by the imperial printing office, the *Wuyingdian*.

The appearance of this type of local history made a subtle but important contribution to the colonization process by helping to equate Xinjiang with the provinces of China proper in the public perception. More tangibly, disgraced officials' work in administration, agriculture, industry, and education made an important contribution to the transformation of Xinjiang from a disunified and partly nomadic territory to a Chinese province. Thus the Qing employment of disgraced officials in Xinjiang in the long term was a more successful part of the colonization process than they had originally intended.

LIFE IN EXILE

Banished scholars and officials occupied an ambiguous position in frontier society. Despite their disgrace, they formed part of the elite in an area lacking a landowning, degree-holding local "gentry" group of the type

32. *SYD* (B) JQ 12/2/6, 66.

33. Songyun's rejected proposal involved a general gazetteer of Ili only; the work eventually produced covered all of Xinjiang.

34. *Xichui Zongtong Shilüe* 1, 1a. This work was Qi Yunshi's draft of the work (*Qinding Xinjiang Shilüe*) later presented to the emperor.

familiar throughout China proper. Considerable personal prestige also attached to at least the more eminent of these exiles by virtue of their former positions.

For local officials exercising authority over the exiles, the appropriate treatment of disgraced former colleagues was complicated. Actual ill-treatment would have been injudicious given the distinct possibility of a subsequent reversal of roles; the seesawing of factional politics, combined with the self-renewal process, made it not unusual for banished officials to attain senior positions following their return from Xinjiang.[35] When Hong Liangji was recalled from exile, Ili military governor Baoning performed nine kowtows to the man whom he had secretly proposed to execute upon a pretext not six months earlier, having assumed this to be the true intention of the authorities in Beijing. Baoning's assumption doubtless resulted from the fresh uncertainties that the recent Heshen debacle had introduced to official life.[36] His subsequent action acknowledged the need to seek to obliterate any ill will that Hong might bear him, particularly if Hong should later attain a position of prominence.[37]

Baoning seems to have been punctilious in his relations with the exiles. He required that banished officials observe such formalities as kneeling in his presence; sometimes they had to remain kneeling for a considerable time before they were permitted to rise.[38] When former Jiangxi governor Chen Huai reported his arrival at Ili to serve a sentence of exile, Baoning reprimanded him for using his former official title; thereafter Chen always presented identifying credentials (*jiaose*) when he called on the military governor.[39] However, other senior Xinjiang officials, including Wenfu, Ürümqi lieutenant governor in the 1760s, Kuilin, Ili military governor in the 1780s, and Songyun, were markedly less formal in their relations with banished officials, possibly because of their own power and prestige.

Edicts sometimes complained of excessive leniency toward the exiles. Baoning, for instance, despite his usual caution, was reprimanded on at

35. See chapter 9.
36. See *Changzhoufu Zhi*, "Renwu Zhuan," 2b.
37. Hong, "Bairi Cihuan Ji," 1a; 3b. That the existence of the proposal is known to us through Hong's poems makes clear that Hong did learn of Baoning's plan.
38. Hong, "Tianshan Kehua," 5a; Hong, "Wanli Hege Ji," 11a.
39. Hong, "Tianshan Kehua," 5a. The jiaose was a form of résumé. For a pro forma, see Huang, *Fuhui Quanshu* 1, 21a–b. Previously Chen Huai had been implicated in the Gansu corruption case but since his subsequent reappointment he had risen to hold the Jiangxi governorship.

least one occasion for sending birthday greetings to the emperor on behalf of disgraced officials at Ili.[40] An 1803 edict particularly discouraged
the formation of close connections between Xinjiang officials and their
exiled former colleagues, implying that it was unsuitable to offer the disgraced officials any opportunity to seek advantage for themselves.[41]
Seven years later, rumors that banished officials in Xinjiang and the
northeast often dined with the local military governors provoked a severe
prohibition against fraternizing. Such behavior, lamented the edict, completely frustrated the intention of giving the banished officials a taste of
hardship:

> When I order [exiles] harshly treated so that they will reform, but
> senior officials [in their place of banishment] on the contrary offer
> them protection, providing for their necessities and facilitating their
> housing arrangements, subsidizing a life of indolence and pleasure,
> [the exiles] completely lose sight of the bitterness of banishment.[42]

Exiled officials were not forbidden to communicate with home; both Ji
Yun and Hong Liangji, for instance, corresponded with their friends and
family during their banishment.[43] Although the governmental postal system was highly organized in the eighteenth century,[44] it was not available
for use by private individuals, far less by exiles.[45] Private postal facilities
existed but were slow and unreliable; moreover as a general rule they
were concentrated in more densely populated areas than the route to

40. *SYD* (T) QL 54/6/1, 247.
41. *QSL* JQ 108, 5a–b, 8/2/9; *QSL* JQ 108, 11a–b, 8/2/11; *SYD* (T) JQ 8/2/21, 109–110.
42. *SYD* (T) JQ 15/7/24, 297–300. The case in question occurred in the northeast. The Jilin military governor had had a house repaired for feiyuan Bengwubu, and had dined with him.
43. On the role of letters in the evidential research movement amongst scholars during this period, see Elman, *From Philosophy to Philology*, 203–204.
44. At the height of the Xinjiang campaign, an urgent communication could be sent from Ili to Beijing (a distance of more than thirty-five hundred miles) in a little more than twenty days, although under normal conditions it took considerably longer. *Qinding Ping-ding Zhunke'er Fanglüe* 49, 22a–b, QL 23/1/26.
45. See, e.g., *QSL* QL 606, 8a–10b, 25/2/2; *GZDQLCZZ* vol. 21, 560, 29/5/25. While in Xinjiang in the 1840s, Lin Zexu maintained a close correspondence with his wife, his sons, and his friends. The military governor, who treated Lin extraordinarily well, some-times helped him send letters, in part through official channels. Lin, "Riji," 438. Lin's immense personal prestige gave him access to government mail services that cannot be regarded as typical for disgraced officials. Normally the enclosure of personal letters with government documents was strictly prohibited.

Xinjiang.[46] Thus the exiles had to devise other ways to maintain contact with their friends and family in China proper.

What little evidence exists concerning how private mail was sent between Xinjiang and China proper suggests a number of possibilities. Exiles might be able to entrust mail to a returning colleague or to an official traveling back to China proper.[47] In 1770 the scholar and future court patron Bi Yuan, then employed as a circuit intendant in Gansu, participated in an inspection tour of the agricultural colonies that took him as far as Ürümqi. On this trip, Bi encountered his fellow Hanlin academician Ji Yun, still serving his term of exile.[48] Perhaps Ji took advantage of this unexpected meeting to send messages home through Bi's good offices, not knowing that he himself would shortly be recalled. Thirty years later, Hong Liangji was able to send letters to his colleagues from Balikun, through which he passed on his way to Ili, in care of someone who was returning to China proper.[49] In addition, servants could sometimes carry correspondence, and merchants traveling between Xinjiang and China proper may also have operated an informal postal service.[50]

Disgraced officials were not normally subject to house arrest or other restrictions within the confines of their place of exile. The case of former assistant magistrate Hong Zhi was a rare exception. Banished in 1788 for cowardice in connection with Lin Shuangwen's uprising in Taiwan, he was later implicated in treasury deficits in Fujian that had arisen prior to his exile. Hong Zhi was imprisoned at Ili in 1796 under a sentence of death that was to be implemented if he failed to repay the monies in question. Not until eight years later, after 90 percent had been repaid, was Hong Zhi permitted to leave his Ili prison to return home.[51]

At Ili exiles were free to leave Huiyuan city on short excursions, but they were required to report their departure at the city gate. Nine times

46. See Cheng, *Postal Communication in China and its Modernization, 1860–1896*, 3.
47. On the use of friends, fellow officials, and servants to carry illicitly acquired funds from Xinjiang to China proper in 1777–1778, see Torbert, *The Ch'ing Imperial Household Department*, 150. The sender was employed in Xinjiang and was not an exile.
48. Bi, "Qiuyue Yinjiaji," 12b–13a.
49. Hong, "Wanli Hege Ji," 6a.
50. For a case in which correspondence carried by a servant had disastrous consequences for the sender, see *Sanfasi* Archives no. 1490, QL 44/9/n.d. See also *SYD* (B) JQ 13/6/24, 323–325, for a case in which an exile sent a servant with messages for his son.
51. *ZPZZ* JQ 9/3/1 (law—exile, packet for JQ 1–9), memorial of Songyun; *SYD* (T) JQ 9/3/28, 215.

each month disgraced officials were obliged to assemble at the military governor's yamen for a de facto roll call.[52]

Former officials in Xinjiang were occasionally sentenced to wear the cangue. This additional humiliation was usually intended to mark continued misdemeanor. Such was the case of Kaitai, sentenced to wear the cangue in perpetuity as a result of his illicit purchase of a concubine. When Kaitai fell ill, he was entrusted to the charge of Futong, a banner colonel to whom he was very distantly connected.[53] Kaitai persuaded Futong to unfasten his cangue and let him live independently. It was general knowledge that the concubine used to visit the liberated prisoner in his house, and she later bore him a son. When Futong was ordered to go to Rehe for an imperial audience, Kaitai's freedom was at an end. Soon afterwards Kaitai drowned himself, leaving his cangue by the side of a well.[54]

Accommodation was usually provided for a newly arrived exile, although at whose expense is not clear. Some exiles stayed in yamen quarters; others occupied separate lodgings. Ürümqi lieutenant governor Wenfu housed Ji Yun within his yamen compound, which Ji regarded as a particular favor. After Wenfu was transferred, Ji moved to a friend's house outside the yamen.[55] At Ili former governor Chen Huai lived in a pavilion to the west of the official residence of councillor Lu Ben. Chen's lodgings were set in several *mu* of land where the flowers were bigger than any seen in China proper. Hong Liangji (see figure 3) was assigned a willow-encircled house in the western part of the city. Its main room was known as the "Huanbi porch" and had columns painted with auspicious inscriptions. This accommodation was in contrast to local rest houses: "[They] are as close as hornets' nests. Apart from an earthen platform there is only a foot or two of space in which the smells of smoke and dust are mingled. On my two journeys, in winter and in summer, I stayed in my cart at night and never stayed in an earthen house (*tufang*)."[56] Hong

52. Hong, "Tianshan Kehua," 4b; Hong, "Wanli Hege Ji," 12b.

53. Kaitai was related to the concubine of Futong's brother-in-law.

54. *SYD* (T) QL 48/n.d., 307–316; *QSL* QL 1186, 14a–15b, 48/8/15. For another example of the canguing of a former official in exile (in this instance a magistrate), see *SYD* (B) JQ 16/9/14, 193.

55. Ji, *Ji Xiaolan Jiashu*, 21, 23. His friend was Tian Baiyan, from Dezhou, in Shandong, according to Ji the youngest son of the scholar Tian Wen (d. 1704). Tian had taught poetry to Lu Jianzeng, also of Dezhou, whose grandson married Ji's eldest daughter. Ji had been exiled for alerting Lu to Lu's imminent arrest.

56. Hong, "Tianshan Kehua," 1a, 3a, 5a. Cf. Ji, "Wulumuqi Zashi," 13a, where Ji Yun refers to emancipist houses as very close "like hornets' nests."

洪
亮
吉

Figure 3. Hong Liangji

was clearly relieved to be assigned to live in the Huanbi porch house, even though it was said to be haunted by another exile who had died there hoping to be recalled.[57]

For some exiles, time must have passed slowly, but there were many ways in which to occupy one's leisure.[58] Literary pursuits were a favorite recreation. Some wrote prose accounts of Xinjiang; others wrote poetry.[59] Because of the potential dangers of the written word, some exiles felt it prudent only to exchange innocuous calligraphy or to write inscriptions.[60] Hong Liangji's friends admonished him to exercise great caution, reiterating the warning given to the Song dynasty poet Su Dong-po, exiled to the south: "If you are visiting from the north, do not ask too many questions; even if you like West Lake do not write a poem about it."[61]

Obtaining reading matter in Xinjiang was not easy. Before 1767, when the examination quota was established at Ürümqi, there were no book-shops, and the only hope was to purchase volumes from local merchants who sold books along with other goods. After 1767, however, special-ized bookshops selling classical texts opened in Ürümqi, although during this period there was still no such incentive for booksellers at Ili.[62] To resolve this problem, exiles brought books with them to share with their fellows; it was customary to distribute these among colleagues before returning to China proper.[63]

Flowers and plants provided a source of interest for some of the exiles. After peonies and peach trees were transplanted to Xinjiang, in some cases by exiles, the flora of Ürümqi gradually began to resemble those in China proper.[64] The poppies that former governor Chen Huai brought from Jiangxi grew to an enormous size at Ili; there is no suggestion that

57. Hong, "Tianshan Kehua," 1a–b.

58. Ji Yun wrote that he had little leisure—hence his Ürümqi poems were written from memory during his return journey. Ji, "Wulumuqi Zashi," preface. Thirty years later, Hong Liangji and his fellow exiles appear to have been kept less busy.

59. On the literature of Xinjiang banishment, see the following section.

60. Hong, "Tianshan Kehua," 4a; Hong, "Wanli Hege Ji," 11b. When Lin Zexu passed through Ürümqi on his way into exile at Ili his autograph was much in demand. Lin, "Hege Jicheng," 9a.

61. Hong, "Tianshan Kehua," 4a. According to one account, an edict was sent to mili-tary governor Baoning specifically prohibiting Hong from writing poetry (and from drink-ing) in exile. Hong, "Qianshu Ili Riji—Fu Chusai Jiwen," 13b.

62. Ji, "Wulumuqi Zashi," 16b.

63. Hong, "Tianshan Kehua," 5a.

64. Ji, "Wulumuqi Zashi," 25a–b. Peonies had been transplanted by an exile named Huang Baotian; a subprefect transplanted peach trees.

they were opium poppies, however.[65] Ji Yun was impressed with the size and variety of the marigolds and chrysanthemums that grew in the ya-men compound where he lived for a time. He planned to send his wife some seeds to plant as a reminder of her exiled husband.[66] Former financial commissioner Gui Jingzhao became an adept chrysanthemum gardener and held a party on the double ninth to celebrate his horticultural success.

Sharing meals helped to pass the time agreeably. Former judicial commissioner Detai used to invite Hong Liangji to dinner and once gave a picnic for him at a scenic spot.[67] Chen Huai, known as an epicure, served roast pheasant at a party held on the double fifth.[68] The exiles ate lamb, the preferred meat of the local Muslims, and sometimes pork or wild boar, although because of Muslim sensibilities pork may well not have been readily available. Many found the locally available fish unsatisfactory, and some exiles raised fish themselves.[69] Cabbage, which grew in abundance, was the principal vegetable.[70] There were fine mulberries, more than an inch long, grapes from Hami, and many different types of local melons. Some fruits could be obtained from China proper but these, of course, were costly.[71] Many exiles particularly enjoyed food prepared in the style of their native areas. The thousands of taels amassed by Gao Wu, an emancipated convict who ran a store specializing in Jiangsu-style delicacies at Ili in 1788, attests to the popularity of the products he sold.[72]

At Ürümqi plays were performed in certain wineshops; in 1768 a seat cost only "a few *qian*." In addition to wine made from local grapes, it

---

65. Hong, "Wanli Hege Ji," 15a. See, however, Fletcher, "Ch'ing Inner Asia," 72, suggesting that the influx of Han Chinese into northern Xinjiang after the Qing conquest may have increased opium use in that region.

66. Ji, *Ji Xiaolan Jiashu*, 21.

67. Hong, "Wanli Hege Ji," 12a; 21a; Hong, "Tianshan Kehua," 3a.

68. Hong, "Tianshan Kehua," 2a–3b, 4b; Hong, "Wanli Hege Ji," 12a, 14b, 21a.

69. Hong, "Tianshan Kehua," 2a–b, 4b. Hong Liangji did not care for lamb and found the thick-skinned, scaleless fish difficult to eat. He enjoyed a dish of pork served by Zhao Bingxian, a fellow countryman also in exile. Hong, "Wanli Hege Ji," 12b. Earlier Ji Yun had noted that fish was little eaten on the frontier because the muddiness of the water made them wormy. Ji, "Wulumuqi Zashi," 13b. In 1842 Lin Zexu received a gift of wild boar meat from the military governor. Lin, "Riji," 438.

70. Hong, "Tianshan Kehua," 2a, 5B.

71. Hong, "Tianshan Kehua," 1b; Hong, "Wanli Hege Ji," 14b. Ji, "Wulumuqi Zashi," 19a; Ji, *Yuewei Caotang Biji* 15, 12a.

72. SYD (T) QL 53/3/19, 445–447. See also Hong, "Tianshan Kehua," 4a. On Gao Wu, see also chapter 9.

was possible to obtain rice wine such as Shaoxing from China proper.[73] The availability of Shaoxing wine and of Jiangsu-style food in Xinjiang may have been in part a response to a demand created by merchants from the Lower Yangzi region of China proper as well as to exiles' gastronomic nostalgia.

Traveling entertainers, considered by Ji Yun to be quite as good as those in Beijing, swarmed to ply their trade on the frontier, and some convicts were themselves talented actors and storytellers.[74] Other activities included gambling, which severely depleted the purses of several exiles.[75] At Ili gambling was banned not long before Hong Liangji's arrival in 1800. Outside the northern gate of Huiyuan city there were markets and numerous brothels.[76] There were temples to visit and festivals, such as those organized by merchant groups, to watch. Yet the familiarity of much of life in exile was belied by its strange ambiance, as Ji Yun's misapprehension concerning the colorful dress of Ürümqi merchants suggested:

> The sheepskin coats are new
>   and cut short at the back;
> For a northerner first seeing them
>   it is a rare sight,
> Dark viridian green and rosy purple,
> So colorful and ornate I mistook them for
>   women coming outside.

Merchants wore these brightly colored clothes, but officials and commoners wore plainer colors. Officials, who wore long robes in public in China proper, wore short jackets for conducting official business and long robes in private at Ürümqi. Ji observed: "This is a military encampment."

However much the exiles sought to replicate normal life, they were

---

73. The existence of grape wine in Xinjiang was recorded in an early nineteenth-century gazetteer: SZJL 9, 344. On the availability of Shaoxing wine in Xinjiang after the conquest, see Zhao, *Huangchao Wugong Jisheng* 2, 29. Joseph Fletcher noted that, although wine was already available in southern Xinjiang by the early eighteenth century, it was the Han Chinese who introduced spirits into northern Xinjiang."Ch'ing Inner Asia," 72.

74. Ji, "Wulumuqi Zashi," 35a–36b.

75. On gambling among exiles in the northeast, see Lee, *The Manchurian Frontier*, 86–87.

76. Hong, "Tianshan Kehua," 4b; Xu, "Xinjiang Fu," 17b.

very much out of their element. The sights and sounds of Xinjiang were a constant reminder:

> People here like animals, and every household has a dog. At night they go and sit on the top of the buildings. Once one barks, the rest all join in and one cannot get any sleep.

> Wealthy merchants all live in the old city. When they close down the evening market by the north and south gates, they play the flute and three-stringed lute for relaxation from their exertions; it is a local custom.[77]

THE EXILE TRADITION

Many earlier exiles had written about their banishment, conjuring up images of alien and remote areas and expressing anguish at their ejection from the heart of political life. Much of this genre of literature, for such it became, focused on the "myth of loyalty and dissent" centered on the third-century B.C. poet Qu Yuan.[78] Qu's enduring reputation in the Chinese cultural tradition was due both to his literary skill and to his persistent loyalty to his ruler despite his banishment, which culminated in his suicide. For latter-day exiles, Qu's example pointed a fresh path to the immortality of which their political disgrace seemed to have deprived them.

The literature of Xinjiang banishment thus formed part of a venerable tradition, and exiled scholars were self-consciously sensitive to their role as its heirs and transmitters. Thus in Ji Yun's preface to his Ürümqi poems, he cited the exiled Tang intellectual Liu Zongyuan's dictum that writing was the only way to repay one's debt to one's country. The reference served both to align his experiences with those of a highly respected predecessor and to legitimate his undertaking. Continuing to adduce historical antecedents, Ji—the editor of the poetry of Song exile Su Dongpo—recalled the poetry of an exiled Tang poet, Wang Changling, in a note to one of his own Ürümqi poems.[79]

---

77. Ji, "Wulumuqi Zashi," 1b, 10b, 17a–b, 14b.
78. See, generally, Schneider, *A Madman of Ch'u.*
79. Ji, "Wulumuqi Zashi," 35a. Wang Changling's well-known frontier songs were written during the years 723–725 when, for unknown reasons, he was on the northwest frontier. The poem referred to by Ji, "Ting Liuren Shuitiaozi," was probably composed in

Apart from his exile poetry, several stories in the collection that Ji Yun published twenty years after his exile as *Yuewei Caotang Biji* are set in Xinjiang. Many of the stories gave detailed descriptions of the city at Ürümqi and its environs. Given Ji's own misinformation about Xinjiang prior to his exile in 1766, he may have been motivated in part by a desire to demystify Xinjiang for later exiles.[80] The use of historical settings to disguise commentary on current affairs is, however, a well-known Chinese literary device and perhaps the remoteness of Ürümqi recommended its use to Ji Yun as a spatial equivalent of antiquity.[81]

Both Ji's Ürümqi poems and his stories have been used as historical sources by a number of scholars, including the influential nineteenth-century exponent of the statecraft school and historian of the frontier, Wei Yuan (1794–1856). Wei included Ji's account in his own compilation of essays on statecraft, and his description of the exiles' riot near Ürümqi in 1768 followed Ji's version extremely closely.[82]

Exile poetry often gave poignant expression to the sufferings of exiles, recalling past joys and raising future hopes in an attempt to blur present sorrow. Yet Hong Liangji, for one, considered that exiles were doomed to repeated suffering.[83] Much of the poetry of former judicial commissioner Li Luanxuan, filled with regret and foreboding, echoed this theme. Shortly after his arrival at Ürümqi he wrote:

> It is meet to reflect upon one's misdeeds
> I dare not think again of home.[84]

Scholars sometimes tried to offer encouragement to their banished friends by comparing them to noted exiles of the past. In this way the stigma of banishment could be converted into a badge of honor. Thus

---

737, after Wang's exile to the south. See Lee, *Wang Ch'ang-ling*, 3; Li, *Wang Changling Shizhu*, 155–156. For a reference in Ji Yun's poems to the exiled Song dynasty poet Su Dongpo, see "Wulumuqi Zashi," 35b.

80. See, e.g., Ji, *Yuewei Caotang Biji*, 13, 37a.

81. On this collection, see Keenan, "The Secret Life of Ghosts: Chi Yün and the *Yüeh Wei Ts'ao T'ang Pi Chi*."

82. Wei, *Shengwu Ji* 4, 33a–b, 6. For Ji's essay, see *Huangchao Jingshi Wenbian* 81, 32b–33a; the accountwas originally published in the late eighteenth century in Ji, *Yuewei Caotang Biji* 20, 4a–6b. Wei, in what appears to be a misprint, assigns this riot to the year 1767. For other uses of Ji Yun as a historical source, see *Xinjiang Tuzhi*, 114, 6a–7b.

83. Hong, "Wanli Hege Ji," 8b. On these themes in the poetry of exile in another culture, see Starn, *Contrary Commonwealth*, 129.

84. Li, "Di Shu." A collection of Li's exile poetry, entitled "Hege Ji," was published shortly after his death.

Huang Pinsan, a fellow exile of Hong Liangji, compared Hong favorably to two distinguished historical figures: Jia Yi of the Han dynasty, banished to what was then the border region of Changsha, and the great Tang statesman Han Yu, banished to Chaozhou in the south. Neither had been recalled from exile as quickly as Hong had.[85] In like vein, the scholar Zhao Yi likened Hong to the poets Li Bai and Su Dongpo, both of whom Chinese literati held in the highest esteem. These exiles were regarded as pioneers of frontier literature because of the works they had composed. Hong, whose exile offered similar scope for scholarly investigation of a hitherto little studied area, would, Zhao suggested, be able to emulate their distinguished example.[86] Zhao half regretted Hong's early recall because it limited his colleague's opportunities to explore and record Xinjiang in more detail.[87]

Other exiles who wrote extensively about Xinjiang during their banishment included the scholars Qi Yunshi and Xu Song. Songyun permitted both these scholars greater freedom of movement than was usual for disgraced officials, in order to facilitate the gathering of information for the language and gazetteer projects.[88] In addition to this officially sponsored work, Qi and Xu each wrote several other works that contributed to the growing body of Xinjiang studies based on research conducted in situ.[89] Even now their writings remain important sources of information on Xinjiang.

85. Hong, "Wanli Hege Ji," 16a–b. Huang, a native of Fujian, had been an assistant magistrate in Hubei. He was recalled in 1801 after three years in exile. *GZD* JQ 6750, 6/11/24.

86. Zhao, *Oubei Shichao*, 2, 193. Hong's diaries of his journeys and his stay in Ili are well known. He wrote a good deal else concerning the frontier area, on occasion relating what he observed to earlier records such as the Han and Tang histories. See, e.g., Hong, "Saiwai Lu," and "Gengshengzhai Wen Jiaji," 1, 16a.

87. Zhao, *Oubei Shichao* 2, 194. For further examples in which Hong's associates evoked past exiles, see, e.g., Hong, "Wanli Hege Ji," 16b–19b. Included in this collection are the writings of the scholar Zhuang Xin, who was familiar with the issue of Xinjiang banishment prior to Hong's exile. In 1787, as magistrate of Xianning, Shaanxi, he had been involved in a search for a returning exile who was wanted to give evidence concerning the impeachment of the Ili military governor. *GZD* JQ 52592, 52/11/30. In 1795 he wrote a new preface to *XJTLSL*, the collection of the laws on Xinjiang convicts compiled by Wu Yixian, a yamen secretary.

88. On Xu, see *Guangxu Shuntianfu Zhi* 103, 12a–b; see also Zhang Qi's 1829 preface to Xu's "Hanshu Xiyu Zhuan Buzhu." On Qi, see Qi's own preface to "Xichui Yaolüe," in which he particularly drew his readers' attention to the fact that his work was based on personal investigation.

89. Their principal works on Xinjiang were: *Xichui Zongtong Shilüe* (the original draft of the official history; written by Qi but published under Songyun's name, it was subse-

Some of those who wrote about Xinjiang may have assumed that no one could or would check the accuracy of their work, but this was unwise in the prevailing intellectual climate that favored evidential research. Banished scholars sometimes expressed informed criticism of the writings of their fellows; Hong Liangji, for instance, criticized one exile author, Wang Yuanshu, for improper inferences and "losing the source in following the stream," and Qi Yunshi accused the author of an earlier account of Xinjiang of reckless inaccuracy, which Qi attributed to inadequate first-hand knowledge.[90]

The scholarly output of the Xinjiang exiles exemplified the type of work that the Ming philosopher Wang Yangming—another eminent predecessor in the exile tradition—had in mind when he suggested that banishment provided the opportunity for self-renewal. As such, however, it did not precisely correspond to the self-renewal for which Qing authorities called, which instead involved the unflagging performance of public service combined with a contrite attitude and depended on external approval for legitimation. Thus, for these exiles, the idea of self-renewal had both a public and a private face, and these did not necessarily coincide.

INFLUENCES ON LATER POLITICAL THOUGHT

The exile of scholars and officials, many of whom were leading lights in the intellectual world of their time, was critically important to the development of literati perceptions of Xinjiang. Although many of these exiles did not spend long years on the frontier, the careful scholarship and investigative research for which they and their colleagues were re-

---

quently renamed *Xinjiang Shilüe*; the two works resemble one another but are not identical); "Xichui Yaolüe" (a descriptive account); "Xiyu Shidi" (a historical geography), and "Xichui Zhuzhici" (a collection of poems). Qi's diary of his journey into exile has been cited in chapter 6. Xu, "Xinjiang Fu" (a poem with explanatory notes); "Xinjiang Shuidao Ji" (A record of the waterways of Xinjiang); and "Hanshu Xiyu Zhuan Buzhu" (Notes on the chapters on the Western Regions in the Han dynastic history). In 1821, after his return from exile, Xu wrote a preface to Hong Liangji's diary of his sojourn in Ili, "Tianshan Kehua," in which he praised the range of Hong's observations. Apparently Xu had not read Hong's diary before his own exile. On Xu, see Zhao, "Xibeixue de Tahuangzhe zhi yi."

90. Hong, "Tianshan Kehua," 5a; Qi, "Xichui Yaolüe," preface.

nowned was extremely valuable. In tracing such influences, it is important to remember that writing on Xinjiang was not absolutely limited to exiles. Although most senior Xinjiang officials were Manchus not known for their high level of scholarship, Chinese scholars occasionally visited Xinjiang in the course of their official duties. One important example was that of Bi Yuan, who as a circuit intendant in Gansu went as far as Ürümqi in 1770. Two *juan* of poems concerning this experience were included in the collection of his poems, "Qiuyue Yinjiaji," published in 1793.

Not only the growing body of literature concerning Xinjiang but also the increasing number of scholars banished there during the Jiaqing reign helped to bring the frontier area into the forefront of literati interest. By the time the Jiaqing Emperor acceded to the throne at the turn of the century, the Qing had ruled Xinjiang for several decades, and the banishment of officials had become more systematic and, perhaps, more commonplace. Familiarity did not so much breed contempt as draw attention to Xinjiang's potential for resolving some of China's problems such as overcrowding due to rapid population growth. In addition, interest in Xinjiang was a natural part of the growing scholarly concern with the issue of China's frontiers. To some degree, this concern originated with the Qianlong Emperor's efforts to promote frontier projects because the frontier was closely associated with the Manchu heritage. The concern gathered momentum in the wake of the domestic rebellions, including the Jahangir uprising in Xinjiang in the 1820s, and the insistent external pressure that faced China from the early nineteenth century.

A number of close connections linked the Xinjiang exiles of the late eighteenth and early nineteenth centuries to later scholars interested in the frontier.[91] Ji Yun, for instance, was a fellow examination graduate (*tongnian*) and close friend of the court patron Zhu Gui, who was in turn both the patron of Hong Liangji and the intellectual forebear of a number of important literati political groups of the early and middle nineteenth century.

The influential scholar Gong Zizhen (1792–1841) was involved with this network of scholars. In 1820 Gong made what was then the revolutionary proposal that Xinjiang become a province as a means of solving some of China's burgeoning problems. The timing of Gong's proposal may have reflected in part a continuing debate concerning the proper

91. See Crossley, "*Manzhou Yuanliu Kao* and the Formalization of the Manchu Heritage."

approach to Xinjiang, at an earlier stage of which the gazetteer project had been mooted.[92] Gong suggested using the expanses of Xinjiang as a source of raw materials for China proper and as a repository for a portion of China's growing population, some of whom, it was already clear, were causing great harm by producing opium instead of food. He recommended reproducing the administrative structure found in China proper in Xinjiang, abolishing the inefficient military agricultural colonies (*tuntian*), and establishing closely regulated commercial links between Xinjiang and China proper.[93] Although this essay was not particularly influential immediately, it held great appeal for later scholars who turned to the northwest frontier as China's only hope in the face of the Opium War and other defeats at the hands of foreigners. Sixty years after it was first published, the essay contributed to the decision to make Xinjiang a province.[94]

Gong's intellectual debt to Hong Liangji, among others, is well known, although he was a child at the time of Hong's banishment.[95] Gong had probably read some of the literature of Xinjiang banishment, for at least some of Qi Yunshi's work had been published soon after Qi's return from Xinjiang in 1811. Gong did not meet Xu Song until 1821, a year after Xu's return from Xinjiang and the publication of Gong's essay. He served with him in the Grand Secretariat, where he was undoubtedly further exposed to the growing interest among Beijing intellectuals in the possibilities offered by the Xinjiang frontier.[96] Xu himself was the center of a group of scholars who gathered in the capital to discuss the northwest frontier and to eat lamb.[97]

Gong Zizhen's intellectual coterie in Beijing was associated with a circle that included the scholar and historian Zhang Mu (1805–1849). Zhang was acquainted with Xu Song as well as with Qi Yunshi's son Qi Junzao (1793–1866), who in the 1840s and 1850s, as one of the ranking officials in the empire, was among other things an important patron of

---

92. On the Xinjiang exiles and the rise of frontier studies see, generally, Chou, "Frontier Studies and Changing Frontier Administration in Late Ch'ing China: The Case of Sinkiang 1759–1911;" see especially chapter 4.

93. Gong, "Xiyu Zhi Xingsheng Yi."

94. Whitbeck, "The Historical Vision of Kung Tzu-chen," 149.

95. See Whitbeck, "Kung Tzu-chen and the Redirection of Literati Commitment in Early Nineteenth Century China," 7–10.

96. Whitbeck, "The Historical Vision of Kung Tzu-chen," 148–149.

97. See Chou, "Frontier Studies," 86.

frontier studies.[98] Zhang edited Qi Yunshi's chronological history of Mongolia, Xinjiang, and Tibet in 1845 and went on to compose a systematic catalogue of the Mongol tribal areas that was much admired by scholars of statecraft and other disciplines.[99]

The historian Wei Yuan was another well-known associate of both Zhang Mu and Gong Zizhen. Wei's familiarity with Ji Yun's descriptions of Ürümqi has been noted above, but he had other sources of information about Xinjiang. He was for a time employed as tutor to the children of the famous general Yang Fang (1770–1846) who had spent a brief spell in exile at Ili following a mutiny among troops under his command. While working for Yang, Wei encountered a number of scholars interested in the northwest.[100] He also shared the interest of the leading scholar and, incidentally, classmate of Ji Yun, Qian Daxin (1728–1804) in the history of the Mongol Yuan dynasty, which naturally involved further study of China's northwest frontiers.[101]

Like Gong Zizhen, Wei advocated that Xinjiang should become a province; these two scholars' writings on the northwest formed a significant part of the section on frontier defense in the widely read collection, *Huangchao Jingshi Wenbian*, that Wei helped to compile. These essays helped compensate for the virtual absence of anything on foreign relations in this collection of writings on practical government and in part awakened Chinese interest in foreign affairs.[102]

Links with the exiles of the Qianlong and Jiaqing periods extended in various ways through these scholars to Lin Zexu. Lin was closely associated with both Wei Yuan and Gong Zizhen and was familiar with at least some of Qi Yunshi's exile writings.[103] He was for a time an active mem-

---

98. Ibid., 120.

99. Mann Jones and Kuhn, "Dynastic Decline and the Roots of Rebellion," 155–156; *ECCP* 47, 134-135. Qi Yunshi had written his chronological history prior to his own banishment to Xinjiang.

100. *ECCP* 884–885; Whitbeck, "Historical Vision," 148; Chou, "Frontier Studies," 113.

101. Qian was a highly respected scholar and, along with Hong Liangji, one of the leading figures in the important Han Learning movement, an important branch of scholarship that was closely linked to the evidential research school in the late eighteenth and early nineteenth centuries. See Elman, *From Philosophy to Philology*.

102. *Juan* 80 and 81 concern frontier defense.

103. On Lin's familiarity with Qi's diary of his journey to Ili, see, e.g., Lin, "Hege Jicheng," 1a. Since irrigation was a key aspect of Lin's work in Xinjiang, he may have been familiar with Xu Song's work on Xinjiang waterways.

ber of a reformist political group whose founders included several disciples of the powerful patron Zhu Gui. Through this group Lin came into contact with the survivors and intellectual descendants of many of those scholars and officials who, as opponents of Heshen's faction over a sustained period, had experienced exile to Xinjiang either first hand or at one remove through their political allies. In addition, as is well known, Lin himself spent several years in Xinjiang in the early 1840s, including some in disgrace, following the early disasters of the Opium War.

The views of Gong, Wei, and Lin on Xinjiang are generally considered to have influenced such key late Qing statesmen as Li Hongzhang (1823–1901), perhaps the leading minister of the late nineteenth century, and Zuo Zongtang (1812–1885), whose suppression of the Muslim rebellion in Xinjiang in the 1860s and 1870s paved the way for Xinjiang's final political incorporation into the empire in 1884.[104] Thus although it would be an exaggeration to claim that the earlier Xinjiang exiles were directly responsible for Xinjiang's integration into the empire, they clearly provided the initial, if indirect, vital intellectual impetus for consolidating the last major addition to Chinese territory in imperial times.

104. See *Zuo Wenxiang Gong Nianpu* 1, 25–26, cited by Chu, *The Moslem Rebellion*, 89. See also Qin, *Zuo Wenxiang Gong Zai Xibei*, 10–12. Zuo's success was partly due to his use of agricultural colonies to supply the troops in Xinjiang, an idea promoted by Lin. Other associates of Lin's who are said to have influenced Zuo's successful methods in Xinjiang included Wang Baixin, a former secretary of Lin's, and Huang Mian, who was in exile at Ili at the same time as Lin. See Chu, *The Moslem Rebellion*, 91; Qin, *Zuo Wenxiang Gong Zai Xibei*, 11–12. See also Whitbeck, "Historical Vision," 149; Kuhn, *Rebellion and Its Enemies*, 183–185.

Chapter Eight
The Lives of the
Xinjiang Convicts

The experience of ordinary convicts sent to Xinjiang had little in common with that of banished officials, except the geographical location of their common place of exile. Most ordinary convicts were enslaved and many, knowing that they were extremely unlikely to return home, tried to escape. Others successfully made new lives on the frontier.

Among the ordinary convicts sent to Xinjiang, some went to remarkable lengths to remain in contact with their relatives and with other exiles in different parts of Xinjiang and China proper. Such tenacity was particularly evident in the case of sectarian exiles, who, as major political offenders, had scant grounds for optimism about their prospects for return. The Qing government was aware that the exile to Xinjiang of this type of offender risked transmitting these criminals' unacceptable religious beliefs to the frontier but felt confident that their primarily folk Buddhist beliefs were incompatible with those of the Muslims who predominated in the areas to which these convicts were sent.[1] Nonetheless, officials had good reason to be vigilant about such exiles, for the closely bonded organization of the religious sects and the relatively high literacy rate of their members made it extraordinarily difficult for the Qing to isolate them completely.[2]

1. See *QSL* QL 1382, 26a, 56/7/13.
2. Even illiteracy apparently did not prevent exiles and their families from corresponding with each other; there are many records of an illiterate's asking someone—a neighbor or an itinerant doctor, for example—to read or write a letter on his behalf. See, e.g., *SYD*

The 1791 case of Liu Zhaokui, an itinerant juggler, illustrates the type of situation with which the Qing had to contend. When Liu returned to his native Weinan county in Shanxi province, after a protracted absence, he had a horse and some money. A relative, the local head of the mutual surveillance system (*baojia*) into which households were organized, became suspicious of Liu's apparent prosperity and reported him to the authorities. It transpired that he was carrying letters from sect exiles throughout southern Xinjiang. Some of these letters seemed innocent enough, but others contained ambiguous wording that suggested they might be coded messages intended to encourage family and sect members still at home. One letter contained the character *gen*, which alerted officials to possible links to a trigram sect; the intended recipients did indeed belong to the Gen trigram sect.[3]

Liu's involvement had begun in 1784 when he became friendly with some Shandongese exiles in the southern Chinese province of Guangxi.[4] He had joined their still flourishing sect. His new friends persuaded Liu to take home some letters and the remains of two fellow sect members who had died in exile. Liu agreed to travel by way of Guangdong in order to make contact with yet other sect exiles. Eventually he reached Shandong, delivered the messages and remains, and spent the winter with the family of one of the exiles with whom he had formed a particularly close relationship. They sent him on to see a woman whose husband had been executed because of his religious activities and whose son, Wang Zichong, had been banished to Kashgar in the far west of Xinjiang for sect involvement. She had heard a rumor that Wang might have died, so she gave Liu four taels—possibly all she could afford—and asked him to take a letter to Wang in exile.

(B) QL 56/8/8, 75 ("I got a neighbor to write a letter [for me to my exiled son]"); *SYD* (B) QL 56/9/6, 84 ("I am illiterate and had to have the letter [from an exiled brother] read to me by an itinerant doctor").

3. The exiles who had sent the letters apparently belonged to another trigram, the Zhen, but were in close contact with Gen trigram members. The two trigrams seem to have been intimately connected. Liu Zhaokui testified that he had overheard Gen trigram discussions when he was at the Shandong home of exiled Zhen trigram sect leader Wang Zichong. *Jixin Dang* (unpaginated) QL 56/7/13. On trigram sects, see Naquin, *Millenarian Rebellion in China*, 63–117.

4. It was unusual for sect offenders to be banished within China proper, but these had been sentenced in 1783 under a temporary ruling, in force from 1781 to 1788, that was implemented because of fears that too great a concentration of sect exiles would "pollute" the frontier areas. This ruling stipulated that sect members not be banished to Xinjiang. *SYD* (B) QL 56/7/n.d., 189–190.

Questioned en route by officials responsible for issuing travel passes to Xinjiang, Liu openly said that he was taking family letters to "his relative" Wang Zichong. None of these officials recalled that Wang, who himself had passed that way on his journey into exile less than two years previously, was a major criminal who ought to be kept completely isolated from any contact with home.

Liu reached Kashgar nine months after he left Shandong. He spent several months in Xinjiang and stayed several weeks with Wang Zichong, who had been operating a business since the death of his beg master. Liu carried messages between Wang and a number of other sect exiles in several locations within Xinjiang, including Aksu, Kuche, and Yarkand. All asked him to take letters to their family and co-religionists in China proper, giving him money for his journey and the horse that was to arouse his relative's suspicion.[5] In addition, Wang wanted Liu to reestablish the sect in Shandong with the help of Wang's cousin.[6]

Liu was transferred from Shanxi to the capital for further interrogation; his ultimate fate is unknown but he was probably put to death. The convicts involved were all punished, in most cases by execution. Their offense was their unrepentant attempt to continue their sect activities despite banishment; no law specifically prohibited exiles from corresponding with their families.

The network of people linked by Liu Zhaokui was so extensive that the impact of its discovery had a profound and long-lasting effect on the Qing authorities. Officials continued to refer to it for many years. In 1801 during the White Lotus Rebellion, another courier between sect members found security at Jiayuguan much tighter than it had been ten years previously. Unable to slip through, he eventually gave himself up to the authorities.[7]

The conditions in which Liu Zhaokui found these exiles were often by no means as poor as the government had intended. Sect leader Wang Zichong, for instance, banished into slavery, had succeeded in establishing a flourishing business after his master's death, although he ought

---

5. *SYD* (B) QL 56/8/8, 51–98.

6. *SYD* (B) QL 56/7/13, 111–117. On this case, see also Naquin, "Connections between Rebellions: Sect Family Networks in Qing China," 355–356.

7. *Jiaobu Dang* JQ 5/9/12, 91–93. On contact and traveling between sect exiles in the northeast and their families and colleagues in China proper, see *QSL* QL 1395, 6b–7a, 57/1/22; *SYD* (T) JQ 24/2/25, 267–269. For another example of suspected contacts between sect exiles within China proper, see *ZPZZ* QL 34/2/7 (law—exile, packet for QL 32–50), memorial of Mingshan.

to have been reassigned to another master immediately.[8] The fact that some of the others were able to provide Liu with money and a horse indicates that their condition was less than abject. Enslaved convicts in particular were theoretically subject to extremely careful regulation, and their masters were required to keep them under control.

STATUS IN EXILE

The most serious offenders, including a majority of convicts exiled for political reasons, were enslaved as a part of their punishment. Those not enslaved were kept under close surveillance by the authorities.

Two principal forms of slavery existed in Qing China: public and private. In the private form, the slave was either sold or born into servitude; he and his family were essentially a chattel of their master.[9] The public form of slavery was imposed by the government as punishment for certain types of criminal activity, particularly in politically oriented cases. The government retained ultimate responsibility for such enslaved convicts but assigned the immediate tasks of supervision and control to others.[10] Such was the case in Xinjiang, where the master had the use but not the ownership of his slave.[11] Thus convict slaves were not permitted to purchase their freedom nor were their assigned masters permitted to sell or manumit them.[12] If a master died or was transferred to a different location, the convict was reassigned to a new master.[13] Government slaves had no legal protection: an official, or their master, or any other free person could abuse or, when the slave had had a death sentence commuted, even kill them with impunity.[14]

8. *QSL QL* 1384, 16b, 56/8/5.

9. See, generally, Meijer, "Slavery at the End of the Ch'ing Dynasty."

10. For a discussion of the development of the law on enslaving Xinjiang convicts, see *XJTLSL* 2, 16a–18b. On the enslavement of criminals generally, see Wei, Wu, and Lu, *Qingdai Nubi Zhidu*, 58–75.

11. See Kawakubo, "Shindai Manshū no henkyō shakai: Shinchō no ryūkei seisaku to henkyō, sono ni," 61. Despite its title, this article concerns Xinjiang as well as the northeast.

12. *DLCY* 76–25. According to this law, the authorities might grant permission to a slave's master for sale or manumission upon being shown good cause, but there is no indication of what amounted to good cause. For a case (originating in the northeast) in which illicit manumission of a slave led to disaster, see *QSL JQ* 176, 12a–b, 12/3/14.

13. *Qinding Pingding Zhunke'er Fanglüe Xubian* 16, 3b–4b, QL 27/3/9; see also *QSL QL* 656, 14b–15b, 27/3/9.

14. See *QCWXTK* 197, p. 6618, cited by Wei, Wu, and Lu, *Qingdai Nubi Zhidu*, 62–63.

In northern Xinjiang most convicts were enslaved to Green Standard soldiers. Since these troops were unable to manage all the convicts, any surplus was enslaved either to Manchu bannermen or Mongol Chahars stationed in Xinjiang or, until 1787, to Xinjiang natives such as the Ölöds. In that year, the practice of enslaving convicts to the Ölöds was terminated because of language problems. The tribesmen's inability to communicate with their slaves made control impossible.[15] Convicts banished to southern Xinjiang were normally enslaved to the local bureaucrats, the begs, until 1828, when a combination of beg inability to control their assigned slaves and changing government needs following suppression of Jahangir's uprising led to some convict slaves' being employed in the local administration.[16]

The nature of personal slavery in Xinjiang is not well documented. Convicts enslaved to the troops generally worked on the governmental agricultural colonies, but they were sometimes assigned other duties. Those enslaved to the Ölöds performed a variety of tasks, including farming and clerical work. Some enslaved exiles worked in the mines and boatyards, as described below. The availability of exiles' children as slaves in the 1760s at Ürümqi, recorded by Ji Yun, suggests that either there were sufficient convicts to supply the market for personal slaves or such slaves were not much in demand; it may also be that the general level of subsistence at that time was often insufficient to support any slaves.[17]

The enslavement of a convict did not extend to those members of his family who voluntarily accompanied him into exile. The crucial distinction between voluntary and mandatory accompaniment was noted on the convict's identification papers, so that the status of the family was known to officials at the exile destination.[18] Family members were registered as free settlers at the place of exile. As such they were not compelled to remain in Xinjiang in the event of the convict's death, although they might do so if they wished. Banner families were enrolled in a banner; others were registered as civilians.[19] However, the exemption of a convict's family from enslavement was not available when banishment resulted from particularly grave crimes, in which event the

15. *QSL QL* 1276, 10b–11a, 52/3/6.
16. Qi, "Qingdai Xinjiang Qianfan Yanjiu," 88.
17. Ji, "Wulumuqi Zashi," 12a. Whether these children were all the offspring of enslaved convicts is not clear.
18. *XJTLSL* 2, 35b.
19. *DLCY* 15–04.

banishment of the entire family was often mandatory, nor was there any exemption for those banished by virtue of collective responsibility.[20]

Children born in exile to enslaved convicts normally had free status. Sons could seek a livelihood elsewhere; daughters could be married or adopted away from the place of exile.[21] There were certain restrictions, however. For instance, the sons of exiles were prohibited dual registration—in their native place as well as in their place of exile—because among other things this might give them the chance to take examinations in two locations. In the most serious cases, severe restrictions were placed on the right of exiles' descendants to sit for the examinations, as in the case of the Lü family exiles in the northeast.

The rationale underlying this restriction was that examination success offered the opportunity to improve one's lot in life; it may also have been intended to deny the sons of well-educated exiles from highly competitive areas such as the lower Yangzi the opportunity of candidacy in a place where their chances of success were far greater than in their native places. Despite all the propaganda about self-renewal, moreover, examination success would present opportunities for self-improvement independent of government control, an outcome that was not the government's intention with regard to its Xinjiang convicts.[22]

The status of Chinese children in Xinjiang depended on their place of birth: those born in Xinjiang were at liberty to move, but those themselves banished by virtue of collective responsibility were not. Even when status was not at issue, Xinjiang officials sometimes sought guidance concerning the appropriate treatment of the younger generation. Thus in 1791 the lieutenant governor at Ürümqi raised the question of two collectively responsible boys who, although born in China proper, had been raised in exile. They had left Xinjiang to earn a living elsewhere. One was fifteen when he was banished with his mother; he was blind and had left his mother's place of exile to become an itinerant fortune-teller. The other was thirteen when banished; at seventeen he, too, had left and become a merchant. The issue was whether they should be executed as

20. *DLCY* 15. Similarly, the exemption from slavery that normally applied to officials, degree-holders, and their families did not apply in the most serious cases, such as rebellion. *DLCY* 45–16. See also *DLCY* 15–01, which prohibited the collectively responsible relatives of rebels from ever establishing an independent household in exile.

21. *DLCY* 15–06.

22. See *DLCY* 76–20, 76-23. As noted in the preceding chapter, Ürümqi but not Ili had an examination degree quota during the period in question.

escaped convicts in the event of their arrest. The emperor's answer demonstrated both the ambiguity of the law and a willingness to interpret it with compassion. If the two boys had intended to escape, they should be put to death. If they had not realized they were not entitled to leave, then they should be returned to their place of exile and kept under close supervision.[23]

Enslaved women convicts and the daughters of collectively responsible exiles could be betrothed by the slave master to other convicts prohibited from returning home.[24] In a memorandum of 1789 the Board of Punishments discussed some of the problems that could arise when the status of convicts differed from that of their spouses. Two enslaved female convicts, Mrs. Tang La and Mrs. Li Liu, had been married by their Ölöd master to other convict slaves. The men had served their term and were entitled to establish themselves independently as farmers. However, Mrs. Tang La was a major criminal in her own right, banished for her involvement in a Muslim uprising some ten years earlier. It was not appropriate to treat her as though she were in exile voluntarily or in a minor case. To separate the two women from their husbands of many years and from their children seemed unconscionable, yet to allow them to become part of an independent establishment would have unduly improved the women's status. The Board decided that the two men should remain where they were, as household servants; the extent to which their theoretically improved status actually made a material difference in their lives is open to question.[25] This case is unusual because the wives' status took precedence over that of the husbands; the only other known instance where this occurred was in the case of imperial princesses.[26]

WORK IN EXILE

The expense of colonizing and defending the new territories was a recurring theme in government documents. The general view was that China

23. *XJTLSL* 2, 24b–25a.
24. *DLCY* 15–13.
25. *XAHL* 1, 60b–61a. Li Liu's file gave no details of the reason for her banishment; presumably her case was analogous to Tang La's, since she was treated in the same way. The women's names indicate that they were now married for the second time. Their first husbands probably died in the rebellion or were put to death for their participation.
26. The issue was raised again in 1806; see *XAHL* 6, 32b–33a.

proper ought not to be expected to support Xinjiang; a related consideration was that the great distances involved high transportation expenses.
The need to promote self-reliance in Xinjiang was at issue from the outset
of the occupation of the new territories.[27] Much of the work performed
by ordinary convicts in exile was a means of accomplishing this goal;
they were often assigned to essential but disagreeable or dangerous tasks
that others were reluctant to undertake.

In northern Xinjiang convicts' work fell into four main categories:
agriculture, industry, defense, and clerical duties. The first two were particularly important to the promotion of self-sufficiency. In southern Xinjiang, where the strength of Muslim influence caused the Qing to pursue
its colonization policy with considerably greater caution than in the
north until the 1830s, convicts enslaved to the begs were not normally
assigned specified tasks by the government.

The introduction of settled agriculture in Xinjiang necessarily began
with land reclamation. For this purpose the government established agricultural colonies for the various groups of settlers throughout the new
territories, as explained in chapter 2.

Land reclamation work was unpopular among free settlers because it
was less lucrative than hiring out one's labor. At times even grants of
land and other incentives failed to induce immigrant settlers to undertake
such work. In the three years from 1785 to 1788, for instance, not one
request to reclaim land was recorded by the authorities.[28]

The principal areas to which convicts were sent were Balikun, Ürümqi,
Tarbagatai, and Ili, all in northern Xinjiang. In addition, 180 convicts
worked in the Hami area, technically part of southern Xinjiang but
strategically located at a key point of entry to the entire frontier region.
Working conditions at both Hami and Balikun were on the whole better
than they were further to the west, and convicts sent to these two locations were usually those guilty of relatively mild offenses.

Many enslaved convicts worked on the military farms (*bingtun* and
qitun) under the garrison troops. In addition, a considerable number of
those not enslaved were assigned to their own agricultural colonies (*fantun* or *qiantun*), where they were subject to general military supervision.
The amount of land allotted such convicts by the government varied in
different locations. At Ürümqi and Ili they received twelve mu (just under

27. See, e.g., ZPZZ QL 27/9/26, (agriculture—opening new lands, packet 31), memorial
of Yongning et al.
28. *SYD* (T) QL 53/2/9, 179.

two acres) of land. An extra plot of five mu was allocated to exiles accompanied by their families to enable them to be self-supporting.[29] By comparison, soldiers received twenty mu (almost three and a half acres) of land that was often of higher quality than that allotted to the convicts.[30] Civilian immigrants, merchant settlers, and forcibly relocated troublemakers such as the silver miners transferred from Yunnan province in 1775–76 were allotted thirty mu (about five acres).[31] At Balikun and Hami there was greater apparent parity between soldiers and convicts; all received an allotment of twenty-two mu of land, although it was not necessarily of equal quality.[32]

The principal crops grown on the agricultural colonies were wheat, barley, peas, and corn.[33] The government issued seed to the soldiers and convicts; one peck (*dou*) of wheat, peas, and barley seed per mu and two and one-half pints (*sheng*) of corn seed per mu.[34] Food was provided for new arrivals until the first harvest.[35]

Convicts at Ili and Ürümqi paid an annual tax of six shi of grain; soldiers had to pay at least twelve shi and sometimes more, depending on the quality of the land. At Balikun, convicts and soldiers paid the same amount of tax.[36]

29. *QSL* QL 653, 7a–b, 27/1/22. See also, e.g., *ZPZZ* QL 40/10/29, (agriculture—opening new lands, packet 23), memorial of Suonuomuceling. One group of thirty-five convicts received an allocation of fifteen mu, but this appears to have been exceptional. See *Xichui Zongtong Shilüe* 7, 5a.

30. See, e.g., *ZPZZ* QL 42/11/12, (agriculture—opening new lands, packet 37), memorial of Suonuomuceling.

31. *SZJL* 105–108. On the resettlement of the miners, see, e.g., *ZPZZ* QL 41/3/20, (agriculture—opening new lands, packet 35), memorial of Yongqing and Yu Jin'ao.

32. See, e.g., *ZPZZ* QL 40/4/1, (agriculture—opening new lands, packet 33), memorial of Yiletu. For an assessment of the ratio of reclaimed land to food supply and the number of people needed to cultivate it, see *HDSL* (1899) 178, 6b.

33. *Qinding Huangyu Xiyu Tuzhi* 32, 1b–25a.

34. *Hubu Zeli* 95, 54b. Cf. *SYD* (B) QL 23/6/9, 359–363, an edict asserting that it was unnecessary to provide seeds or tools for the soldiers' convict slaves. The relocated silver miners received 1.2 shi of wheat, barley, and corn seed for their thirty mu of land. *ZPZZ* QL 41/3/30, (agriculture—opening new lands, packet 35), memorial of Yongqing and Yu Jin'ao.

35. *QSL* QL 653, 7a–b, 27/1/22.

36. On the taxation of convicts see *Xinjiang Tuzhi* 30, 2b, possibly based on *SZJL* (a gazetteer of Ürümqi and other locations in eastern Xinjiang) 4, 128–129. Cf. *Xichui Zongtong Shilüe* 7, 4b–5b, which gives the much lower figure of eight sheng per mu payable by emancipists and certain convicts, making an annual total of just under one shi. The reason for the discrepancy is unclear. Land allotment was the same at Ili and Ürümqi, but production quotas were higher at Ili. Nevertheless, the higher tax figure appears to relate to Ürümqi.

By comparison, civilian immigrants received loans for seeds, housing, and livestock, and a tax exemption for six years, at which point the loans also fell due. Qing policy towards its free settlers in Xinjiang thus generally followed the pattern set in regions to which they had previously encouraged immigration, for instance Sichuan and southwest China.[37]

Graduated annual productivity targets were set for each location; meeting or exceeding these resulted in rewards for all concerned, including responsible officials.[38] Conversely, failure to meet the basic target brought punishment. There were two standards, one for Ili and one for Ürümqi.[39] At Ili the basic target for convicts was 9 shi and at Ürümqi it was 6.6 shi; for soldiers it was 18 and 15 shi respectively, although there was some variation to take account of the uneven quality of the land.[40] If convicts met or exceeded the targets, they received a reward of flour or grain; soldiers received a supplementary food allowance (yancaiqian) and the responsible officials received merit points on their records (yixu). There was also a higher target, which brought double the basic reward, and a minimum required level at which no reward was given.[41]

This system met with only partial success, because, on the one hand, officials sometimes exaggerated their harvest reports, and, on the other, the troops devoted more energy to farming than to military training.[42] Some scholars believe this imbalance contributed to the Xinjiang troops' lack of preparedness at the time of Jahangir's uprising in the 1820s.[43]

The government issued one set of agricultural implements to every six convicts and to every three soldiers. The details of such a "set" give some sense of the agricultural procedures and technology of the late eighteenth

37. See Entenmann, "Migration and Settlement in Sichuan, 1644–1796," 79–80, 121–122; Lee, "State and Economy in Southwest China, 1400–1800," 64.

38. Productivity targets and taxes were both measured in fine grain (xiliang, i.e., grain that could be used for food). Because a proportion of the overall amount harvested was not xiliang, the total quantity of grain harvested had to exceed the targets.

39. The targets at virtually all the tun corresponded to one of these standards. See ZPZZ 40/4/1, (agriculture—opening new lands, packet 33), memorial of Yiletu.

40. See HDSL (1899) 178, 17a–18a. Cf. Huang, The Peasant Economy and Social Change in North China, 59. On the measurement of grain by shi, see Ch'üan and Kraus, Mid-Ch'ing Rice Markets and Trade, 97–98.

41. ZPZZ QL 40/4/1, (agriculture—opening new lands, packet 33), memorial of Yiletu. For examples of annual reports on harvests and rewards, see, e.g., ZPZZ QL 43/11/6, (agriculture—opening new lands, packet 37), memorial of Suonuomuceling; ZPZZ QL 45/11/7, (agriculture—opening new lands, packet 37), memorial of Kuilin.

42. See SZJL 4, 123–124.

43. See Luo, Qing Gaozong Tongzhi Xinjiang Zhengce de Tantao, 238.

century, since each was composed of one plowshare, two pitchforks, one axehead, one billhook, two sickles, one hoe, two harnesses, one lasso, two spades, two bridles, two saddles, five bowstrings, one hobbling rope, one girth, and two saddle cloths. The iron from which the tools were manufactured came from the Xinjiang mines but—in one small illustration of the difficulties besetting the quest for self-reliance—leather and hemp were supplied from China proper.[44] One exile noted that in the early days of colonization when the Ili military governor sent out an order for spades, no one knew what a spade was and they had to be ordered from China proper.[45]

Every three convicts were issued an ox, except at Balikun where the issue was either an ox or a horse; every two soldiers were issued two animals, either horses or oxen, supplied from Ili.[46] In comparison with practices in China proper, this ratio seems to have been high. In 1890 farm laborers in Shandong province had only one draft animal for every four farm laborers.[47] The high ratio in Xinjiang may have been due both to the relative availability of horses in Central Asia and to the government's active involvement in developing agriculture on the frontier in the earlier period.

Not all those banished to Xinjiang proved effective farmers. The government recognized that land reclamation was strenuous work and assigned older or frail convicts to more appropriate tasks, exempting them from tax requirements and issuing only half rations.[48] However, even those who were physically strong enough for farming were not necessarily very successful at it. In 1804 Ili military governor Songyun found that convicts assigned to farms attached to the mines were so inexperienced that they could not produce enough food for the miners.[49] It is unclear whether this situation arose as a result of the convicts' unfami-

44. *SZJL* 4, 129. Funds for repairs were set aside by the government; see *Hubu Zeli* 95, 55a.

45. Ji, "Wulumuqi Zashi," 14a.

46. *SZJL* 4, 126–129. On animal allocation, see also, e.g., *ZPZZ* QL 41/3/13, (agriculture—opening new lands, packet 35), memorial of Yongqing. A certain proportion of the animals were expected to become unfit for use—30 per cent of the horses and 15 percent of the oxen; it is not made clear over what period of time. Officials were held responsible if this allowance were exceeded.

47. Huang, *The Peasant Economy and Social Change in North China*, 152.

48. *Hubu Zeli* 95, 64b–65a.

49. *SYD* (T) JQ 9/7/28, 467. The food shortages at the mines that resulted from the convict farmers' inexperience were sufficiently serious that Songyun replaced them with several thousand Muslims to supply the necessary skilled labor.

liarity with farming of any kind or because the crops planted in Xinjiang differed from those harvested in their native place. For instance, a southerner accustomed to growing rice probably lacked expertise in growing wheat, and the evidence is insufficient to justify a presumption that the majority of convicts had any experience of farming at all.[50] Such issues appear not to have been given much advance consideration in the government's colonization plans.[51]

The development of industry, in particular the extraction of minerals, was an essential aspect of the pursuit of self-sufficiency in Xinjiang. Convicts assigned to mining worked primarily in the lead and iron mines in Ili and Ürümqi, providing the raw material for agricultural tools and military supplies.[52] At the iron mines a high level of extraction was necessary because of wastage; the yield of usable iron from the Ürümqi mines, for instance, amounted to only 13 percent of what was extracted.[53] Initially at least 150 convicts worked in these iron mines; another 100 worked in two lead mines in the late 1760s. The numbers varied with fluctuating demand over the years, and attempts to maintain fixed quotas for convict labor seem not to have been wholly successful.[54] There appears to have been no thought of extracting lead or iron for export to other parts of China.

Some convicts were employed in the copper and gold mines, although because of the high value of these minerals this was relatively unusual.[55] In 1776 70 were assigned to the copper mines; half to work in the mines

50. See Antony, "Peasants, Heroes and Brigands," for evidence that very few bandits in south China—undoubtedly one source of Xinjiang convicts—were actually farmers, though many may have been rural dwellers. Some, for instance, were beggars, fishermen, or servants.

51. Cf. Chu, *The Moslem Rebellion*, 91, 94: Zuo Zongtang favored the use of a native army in the northwest because he thought that southerners would be afraid of going to the northwest and that unlike local troops they might not be willing to eat wheat, barley, and other northern foods.

52. *Xichui Zongtong Shilüe* 8, 2b–4a. On Qing fears regarding the convict miners see, e.g., *QSL QL* 917, 7b–8a, 37/9/19. On the Qing sense that miners generally were bad elements, see Sun, "Mining Labor in the Ch'ing Period." Theft from the mines by Ölöds and others, including escaped convicts, was a continuing problem. See *Qingdai de Kuangye* 2, 526–530.

53. Ji, "Wulumuqi Zashi," 22a.

54. *Qingdai de Kuangye* 2, 521–522.

55. See, however, *ZPZZ JQ* 2/1/21, (law—exile, packet for JQ 1–9), memorial of Changling and Tuolun, proposing to use convict labor in the copper mines; see also *Xichui Zongtong Shilüe* 8, 4a.

and half to farm nearby land to supply the miners. A few were sent to mine coal in the mountains due to a shortage of firewood. The Qing also employed skilled convicts to make materials such as roof tiles for the cities they built in Xinjiang after the conquest.

At least 500 convicts worked on the Ili River, which was an important communication artery within Xinjiang. Some were employed as sailors and trackers on the boats used primarily to transport grain. Others worked in the boatyards, where the boats were patched every three years and overhauled every five. A few served as ferrymen, transporting people and goods across the river, and every year some convicts were assigned to guard duty at the dykes at Huiyuan city when floods eroded the protective embankments.[56]

Military service was not generally required of convicts banished to Xinjiang, although some emancipists were enlisted in the army. However, such exiles were very occasionally chosen to perform particularly hazardous missions during military emergencies. Such emergencies occurred only rarely before 1820, and naturally convicts were not deployed to suppress the exile riot of 1768. However, in 1765 during a Muslim uprising at Ush, twelve Ili convicts were delegated to scale the walls of a besieged city with the collapsible "cloud ladders" (*yunti*). If they survived, their reward was to be emancipation and enlistment in the Green Standard army.[57] This precedent was followed in the 1820s when two thousand convicts were enlisted to help suppress Jahangir's uprising.[58] Afterwards military governor Changling requested that they be granted permission to return home.[59] Yet this use of convicts did not necessarily imply that the government took their loyalty for granted, even against the native Muslims of Xinjiang; it was, rather, an action of last resort.

Some literate convicts worked as clerks in various yamen offices. Convicts Zhang and Wang, enslaved to the Ölöds, were employed as records

56. *Qingdai de Kuangye* 2, 384–385; *Xichui Zongtong Shilüe* 8, 6b; Qi, "Qingdai Xinjiang Qianfan Yanjiu," 87, citing Gefengge, "Yi Jiang Hui Lan." See also Wei, Wu, and Lu, *Qingdai Nubi Zhidu* 71.

57. Nayancheng, *A Wencheng Gong Nianpu* 3, 30A–b, QL 30/8/23. For an illustration of a cloud ladder, see Kierman and Fairbank, eds., *Chinese Ways in Warfare*, 165.

58. *Xinjiang Tuzhi* 109, 10b. For further examples in the nineteenth century, see Qi, "Qingdai Xinjiang Qianfan Yanjiu," 91.

59. Guilun, *Chang Wenxiang Gong Nianpu* 3, 45a.

copyists in the prefect's yamen at Ili. After they took advantage of their position to warn a fellow convict of his impending arrest, with the result that he committed suicide, each was flogged and sentenced to a spell in the cangue.[60] The assignment of enslaved convicts to office work was unusual, however, and in 1801 an edict forbade the employment of such exiles as personal servants (*changsui*) in any yamen. This prohibition was ordered both because of the risk involved in allowing these major criminals access to official business and because the work was not regarded as sufficiently onerous.[61]

Many convicts doubtless felt little enthusiasm for their assigned tasks. At least one hated farming so much that he risked and lost his life attempting escape.[62] The unpleasantness, often tempered with peril, of many of the duties required of convicts symbolized their continued status as criminals who owed their very existence to imperial "benevolence."

Qing authorities frequently referred to the opportunity for self-renewal furnished ordinary convicts, as well as banished officials, by their exile. Yet for many common exiles the idea of self-renewal must have lacked the moral impact it had for intellectuals, who were steeped in Neo-Confucian values. The hard labor and exemplary behavior required of ordinary convicts did eventually lead to emancipation, except in the most serious cases. That prospect, and the hope of establishing a new life on the Xinjiang frontier, in practice amounted to a form of self-renewal. In the meantime convicts had to find whatever ways they could of alleviating their punishment.

LIFE IN EXILE

Such knowledge as we can glean of the lives of ordinary convicts comes only from official documents and from occasional observations recorded by such exiled scholars as Ji Yun. The dearth of first-hand accounts by convicts in exile has certain obvious disadvantages for the historian. Officials, though generally accurate in their reports, were concerned only intermittently with those aspects of convicts' lives for which they were

60. *SYD* (T) QL 53/2/9, 157.
61. *QSL* JQ 85, 11a–b, 6/7/12. On the role of the changsui, see Ch'ü, *Local Government*, 74–92.
62. Ji, *Yuewei Caotang Biji* 7, 33a. The exile was arrested twenty days after his escape and put to death.

not directly responsible.[63] Nonetheless, it is possible to gain from these documents a general sense of how ordinary convicts lived in Xinjiang.

The same considerations that forced the Qing to make adequate provision for the journey across China governed convicts' treatment once in exile. The government had to maintain them in reasonable condition in order to extract the maximum return for the considerable investment involved in transporting them to the frontier. In 1758, as the first convicts arrived in Xinjiang, however, the political need to demonstrate that the new territories could be financially self-reliant and that the transportation of convicts to Xinjiang would prove cost-effective sometimes relegated these requirements to second place.[64]

Thus in that year it was ordered that no separate provision was to be made to accommodate slaves, who could construct their own frontier-style earthen houses.[65] However, many convict slaves were probably given at least temporary shelter by their masters, otherwise the extremely cold Xinjiang winter weather would certainly have killed them. In general, settlers built their own accommodation, but there is little information on how convicts lived. In 1770 when Ji Yun noted that the farming convicts generally lived on the land they worked, and that in winter at least the married exiles came to the city to wait for spring, he was presumably referring to those who were not enslaved.[66]

At least at Hami, the government did provide convicts with housing.[67] There were thirty houses for married convicts and seven for unmarried ones; these had been constructed by local officials. Elsewhere at Hami there were earthen houses for convicts and soldiers.[68]

In some areas the authorities issued a monthly ration to convicts; at

63. Most of the information that Ji Yun provides is confirmed by other sources. However, it is not always possible to determine the extent to which the anecdotes concerning the exiles featured in some of his ghost stories can be regarded as reliable historiographical sources.

64. See, e.g., *SYD* (T) *changben* QL 23/6/21, 121, referring to censorial objections to the expenses involved in colonizing Xinjiang; see also *SYD* (T) QL 23/12/11, 230–232; *Qinding Pingding Zhunke'er Fanglüe Xubian* 15, 30b, QL 27/2/26.

65. *SYD* (B) QL 23/6/9, 359. Probably the earthen houses to which this edict referred were the same ones Hong Liangji found so unappealing fifty years later.

66. Ji, "Wulumuqi Zashi," 13a.

67. On the construction of housing for soldiers in the Ürümqi area, see *HDSL* (1899) 178, 13a–b. On other government housing, see also, e.g., *Qinding Huangyu Xiyu Tuzhi* 34, 5b–6a; the government-constructed housing referred to in this text was apparently not used for convicts.

68. *Hami Zhi* 43, 7a, 8a.

others they left them to provide for themselves. At Hami and Balikun, convicts received 30 *jin* (approximately 18 kilograms) of flour each month, with a supplement of 10 jin per month during farming season.[69] Thus the daily allowance was equal to approximately 600 grams. This compared with 840 grams (later reduced to just under 700 grams) of grain issued each day to convicts in transit; the extra allowance during farming season brought the farmers' rations into line with the provisions issued to convicts in transit. Those accompanied by their families received in addition 30 jin of flour for adults and 15 for children each month.[70] Convicts who were too old or infirm to support themselves were issued a half ration.[71] The ration was the same at Balikun.[72] At Ürümqi and Ili food was apparently not issued to convicts because they were expected to support themselves from the land allocated to them. As noted above, in those locations convicts accompanied by their families normally received additional acreage.

At Hami clothes were issued to ordinary convicts. The annual allowance consisted of one shirt, two pairs of unlined trousers, two pairs of shoes, and one pair of woolen footwraps. Every two years they received a jacket and a woolen hat, and every three years a sheepskin coat.[73] This apparently was considered too lavish by the Qing government, since in 1767 the annual clothing budget per convict was almost halved from 10.3 taels to 5.5 taels and by 1780 it had plummeted to 1.92 taels.[74] At

69. On the jin, see Ch'üan and Kraus, *Mid-Ch'ing Rice Markets and Trade*, 79.

70. Until 1767 the Hami convicts were permitted to reclaim additional land to support themselves and their families, but in that year it was ordered that the harvest from the additional land should be handed over to the government and used to issue the convicts a set amount. *Hami Zhi* 42, 6a–7a; see also ibid., 18, 1a–b. At Hami in the early nineteenth century, each household was estimated to consist of two "large mouths" (*dakou*)—able-bodied men—and eight "small mouth" (*xiaokou*), presumably the convict's wife and their children. This seems large by comparison with the average of three or four per civilian household recorded in the official gazetteer (*Qinding Huangyu Xiyu Tuzhi*) a dozen or so years after the conquest. See Luo, *Qing Gaozong Tongzhi Xinjiang Zhengce de Tantao*, 232.

71. Qi, "Qingdai Xinjiang Qianfan Yanjiu," 89, citing *QSL*.

72. Prior to 1785 the Balikun convicts received less government food issue than those at Hami, but in that year food distribution was equalized in the two locations. See *SYD* (T) QL 50/6/2, 147–148; *SYD* (T)QL 50/8/23, 327–331; *SYD* (T) QL 50/9/n.d., 565.

73. *Hami Zhi* 20, 2a.

74. *Hami Zhi* 42, 6b. Cf. ibid., 20, 2a, the annual actual cost given for clothing issue per convict is 2.43 taels; Cf. also *SYD* (T) QL 50/8/23, 330, which refers to the Tarnaqinq (Hami) regulation budget of 1.92 taels for clothing. This figure may exclude the sheepskin coat, which cost 2 taels (0.66 taels per year).

Balikun after 1780 there was also an annual budget of 1.92 taels for convicts' clothing.[75] As we shall see, clothing for convicts working in the mines at Ili was sometimes contributed by other convicts; no other information has come to light concerning clothing issued to convicts at Ili or Ürümqi.

Convicts were kept under close control. A convict slave's master was responsible for ensuring that the slave did not escape; the presence of convicts who were not enslaved was checked by means of a periodic roll call.[76] Even free settlers were not permitted to leave the area. At the *tun* anyone arriving after sunset was checked; within the city, soldiers patrolled the alleyways at night. This was partly to guard against clandestine assignations. In the 1760s, when male convicts far outnumbered women, marriage disputes were so common that the subprefect's office appointed two women to arrange matches, and all others were forbidden.[77]

The convicts brought a variety of talents to Xinjiang. Some, such as those whom the government employed making industrial ceramics, were skilled craftsmen. Convict Fang Zheng was known for his abilities as a repairer of clocks.[78] Others possessed medical knowledge, as in the case of the wife of one exile who cured an ailing lieutenant stationed at Ürümqi. Carpenter Liu, a popular comic lead actor at Ürümqi in the 1760s, may well also have been an exile.[79]

Ji Yun, who was particularly interested in storytelling and in acting, found a number of skilled exponents among the exiles at Ürümqi in 1768:

> There are several troupes of actors; among the exiles, those who can do *kunqu* have collected themselves into a group. The best of them is Cheng Si of Hangzhou. . . . There are several troupes of boys who sing. The best is "Peiyu Peijin" but recently the Xinjiao group, made up of the sons of exiles at Changji, has almost matched them.[80]

75. *SYD* (T) QL 50/8/23, 327-331; *Hubu Zeli* 95, 63a–b.

76. See Wei, Wu, and Lu, *Qingdai Nubi Zhidu* 71. How frequently officials held roll calls for common convicts in Xinjiang is not known. In the 1770s in the northeast, exiles had to answer a roll call every five days. Chen, "Ji Lü Wancun Zisun," 2.

77. Ji, "Wulumuqi Zashi," 12a, 15b. For similar problems on another frontier, see Entenmann, "Migration and Settlement in Sichuan," 123.

78. Ji, "Wulumuqi Zashi," 10a, 35b.

79. Ji, *Yuewei Caotang Biji* 14, 2b.

80. Ji, "Wulumuqi Zashi," 35a.

Convict He Jineng was particularly accomplished in singing love songs from Hubei, and Ji was moved by his rendering of "Red Silk Trousers." Ji also admired the realistic narration done by the convict storyteller Sun Qineng.[81] A few years later Bai Er, at the time one of Beijing' most famous "female lead" actors, was banished to Xinjiang, where he perhaps continued to ply his art.[82]

In 1775 the Qianlong Emperor expressed his disapproval of the wineshops and theaters that were flourishing on the frontier and threatened to punish senior Xinjiang officials if they failed to close such establishments. Yet troupes of actors continued to thrive. In 1808 Ili military governor Songyun suggested limiting admission to the two acting troupes then resident at Ili, because of the risk that the sons of soldiers and farmers would join the troupes and become corrupted. Responding to Songyun's memorial, the Jiaqing Emperor reminded him of the earlier prohibition and ordered that the troupes be disbanded. The emperor observed that it was impossible to avoid "corruption" as long as such troupes continued to exist.[83]

Selling food was a common occupation among exiles and could be quite profitable. As noted elsewhere, convict Gao apparently raised several thousand taels by selling Jiangsu-style delicacies at Ili. His clientele doubtless included homesick exiles and lower Yangzi merchants trading on the frontier. Gao was wealthy enough to lend money to others; just before his departure for home he called in loans of more than three hundred taels from a single creditor. This was Yu Shihe, nephew of the former ranking Grand Councillor Yu Minzhong. Yu Shihe was banished in 1780 for trying to appropriate a large part of his deceased uncle's very considerable estate.[84] During his eight years in exile—when by his own account he had no money—he frequently bought on credit from convict Gao. When Gao claimed his money, Yu promised to arrange payment in Jiangsu since he too was bound for home.[85]

The advent of Han Chinese settlers and exiles introduced a fresh range of religious and ritual beliefs to the frontier, where Islam and, in the

81. Ibid., 36a.
82. Mackerras, *The Rise of the Peking Opera*, 89–90.
83. *QSL* JQ 194, 1b–2b, 13/4/1.
84. He was banished "as a warning to unfilial sons" (his uncle had contributed to his upbringing). *SYD* (T) QL 45/7/12, 63.
85. *SYD* (T) QL 53/2/19, 445–448. Yu's debt was calculated in *yuansiyin*, a form of money that circulated in Jiangsu and Zhejiang. On this case, see also chapter 9.

north, the Tibetan lamaist branch of Buddhism were already prevalent. The Qing had no objection to orthodox festivals and religious beliefs among the immigrants. In the 1760s Ji Yun found that religious and ritual activities at Ürümqi were much like those in China proper except that there was no "spring-welcoming" festival. The agricultural colonies held a lion dance competition at New Year, which in 1770 was won by the team of dancers from Changji, one of the locations to which convicts were sent. Children dressed up; lanterns were lit; women let down their hair and there was much noise and bustle.[86]

At Ili in 1788 the military governor became very suspicious of activities in several temples to the goddess of fertility. He converted the temples into public buildings and had the Buddhist texts and images destroyed. The events that aroused his suspicion—men and women mingling at nocturnal meetings, burning incense, and reading sutras—suggest that he was concerned about improper religious sects, whose nefarious activities often took such forms.[87] Although most sect exiles were sent to the remote isolation of southern Xinjiang, they may have had contact with some of their confreres at Ili.

As with the native sects, the religious ardor of Catholic converts was not necessarily dampened by exile to Xinjiang. According to a missionary report sent to Rome in 1807, one of the imperial princes exiled two years previously had been preaching openly at Ili. When subjected to threats from the authorities, he declared that only death could silence him. The high rank formerly held by this exile perhaps lent force to the example his outspokenness presented to other Catholic exiles.[88] To the authorities it demonstrated that even banishment to Xinjiang was not universally intimidating.

CRIME IN EXILE

The banishment of convicts to the Xinjiang frontier did not always achieve the goal of rehabilitation. Some convicts, unreformed, escaped from Xinjiang; others committed further crimes while there. In either

---

86. Ji, "Wulumuqi Zashi," 8a, 34a–b.
87. Temple gatherings such as these also gave rise to fears about promiscuity. See, e.g., Naquin, *Millenarian Rebellion in China*, 47–49.
88. *Nouvelles Lettres édifiantes* 4, 135–162.

case, the criminal's recapture was usually followed by immediate execution; there was no second chance.[89]

Convicts began to escape from Xinjiang as soon as the system of banishment was instituted in 1758. A report submitted in the fourth month of Qianlong 31 (1766) named six convicts who had escaped in the previous year and were still at large; in the current year, seventeen had already escaped and had not yet been recaptured.[90] In the last three months of Qianlong 50 (1785–86) fourteen convicts escaped; a report from the third month of Qianlong 51 noted that twelve of those who had escaped during the preceding year were still at large.[91] Many were never recaptured.

Their less fortunate comrades often gave pitiful accounts of their experiences. Convict Zhou Shiyuan, recaptured after having reached Suzhou near Jiayuguan in China proper, testified that he escaped from Ürümqi because life on the agricultural colony was unbearable. He escaped with another convict, but they then parted company. Zhou found that life as a fugitive was no better, however, and became so cold and hungry that he tried to kill himself; he was then arrested and put to death. A proclamation concerning Zhou Shiyuan was made at Ürümqi to deter others.[92] The inhospitable terrain between Xinjiang and China proper doubtless claimed many other lives. The corpse that Ji Yun's servant discovered in the mountains was nothing remarkable.[93]

It was not only cold, hunger, and official vigilance that the escaped convict had to fear. A convict who betrayed an escaped fellow was rewarded by immediate registration as a civilian in Xinjiang; an emancipist who did so was permitted to return home.[94] The authorities doubtless

89. For edicts on punishment for escaped convicts, see *XJTLSL* 2, 23a–24a.

90. *QSL* QL 759, 6b–7b, 31/4/18. The annual provincial reports concerning escaped convicts included information on convicts who had absconded from their place of exile as well as those who had fled en route. In addition to reports made by officials in the convict's native province, officials in Xinjiang were also required to report escapes. *QSL* QL 755, 24b–25a, 31/2/27. This system made it more difficult for officials to conceal escapes in the hope of avoiding punishment.

91. *SYD* (T) QL 50/9/2, 475 (four escaped); ibid., 50/9/20, 625 (one escaped); ibid., 50/10/6, 31 (one escaped); ibid., 50/10/19, 127 (two escaped); ibid., 50/10/22, 149 (three escaped); ibid., 50/11/23, 311 (one escaped); ibid., 50/12/5, 486 (two escaped); ibid., 51/3/4, 377–378 (noting that twelve of the convicts who had escaped during the previous year were still free).

92. *GZDQLCZZ* vol. 28, 579–580, 32/11/15. For another case in which an escaped convict pleaded hardship in mitigation, see *GZDQLCZZ* vol. 28, 204, 32/9/23.

93. See chapter 1, text accompanying n. 6.

94. *HDSL* (1899) 745, 11b (1786).

hoped that the rewards for informing would discourage convicts from conspiring to escape in groups; although these hopes seem to have been largely realized, few instances of betrayal were actually recorded.

Preventing convicts from escaping was in the interests of all concerned. The punishment for those responsible was flogging for the slave's master if he was not an official, at the rate of fifty strokes per escape.[95] If the convict had been enslaved to an official, the master was subject to a fine. The amount of the fine and the extent of responsibility—that is, whether all pertinent officials or only the person directly responsible for the convict were punished—depended on the number of escapes during the year. The fine when one convict escaped was three months' salary. This amounted to only a small proportion of the official's annual income, given the much higher level of the *yanglian* salary supplement, not to mention illicit sources. If up to five escaped, the responsible official's superior was also fined one month's salary; if twenty escaped, the ranking official (the military governor at Ili or lieutenant governor at Ürümqi) was also fined one month's salary. In all cases fines were subject to pro rata increases if greater numbers of convicts escaped.[96]

Some convicts carried on their old ways of murder, robbery, forgery, and brawling in exile. In 1765 Balikun officials reported the execution of convict Cao Sixi for the murder of convict Xu Sanzi in a dispute over a two-tael loan.[97] In 1774 convict Ma De, who had already served fifteen years for robbery, was executed after he became involved in a dispute about irrigation with a civilian named Zhang and killed him.[98]

Qing authorities exercised little direct control over enslaved convicts in southern Xinjiang, primarily because there the Qing presence was far less well established than in northern Xinjiang. Most of the responsibility for the convicts was delegated by the central government to the begs.

---

95. Whether the full quota of strokes was actually applied is unclear. In practice fewer strokes may have sufficed, as when criminals sentenced to "one hundred blows with the heavy bamboo" received only forty blows. See Bodde and Morris, *Law in Imperial China*, 77. Moreover, some may have been able to commute their punishment to a fine.

96. *XJTLSL* 2, 28a–b.

97. *GZDQLCZZ* vol. 24, 185–186, 30/i2/12. Cao's master was sentenced to eighty heavy blows for "doing what ought not to be done" (*DLCY* 386), or, in this case, not doing what ought to be done, in other words failing to keep his slave under control.

98. *GZDQLCZZ* vol. 37, 45, 39/9/28. Convict Kang Tingyan, enslaved in Heilongjiang, ground pulverized cakes made of arsenic and persimmon compresses to spread on his skin sores but did not destroy what he did not use. His master's mother and another convict slave found them and ate them and died of arsenic poisoning. Kang was executed for this accidental killing. *QSL* JQ 215, 21a–b, 14/7/9.

However, in 1797 Qing officials expressed concern about the volatile situation created by the high proportion of convict slaves to begs—two or three to one.[99] Events soon justified their anxiety. When the wife of beg Yibulayimu of Yarkand and her five-year-old grandson upbraided their slave Zheng Yaozu, a former river pirate, for his continuing insubordination, Zheng struck the little boy several times on the face with a whip. The beg's wife and the little boy fled. When the beg returned he asked the government to punish Zheng, who was sentenced to death.[100] This case may be more complex than it appears on the surface, since beg Yibulayimu himself had previously served a sentence of banishment at Ili for high-handedness in dealing with Muslims under his authority.[101]

Occasional instances of crime among ordinary convicts were to be expected and were relatively easy to control. More alarming was the risk that groups of convicts might combine in joint action against the authorities. The fear of this eventuality lay behind the frequent legislative amendments that aimed to avoid too high a concentration of convicts in any single area and prompted attempts to organize mutual surveillance among convicts.[102]

These fears crystallized when a gathering of convicts and officials turned into a massacre and revolt. In 1768, at the mid-autumn festival, officials at the Changji agricultural colony, west of Ürümqi, held a hillside picnic for the exiles:

> Men and women were sitting together. The officials got drunk and forced some of the women to sing songs. In an instant there was an uproar; they stabbed the officials and killed them, robbed the arsenal of weapons and occupied the city. The report reached Ürümqi [the next morning] and Grand Secretary Wenfu hastily assembled troops. At that time, the soldiers were dispersed among various colonies and only 147 men were in the city, but they were all crack troops.[103]

The authorities estimated that some 200 convicts were involved. Lieutenant governor Wenfu and his troops surrounded the rebels, killing

---

99. ZPZZ JQ 2/1/21 (law—exile, packet for JQ 1–9), memorial of Changlin and Tuolun).
100. ZPZZ JQ 2/3/20 (law—exile, packet for JQ 1–9), memorial of Jifeng'e.
101. SYD (B) QL 59/4/27, 238.
102. QSL QL 791, 19b–21a, 32/17/30.
103. Ji, *Yuewei Caotang Biji* 20, 4a. Presumably "singing songs" was a euphemism and the drunken officials in fact tried to assault the women.

100 and capturing 30 alive, with some loss of life on the government side. The ringleaders were slowly cut to death; the rest were beheaded immediately and their corpses exposed. The wives and young sons of the rebels were enslaved to the soldiers who had suppressed the uprising; all who were more than nine years of age were put to death. In the attempt to restore local order, the government replaced livestock and other possessions seized by the rebels from civilians in the vicinity.[104]

The Changji uprising erupted in a location where, according to one account, although there were more than 3,000 troops, there were also at least 1,600 convicts.[105] The riot occurred only a year after the "changee" system was introduced, a modification that reflected Qing awareness that too many criminals were arriving in Xinjiang; it focused official attention even more sharply on the critical need to avoid undue concentrations of convicts in a single area.[106] In addition, the Changji uprising, the only one of its kind to occur during the eighteenth century in Xinjiang, took place within ten years of the inception of the banishment system, and the fact that frontier society was still in its formative period may have made it possible for officials and convicts to mix at a social occasion.[107] The sudden and violent transformation of a seasonal celebration indicates the high level of barely suppressed tension that characterized relations between these groups.

MISTREATMENT OF CONVICTS

Common people in Qing China were always vulnerable to mistreatment at the hands of officials. This situation was exacerbated when crimes were committed against convicts, who had no recourse whatsoever.

The accusations leveled against Ili military governor Kuilin in 1788 included several allegations of the torture and murder of ordinary exiles. The case of convict Liu Si was an extreme example. Kuilin was said to have ordered Liu's hands, feet, and penis cut off, the extremities thrown

---

104. *QSL* QL 818, 19b–21b, 33/9/9; *ZPZZ* QL 33/10/11, (agriculture—opening new lands, packet 32), memorial of Wenfu.

105. See Qi, "Qingdai Xinjiang Qianfan Yanjiu," 93, citing Wei, *Sheng Wu Ji.*

106. See *HDSL* (1899) 721, 18b–19b.

107. In Heilongjiang in 1813 officials foiled an uprising allegedly plotted by a group of exiles. See, e.g., *QSL* QL JQ 266, 16b–18a, 18/2/19; ibid., 266, 21a–23a, 28/2/24; ibid., 267, 19a–20b, 18/3/21; ibid., 268, 19a–20a, 18/4/26.

into the river, and the penis stuffed into his mouth. The complaint, probably filed more for political reasons than out of any concern for convict welfare, stated that Kuilin had failed to report his actions to the authorities in Beijing. Kuilin's response was revealing. Although he admitted that he had been wrong not to make a report, he did not completely deny the accusation of torture and explained why he had taken such measures:

> Liu Si...stole a sheep and stabbed someone and was repeatedly arrested and tried. He was so bad that I decided ordinary punishment would not suffice to instil dread in the other convicts. I ordered his hands and feet cut off and thrown into the river because of the stabbing, as a warning to the other convicts. This is the truth.[108]

Kuilin was also accused of causing the death of two others while they were wearing the cangue. One was Zhang San, undergoing punishment because, in a drunken rage, he hit someone and later threatened to murder his Ölöd master and the master's son. The second was Yao Yi, an emancipist who was incarcerated after an altercation with some soldiers. His continued unruliness, including intimidation of his guard, prompted Kuilin to order him put in the cangue. Yao died because Kuilin refused to allow Yao's family or friends to bring food to him.[109]

Kuilin was not unique in his ill-treatment of convicts. In 1808 a battered corpse discovered in the Ili granary was identified as that of convict Tang Jiawa, the slave of a clerk in the grain office. It transpired that Tang, who had been reported as a fugitive in an attempt to conceal his disappearance, had been punished for committing a number of robberies; the injuries on his corpse suggested that he might have died from abuse by the responsible official.[110]

The contributions ordinary convicts made to the colonization of Xinjiang must have been small comfort to these unwilling immigrants. Far from home, with little prospect of return, most faced years of punishment before they could even begin to hope to improve their situation. Those who escaped from exile normally remained fugitives until their recapture; those who were recaptured were almost always executed. For the many who were too daunted to attempt such desperate ventures, their only prospect was death, even beyond which their exile would endure.

108. *SYD* (T) QL 53/2/9, 153. Kuilin denied the other accusation.
109. *SYD* (T) QL 53/2/9, 156.
110. *SYD* (B) JQ 13/7/5, 97.

Chapter Nine

The End of Exile

Part of the Qing's stated purpose in banishing exiles to Xinjiang, as demonstrated by the focus on self-renewal, was that the period of actual punishment should eventually come to an end. Once an offender had completed the process of rehabilitation, the expectation was that he should put his criminal past behind him, with the proviso that he would be liable for more severe punishment than others in the event of further transgression. This was true even for ordinary convicts compelled to remain on the frontier for the rest of their lives, as well as for banished officials permitted to return to China proper.

Yet many exiles were profoundly concerned about their prospects and about the fate of their remains should they die in Xinjiang. The scholar Hong Liangji, for instance, who fully expected to end his days on the frontier, took the precaution of purchasing a burial plot at Ili soon after his arrival there. He, at least, need not have done so.[1] It was sometimes possible for the remains of exiles who died in Xinjiang to be returned to China proper, for burial among their ancestors' graves. Thus former magistrate Chen Shichang, returning from exile in Xinjiang to his native Jiangxi province, carried home the "teeth and hair" of a deceased exiled fellow countryman.[2]

Other than through death, the end of the formal term of exile occurred

1. Hong, "Gengshengzhai Wen Yi Ji," 3, 12a.
2. Hong, "Wanli Hege Ji," 5a.

in one of three ways: through the lapse of time, upon the proclamation of an amnesty or an imperial pardon, or upon payment to the government of a substantial sum of money known as a "contribution"(*juanshu*). The differential treatment accorded ordinary convicts and banished officials came into starkest relief with respect to the termination of punishment, for officials had far greater opportunities to hasten the moment of release by virtue of the much greater wealth and political influence at their disposal.

There were, however, partial exceptions to this general principle, as illustrated by the case of convict Gao, who had been banished into slavery by virtue of collective responsibility after his father, himself a slave, had killed his master's mother. Gao attained civilian status after eight years of mine work at Ili and established a business selling Jiangsu-style food. Subsequently, and apparently in breach of the prevailing regulations, military governor Yiletu granted him permission to escort home the coffin of his deceased mother.[3] Before Gao could leave, however, Yiletu was replaced by Kuilin, who imposed a ban on Gao's entering the city as punishment for an alleged breach of the peace. Gao, anxious about a possible revocation of his travel pass, used intermediaries to offer Kuilin a bribe of two thousand taels.[4] This sum, a colossal one for most commoners, apparently represented part of the profits of the business. When Kuilin learned of the bribe, he confiscated the money and used it to fund some city repairs.[5]

Gao had already left Xinjiang for his native province of Jiangsu with his mother's coffin when these events came to the attention of officials in Beijing; he traveled some of the way with another Jiangsu returnee, the well-connected exile Yu Shihe, who owed Gao money.[6] Gao was not traced until he reached home. There the commercial success that in Xinjiang had brought him powerful contacts was no longer of significance. He was arrested and sent back, this time to Ürümqi, with a special injunction that he was never to be allowed to return home again.[7]

3. Despite the exceptional nature of the permission, once it had been granted the officials in Xinjiang apparently did not think it appropriate to revoke it. *SYD* (T) QL 52/11/28, 404.

4. The actual offer of the bribe was made on Gao's behalf by convict Pang, who "knew about such things." Pang did not approach Kuilin directly but spoke to his brother.

5. *SYD* (T) QL 53/3/19, 446.

6. As noted in the preceding chapter, Yu was the nephew of a senior Grand Councillor and was in Gao's debt for several hundred taels.

7. *SYD* (T) QL 53/3/19, 449. Yu's debt to Gao was seized by the government. Kuilin's

THE DURATION OF PUNISHMENT

The issue of the duration of punishment for the Xinjiang exiles greatly exercised Qing officials. Frequent changes in the laws reflected the wish to clarify distinctions between different punishments without detracting from the broad purposes of, on the one hand, colonization of the new frontier and, on the other, providing a vehicle for the exiles' moral regeneration. These laws sought to differentiate between offenders with commuted sentences and those with increased ones and between the Xinjiang exiles and their counterparts in China proper. Although the technically less serious sentences of the exiles within China proper were for life, banishment to Xinjiang was not initially permanent, in part because Xinjiang's extreme remoteness seemed to distinguish it from exile destinations in China proper; the view was sometimes expressed that lifelong banishment to such a place might be unduly severe.[8]

After 1766, for common convicts, and 1764, for banished officials, minimum terms were established that attempted to address these various issues. These depended on the original crime and sentence and on behavior in exile. For neither group did they carry, however, a guarantee concerning the maximum term. This open-endedness, and frequent changes in the laws governing duration, enhanced the general atmosphere of uncertainty surrounding a sentence of banishment.[9]

For ordinary convicts, the shortest possible term was initially three years; this applied to those with increased sentences. For other convicts it was five years, but this was later extended to ten.[10] In practice few served less than a decade and most served even longer. Emancipation then depended on official confirmation that during those years the convict had manifested a sufficient degree of repentance by working assiduously and behaving well; for the most serious convicts, such as those banished in

---

acceptance of the bribe was one of eleven counts of impeachment leveled against him. Although Kuilin appeared not to have misappropriated Gao's money, some of the other counts were proven, on which, see chapter 8. Kuilin was dismissed and fined; he did not again attain high office. Kuilin's lenient treatment was probably due to his being a first cousin of the influential Manchu official Fukang'an.

8. See, e.g., *QSL* QL 941, 38b, 38/8/27.

9. For a detailed account of the changes in the laws governing the duration of banishment in Xinjiang for ordinary convicts, see Waley-Cohen, "Stranger Paths of Banishment," 264–278.

10. *DLCY* 45–33.

rebellion cases, emancipation was forever out of reach, regardless of conduct.

Work in the mines or in the boatyards that built and serviced the fleet of grain transport vessels on the Ili River was so terrible that, for those who survived, it generally reduced the length of a term of banishment and for some even provided a means for eventual return home. These privileges also applied to others who provided support services for mining projects in the form of food, money, and clothing. Upon the expiration of eight—later reduced to five—years, such convicts were entitled to register as civilians within Xinjiang, and, with some exceptions, were permitted to return home after a further spell of eight to twelve years working in the mines.[11]

The opportunity to work in the mines was not universal and was restricted to convicts whose behavior was unimpeachable.[12] In some locations quotas existed; for instance, at the Ürümqi iron mines no more than 200 convicts were employed at any given time.

Of these convicts, 150 actually worked in the mines, while 50 farmed nearby land to provide for them. Up to 100 others, often those too frail to perform such arduous labor, could contribute up to thirty taels—a substantial sum few could afford—to the expenses of operating the mines. The amount paid determined the extent of the benefit. Thirty taels limited the term to fifteen years; after this term, convict slaves could register as civilians and others could return home. A later amendment, introduced to reflect the inability of many convicts to contribute so much, permitted payments of ten or twenty taels. A contribution of ten taels led to a total term of seventeen years; a contribution of twenty taels meant a term of sixteen years.[13]

In addition, 40 other convicts were permitted to reduce their terms by making annual contributions in the form of clothing for the use of the Ürümqi mineworkers.[14] This contribution consisted of five felt caps, five

11. *DLCY* 45–33. The exact length of time depended on the gravity of the crime. Those excluded from this avenue were convicts guilty of the most serious crimes, who in any event were not supposed to be assigned to mine work.

12. *SYD* (T) QL 49/4/15, 126.

13. *SYD* (T) QL 49/7/21, 149–152. See also *QSL* QL 1211, 8b–9a, 49/7/2; *Qingdai de Kuangye* 2, 385, 521–522.

14. It is unclear whether these 40 were part of the 100 contributors or separate from them. The quota of 40 and the specified quantity of clothing were presumably calculated on the basis of supplying 200 convicts.

leather jackets, five leather robes, five pairs of leather shoes, ten pairs of leather boots, ten blue cotton undershirts, ten pairs of unlined blue cotton trousers, five pairs of cotton socks, five belts, and ten cotton towels.[15] The adoption of this incentive system demonstrates the force of Qing concerns about self-sufficiency in Xinjiang. Yet those who earned the right to return in one of these ways were a small minority of the Xinjiang convicts.

By the early nineteenth century, Qing officials had become aware that to deny the vast majority of convicts all hope of returning to China proper gave inadequate motivation for good behavior. Moreover, since the advent of hundreds of thousands of civilian immigrants, the need for colonists in Xinjiang had subsided. In 1806, therefore, the government issued a set of detailed regulations that restored to most convicts the hope of eventual return. These regulations divided the convicts into categories based on their age and the length of time already served in Xinjiang and allowed most to return home upon reaching the age of seventy or completing fifteen to twenty years in Xinjiang. The requirement of good behavior remained in force.[16]

Banished officials were covered by separate regulations, because for them, in contrast to the ordinary convicts, the end of exile usually meant return to China proper. For those whose sentences had been increased from simple dismissal, beatings, or penal servitude, the minimum term was three years; for those whose sentences had been increased from one of the less extreme forms of exile (liu or chongjun), it was ten years.[17] Those whose sentences had been commuted from a death sentence were

15. *Hubu Zeli* 95, 64a. See also *DLCY*, note following 45–33, *juan* 6, p. 162.

16. *QSL JQ* 156, 10b–13b, 11/1/9. For details of these regulations, see appendix 3.

17. *DLCY* 45–18. Intercalary months were not included in the calculation of the amount of time served, nor was the time required for the journey into exile. When a death sentence was first commuted to exile within China proper and then increased to Xinjiang banishment, the ten-year minimum term applied. See *XAHL* 6, 14a–16b. Officials could pay a sum of money in lieu of suffering corporal punishment. From 1782 to 1801, those officials originally sentenced to exile within China proper were first required to serve ten years in Xinjiang and then to return to China proper to serve their original sentence. This was later abandoned both because Xinjiang banishment was felt to be harsher than other forms of exile and because it was felt that the imposition of a double exile was too severe. See *DLCY*, discussion following 45–18, *juan* 6, p. 154. For some of the edicts on this subject, see *SYD* (T) *QL* 38/8/11, 130–131; *QSL QL* 941, 38a–39a, 38/8/27; *QSL QL* 1158, 4a–b, 47/6/7; *SYD* (T) 50/n.d. (third month), 561–563. See also *SYD* (B) *QL* 59/4/ 27, 189.

threatened with lifelong exile, yet most of these were eventually released, in some instances even when the original sentence explicitly forbade the possibility of return.[18]

Supervision of convict labor in the mines and boatyards offered some banished officials the possibility of achieving a reduction in term, but such exiles risked responsibility for any shortfall in operating funds.[19] The system of assigning some of the burden of financing such projects to these exiles was introduced in 1789 when it became clear that few convicts would be able to raise sufficient money to relieve the government of this expense.[20] Secondment to these types of often gruelling, but potentially advantageous, work was restricted to those who showed a suitable degree of contrition and, almost certainly, to those who were well connected.

Few banished officials served less than three years in Xinjiang. Many served for at least five years, although relatively few remained beyond ten. Those who did return after fewer than three years in exile were normally well known or senior officials whose political connections contributed to their early release. Such was almost certainly true in the cases of the Hanlin academician Ji Yun, recalled after only a year in exile, and the army general Mingliang, transferred to assist in military campaigns after less than a year. Thus the removal from the corridors of power effected by a sentence of banishment was sometimes only very short-lived.

Upon the expiration of the minimum term—sooner or later, perhaps depending on the exile's personal influence—the ranking official in the place of exile submitted to the emperor a request for permission for the exiled official to return home.[21] The request was not automatically approved. Theoretically approval depended on whether the exile had demonstrated, through hard work and a repentant attitude, that he had

18. See QSL QL 1456, 20a–21b, 59/7/9. See also undated qingdan from the late Jiaqing or early Daoguang period, located in ZPZZ (law—exile, packet for JQ 10–18). Cf. QSL JQ 358, 13b–14b, 24/5/18, adding six years to the terms of ten officials who had already served almost nine years in exile.

19. It was considered too risky to allow exiles to draw from government funds. An edict of 1795 (QSL QL 1478, 4a–b, 60/5/1) appears to abrogate the contributions system at the mines, yet it is still covered in regulations issued in 1865. Hubu Zeli 95, 63b–64a.

20. Qingdai de Kuangye 2, 521.

21. For some examples, see ZPZZ QL 32/3/21 (law—exile, packet for QL 32–50), memorial of Wudashan; GZD JQ 8523, 7/7/16; ZPZZ JQ 9/1/10 (law—exile, packet for JQ 1–9), memorial of Songyun; ZPZZ JQ 10/11/16, (law—exile, packet for JQ 10–18), memorial of Songyun; GZD JQ 12317, 13/10/28; GZD JQ 12479, 13/11/16; GZD JQ 18029, 20/3/4.

achieved self-renewal; in practice, a number of other factors, such as the government's control agenda and the exile's political connections, were certainly relevant. For example, when the twenty-one officials banished in the aftermath of Heshen and Fukang'an's vendetta against Chai Daji had spent three years in exile, the military governor submitted requests on their behalf. All were ordered to remain in Xinjiang. One, a former first captain (*dusi*) in the Green Standard army, was to serve for ten more years, eleven junior officers were to serve for six more years and the remaining nine exiles for three more years. Upon the expiration of the further term, they were to be allowed home.[22] The length of their terms undoubtedly related to their unfortunate former association with Chai Daji. Other responses that did not immediately approve requests for feiyuan to return from Xinjiang either stipulated reapplication after a further period of years or consisted of an outright denial.[23]

AMNESTIES AND PARDONS

The practice of proclaiming amnesties (*she*) existed in China from the early imperial period. Some reduced or cancelled criminal sanctions; others involved benefits such as tax remissions. Under the Qing some form of amnesty was issued in most years.[24]

Amnesties were granted for two principal reasons. The first was the commemoration of an important event, such as the emperor's birthday or an imperial tour. The second was the alleviation of a natural calamity such as a flood or drought; the granting of an amnesty in such circumstances stemmed from the traditional Chinese belief that cosmic harmony was affected by imperial injustice. According to this belief, the only way to relieve natural disasters was to release exiles and other prisoners in order to restore heavenly equilibrium.

Amnesties were frequently limited in application to particular loca-

22. *SYD* (B) QL 57/9/19, 137. On this case, see chapter 5, text accompanying n. 8.

23. See, e.g., *GZD* JQ 10067, 13/2/25, ordering former magistrate Liu Jiaying to remain in exile for a further six years (having already served three years). The edict stipulated that a further request should be submitted on Liu's behalf at the expiration of the six-year extension. For an 1816 ruling on this issue, see *XAHL* 6, 17b–18a.

24. McKnight, *The Quality of Mercy*, xi, 12–36. For a list of amnesties granted from 1621 through 1785, see *QCWXTK* 210. Such amnesties were separate from the annual assize system discussed in chapter 4.

tions or to particular types of criminals. For example, in the case of floods, only those in the inundated provinces were covered by an amnesty intended to encourage better weather conditions. Similarly, the Qianlong Emperor sometimes ordered the release of criminals in the provinces he visited on an imperial tour.[25]

In 1778, when a limited amnesty extended only to those serving a sentence of life exile within China proper (*jun* or *liu*) who had completed at least ten years of their term,[26] the question of its application to the Xinjiang convicts arose, since it extended to some exiles in the northeast.[27] The problem was that, on the one hand, it seemed inappropriate to exclude the Xinjiang convicts altogether but, on the other, it was inconvenient and expensive to send them home. In the event, of the convicts who had spent at least ten years in exile, only those more than seventy years old and the disabled were allowed to return home, on the ground that they could not work. The rest were to settle in Xinjiang with civilian status.[28]

For the majority of Xinjiang exiles, avoiding or reducing a term of banishment through an amnesty was extremely unlikely.[29] Many of the crimes punishable by banishment to Xinjiang were incorporated in the long lists of crimes statutorily excluded from the operation of general amnesties.[30] The exclusion covered, for instance, those convicted of one of the ten great evils, of improper religious activity, and of robbery or desecration of graves.[31] Also barred were those sentenced by virtue of collective responsibility.[32]

25. See, e.g., *QSL* QL 1204, 16a, 49/4/7.
26. On the implementation of this amnesty, see *XKTB* QL 44/8/4, packet 258, memorial of Yinglian.
27. *XKTB* QL 44/2/15, packet 258, memorial of Yinglian.
28. *QSL* QL 1048, 16b–17a, 43/1/11.
29. Although exiles in China proper might benefit from a general amnesty granted before their arrival in exile (provided they had not deliberately procrastinated), exiles en route to Xinjiang were usually excluded because of the gravity of their crimes. See, however, *DLCY* 17. See *SYD* (B) JQ 13/2/18, 139–141, for an example in which two officials traveling into exile at Ürümqi were granted a reduced sentence as a result of an amnesty, although a third was not.
30. *DLCY* 16.
31. *DLCY* 16; *HDSL* (1899) 733, 2a–5a. *QCXWXTK* 250, p. 9955, suggests that only those Xinjiang convicts sentenced in religious and treason cases were never permitted to benefit from amnesties. On the effects of the exclusionary rules, see also McKnight, *The Quality of Mercy*, 110.
32. *XJTLSL* 2, 7b. The exclusion of the collectively responsible was usually specified in individual laws. See also *DLCY*, commentary following 281–12, *juan* 31, p. 770.

Officials banished to Xinjiang were occasionally the objects of partial amnesties. In 1794 an imperial edict ordered a general review of the cases of several hundred officials serving sentences of banishment in Xinjiang. The Grand Council's 1794 recommendations affected 260 former officials, both civil and military, and provide an insight into the many ways such exiles might be treated.[33]

The Grand Council recommended seven different clemency measures: immediate return home; immediate reduction of sentence to beating (*zhang*), which might be avoided through monetary redemption; immediate reduction of sentence to a maximum of three years' penal servitude (*tu*) within the exile's native province; return home after completing three years of banishment in Xinjiang; reduction of sentence to penal servitude after completing three years in banishment in Xinjiang; reduction of sentence by one degree (in effect, that is, reduction to penal servitude) after three more years in Xinjiang; and submission of further requests for instructions after three more years in Xinjiang.[34] The two principal factors apparently taken into consideration by the Grand Council were the length of time served and the gravity of the crime.

The emperor approved most, but not all, of the recommendations. For example, Mengtai, an imperial family member held responsible for the spoilage of sacrificial silk, was ordered to remain in exile for at least six further years despite being recommended for immediate return home. Mengtai had already spent ten years in exile; his unusually long banishment suggests that his case may have been more complicated than appears from available information.[35]

In the sixth month of 1795 a drought in Rehe and the capital area prompted further review of the sentences of officials and bannermen serving terms of exile in Xinjiang, in an attempt to produce rain. They were allowed home if their crime had been relatively minor. Three months later former provincial commander-in-chief Gao Cha, banished more

33. *SYD* (B) QL 59/4/27, 195–284. On the degrees by which punishments were reduced, see Bodde and Morris, *Law in Imperial China*, 101–102. See appendix 4 for a tabulation of the period of exile already served by some of the disgraced officials in Xinjiang in 1794. On regulations introduced in the mid-nineteenth century that enabled banished officials to purchase a reduction in term in certain circumstances, see Chou, "Frontier Studies," 71–72.

34. The 260 were not the full complement of officials then serving sentences of banishment in Xinjiang; for unstated reasons the cases of some 190 more were not reviewed at that time.

35. *QSL* QL 1457, 7a–b, 59/7/7.

than two years earlier because of his failure to report malingering by two of his relatives, was permitted to return home immediately despite an earlier order reducing his sentence to forced labor after completing three years in exile. It seems unlikely that an amnesty issued for so specific a purpose would have been delayed for three months, even taking into account delays in communications between Xinjiang and the capital, but it may be that reconsideration of Gao's case occurred as a result of this order. It is even more likely that Gao found some way of exerting influence to obtain his release.[36]

Compared with the relatively routine granting of amnesties, imperial pardons were highly unusual. Usually those who received the benefit of such imperial clemency were known personally to the emperor, or perhaps a family member had demonstrated exceptional virtue. In practice it sometimes proved expedient to invoke the emperor's ultimate authority in this way to resolve a political impasse.

Such may well have been the true reason for the release of the scholar Hong Liangji, banished to Xinjiang in 1799 after his death sentence was commuted, as described in chapter 5. Hong's term of fewer than three months in exile was one of the shortest on record. The ostensible reason for his exceptionally prompt recall was the protracted drought in the area around the capital. None of the usual measures had yet proved effective. The release of a major political prisoner such as Hong was a last resort. By all accounts it was immediately successful, for rain is said to have fallen in Beijing the same day.[37]

Scholars have yet to discover the true nature of the debate that undoubtedly preceded the order for Hong's execution and his subsequent exile and release. It certainly related to the intense power struggle between the then still powerful supporters of the fallen imperial favorite, Heshen, and their newly ascendant opponents, with whom Hong was affiliated. Heshen's supporters may have preferred not to risk creating a sympathetic rallying point for their rivals by executing Hong, and their opponents were probably unwilling to sacrifice one of their number who had had the courage openly to express the private opinions so many of them held.[38]

36. See *QSL* QL 1481, 10b–11a, 60/6/25; *QSL* QL 1481, 10b–11a, 60/6/25; *SYD* (B) 60/9/28, 301.

37. See, e.g., *ECCP* 374.

38. For a discussion of this case, see Elman, *Classicism, Politics, and Kinship*, 284–290.

In at least one instance a pardon was granted as a single, small incident in a larger trend towards the promotion and preservation of Manchu culture.[39] In 1775 Chengfang, a Manchu, was sentenced to banishment to Xinjiang because of his activities as a beggar chief. His mother, a member of the imperial clan, was outraged by her son's activities. She destroyed his beggar's placard with a stick and refused to allow him to continue this way of life. The emperor praised her for her attention to the importance of Manchu "face" and awarded her a roll of satin. Noting her advanced age—she was more than seventy years old—the emperor pardoned Chengfang and expressed the hope that his mother's example would inspire other young members of the banners.[40]

In 1794 a pardon was granted because of the exiles' prominent connections. The emperor allowed the banished sons of the corrupt official Wang Danwang to return from Ili; Wang's younger sons who were still in prison in Beijing awaiting banishment were excused from exile. The order of clemency occurred after the National History Office submitted to the emperor a draft official biography of Wang's father, whose career had culminated in a governorship.[41]

However, in the confused political ambiance of the turn of the century, even the best connections were no guarantee of a pardon. In 1800 Adis, the son of Agui—who until his death three years earlier had been the ranking official in the empire and a leading rival of Heshen—was banished to Ili for bungling in the campaign against the White Lotus rebels. The edict expressed formal regret at banishing the son of so meritorious an official but took pains to make clear that Adis's continuing incompetence was inexcusable on any grounds.[42]

Amnesties and pardons were an unreliable source of relief for the Xinjiang exiles. The crimes of many ordinary convicts had carried them beyond the scope of any amnesty, and even the less serious criminals could not be certain that the next proclamation would extend to them.

39. See, generally, Crossley, "*Manzhou Yuanliu Kao* and the Formalization of the Manchu Heritage."
40. *SYD* (T) QL 40/4/19, 46.
41. *Qing Shi Gao* 339, p. 11075.
42. *QSL* JQ 66, 1b–2b, 5/i4/16. Adis was banished at the request of commander-in-chief Lebao, the son of Wenfu whom Agui had succeeded as commander of the army fighting the Jinchuan more than a quarter of a century before, following Wenfu's death in battle. In requesting Adis's banishment, Lebao may have been settling an old score, but no evidence has yet come to light to support this hypothesis.

For banished officials, political connections might be their best hope, but there was no guarantee that these would prove sufficiently potent to save them.

CONTRIBUTIONS

Although statutorily ineligible for monetary redemption of their crime, Xinjiang exiles could sometimes contribute very large sums to the state in exchange for permission to return home before their term expired.[43] By 1736 this procedure, *juanshu*, which originated in the Kangxi period, was being used specifically to finance the Xinjiang military campaigns. Although originally intended as a temporary measure, it proved too useful to be discontinued.[44]

An application to make such a contribution was normally made by a member of the exile's family.[45] The relationship had to be close; the application of the married elder sister of exile Miu Yuanchun was refused on the ground that to grant permission would set a dangerous precedent to other "outer" relatives.[46] Applications were sent by the governor or governor-general of the exile's native province to the emperor, whose approval was required.[47] Payment in full within a time limit of two months was required before the exile was permitted to return.[48] Those convicted of very grave crimes were excluded from this system.

Complicated formulae based on the offender's status and the severity of his punishment were used to calculate the amount of the contribution. For banishment to Xinjiang, the amount payable for officials of the first and second ranks was 12,000 taels; for the third and fourth ranks, 9,600 taels; for the fifth and sixth ranks, 7,200 taels; for the seventh to ninth

43. On the monetary redemption of punishment, see chapter 4. At least after 1805, officials who redeemed their crimes through large contributions subsequently had to make a further payment to purchase the right to be restored to office. See Metzger, *Internal Organization*, 308.

44. QCWXTK 209, pp. 6729–6730; QCXWXTK 255, p. 10003.

45. In those rare cases in which the request was submitted prior to exile, it usually came from the criminal himself.

46. SYD (T) JQ 18/4/18, 175. Miu was allowed home two years later, having served three years in exile. GZD JQ 17790, 20/2/9.

47. Officials probably first required evidence of an applicant's ability to pay the amount proffered, because of the risk of punishment for the official in the event of default; possibly some tested that ability by forwarding the application only upon receipt of a bribe.

48. *Huidian* (1899) 56, 12b.

ranks and *jinshi* and *juren* degree-holders, 4,800 taels; for *gongsheng* and *jiansheng* degree-holders, 2,400 taels; and for ordinary people, 1,200 taels.[49] Although these were sometimes the amounts paid, in several cases the amounts were in fact substantially higher, and sometimes an application that proffered only the minimum was rejected for no apparent reason.[50]

Ordinary people, other than members of wealthy families who did not themselves hold any degree or official position, could seldom have raised sufficient funds to make such a contribution. The majority of commoners would not have seen 1,200 taels in a lifetime. For example, the annual wages of a relatively well-paid worker such as a bondservant in a prince's household amounted to under 50 taels (in money and grain).[51]

The stipulated amounts were significant even in comparison to official salaries and salary supplements. During this period official salaries did not exceed 200 taels per annum, and even the highest annual integrity-nourishing supplements payable to the most senior officials amounted to only 12,000 taels, equivalent to the minimum contribution payable by

49. See *QCWXTK* 209, p. 6731; Boulais, *Manuel du code chinois*, 15–16. In theory one could make a contribution to avoid even a death penalty. For this the basic figures—often as much or even more than those stipulated for Xinjiang banishment—were: officials of the third or higher rank, 12,000 taels; the fourth and fifth ranks, 5,000 taels; the sixth rank, 4,000 taels; the seventh to ninth ranks and jinshi and juren degree-holders, 2,500 taels; *gongsheng* and *jiansheng* degree-holders, 2,000 taels, and ordinary people, 1,200 taels. Exile within China proper cost 40 percent less than a death sentence, and forced labor 60 percent less. *QCWXTK* 209, p. 6731. *Huidian* (1899) 56, 12a–b. Cf. *QCXWXTK* 255, p. 10003. The basic law also covered banishment to the northeast, but not banishment to Xinjiang since the law was passed in 1734, prior to the conquest of Xinjiang. Xinjiang contributions were twice those required for the northeast (see *GZD JQ* 9939, 13/2/11). Northeast exiles paid slightly less than China proper exiles although banishment to the northeast was a more serious punishment. This was because China proper exiles could avoid exile by this means altogether, whereas northeast exiles could make a contribution only after arrival in exile; there is no evidence of any apportionment based on the amount of time already spent in exile.

50. In the event of a decreased sentence, such as execution commuted to banishment, the amount payable was normally that applicable to the original sentence. *HDSL* (1899) 724, 14b. For an example, see *GZDQLCZZ* vol. 36, 458, 39/8/24. Those whose Xinjiang banishment represented an increased sentence, and who after the expiration of their term in Xinjiang were to be remitted to China proper to serve their original sentence, were sometimes able to avoid serving their original sentence by making a contribution. For these exiles, the amount payable was based on the original sentence because the Xinjiang sentence had already been served. *ZPZZ JQ* 9/12/23 (law—exile, packet JQ 1–9), memorial of Weishibu.

51. See Naquin, *Millenarian Rebellion in China*, 281–282.

such an official. Expenses, too, were high for officials; one eighteenth-century governor-general ("noted for his frugality") estimated that his annual living expenses were at least 6,000 taels.[52]

Large contributions were rarely accepted before at least a portion of the term in Xinjiang had been served. In 1792 the Qianlong Emperor affirmed the general principle that criminals must go into exile before an application would be approved and could return only after the contribution had been paid in full. The alternative would have permitted offenders to "wait in comfort at home," which was clearly undesirable.[53]

However, the ill health or extreme old age of a criminal might justify his being excused from proceeding to Xinjiang. In 1787 the adoptive grandmother of Wu Chengxu, a former *daotai* (fourth rank) sentenced to banishment for his subordinate's misdeeds, applied to make a contribution of 30,000 taels in two installments on his behalf. She asserted that exile would aggravate Wu's ailments—he suffered from asthma and from numbness in his left arm—in addition to leaving her bereft of filial support in her old age. Her offer, far more substantial than required by the regulations, was accepted and Wu did not go into exile. An annotation on the approved request earmarked the money for the Imperial Household Department (*Nei Wu Fu*), which probably meant that it reached either the emperor himself or, more likely, the minister Heshen.[54]

The deciding factor in Wu Chengxu's case was not necessarily the plea for humanitarian consideration. As the following cases demonstrate, some applications that were supported by substantial offers of money were accepted even without such a plea, whereas others that pleaded the exile's ill health but offered little more than the minimum contribution were rejected.

Shen Shu, formerly a vice-president at the Board of Punishments (fifth rank), returned from exile in Xinjiang after his brother contributed 25,000 taels to the treasury of his native Guangdong. No humanitarian

52. Zelin, *The Magistrate's Tael*, 37–38, 137, 145, 154, 279; see also 293–298 on increases in the cost of living during the Qianlong and Jiaqing reigns.

53. *SYD* (T) QL 57/5/20, 191. See also *SYD* (B) QL 56/11/21, 159: Yushan, formerly a magistrate in Henan, was sentenced to banishment for his involvement in a murder. Although he was allowed to avoid exile by making a contribution of 25,000 taels, (a huge sum in proportion to his status), he was imprisoned at the Board of Punishments in Beijing pending payment in full by his son.

54. *GZD* QL 51476, 52/8/6. See text accompanying n. 66 on money paid to the Imperial Household Department.

grounds were raised in this case, which may, however, have received support from local officials hoping to gain access to the money.[55]

In 1787, however, former prefect Shi Guanglu (fourth rank), banished for causing delays in the transport of military supplies, applied for permission to pay a mere 10,000 taels to exchange his sentence for a term served at his own expense in Fujian. Shi, like Shen, did not accompany his offer with any excuses. Perhaps because it exceeded the minimum applicable to an official of his rank by only 400 taels, he was ordered to proceed to Xinjiang.[56]

During the Jiaqing period, Zhou E, a former Suzhou prefect, was banished for mishandling a major criminal case. In 1808 Zhou's elder brother applied for permission to pay the minimum 9,600 taels into the Suzhou treasury in exchange for his return. Permission was denied even though the application was supported by the assertion that Zhou's already poor health had been exacerbated by his exile.[57] When a further application, supported by an increase of the proposed contribution to 10,600 taels, was submitted a few years later, requesting permission for Zhou to work on the Nanhe water conservancy project, the edict rejecting it commented: "When the case is serious, then ten times the required amount of contribution is not enough to bring about clemency. [If it were, then] wealthy families could all have the good fortune to achieve clemency. How could we maintain law and order?"[58]

This declaration, which no doubt formed part of the Jiaqing Emperor's attempts to promote a public image of state incorruptibility, seemed on the face of it to be consistent with the rejection two years earlier of Zhang Chengji's application. Less than a year after Zhang, formerly governor of Jiangxi (second rank), arrived in Xinjiang, he applied to contribute 30,000 taels to be allowed to return home. He supported his request by noting that his adoptive aunt (*guoji bomu*) was now more than eighty years old and in poor health. His request was rejected: not only was it made too soon but the relationship was too tenuous.[59] Yet within a year

55. *GZDQLCZZ* vol. 17, 778, 28/5/21. Shen's crime was not specified in this document.

56. *SYD* (T) QL 52/12/11, 525.

57. *GZD* JQ 9939, 13/2/11; the rejection is at *SYD* (B) 13/2/26, 237.

58. *SYD* (B) JQ 14/2/17, 259. The result of another request submitted in 1815 is unknown. See *GZD* JQ 18029, 20/3/4. This document also refers to yet another unsuccessful request submitted in 1811.

59. *QSL* JQ 176, 22a–23a, 12/3/17. For a similar example, see *QSL* JQ 173, 15a–b, 12/1/20.

he was one of several senior officials serving sentences of banishment in Xinjiang who were ordered to proceed at their own expense to work on the Nanhe water conservancy project, to which Zhou E had been refused permission to transfer. Other officials covered by this order included Yan Jian, formerly and subsequently governor-general of Zhili; Taifeiyin, formerly a capital official and associate of Heshen, later governor of Guangxi, and Li Luanxuan, formerly judicial commissioner of Yunnan and later governor of that province.[60]

At a time when factionalism was a potent force in national politics, this type of reassignment of exiles almost certainly represented a useful form of compromise in sensitive cases. The Nanhe project was notorious for providing ample opportunity for graft, and the lavish life-style of its officials made it a surprising destination for those in genuine disgrace.[61] Using political influence and bribery was quite possibly the only means of achieving a transfer there. Such considerations surely affected the decision to move these four officials from Xinjiang; in comparison with the luckless Zhou E, all were high-ranking and hence well connected to the influential.

On rare occasions officials originally subject to Xinjiang banishment who had been permitted to take up alternative employment within China proper—most commonly water conservancy work for civil officials and army service for military officers—could then make a contribution to avoid such alternative employment.[62] Yongqing, formerly financial commissioner of Hubei province (second rank), suffered from an eye disease that limited his ability to work. His sentence of banishment to Xinjiang was commuted, and he was ordered to proceed to Zhejiang to help in coastal defense work. Yongqing later asserted that his disease rendered him unable to perform even this less arduous assignment. He was permitted to make a contribution of 50,000 taels in two instalments to the coastal defense work project and to return home once the payments had been made.[63]

60. QSL JQ 193, 17a–b, 13/3/21.
61. See "Daoguangshi Nanhe Guanli zhi Chitai." I am grateful to Randall Dodgen for this reference.
62. For examples of employment within China proper an alternative to Xinjiang banishment, see QSL JQ 59, 21b, 5/2/9; ibid., 84, 36b–37a, 6/6/27; ibid., 193, 17a–b, 13/3/21.
63. Yongqing was banished for negligence relating to a case involving the live burial of several people. GZD QL 50779, 52/4/28; SYD (T) QL 52/5/18, 26. Yongqing's age is not stated; it is unlikely to have been a factor. The memorial and edict concern his infirmity only.

In at least one case the amount paid suggests that the criminal may have been a commoner. Zhao Bing, banished in 1793 as a slave—a fate from which officials and their families were normally excluded—worked for a time in exile in the mines and eventually attained the status of a civilian (*min*). In 1801 his mother, then already more than eighty years old, applied to make a contribution of 1,200 taels to secure Zhao's return. Her application was rejected. The rules required that the sum contributed be doubled once there had been a rejection.[64] Three years later, she was permitted to contribute 2,400 taels and Zhao, then sixty-five years old himself, returned home.[65] No suggestion of bribery or political connections has come to light in Zhao's case.

Both the substantial sums involved in contributions and the payment of the funds either to the Imperial Household Department or to provincial treasuries bring to mind another form of crime-related payments that began to be made in the Qianlong period. These were the "self-imposed fines" paid by certain officials who expressed a desire to atone for their as yet unpunished negligence in this way (*zixing yizui*). These sums, ranging from ten thousand to more than one million taels, were managed by a Secret Accounts Bureau within the Imperial Household Department that was under the control of Heshen and Fukang'an. These payments essentially constituted a form of blackmail perpetrated by these two senior ministers.[66]

Yet there were important differences between contributions and the self-imposed fines. First, self-imposed fines involved far more money than did contributions and were often paid by colleagues rather than relatives. Second, the fines were usually shrouded in secrecy—they are known through the "Records of the Secret Accounts Bureau" (*Miji Dang*)—in contrast to the open regulations that governed the system of contributions. Third, the fines were paid for offenses as yet unpunished, whereas contributions involved sentences already imposed and usually partially served.[67] Finally, a contribution, once approved, ensured release, but the

64. Cf. Zhou E's case (text accompanying nn. 56 and 57).
65. ZPZZ JQ 9/3/1 (law—exile, packet for JQ 1–9) memorial of Songyun; SYD (T) JQ 9/3/28, 211.
66. "Miji Dang," cited by Chang, "The Economic Role of the Imperial Household in the Ch'ing Dynasty," 263–266. Chang has calculated that almost 3.5 million taels were paid in this way by thirty-two officials between 1780 and 1795. See also Torbert, *The Ch'ing Imperial Household Department*, 120.
67. See Chang, "Economic Role," 264–265.

payment of a self-imposed fine was no guarantee that punishment could be avoided altogether.

A case illustrating how unreliable a means of escaping punishment the self-imposed fines could be was that of former financial commissioner Gui Jingzhao. An offer made in 1793 by Grand Councillor Agui to pay a self-imposed fine on Gui's behalf was accepted.[68] In the same year, however, Gui was banished to Xinjiang for failure to expose high-level corruption in Zhejiang and was expressly prohibited from making a large contribution. In 1794, as part of the general review of the sentences of banished officials in Xinjiang described in the preceding section of this chapter, the Grand Council proposed that Gui should remain in exile an additional three years before requesting consideration for return.[69] As noted above, such requests were no mere formality and were often denied.[70] However, one year later, perhaps partly due to his earlier payment and his high connections, Gui was permitted to make a contribution in exchange for permission to return home after only two more years.[71]

The fairly frequent rejection of juanshu applications, couched in terms of principle, suggests that more subtle considerations than the purely venal were at play. Political jockeying by an applicant's supporters at court undoubtedly often played a part in the decision-making process, as in the case of requests to permit an exile to return home upon the expiration of his full term. Moreover, there was some moral advantage to be derived by the state from the appearance of indifference to offers of money in exchange for exoneration from punishment. In contrast to the open regulations governing juanshu, however, the secrecy surrounding the self-imposed fines substantially diminished the potential for any moral advantage. Possibly in part because of the enormous revenue from the self-imposed fines, the comparatively small sums proffered as juanshu in

68. "Miji Dang" 4a.

69. SYD (B) QL 59/4/27, 282.

70. Three other officials who paid self-imposed fines were banished to Xinjiang but served relatively short terms. These were Muhelin (nine months in exile), Yade, and Wenshou (two years in exile).

71. SYD (B) QL 60/9/28, 301. This permission came three months after a further general review of the sentences of Xinjiang exiles was ordered because of a drought in Rehe and the capital area. QSL QL 1481, 10b–11a, 60/6/25. The order did not state precisely when Gui was to return. Hong Liangji's references to Gui in his exile diary of 1800 suggest that in fact Gui was still at Ili. Hong does not specifically state that he encountered Gui at Ili in 1800, however, and Gui may indeed have returned by then and Hong may have been merely reporting hearsay.

each individual case were insignificant enough for their rejection to have had little impact on either the state treasuries or the private purses of wealthy top officials.

Both the contributions and the self-imposed fines were initiated to meet particular needs—contributions eased the cost of military campaigns, and the fines helped cover the expenses of particular officials' luxurious living. Yet both continued into the nineteenth century, long after their initial purpose had been fulfilled, for they furnished a source of revenue that officials, having once tapped, were unwilling to relinquish.[72] Thus both contributed to the commercialization of public life and of the judicial process that reached acute proportions during the declining years of the dynasty.

THE IMPACT OF BANISHMENT ON DISGRACED OFFICIALS

The careers of disgraced officials who eventually resumed public service can be divided into two main groups. Some went on to hold positions that surpassed those held prior to banishment; others never again achieved so high a level. Among the former, some returned to China proper immediately upon the expiration of their term, whereas others, mainly Manchus, remained in Xinjiang, either for the rest of their working lives or for a period of interim employment prior to their return to China proper.

Ji Yun's career following his return from exile in 1771 was extremely successful, not least because he was one of the few Han Chinese to become a court favorite.[73] Two years after leaving Ürümqi, he was appointed joint chief editor of the Imperial Manuscript Library, a position that he occupied for many years and that brought him both honor and chastisement. Towards the end of his life he was at different times president of the Censorate, of the Board of War, and of the Board of Ceremonies.[74]

---

72. On the heavy use of the contribution system to raise money in the mid-nineteenth century, see Qi, "Qingdai Xinjiang Qianyuan Yanjiu," 8; for an order to pay a self-imposed fine a decade after Heshen's demise, see *SYD* (B) JQ 14/6/29, 352–354.

73. See Guy, *The Emperor's Four Treasuries*, 48.

74. *ECCP* 120–123. Such success carried the risk of further punishment. According to Ji, on one occasion he thought that he might be banished again. Working in Beijing during the summer, he was unable to bear the unusually intense heat and removed his long robes. An unheralded visit by the emperor took him by surprise and he hid by a kang. Some time later when all fell quiet he found someone sitting on the kang and enquired whether "the

Ji's rise was relatively unusual for his time, but later such postexile success became more common. For instance, Shaanxi governor Qin Cheng'en, exiled in 1799 for ineptitude in the White Lotus campaign, served three years before returning to resume a successful career culminating in a governor-generalship.[75] Yunnan judicial commissioner Li Luanxuan, banished in 1806 for mishandling a criminal case, eventually resumed his official career and became governor of Yunnan shortly before his death in 1817.[76]

The increased frequency of restoration to high office after banishment to Xinjiang in the Jiaqing period reflected two trends. First, the larger number of officials suffering such punishment reduced the impact of public humiliation. Second, the tense, superficial political stability created by Heshen's predominance in the late eighteenth century was replaced after his death by much greater fluctuations in the struggle for power.

Some disgraced officials of considerable seniority returned to take up appointments in China proper but never again matched their earlier position. For example, neither former governor-general Wu Xiongguang, recalled after only one year in exile, nor former governor Chen Huai rose above the fourth rank after their return.[77] Former judicial commissioner Xu Song never rose above the position of a prefect following his recall from Xinjiang, although his scholarship was much acclaimed.[78]

The undistinguished postexile careers of these officials was partly attributable to the nature and gravity of their crimes. Wu Xiongguang had been banished for a political offense—failure in office—Chen and Xu

---

old boy" (*laotouzi*) had left. It was the emperor himself, who was not amused. Only Ji's ready wit saved him from punishment. Ji, kowtowing, explained that "laotouzi" denoted the utmost reverence. "*Lao*" referred to the emperor's venerable status as ruler; "*tou*," similarly, denoted his position as supreme head; "*zi*" implied that he was the father of the people and was also used in the respectful sense of "master," as it had been used by the Song dynasty Neo-Confucians in referring to Confucius and Mencius. Ji, *Ji Xiaolan Jiashu*, 37. Although the veracity of this anecdote cannot be confirmed, Ji's wit was famous and was much appreciated by the Qianlong Emperor.

75. *Qing Shi Gao* 355, pp. 11177–11178.

76. *Guochao Qixian Leizheng Chubian* 196, 1a–2a.

77. On Wu, see *Qing Shi Gao* 357, p. 11324. He was later honored at a banquet, however. Chen Huai had been implicated in the Gansu corruption case and was sentenced to work for a time on a water conservancy project. Thus when he was banished to Xinjiang he had already fallen and risen again once, as the emperor pointed out. *Qingshi Liezhuan* 27, 38b–40a. Another exile, former governor Wu Shigong, banished to Balikun in 1761 in a corruption case, was permitted to return home after a year; he died not long afterwards. *Qing Shi Gao* 309, p. 10617; QSL QL 662, 10a–11a, 27/5/24. Wu was permitted to pay a sum of money to purchase his return because he was too old and frail to work effectively.

78. *Qing Shi Gao* 486, p. 13414.

had both been banished for corruption. On the other hand, Li Luanxuan and Qin Cheng'en, whose subsequent distinction has been noted, had both been banished for far less serious offences involving incompetence but without corrupt intent.

Yet even in political cases regarded as extremely grave, the Qing may have been prepared to disregard tainted connections when it suited them, as demonstrated by the case of Fang Guancheng (1698–1758). Fang had spent part of his youth with his father and grandfather in exile in Heilongjiang. They were scholars who had been banished for collective responsibility in the famous Dai Mingshi sedition case of the Kangxi period.[79] This case lingered in official memory until 1780 (almost a quarter century after Fang's death) when a query was raised concerning a possible relationship between Dai Mingshi and a target of the Qianlong literary inquisition, Dai Shidao.[80] Nonetheless the public careers of Fang Guancheng and his son, Fang Weidian, were highly successful; each culminated in a governor-generalship.

The appointment of exiles to official positions within Xinjiang was governed by a number of considerations. In the first place, there were certain advantages, such as economy, to the appointment of officials already in situ, and it was a matter of concern that officials conversant with local conditions be allowed to remain.[81] Furthermore, the problem caused by the unpopularity of frontier appointments among officials could be resolved in part by the appointment of those in a weak position to protest by virtue of their—albeit now expiated—disgrace.[82] A re-

---

79. *ECCP* 235. Fang Guancheng's father was Fang Shiqi and his grandfather was Fang Dengyi. They were exiled in 1711. Dai Mingshi, who was executed, had referred to the seditious writings (about the late Ming) of Fang Xiaobiao, the father of Dengyi and great-grandfather of Fang Guancheng. By 1711 Fang Xiaobiao had died; he was convicted posthumously and his descendants (including the well-known scholar Fang Bao) were banished or imprisoned.

80. On this see *Qingdai Wenzi Yu Dang*, vol. 2, 485–519. Dai Shidao came from a different part of Anhui province from Tongcheng, the home of Dai Mingshi and the Fang clan, and no actual connection was established; the Dai Mingshi case files were found to have been destroyed. *SYD* (T) QL 45/7/n.d., 66. Dai Mingshi's works were proscribed as part of the literary inquisition.

81. See, e.g., *SYD* (T) QL 38/9/5, 142–143; *SYD* (T) QL 43/3/24, 501; *SYD* (B) QL 59/6/8, 61–62; *SYD* (B) JQ 11/3/14, 227.

82. In 1789 an official (not an exile) newly arrived to take up a position at Ili requested immediate reinstatement to his former position in Beijing on the ground that he knew nothing about local conditions. The emperor, noting that many officials were unwilling to go to Xinjiang, insisted that those appointed to such posts must remain for a minimum of four years in order to acquaint themselves with local conditions. *QSL* QL 1337, 16b–17a, 54/8/21.

quirement that the appointment of disgraced officials receive imperial approval suggests that the central government was unwilling to relinquish close control of appointments from the ranks of exiles or of the frontier administration in general.[83]

It was mainly banished Manchus and Mongols who reentered public service through positions in Xinjiang, for few Han Chinese held senior positions on any frontier. In 1767, shortly after Hunan governor Changjun was dismissed and sent to Kashgar, he was transferred to a post at Kalashar.[84] Former governor-general Yude, banished to Ili in 1806, was transferred in the following year to serve as imperial agent at Ush.[85] In 1810 former governor-general Tiebao was awarded the third rank after a year in exile at Ürümqi and transferred to a senior post at Kashgar.[86] Later he was recalled to high civil office at Beijing. All three were Manchus.[87] Hening, a Mongol, was banished to Ürümqi in 1801 following his dismissal as governor of Shandong for mishandling a criminal case. He served in various posts in Xinjiang between 1802 and 1808, when he was recalled to China proper, subsequently attaining senior positions in Beijing and the provinces, including Board president, acting governor-general and, briefly, Grand Councillor.[88]

The positions of councillor (*canzan dachen*) and commandant (*lingdui dachen*) both carried great responsibility in Xinjiang and frequently seem to have been used as ports of reentry into officialdom for high-ranking Manchu and Mongol exiles. Thus Shandong governor Changling, dismissed in 1809 and banished to Ili for failing to discover misappropriations of public funds, was appointed councillor at Khobdo in Mongolia with the rank of a junior bodyguard only three months after his arrival in exile. Later he rose to the governor-generalship of Shaanxi and Gansu. In 1814 he was again sentenced to banishment to Ili in connection with the Eight Trigrams rebellion of the previous year. The subsequent discovery that he had suppressed an uprising in Shaanxi early in 1814 led to his

83. See *Huidian* (1818), 5b.

84. *Guochao Qixian Leizheng Chubian* 172, 32b.

85. *Guochao Qixian Leizheng Chubian* 188, 11a. Six months after his transfer, Yude became ill and returned to China proper, where he died within a year.

86. *Qing Shi Gao* 353, p. 11281.

87. On another Manchu, former governor Gaoqi, see *Guochao Qixian Leizheng Chubian* 313, 25a–34a.

88. *Guochao Qixian Leizheng Chubian* 100, 36a–39b. Hening changed his name to Heying in 1820 for reasons of taboo; the personal name of the Daoguang Emperor, who succeeded to the throne in that year, was Minning.

punishment being reduced to demotion.[89] Before the end of the year he was awarded the rank of governor-general and sent to Ili as a councillor. Two years later he became military governor.[90]

Certain relatively junior banished officials could, after a number of years, be recommended for local vacancies by Xinjiang officials. Only those banished for "public" crimes, which generally included shortcomings devoid of corrupt intent, were eligible for such appointments.[91]

In 1773 this system of recommendation was temporarily abandoned because it tended to provide excessive scope for advancement. Moreover, sometimes the only posts available in Xinjiang were senior to those held at the time of banishment. The recommendation system was reinstituted in 1794 for several reasons. First, it was a waste of talent to exclude so many qualified officials from government; second, imperial favor could annul disgrace and permit exiles to make a fresh start once they had expiated their crimes, and third, the number of banished officials in the Xinjiang settlements was reaching unacceptably high levels.[92] Thereafter proposals to appoint disgraced officials who had served for a number of years in exile to posts in Xinjiang continued to be submitted, and most were confirmed.[93]

Many exiles never resumed their official careers, either from choice or from lack of opportunity. Hong Liangji worked as a teacher, traveled extensively, and devoted his energies to letters after his return from exile; he died within ten years.[94] His outspoken criticisms impinged too much

---

89. The sentence was announced before his victory became known. *ECCP* 67.

90. See Guilun, *Chang Wenxiang Gong Nianpu* 1, 72a; 2, 32b; *ECCP* 67–69. Others whose early postexile appointments were to one of these positions included Hening, Tiebao, and former governor Yijiang'a.

91. *QSL* QL 935, 15a–b, 38/5/21. For two cases exemplifying this distinction, see *QSL* QL 947, 18a–19a, 38/11/24; *SYD* (T) QL 41/2/27, 203. Regulations provided that disgraced officials banished for "public" crimes might receive an imperial audience prior to reinstatement but whether this occurred as a matter of course is unclear. Given the distances involved it would seem to have been impractical for Xinjiang exiles who were to be appointed to positions in that region.

92. *QSL* QL 1445, 4a, 59/1/18; *SYD* (B) QL 59/4/27, 190–191. Cf. *QSL* QL 1445, 4b–5a, 59/1/18, for an edict preferring the appointment to a Xinjiang vacancy of a candidate selected in Beijing to that of a feiyuan at Ili. The reason given was that such an appointment would replace punishment with promotion.

93. See, however, *QSL* JQ 295, 9b–10a, 19/8/19, for the proposal to appoint former education commissioner Xu Song to the post of clerk (*bitieshi*) with responsibility as an assistant in charge of grain affairs in Ili. This proposal was rejected on the ground that Xu, who had been banished for corruption, had served only a year of his term.

94. See *ECCP* 374.

on imperial sensibilities, and angered too many of the still powerful targets of his attack, to allow any resumption of official duties, despite the speed of his recall. Former magistrate Zhou Gongxian, banished in 1782 for unsatisfactory performance in office, spent ten years in exile. After his return he retired to the country and led a quiet life, associating with other scholars but showing no interest in official life.[95] Song Yu, a Han bannerman who held the jinshi degree, returned home after a decade in exile at Ürümqi. He devoted his remaining years to poetry and wine and no longer sought official position.[96]

It was a small irony that contacts made in exile could later prove useful to disgraced officials for whom no reappointment was forthcoming.[97] After Qi Yunshi returned from exile he was employed as a secretary by Songyun, who had been transferred from the Ili military governorship to be governor-general of Jiangsu, Jiangxi, and Anhui provinces.[98] Song-yun's treatment of Qi Yunshi is another example of the lenient attitude for which he was sometimes reprimanded.

For some the return from Xinjiang was tinged with sadness. Former judicial commissioner Li Luanxuan, banished in 1806, was racked with homesickness and guilt, for as a result of his exile he had been unable to care for his elderly father and his family despite the sacrifices they had made to advance his career.[99] As we have seen, Li left Ürümqi after two years but he never saw his father alive again; soon after his transfer to China proper he was permitted to return home to carry out mourning rituals. His sense of achievement concerning his career successes following his exile was attenuated by his grief.[100] In another case, former magistrate Chen Shichang returned from exile knowing that his wife had been killed and his sons maimed, presumably by the very bandits whose capture of Chen himself had led to his exile.[101]

95. *Guochao Qixian Leizheng Chubian* 232, 43a–b.
96. *Yutianxian Zhi* 18, 11b–12a.
97. Following dismissal and banishment, an official could sometimes repurchase appointment. See Metzger, *Internal Organization*, 307–308. Repurchase was apparently not necessary if the emperor ordered reappointment, nor was it necessary for restoration of title without actual appointment to office. A ruling of 1770 excluded officials who had served sentences of banishment in Xinjiang following commutation of a death sentence from the right to repurchase appointment. *HDSL* (1899) 86, 18a–b.
98. *ECCP* 135. Qi subsequently taught in various academies.
99. Li, "Xiangfeng Xing."
100. See biographic packet in *Guoshi Guan Dang*, material dated Daoguang 2/7.
101. Hong, "Wanli Hege Ji," 3a.

The cycle of disgrace, self-renewal, and full or partial restoration of status that characterized banishment to Xinjiang offers an illustration of the volatility of the social structure in Qing China. It was possible to fall from high office and to plumb the depths of public humiliation, only to recover or even surpass one's earlier position at a later stage. For the vast majority of banished officials this process did not involve the loss and reacquisition of elite status but rather the temporary setting aside of the power and prestige associated with it. The vicissitudes of public life, however, meant that none could be wholly confident that the cycle would turn full circle.

THE IMPACT OF BANISHMENT ON ORDINARY CONVICTS

For most ordinary convicts, banishment endured for life, and they were never permitted to leave the frontier. However, except in the most serious cases, once the formal term of exile expired, convicts were considered to have worked out their criminality and to have renewed themselves. At that point they became eligible for emancipation, with the exception of those banished in sect and rebellion cases.[102] Considerable numbers of convicts were emancipated each year. In a single location in the Ürümqi area alone, for instance, almost 800 former convict households registered as civilians between 1767 and 1805.[103]

From 1766 to 1770, only those convicts accompanied by their families were eligible for emancipation because Qing officials in Xinjiang, perhaps seeking to learn from the experience of their counterparts in Taiwan, feared that for the single the temptation to escape would be irresistible.[104] Thus by 1770, 235 households—convicts with their families—had attained civilian status at Ürümqi, but several hundred more convicts had been denied registration as civilians solely because of the family requirement.

Proposing to amend the regulations, lieutenant governor Bayanbi observed that to foreclose all hope for unmarried convicts of rejoining free society effectively barred them from any incentive for self-improve-

---

102. *DLCY* 45–33.

103. Qi, "Qingdai Xinjiang Qianfan Yanjiu," 90, citing *SZJL*.

104. Late nineteenth-century evidence suggests that official fears were justified and that convicts accompanied by their families in fact were much less likely to attempt escape. See Meijer, *The Introduction of Modern Criminal Law in China*, 145.

ment. He further suggested that the restriction was unfair because many might have remained unmarried only because of extreme poverty. Although the fear of possible escapes was justified, Bayanbi implied that the government should have more faith in the efficacy of its own system.[105] As the result of his proposal, from 1770 hard work and good behavior became the principal criteria for emancipation for convicts who had served the requisite amount of time in banishment, irrespective of the presence or absence of their families. In fact, those accompanied by their families were denied emancipation if they had been indolent or insubordinate.[106]

Upon emancipation, eligible civilian exiles registered as residents of Xinjiang and were settled wherever arable land was available. They could not choose where they settled but were relocated by the Xinjiang authorities and given twelve mu of land.[107] Emancipists were treated like voluntary civilian settlers in that they received government loans for seeds, livestock, and housing, but the value was only half that given other civilians, and their grace period before repayment was three, rather than six, years. Like voluntary immigrants, they paid tax of eight sheng per mu, but their initial exemption was for only a year.[108] In the mixed society of the Xinjiang frontier, emancipists thus constituted an intermediate group between free settlers and convicts.

Exiled soldiers entered the army upon emancipation. Manchus joined the banner troops; others joined the Green Standard army.[109] When these units were transferred to China proper, the emancipists went with them.[110]

105. ZPZZ QL 35/1/4 (law—laws, packet for QL 35–39), memorial of Bayanbi.

106. QSL QL 851, 5a–b, 35/1/26. See also QSL QL 875, 10a–11a, 35/12/23.

107. ZPZZ QL 35/1/4 (law—laws, packet for QL 35–37), memorial of Bayanbi; GZD QL 32498, 42/9/8.

108. See ZPZZ QL 43/5/24 (agriculture—opening new lands, packet 37), memorial of Suonuomuceling. Cf. Xichui Zongtong Shilüe 7, 3a, citing a 1772 order to the effect that civilians had only three years before their loans fell due. Since the above-cited memorial was submitted six years after this order, it is possible that the regulations changed during that time, but no evidence on this has come to light. On tax, see ibid., 5a.

109. Nayancheng, A Wencheng Gong Nianpu 3, 50a, QL 31/10/22. Cf. HDSL (1899) 745, 7a (1772).

110. The members of one group of almost two hundred Mongol soldiers of the bordered blue banner were enrolled in the Green Standard army and transferred to fill vacancies in China proper as needed. QSL QL 768, 18a–19b, 31/9/14. These exiles were still in Xinjiang in 1770, when Ji Yun noted that "local people call them "blue-banner men" (lanqi); although they are registered as residents of the western regions, their way of life is really different from that of westerners." Ji, "Wulumuqi Zashi," 13a.

Qing officials apparently lacked confidence that the self-renewal crowned by emancipation would be lasting. Thus emancipation did not obliterate an ex-convict's origins. As on other frontiers, Xinjiang authorities continued to identify settlers by their native place.[111] Those who committed further offences were subject to more severe punishment than were free settlers. Moreover, officials often worried that emancipists would attempt to abscond. In 1767 the authorities, expressing concern about their growing numbers, organized a mutual surveillance (*baojia*) system for emancipists at Changji near Ürümqi, in the hope that this would help to prevent homesick emancipists from attempting to escape and to control the behavior of those who remained. The exiles at Changji rioted in the following year, but the extent of emancipist involvement is undocumented.

For many ordinary convicts, banishment, even when accompanied by enslavement, might prove only a temporary—although not necessarily brief—interlude, followed by readmission to the society of good people, albeit still far from one's original home. For some of those who had been driven by poverty to break the law in China proper, life in Xinjiang may have offered greater chances for survival than they could ever have hoped to receive in their native place; the hardships experienced by exiles' families who remained in China proper were undoubtedly sometimes as terrible as those suffered by the wives and children who went to Xinjiang.[112]

The Qing sought to establish a context of conditional self-renewal for all the Xinjiang exiles, even those whose humble social level and limited education made it unlikely that they themselves would be specifically concerned with Neo-Confucian ideals. Through this approach the Qing seemed to perpetuate the classic assumption that the ordinary person had as much potential for moral cultivation as the educated scholar-official. Yet except to the extent that law and order were adversely affected by any failure to achieve rehabilitation through compliant behavior, the Qing were undoubtedly more concerned with their own overall goals in Xinjiang than with the individual moral redemption of thousands of exiled commoners. For ordinary convicts who had been enslaved, emancipation from servitude was presumably of some significance, but for

---

111. See Lee, "State and Economy in Southwest China, 1400–1800," 75; *HDSL* (1899) 744, 24a–b.

112. See, e.g., *SYD* (B) QL 56/8/8, 73; *SYD* (B) 56/8/n.d., 112.

others the change of status from convict to emancipist did not necessarily have any meaningful impact. Yet by giving even their exile a specifically moral context, the Qing created a situation in which the punishment provided a medium through which the emperor could display the ideal benevolence of a Confucian ruler, thus lending support to the Manchu claim to legitimacy.

One important effect of this approach was that banishment to Xinjiang produced dual forms of self-renewal: public and private. Public self-renewal derived from an opportunity bestowed by the emperor and, as a result of the requirement of imperial confirmation, was subject to manipulation by powerful politicians pursuing their own personal agendas, particularly when former colleagues were involved. The limited philosophical relevance to ordinary convicts of this type of self-renewal has been discussed above.

For many banished officials, too, the idea that officially authorized self-renewal had moral force was ultimately unconvincing. Many of those disgraced and punished as the result of factional struggles cannot have felt that they had sunk to an abased moral level or that the type of public self-renewal called for in imperial edicts had any significance beyond the practical one of leading to restoration of status. Neither Ji Yun nor Hong Liangji, for instance, expressed the slightest remorse or contrition in their many writings about their exile experiences, except to the extent that the uncertainty of their prospects caused great anxiety. For other exiles whose transgressions had actually been motivated by criminal intent, banishment to Xinjiang often constituted only a relatively short-term setback that, for the well connected and affluent at least, could sometimes be mitigated through political or financial influence. For these exiles, too, public self-renewal, although practically necessary, can have had little moral importance.

Yet some, enmeshed in the concepts of absolute loyalty to emperor and state instilled by long years of training, may have been highly susceptible to this approach. One such example was former judicial commissioner Li Luanxuan, openly tormented by the thought of the shame he had brought upon his family. For Li and others like him—for he was undoubtedly far from unique—the public form of self-renewal in which a term of banishment culminated reinforced their bond with the state.

For many banished officials, however, a meaningful form of self-renewal took on a more private level. Exiles' investigation of Xinjiang and their literary output provided an ideal vehicle for such personal cultivation as Wang Yangming had proposed. The detailed accounts written by exiles such as Ji Yun and Hong Liangji certainly fall into this category. So did the poetry of Li Luanxuan, although in his case the two types of self-renewal were conflated as a result of his apparent subscription, either spontaneous or through intimidation, to the public version of self-renewal proposed by the government. Li's attitude embodied precisely that combination of shame and constructive energy that the Qing sought to foster among their Xinjiang exiles. His death shortly after his elevation to a governorship deprived him of the final glory he so painfully sought and symbolized the uncertainty of so many official careers under the Qing.

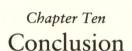

Chapter Ten
Conclusion

The Qing conquest and annexation of Xinjiang were the acts of a dynasty at the height of its power. The institution of a system of exile designed to achieve at a stroke the multiple goals of punishment, colonization, controlled rehabilitation, and the removal of offenders from the Chinese heartland exemplified the Qing's ability to adapt ancient practices to contemporary circumstances. At the same time it fulfilled the perennial ambition to accomplish several ends by a single means (*yi ju liang de*).

Chinese law, like that of other cultures, reflects societal values. Thus the availability of exile as a punishment that could be invoked both to mitigate more extreme measures and to increase the applicable penalties in particularly egregious cases embodied highly esteemed classical principles: the exercise of clemency by a benevolent ruler and the severe punishment of those whose conduct threatened the state or violated the cosmic order. Similarly, Qing law reflected Confucian social attitudes in, on the one hand, the differential treatment of offenders based on their status, and, on the other, the assumption that all but the very worst transgressors were capable of rehabilitation.

In the context of banishment to Xinjiang the Qing explicitly invoked the idea, integral to both traditional jurisprudence and orthodox ideals, that punishment could serve as a route to self-renewal. Yet the government's purpose was quite distinct from that of a personal, moral goal. By seeking to convert the process of private self-cultivation into a public one subject to external approval, the Qing preempted, for the purposes of political and social control, the highly moral language of Neo-Confucian philosophy. The Qing's invocation of such justifications for their Xinjiang exile policy reflected primarily on the dynasty's own perception of its public image.

The government's desire—and even its ability—to judge the moral rehabilitation of those it banished to Xinjiang was not universally accepted, although it may have convinced a majority of officials. Even allowing for an element of self-interest, the lenient treatment often accorded "disgraced" former colleagues by such powerful officials as Songyun cannot be reconciled with other than pro forma deference to the Qing policy of setting Xinjiang banishment within a moral framework. Moreover, the cynical use to which exile was put during the Heshen period must have confirmed the ambivalence of these highly educated and knowledgeable men towards the Neo-Confucian claims made for the system.

The concept of self-renewal was not, however, completely devoid of meaning even for those who did not subscribe to the Qing's pretensions. Many scholarly exiles took advantage of the time they were forced to spend on the frontier to study and to write, revitalizing their own quest for personal cultivation as had been suggested by such eminent predecessors as the exiled philosopher of the Ming dynasty, Wang Yangming.

Moral considerations could not have had much significance for many ordinary convicts. For the most serious offenders among them, including sectarians banished precisely because of their rejection of Confucian tenets, the virtual lack of any hope of emancipation negated the relevance of self-renewal. For others, whatever the actual impact of emancipation may have been, that prospect, so long held out as an incentive to good behavior, can be characterized as a practical form of rehabilitation, although it lacked the self-generated moral force upon which such a change theoretically depended.

To a considerable extent, the system of banishment to Xinjiang from 1758 through 1820 mirrored the Qing dynasty's gradual transition from strength to weakness, as the dynamic experimentation that marked the early decades of the system gave way to stasis in the face of other, urgently pressing, problems. Moreover, the general rise in criminal activity caused by demographic growth, the spread of heterodox religious groups, and the increase of political factionalism and bureaucratic corruption all provided sources for the exile population of Xinjiang. At the same time, the success of voluntary immigration policies reduced the importance of colonization, although Xinjiang continued to be used as a repository for both common criminals and political offenders in the later nineteenth and twentieth centuries.

The complex goals of the Qing system of banishment to Xinjiang inevitably conflicted with each other. First, they produced an ambiguous attitude towards the region's status: officials sought, on the one hand, to demonstrate the success of colonization by declaring Xinjiang a part of China proper and, on the other, to affirm the distinction between the frontier and the heartland to make clear that banishment to Xinjiang was the most severe form of exile and, indeed, the most severe of all punishments other than death. Second, the need for security on the frontier was threatened, at least potentially, by the deliberate importation of criminal elements, particularly those who had been banished in cases involving such offenses as rebellion or heterodox religious activities. The Qing took a calculated risk in using these exiles for colonization purposes, although, with very few exceptions, no adverse consequences ensued. Third, the government's subsidized removal of certain commoner convicts' entire families to the frontier, undertaken with a view to rapid colonization and in the hope that it would discourage attempts to escape, clearly diminished the severity of the punishment; the extent to which a sentence of banishment inflicted suffering on these exiles remains open to some doubt. Fourth, in contrast, the enforced dispersal of families in the most serious cases was contrary to the integrity of the family unit in orthodox Confucianism. Thus, in its treatment of these offenders, the state acted in opposition to the very beliefs that it purported to defend. All these various contradictions reflect a somewhat equivocal attitude towards banishment to Xinjiang on the part of the Qing, who, although concerned to demonstrate their deep devotion to traditional Confucian ideals, did not scruple to set these aside to meet particular exigencies.

The Qing's use of exiles to colonize and administer Xinjiang was only a qualified success. Particularly in the decades immediately following the conquest, the influx of ordinary convicts into northern Xinjiang provided a useful labor source, notably for agriculture and mining. Likewise, the employment of banished officials in the frontier bureaucracy and elsewhere spared the government the expense of new appointments and provided a high level of administrative experience. The deployment of exiles in these various capacities went some way towards achieving the Qing goal of self-sufficiency for Xinjiang, although the numbers involved were always too low to tip the balance in favor of fulfilling this unrealizable ambition.

Although neither self-renewal for exiles nor self-sufficiency for Xinjiang came to full fruition, the scholarly and evocative studies of the frontier made by banished officials did have a significant influence on later Chinese intellectuals and thus contributed to the region's formal integration into the empire. In this way the system of banishment ultimately played an important, although unintended, role in the process of colonization.

Yet in the long term, the conquest of Xinjiang succeeded only in a political sense. Acculturation eluded the Qing as it had earlier dynasties: even today Xinjiang retains its intensely Central Asian ambiance, and Muslim resistance to Beijing continues. Current policies towards the region echo those of the Qing in many respects, including the desire to maintain it as a defensive shield and the effort to increase its Han Chinese population.

Successive governments of the People's Republic have continued to exile political and criminal offenders to Xinjiang. Numerous intellectuals, often the victims of factional disputes, were banished there in the aftermath of the anti-rightist campaign of 1957–1958 and during the Cultural Revolution of 1966–1976. Some eventually returned to the heartland and assumed senior government positions, as their Qing predecessors had done. By the early 1980s, as the Chinese population surpassed one billion, tens of thousands of common criminals had been sent to labor camps in Xinjiang and "given the opportunity to reform," as part of the authorities' response to the growing lawlessness of modern China. Thus the conventional wisdom, that the past teaches us much about the present, holds true for the study of banishment to Xinjiang despite the Chinese revolutions of the twentieth century.

The Application of Collective Responsibility under the Qing

A number of laws in the Qing code provided for the punishment, by virtue of collective responsibility, of the relatives of the principal offenders in major criminal cases. In that event the family members received a punishment less horrible than that meted out to the main culprits. Thus, for example, when the latter suffered death by slow slicing with exposure of the severed head (*lingchi xiaoshi*), the relatives might suffer decapitation (*zhan*), regarded as a less severe form of execution. However, often in such cases at least some of the relatives were not executed but were condemned to banishment, the newly reintroduced punishment of castration, or enslavement, or to a combination of these punishments.

The extent to which collective responsibility applied depended on the nature of the offense, which in virtually every instance was to some degree political. The net was cast widest in sentences imposed by reference to the rebellion and treason laws. In such cases the collectively responsible relatives included wives and concubines, children, grandchildren, siblings, parents, grandparents, paternal uncles and brothers' sons, and other residents of the principal's household. In most other cases to which it applied, collective responsibility was limited to the offender's wife and children.

There were a few exemptions to the collective responsibility rules. For instance, in certain situations it was considered unreasonable to invoke collective responsibility to punish a person who had lived separately from his family for some time and who clearly had no connection with the criminal relative. Such people might be exempted from punishment. This type of clemency, however, was discretionary. Thus in 1784, the relatives of a Muslim involved in an uprising in Gansu were put to death although they had been living in Xinjiang for several years and asserted total ignorance of the events in Gansu (*Sanfasi* Archives no. 1428,

QL 49). In that particular case, the disinclination to clemency was probably attributable in large measure to the Qing's extreme nervousness about Muslim unrest.

Another potential exemption was available to married women. The married (or betrothed) sisters and daughters of major criminals ceased to be part of their natal family upon their marriage and became part of their husband's, so they were not implicated in crimes committed by members of their own families. Betrothal to a criminal, however, was not treated as sufficient connection for the imputation of collective responsibility provided the marriage had not yet taken place (*weicheng*). Sons and grandsons adopted out of a family were treated analogously to women who had married out and were not held collectively responsible.

Collective responsibility proved a useful tool for social and political control. By enabling the government to root out possible sources of disruption, the doctrine of collective responsibility allowed the government to appear to be conspicuously promoting public welfare by enforcing the law and maintaining social order. It also presented the politically influential with a chance to extirpate a rival's entire family, thus obstructing any prospects for restoration and revenge. At the same time, because the majority of collectively responsible offenders were not executed, the doctrine offered the government an opportunity whose impact was double-edged. On the one hand, abstaining from putting people to death when they "deserved" to die manifested a degree of official tolerance in the face of antisocial activity. Yet, on the other, keeping them alive on condition of good behavior perpetuated a damoclean threat that, it was hoped, would foster a submissive attitude among actual or potential dissidents.

Appendix Two

The Case of
Lü Liuliang's Descendants

Lü Liuliang was a scholar who lived from 1629 to 1683, his life thus spanning the dynastic transition from Ming to Qing. His political loyalties, some of which he committed to writing, remained with the overthrown Ming. The persecution of his family resulted from the discovery of these writings some fifty years after his death, after they were claimed as inspiration by a failed licentiate who attempted to incite an eminent general to rebellion.

The Lü Liuliang case was so extreme, and imperial involvement so intense, that it became a cause célèbre. For mid-Qing emperors and officials, repetition of this episode was to be avoided at all cost, and for antidynastic activists in the late Qing, it served as a prime example of Manchu oppression of their Chinese subjects.

In 1730 some of Lü's anti-Manchu writings came to the notice of the Yongzheng Emperor when a failed licentiate, citing Lü's writings as his inspiration, proposed to the eminent general Yue Zhongqi that Yue should lead a rebellion. In the aftermath of this episode, the corpses of Lü and his son were disinterred and dismembered and their skulls exposed in public. The emperor justified his extreme severity on the ground of filial piety, asserting that Lü had insulted his father, the Kangxi Emperor. One of Lü's surviving sons was put to death for treason and Lü's grandsons, originally also sentenced to death, were banished to Ninguta in Jilin province together with members of several other Lü households. The total number of people banished exceeded one hundred. Clemency was shown because of the numbers involved; even in extreme cases emperors generally preferred to avoid mass execution because this reflected poorly on their own record as benevolent rulers.

The exiled Lü's were enrolled in the banners and were permanently forbidden to take the civil service examinations or to purchase a degree that could lead to official position. Forty years later, in 1775, it transpired that through an error on the part of officials at the Board of Civil Office, Lü Liuliang's grandson, Lü Yijian, and his great-grandson, Lü Fuxian, had purchased jiansheng degrees. The investigation of this case brought to light evidence of their life in exile in eighteenth-century Manchuria. The details of this case were discovered in the Qing archives by the well-known scholar Chen Yuan; on whose article; "Ji Lü Wancun Zisun" much of the following is based.

Far from living in abject poverty, they had relinquished the traditional scholarly distaste for commercial occupations and successfully carried on a variety of trades. Several now owned substantial property in Ninguta. Lü Yijian, the grandson of Lü Liuliang, had studied medicine and at one time had been a medical officer in Ninguta. He owned a house with thirteen rooms but apparently little capital, for he had to borrow from two nephews to raise the 125 taels needed to purchase the degree. This he asserted that he had wished to do in order to avoid having to answer a roll call every five days, a restriction imposed upon exiles but not upon degree holders. Lü Fuxian, the great-grandson of Lü Liuliang, pursued his studies for some time but then turned his attention to business. He traded fox and sable furs and also sold hot water in the village where he lived. Lü Fuxian also lent money at 20 percent interest. His property included an enormous house ("165 rooms"), the hot water shop in the village, and several thousand mu of land.

Two other members of the Lü family in Ninguta, nephews of Lü Yijian, were also successful businessmen, presumably closely associated with one another. One operated a medicine business and also sold grain and salt. He owned a 28-room thatched house, 300 taels of silver, and the medicine shop. It was he who had lent Lü Yijian a little more than 60 taels to enable him to purchase a degree. The other had a bakery, was involved in the lucrative ginseng and fur trades, and was also a moneylender. His property amounted to a 35-room house, several thousand mu of land, and a huge, although unexplained, amount of salt—twenty-five thousand jin or about fifteen thousand kilograms. He took a mortgage on Lü Fuxian's house, originally priced at 300 taels, for 125 taels and also lent Lü Yijian 60 taels. An inventory of the property of these four men, made at the time of the investigation, showed that they owned additional assets in the form of cash, animals, and equipment.

As exiles the Lüs were not permitted to leave Ninguta. They entrusted their funds, and the requisite family history, which covered three generations—presumably including the infamous Lü Liuliang himself—to others, commissioning them to take it to the capital and purchase the degrees on their behalf. One of these agents was a worker at the family bakery; the other was a man from Jiangsu province, visiting Ninguta to buy ginseng to take to the capital. The plan was that they would send the degree certificates to Shengjing, the capital of Fengtian, to a third person, who would hand them on to a distant Lü relative, who in turn would send it on to Lü Fuxian in Ninguta.

Although the purchase of the degrees duly took place, someone eventually realized—who is unclear—that Lü Yijian and Lü Fuxian were directly descended from Lü Liuliang and as such were absolutely banned from making such a purchase. The scheme collapsed and all the protagonists were punished.

Official proposals to put Lü Yijian and Lü Fuxian permanently in the cangue were rejected by the Qianlong Emperor as insufficiently severe. They and their families were sent into slavery to the even remoter regions of the far northeast frontier, in Heilongjiang. Their wealthy relatives were sentenced to three months in the cangue at Ninguta and then sent to Heilongjiang with their families for hard labor. In 1799 they were specifically excluded from an amnesty allowing many other exiles in the northeast to return home (see *QSL JQ* 41, 31b–33a, 4/3/29). Despite their degraded status, members of the Lü family became the most highly respected teachers, according to information given to the scholar Zhang Binglin, who visited Qiqihar in the early twentieth century (see Xie, *Qingchu Liuren Kaifa Dongbei Shi*, 78). The two agents were sentenced to two months in the cangue at Ninguta (doubtless to deter would-be imitators) followed by a beating. The negligent officials at the Beijing Board of Civil Office who had failed to check the Lü documents carefully enough to observe the Lü Liuliang connection were subject to administrative punishment.

The 1806 Regulations Concerning the Right of Ordinary Convicts to Return from Xinjiang

By the early nineteenth century, Qing officials realized that it was counterproductive to deny convicts all hope of returning to China proper. Convicts had little cause for good behavior without the ultimate reward of return. The resulting regulations on the length of the term of banishment were intended by the government to restore incentives for self-renewal.

Regulations issued in 1806 divided the Xinjiang convicts into categories based on age, good behavior—which was always a prerequisite to permission to return home—and term already served. The most serious criminals were excluded from the right to return under these regulations. Slaves more than seventy years old were eligible for return home. Slaves less than seventy years old who had served at least twenty years were eligible for transfer to their native provinces to serve a three-year sentence of banishment (tu); those who had worked in the mines might be permitted to redeem such a three-year sentence. Slaves who had achieved civilian status, and non-slaves who had achieved civilian status but had not earned the right to return home by working in the mines, were eligible for return home once they reached the age of seventy. These convicts who had become civilians and were less than seventy years old but had served at least fifteen years were eligible for transfer to serve for three years in their native provinces. Those who were neither seventy years old nor had served the required term were eligible either for return or for transfer to serve a further three year sentence in China proper upon the expiration of that term, depending on their age. Convicts more than seventy years old who had continued to work in the mines after emancipation received a three-year reduction in term; those less than seventy served the requisite amount of time and were then eligible to return home. Anyone who

226

preferred to remain in Xinjiang might do so provided he was able to support himself (*QSL* JQ 156, 11/1/9).

These regulations illustrate the toughness of the system of banishment to Xinjiang. For many convicts, emancipation was only a distant prospect. Indeed some convicts elected to continue to work in the mines—an employment that admittedly was often at best gruelling—into their seventies, in the hope of achieving a reduction in term and even a chance to return home. However, although these regulations enabled convicts of advanced age to return to China proper, it is open to question whether they were all able to survive the arduous return journey, even when the government gave them the travel money (see *XAHL* 6, 32a–34a).

Appendix Four

Period of Exile Already Served by Disgraced Officials in Xinjiang in 1794

Years in Exile	Numbers of Exiles in Category						
	A	B	C	D	E	F	G
1	0	0	0	0	2	1	12
2	0	0	0	2	20	9	14
3	0	0	0	0	0	8	9
4	0	0	2	0	0	8	7
5	1	0	0	0	0	17	13
6	0	0	0	0	0	57	7
7	2	1	1	0	0	1	5
8	0	1	1	0	0	3	5
9	0	0	0	0	0	0	1
10	4	0	1	0	0	2	13
11–15	0	1	5	0	0	2	9
16–20	1	1	1	0	0	0	4
21–25	1	0	0	0	0	0	1
26–30	0	0	0	0	0	0	2
30 +	1	0	1	0	0	0	0
Total	10	4	12	2	22	108	102

Source: SYD (B) QL 59/4/27, 195–284.

Explanation of Categories: A = Immediate return home; B = Immediate reduction to beating; C = Immediate reduction to penal servitude; D = Return after completing three years in Xinjiang; E = Reduction to penal servitude after three years in Xinjiang; F = Reduction by one degree after three more years in Xinjiang; G = Submission of request for instructions after three more years in Xinjiang.

Glossary of Terms and Book Titles Not Listed in the Bibliography

ancha 安插 (resettlement)
bagong 拔貢 (first-class senior licentiate)
baizhou qiangduo 白晝搶奪 (plundering)
banfang 班房 (informal jail)
banshi dachen 辦事大臣 (imperial agent)
bao 包 (packet)
baojia 保甲 (mutual surveillance system)
bazong 把總 (sublieutenant)
beg 伯克 (Muslim local official)
bianwai 邊外 (beyond the borders)
bianyuan 邊遠 (to a distant frontier)
bingfang 兵房 (office of military affairs in local yamen)
bingpai 兵牌 (identification tags)
bingtun 兵屯 (military agricultural colony for Green Standard soldiers)
bitieshi 筆帖式 (clerk)
bo ke 伯克 (beg)
bu dao 不道 (massacre or murder by magical means)
bu mu 不睦 (acute family discord)
bu xiao 不孝 (lack of filiality)
bu yi 不義 (incest)
bu ying wei 不應爲 (doing what ought not to be done)
buzhengshi 布政使 (financial commissioner)
cangshi 倉石 (standard imperial granary measure)
canjiang 參將 (lieutenant colonel)
canling 參領 (regimental commander)

canzan dachen 參贊大臣 (councillor)

Chahars 察哈爾 (nomads from Inner Mongolia)

changben 長本 (Grand Secretariat edition of imperial edicts)

changsui 長隨 (personal servant)

chejiasi 車駕司 (remount office, Board of War)

chi 笞 (beating with a light stick)

chi 赤 (reddish brown)

chongjun 充軍 (military exile under the Ming and Qing)

chufen zeli 處分則例 (administrative regulations)

chujun 出軍 (military exile under the Yuan)

congfan 從犯 (secondary offender)

da bujing 大不敬 (great lack of respect)

Daghurs 達呼爾 (natives of the northeast)

Dalisi 大理寺 (Court of Judicature)

dangchai 當差 (government service)

daotai 道台 (circuit intendant)

Da Qing Lü Li 大清律例 (the penal code of the Qing)

dianda 殿達 (palace official)

dianshi 典史 (district jailwarden)

difa Ili Wulumuqi dengchu 遞發伊犁烏魯木齊等處 (under deportation to Ili and Ürümqi)

diaoyong 調周

dou 斗 (whorls on fingerprints)

Duchayuan 都察院 (Censorate)

dusi 都司 (first captain)

dutong 都統 (lieutenant governor)

e'ni 惡逆 (parricide)

ershi 二十 (twenty)

ewai waiwei 額外外委 (sergeant)

fa 罰 (fine)

fafeng 罰俸 (salary fines)

fan 犯 (criminal)

fantun 犯屯 (criminals' farms)

fangben 方本 (Grand Council edition of imperial edicts)

fangbian 防弁 (low-level military official)

Fanglüe Guan 方署館 (Office for compiling records of campaigns)

fangyu 防禦 (platoon captain)

fapei 發配 (banishment)

feiyuan 廢員 (disgraced official)

fen 分 (cash)

fenbie 分別 (as appropriate)

fudutong 副都統 (deputy lieutenant governor)

fujiang 副將 (colonel)
fujin 附近 (very near)
gaiqian 改遣 (sent [to China proper] instead)
gaitu guiliu 改土歸流 (returning natives to regular administration)
gen 艮 (trigram)
gezhi 革職 (outright dismissal)
gezhi liuren 革職留任 (dismissal with retention of duties)
gongsheng 貢生 (degree-holder)
guanfan 官犯 (criminal of official status)
guoluzi 嘓嚕子 (Sichuanese rebel)
guoji bomu 過繼伯母 (adoptive aunt)
hanjun 漢軍 (Han bannerman)
haoxian 耗羨 (meltage fee)
hong 行 (merchant company)
huanji 緩急 (degree of urgency)
huanjue 緩決 (assizes deferral category)
Hui 回 (Muslim)
huitun 回屯 (Muslim colonies)
Huizei 回賊 (Muslim bandit)
hutun 戶屯 (civilian farms)
ji 己 (sixth [volume])
jia hao 枷號 (cangue)
jiangjun 將軍 (military governor)
jiansheng 監生 (degree-holder)
jianyu 監獄 (prison)
jiaofei 教匪 (sectarian rebel)
jiaose 脚色 (résumé)
jiaoxi 教習 (teacher)
jiaoyu 教諭 (schools director)
jia yi liu 加役流 (exile with added labor)
jiangji liuren 降級留任 (demotion with retention of duties)
jibian 極邊 (to the furthest frontiers)
jiduwei 騎都尉 (cavalry commandant)
jinbian 近邊 (to a nearby frontier)
jinshi 進士 (degree-holder)
jin 斤 (measure)
juan 卷 (part of book)
juanshu 捐贖 (contributions)
jun 軍 (military exile—the punishment)
junfan 軍犯 (military exile—the convict)
juntai 軍台 (military postal station)
junxiao 軍校 (adjutant?)

juren 與人 (degree-holder)
kaozheng 考證 (evidential research)
kouwai 口外 (beyond the borders)
kuchai 苦差 (hard labor)
kunqu 昆曲 (type of opera)
langzhong 郎中 (departmental director)
lanqi 藍旗 (blue banner)
laotouzi 老頭子 (old boy)
li 里 (mile)
li 例 (substatute)
liangmin 艮民 (good people)
liangyi 量移 (measured transfer)
Lifan Yuan 理藩院 (Court of Colonial Affairs)
lingchi 凌遲 (slow slicing)
lingchi xiaoshi 凌遲梟示 (slow slicing with exposure of the severed head)
lingdui dachen 領隊大臣 (commandant)
liu 流 (exile)
liu bu 六部 (six boards)
Liu bu chufen zeli 六部處分則例 (Administrative Regulations of the Six Boards)
lü 律 (statute)
lüli 律例 (laws)
Lüliguan 律例館 (legislative office)
Miao 苗 (a minority people)
mi 米 (grain)
min 民 (ordinary people)
mintun 民屯 (civilian colonies)
mou dani 謀大逆 (treason)
moufan 謀反 (rebellion)
moupan 謀叛 (disloyalty)
mousha 謀利 (deliberate homicide)
mu 畝 (measure of land)
nashu 納贖 (redemption)
neidi 內地 (China proper)
neiluan 內亂 (insurrection)
nianpu 年譜 (chronological biography)
nucai 奴才 (slave)
Ölöds 額魯特 (natives of Xinjian)
Peiyu Peijin 佩玉佩金 (troupe of singers)
pingfan 平犯 (ordinary offender)
pingren 平人 (ordinary person)
qi 箕 (open wavy lines on fingerprints)
qian 錢 (money)

qiangdao 強盜 (robbery with violence)

qiantun 遣屯 (criminals' farms)

qianxi 遷徙 (form of exile)

qitun 旗屯 (banner farms)

qianzong 千總 (lieutenant)

qianzong waiwei 千總外委 (ensign)

qiedao 竊盜 (stealing)

qiezei 竊賊 (thieves)

Qingdai Fazhi Dang'an 清代法制檔案 (Archives of the Qing Legal System)

qingdan 清單 (list)

qingshi 情實 (assizes execution category)

qiushen 秋審 (autumn assizes)

qusi yijian zhi feitu 去死一間之匪徒 (criminals a fraction away from death)

San Liu Dao Li Biao 三流道里表 (table of destinations for exiles)

she 赦 (amnesty)

sheng 升 (pint)

shi 石 (measure)

shi e 十惡 (ten great evils)

shier 十二 (twelve)

shoubei 守備 (second captain)

shoushu 收贖 (redemption)

Shuihuzhuan 水滸傳 (novel by Shi Nai'an)

shuyuan 書院 (academy)

shuzui 贖罪 (to expiate one's crime)

si 死 (death penalty)

si 巳 (sixth [volume])

Sibos 錫伯 (natives of northeast China)

Solons 索倫 (natives of northeast China)

sui 歲 (years)

tian 天 (section of periodical)

tidu 提督 (provincial commander-in-chief)

ting 廳 (independent subprefecture)

"Ting Liuren Shuitiaozi" 聽流人水調子 (poem by Wang Changling)

tongpan 通判 (second-class subprefect)

tongnian 同年 (classmate)

tongzhi 同知 (first-class subprefect)

tu 徒 (penal servitude)

tufang 土房 (earthen house)

Tu Liu Qianxi Difang 徒流遷徙地方 (Places of Exile)

tun 屯 (military agricultural colony)

tuntian 屯田 (military agricultural colony)

waiqian 外遣 (banished beyond the borders)

waiwei 外委 (corporal?)

weicheng 未成 (not yet married)

weifei 為匪 (troublemarkers)

weisuo 衞所 (Ming garrison)

wenzi yu an 文字獄案 (literary inquisition case)

Wu Jun Dao Li Biao 五運道里表 (Table of Military Exile Destinations)

wuluren 無祿人 (unsalaried person)

Wuyingdian 武英殿 (imperial printing office)

xian 縣 (county)

xiancheng 縣丞 (assistant magistrate)

xiaoli shuzui 効力贖罪 (to expiate one's crime by exerting oneself)

xiaoqi 驍騎 (first-class private)

xiaoqixiao 驍騎校 (lieutenant)

xie bangzi 鞋幫子 (the side of a slipper)

xiedou 械鬥 (communal feuder)

xiefujiang 協副將 (assistant colonel)

xie jiao 邪教 (heterodox religion)

xieling 協領 (regimental colonel of a provincial garrison)

xiliang 細糧 (fine grain)

Xingbu 刑部 (Board of Punishments)

xingfang 刑房 (office of justice in a local yamen)

Xinjiang gaifa neidi qianfan 新疆改發內地遣犯 (Xinjiang changee)

xinjiao 新教 (troupe of singers)

xiongfan 兇犯 (evil criminal)

xiyu 西域 (Western regions)

xiyu duhu 西域督護 (protector-general of the Western regions)

"Xiyu Tongwen Zhi" 西域同文志 (work sponsored by Fuheng)

Xuannan 宣南 (poetry club)

xundao 訓道 (subdirector of schools)

xunjian 巡檢 (sub-district magistrate)

yancai 鹽菜 (salt vegetables)

yancaiqian 鹽菜錢 (food allowance)

yandashi 鹽大使 (tea and salt official examiner)

yanglian 養廉 (integrity-nourishing salary supplement)

yanzhang 烟瘴 (insalubrious area)

yi ju liang de 一舉兩得 (to achieve multiple ends by a single means)

yixu 議敘 (merit point)

youji 游擊 (major)

yuan 圓 (money)

yuansiyin 元絲銀 (type of money)

yunti 雲梯 (cloud ladder)

zhang 杖 (beating with a heavy stick)

zhanyuan 站員 (postal station inspector)
zhaomo 照磨 (correspondence secretary)
zhemo chaishi 折磨差使 (grindingly hard labor)
zhen 震 (trigram)
zhifu 知府 (prefect)
zhi shu you wei 制書有違 (disobeying imperial orders)
zhixian 知縣 (county magistrate)
zhizhou 知州 (department magistrate)
zhongdi xiaoli 種地効力 (to exert oneself farming)
zhongfan 重犯 (major criminal)
zhongshu 中書 (clerk)
Zhongshu Zhengkao 中樞政考 (Regulations of the Board of War)
zhou 州 (department)
zhoutong 州同 (first-class assistant department magistrate)
zhuanbao 傳包 (biographic packet)
zhushi 主事 (secretary)
zixin 自新 (self-renewal)
zixin zhi lu 自新之路 (the path to self-renewal)
zixing yizui 自行議罪 (acknowledgement of one's crimes)
zongbing 總兵 (brigade general)
zongdu 總督 (provincial governor-general)
zongshang 總商 (merchant)
zongshi 宗室 (imperial family member)
zui 罪 (crime)
zuoling 佐領 (company commander of a provincial garrison)
zuoza 佐雜 (petty official)

Glossary of Personal Names

Adis　阿迪思
Agui　阿桂
Aibida　愛必達
An Lushan　安祿山
Asiha　阿思哈
Bai Er　白二
Bai Juyi　白居易
Bao Yang (Mrs.)　鮑楊氏
Baoning　保寧
Bayanbi　巴彥弼
Bengwubu　綳武布
Bi Yuan　畢沅
Cao Sixi　曹四喜
Chai Daji　柴大紀
Chai Dajing　柴大經
Chai Jijia　柴際甲
Changjun　常鈞
Changlin　長麟
Changling　長齡
Chaoquan　朝銓
Chen Hongmou　陳宏謀
Chen Huai　陳淮
Chen Huizu　陳輝祖
Chen Shichang　陳世昌
Chen Yin　陳寅

Chen Zhili　陳執禮
Chengfang　成方
Cheng Si　程四
Dai Mingshi　戴名世
Dai Shidao　戴世道
Detai　德泰
Emida　鄂彌達
Fan Shishou　范時綬
Fang Bao　方苞
Fang Dengyi　方登嶧
Fang Guancheng　方觀承
Fang Shiqi　方式齊
Fang Shouchou　方受疇
Fang Weidian　方維甸
Fang Xiaobiao　方孝標
Fang Zheng　方正
Fukang'an　福康安
Fulehun　富勒渾
Futong　富通
Gaoqi　高杞
Gao Wu　高五
Gong Zizhen　龔自珍
Gui Jingzhao　歸景照
Guotai　國泰
Hailu　海祿

236

Han Yu　韓愈
He Jineng　何奇能
Hening　和寧
Heshen　和珅
Heying　和瑛
Hong Zhi　洪智
Huang Baotian　黃寶田
Huang Mian　黃冕
Huang Pingsan　黃聘三
Huang Wenfu　黃文甫
Jahangir　張格爾
Jia Yi　賈誼
Jiang Sheng　姜晟
Jifeng'e　奇豐額
Jinchang　晉昌
Jing'an　景安
Kaitai　開泰
Kang Jitian　康基田
Kang Tingyan　康廷燕
Kuilin　奎林
Le'erjin　勒爾謹
Li Bai　李白
Li Dangui　李丹桂
Li Erman　李二滿
Li Erxiao　李二小
Li Liu (Mrs)　李劉氏
Li Luanxuan　李鑾宣
Li Shiyao　李侍堯
Li Xuancai　李選才
Lin Shuangwen　林爽文
Liu (carpenter)　劉
Liu Jiaying　劉嘉穎
Liu Si　劉四
Liu Tongxun　劉統勳
Liu Zhaokui　劉照魁
Liu Zongyuan　柳宗元
Lu Ben　盧本
Lu Jianzeng　盧見曾
Lü Fuxian　呂敷先
Lü Liuliang　呂留良
Lü Yijian　呂懿兼
Ma De　馬德

Mengtai　蒙泰
Mi Tianxi　米天喜
Mingliang　明亮
Mingshan　明山
Miu Yuanchun　繆元淳
Muhelin　穆和闐
Nayancheng　那彥成
Ni Hongwen　倪宏文
Pang (convict)　龐
Qi Junzao　祁寯藻
Qu Yuan　屈原
Qian Daxin　錢大昕
Qianqi　錢琦
Qin Cheng'en　秦承恩
Qingbao　慶保
Rao Yuxiang　饒玉相
Sengbaozhu　僧保住
Shen Shu　沈澍
Shi Guanglu　施光輅
Shi Zhonghe　石中和
Shuhede　舒赫德
Shun　舜
Songyun　松筠
Song Yu　宋昱
Suonuomu　索諾木
Suonuomuceling　索諾木策凌
Suchang　蘇昌
Su Dongpo　蘇東坡
Sun Chengbao　孫宬褒
Sun Qineng　孫七能
Sun Shiyi　孫士毅
Taifeiyin　台斐音
Tang Jiawa　唐家娃
Tang La (Mrs)　唐喇氏
Tian Baiyan　田白岩
Tian Wen　田雯
Tiebao　鉄保
Tuolun　託倫
Wang Baixin　王柏心
Wang Changling　王長齡
Wang (convict)　王
Wang Danwang　王亶望

Wang Erlou　王二樓
Wang Li (Mrs.)　王李氏
Wang Liyuan　王荔園
Wang Lun　王倫
Wang Tingkai　汪廷楷
Wang Tingxi　汪廷熙
Wang Yuanshu　王元樞
Wang Zichong　王子重
Wei Keyu　衞克堉
Wei Peijin　韋佩金
Weishibu　倭什布
Wei Yuan　魏源
Wei Zhiyi　韋執誼
Wenfu　溫福
Wenning　文寧
Wenshou　文綬
Wu (family)　吳
Wu Chengxu　吳承緒
Wudashan　吳達善
Wu Shigong　吳士功
Wu Xiongguang　吳熊光
Wu Yasan　吳亞三
Wu Yulin　烏玉麟
Wu Zhaoping　吳昭平
Xia Si　夏四
Xie Huan　謝環
Xingkui　興奎
Xu Buyun　徐步雲
Xu Mingbiao　徐名標
Xu Sanzi　徐三子
Xu Wu　徐午
Yade　雅德
Yan Jian　顏檢
Yan Shiying　顏時英
Yang Fengyuan　楊逢源
Yang Jingsuo　楊景索
Yang Xiang　楊香
Yao Yi　姚義

Yibulayimu　依布拉依木
Yijiang'a　伊江阿
Yiletu　伊勒圖
Yimian　宜綿
Yin Changlin　尹昌霖
Yinglian　英廉
Yongning　永寧
Yongqing　永慶
Yude　玉德
Yu Jin'ao　俞金鰲
Yu Minzhong　于敏中
Yu Shihe　于時和
Yu Wenyi　余文儀
Yue Zhongqi　岳鍾琪
Yushan　玉山
Zhang (convict)　張
Zhang Binglin　章炳麟
Zhang Chengji　張誠基
Zhang Mu　張穆
Zhang Qi　張琦
Zhang San　張三
Zhang Xuecheng　張學誠
Zhang Tianqiu　張天球
Zhao (old Mrs.)　老趙氏
Zhao Bing　趙炳
Zhao Bingxian　趙炳先
Zhao Yi　趙翼
Zheng Tai　鄭泰
Zheng Yaozu　鄭耀祖
Zhou E　周鍔
Zhou Gongxian　周恭先
Zhou Shiyuan　周世元
Zhou Wan　周琬
Zhu Gui　朱珪
Zhu Yun　朱筠
Zhuang Xin　莊炘
Zuo Zongtang　左宗棠

Glossary of Place-Names

Aksu 阿克蘇
Anding 安定
Anping 安平
Ansu 安肅
Anxi 安西
Balikun 巴里坤
Baxian 巴縣
Binzhou 邠州
Caibashihu 蔡巴什湖
Changji 昌吉
Changsha 長沙
Changwu 長武
Chaozhou 潮州
Dezhou 德州
Didao 狄道
Dunhuang 敦煌
Fuqiang 伏羌
Fuyi 撫彝
Ganzhou 甘州
Gaolan 皋蘭
Gaotai 高台
Gongchang 鞏昌
Gulang 古浪
Gutian 古田
Hami 哈密

Hangzhou 杭州
Heping 和平
Hezhou 河州
Huanbi 環碧
Huazhou 華州
Huining 惠寧
Huiyuan 惠遠
Huizhou 惠州
Huozhou 霍州
Ili 伊犂
Jiangning 江寧
Jiayuguan 嘉峪関
Jinchuan 金川
Jingning 靜寧
Jingzhou 涇州
Kalashar 哈喇沙爾
Kashgar 哈什噶爾
Khobdo 科布多
Kuche 庫車
Lanzhou 蘭州
Liangzhou 涼州
Liaodong 遼東
Liaoyang 遼陽
Longde 隆德
Majiling 馬蹟嶺

239

Moushan　牟山
Muguomu　木果木
Nanchang　南昌
Nanhe　南河
Nanping　南平
Ninguta　寧古塔
Ningyuan　寧遠
Pingfan　平番
Pingliang　平涼
Qingshui　清水
Qinzhou　秦州
Qiqihar　齊齊哈爾
Quanzhou　泉州
Rehe　熱河
Shandan　山丹
Shangyangbao　尙陽堡
Shengjing　盛京
Shenyang　瀋陽
Shu　蜀
Suzhou　肅州
Tarbagatai　塔爾巴噶台

Tarnaqin　塔爾納沁
Tianshan Beilu　天山北路
Tianshan Nanlu　天山南路
Tianshengdun　天生墩
Toksun　托克孫
Tongcheng　桐城
Turfan　吐魯番
Ürümqi　烏魯木齊
Ush　烏什
Wang Hei'er　王黑兒
Weiyuan　渭源
Wuchang　武昌
Wuwei　武威
Wuyuan　武緣
Yarkand　葉爾羌
Yongchang　永昌
Yongding　永定
Zhangye　張掖
Zhangzhou　漳州
Zhengding　正定

Bibliography

"Annan Tuohui Changtu An" 安南脫回廠徒案 (The case of the Annan miners who fled back [to China]). *Shiliao Xunkan* 史料月刊, 21–22. Peiping: Palace Museum, 1930–31.

Antony, Robert J. "Peasants, Heroes and Brigands: The Problems of Social Banditry in Early Nineteenth-Century South China." *Modern China* 15, no. 2 (April 1989): 123–148.

Balazs, Etienne. *Le Traité juridique du "Souei-Chou."* Leiden: E. J. Brill, 1954.

Bartlett, Beatrice S. *Monarchs and Ministers: The Founding and Growth of the Grand Council in Mid-Ch'ing China, 1722–1820.* Berkeley and Los Angeles: University of California Press, forthcoming.

Benedict, Carol. "Bubonic Plague in Nineteenth-Century China." *Modern China* 14, no. 2 (April 1988): 107–155.

Bernstein, Thomas. *Up to the Mountains and Down to the Villages: The Transfer of Youth from Urban to Rural China.* New Haven: Yale University Press, 1977.

Bi Yuan 畢沅. "Qiuyue Yinjiaji" 秋月吟笳集 (Yinjia collection of the autumn moon). In *Lingyanshanren Shiji* 靈巖山人詩集 (Collected poems of the man of Lingyan Mountain), 25. 1799.

Bodde, Derk. "Age, Youth and Infirmity in the Law of Ch'ing China." In *Essays on China's Legal Tradition*, edited by Jerome A. Cohen, R. Randle Edwards, and Fu-mei Chang Chen, 137–169. Princeton, N.J.: Princeton University Press, 1980.

———. "Prison Life in Eighteenth-Century Peking." *Journal of the American Oriental Society* 89, no. 2 (April–June 1969): 311–322.

———. "The State and Empire of Ch'in." In *CHC* vol. 1, edited by Denis C.

Twitchett and Michael Loewe, 20–102. Cambridge: Cambridge University Press, 1986.

Bodde, Derk, and Morris, Clarence. *Law in Imperial China, Exemplified by 190 Ch'ing Dynasty Cases Translated from the Hsing-an Hui-lan, with Historical, Social, and Juridical Commentaries.* Cambridge: Harvard University Press, 1967.

Borei, Dorothy V. "Economic Implications of Empire-Building: The Case of Sinkiang." Paper presented at the Mid-Atlantic Region of the Association for Asian Studies, Indiana University of Pennsylvania, October 1988.

———. "Images of the Northwest Frontier: A Study of the Hsi-Yü Wen Chien Lu." *American Asian Review* 5, no. 2 (Summer 1987): 26–46.

———. "Strategic and Economic Integration of the Northwest during the Ch'ing Period." Paper presented at the New England Conference of the Association of Asian Studies, Harvard University, October 1989.

Boulais, Gui. *Manuel du code chinois.* Shanghai: Imprimerie de la Mission Catholique, 1924. Reprint. Taibei: Chengwen, 1966.

Brunnert, H. S., and Hagelstrom, V. V. *Present Day Political Organization of China.* Shanghai: Kelly and Walsh, 1912. Reprint. Taibei: Chengwen, 1971.

Bünger, Karl. "Genesis and Change of Law in China." *Law and State* 24 (1981): 66–89.

Cai Shenzhi 蔡申之. *Qingdai Zhouxian Gushi* 清代州縣故事 (Stories from counties and departments of the Qing dynasty). Hong Kong: Longman, 1968.

Campion, Emile. *Etudes sur la colonisation par les transportés anglais, russes et français.* Rennes: F. Simon, 1901.

Chang Chung-li. *The Chinese Gentry: Studies on Their Role in Nineteenth-Century Chinese Society.* Seattle: University of Washington Press, 1955.

Chang Te-ch'ang. "The Economic Role of the Imperial Household in the Ch'ing Dynasty." *JAS* 31, no. 2 (February 1972): 243–274.

Chang Wejen (Zhang Weiren). "The Grand Secretariat Archive and the Study of the Ch'ing Judicial Process." *CSWT* 4, no. 5 (June 1981): 108–120.

Changzhoufu Zhi, Renwu Zhuan 常州府志, 人物傳 (Gazetteer of Changzhou Prefecture, biographies). In *Hong Beijiang Xiansheng Yiji* 洪北江先生遺集 (Bequeathed writings of Mr. Hong Beijiang). Shoujing Tang, 1877–1878.

Chen, Fu-mei Chang. "The Influence of Shen Chih-ch'i's *Chi-chu* Commentary upon Ch'ing Judicial Decisions." In *Essays on China's Legal Tradition*, edited by Jerome A. Cohen, R. Randle Edwards, and Fu-mei Chang, 170–221. Princeton, N.J.: Princeton University Press, 1980.

———. "Local Control of Convicted Thieves in Eighteenth-Century China." In *Conflict and Control in Late Imperial China*, edited by Frederic Wakeman, Jr., and Carolyn Grant, 121–142. Berkeley and Los Angeles: University of California Press, 1975.

———. "On Analogy in Qing Law." *HJAS* 30 (1970): 212–224.

Chen, Paul Heng-ch'ao. *Chinese Legal Tradition under the Mongols*. Princeton, N.J.: Princeton University Press, 1979.

Chen Yuan 陳垣. "Ji Lü Wancun Zisun" 記呂晚村子孫 (The descendants of Lü Liuliang). In *Wenxian Tekan* 文獻特刊 (Special historical publications), "Lunshu" 論述, 1–4. Taibei: Palace Museum, 1967.

———. "Ji Xu Song Qianshu Shi" 記徐松遣戍事 (On the banishment of Xu Song). *Guoxue Jikan* 國學季刊 5, no. 3 (1935): 141–150.

Cheng Ying-wan. *Postal Communication in China and its Modernization, 1860–1896*. Cambridge: Harvard University Press, 1970.

Cheng'an Suojian Ji 成案所見集 (Collection of seen leading cases). Four successive collections, covering 1736–1805. Compiled by Ma Shilin 馬世璘. Edition of 1805 compiled by Xie Kui 謝奎.

Ching, Julia, trans. and annotator. *The Philosophical Letters of Wang Yangming*. Canberra: Australian National University Press, 1972.

Chou, Nailene. "Frontier Studies and Changing Frontier Administration in Late Ch'ing China: The Case of Sinkiang 1759–1911." Ph.D. diss., University of Washington, 1976.

Ch'ü T'ung-tsu. *Law and Society in Traditional China*. Paris and The Hague: Mouton, 1961.

———. *Local Government in China under the Ch'ing*. Cambridge: Harvard University Press, 1962. Reprint. Stanford, Calif.: Stanford University Press, 1969.

Chu Wen-djang. *The Moslem Rebellion in Northwest China, 1862–1878: A Study of Government Minority Policy*. The Hague and Paris: Mouton, 1966.

Ch'üan, Han-sheng, and Kraus, Richard A. *Mid-Ch'ing Rice Markets and Trade: An Essay in Price History*. Cambridge: Harvard University Press, 1975.

Cohen, Paul A. *China and Christianity: The Missionary Movement and the Growth of Chinese Antiforeignism, 1860–1870*. Cambridge: Harvard University Press, 1963.

Cranmer-Byng, J. L., ed. *An Embassy to China: Lord Macartney's Journal*. London: Longmans, 1962.

Crossley, Pamela Kyle. "*Manzhou Yuanliu Kao* and the Formalization of the Manchu Heritage." *JAS* 46, no. 4 (November 1987) 761–790.

———. *Orphan Warriors: Three Manchu Generations and the Ending of the Qing World*. Princeton, N.J.: Princeton University Press, 1990.

———. "The Qianlong Retrospect on the Chinese-Martial Banners." *LIC* 10, no. 1 (June 1989) 63–107.

"Daoguangshi Nanhe Guanli zhi Chitai" 道光時南河官吏之侈汰 (The extravagance of officials at Nanhe in the Daoguang period). In *Chunbingshi Yecheng* 春冰室野乘 (Unofficial annals of Chunbing Lodge), pt. 1, 52a–54a. In *Guanzhong Congshu* 関中叢書 (Collectanea from within the passes), compiled by Song Liankui 宋聯奎, vol. 94. Shaanxi: Tongzhiguan, 1935.

Daqing Lichao Shilu (QSL) 大清歷朝實錄 (Veritable records of successive reigns of the Qing dynasty). Tokyo, 1937–1938.

Daqing Lüli Huitong Xinzuan 大清律例會通新纂 (Comprehensive new edition of the Great Qing Code [1873], attributed to Yao Yuxiang [姚雨薌]). With original commentary by Shen Zhiqi 沈之奇 and added commentary by Hu Yangshan 胡仰山, ed. Beijing, 1873. Reprint. Taibei: Wenhai, 1964.

de Groot, J. J. M. *Sectarianism and Religious Persecution in China.* Amsterdam: Johannes Müller, 1903.

de Quincey, Thomas. *Revolt of the Tartars or, Flight of the Kalmuck Khan.* Boston: Leach, Shewell and Sanborn, 1896.

Dreyer, Edward. *Early Ming China: A Political History, 1355–1435.* Stanford, Calif.: Stanford University Press, 1982.

Edwards, R. Randle. "Ch'ing Legal Jurisdiction over Foreigners." In *Essays on China's Legal Tradition*, edited by Jerome A. Cohen, R. Randle Edwards, and Fu-mei Chang Chen, 223–269. Princeton, N.J.: Princeton University Press, 1980.

Ekirch, A. Roger. *Bound for America: The Transportation of British Convicts to the Colonies, 1718–1775.* Oxford: Clarendon Press, 1987.

Elman, Benjamin A. *Classicism, Politics, and Kinship: The Ch'ang-Chou School of New Text Confucianism in Late Imperial China.* Berkeley and Los Angeles: University of California Press, 1990.

———. *From Philosophy to Philology: Intellectual and Social Aspects of Change in Late Imperial China.* Cambridge: Harvard University Press, 1984.

Entenmann, Robert. "Migration and Settlement in Sichuan, 1644–1796." Ph.D. diss., Harvard University, 1982.

Fang Bao 方苞. "Yuzhong Zaji" 獄中雜集 (Miscellaneous notes written in prison). 1851. Reprint. In *Fang Bao Ji* 方苞集 (Works of Fang Bao), edited by Liu Jigao 劉季高, 709–712. Shanghai: Shanghai Guji Chubanshe, 1983.

Farquhar, David. "The Ch'ing Administration of Mongolia up to the Nineteenth Century." Ph.D. diss., Harvard University, 1960.

Fisher, Thomas S. "Lü Liu-liang (1629–1683) and the Tseng Ching Case (1728–1733)." Ph.D. diss., Princeton University, 1974.

Fletcher, Joseph F. "China and Central Asia 1368–1884." In *The Chinese World Order*, edited by J. K. Fairbank, 206–224. Cambridge: Harvard University Press, 1968.

———. "Ch'ing Inner Asia c. 1800." In *CHC* vol. 10, pt. 1, edited by John K. Fairbank, 35–106. Cambridge: Cambridge University Press, 1978.

———. "The Heyday of the Ch'ing Order in Mongolia, Sinkiang and Tibet." In *CHC* vol. 10, pt. 1, edited by John K. Fairbank, 352–408. Cambridge: Cambridge University Press, 1978.

Forbes, Andrew D. W. *Warlords and Muslims in Chinese Central Asia: A Political History of Republican Sinkiang, 1911–1949.* Cambridge: Cambridge University Press, 1986.

Fu Lo-shu. *A Documentary Chronicle of Sino-Western Relations, 1644–1820.* Tucson: University of Arizona Press, 1966.

Gillen, Mollie. "The Botany Bay Decision, 1786: Convicts, Not Empire." *English Historical Review* 97 (1982): 740–766.

von Glahn, Richard. *The Country of Streams and Grottoes: Expansion, Settlement, and the Civilizing of the Sichuan Frontier in Song Times.* Cambridge: Harvard University Press, 1987.

Glaser, Daniel, ed. *Handbook of Criminology.* Chicago: Rand McNally, 1974.

Gong Zizhen (Kung Tzu-chen) 龔自珍. "Xiyu Zhi Xingsheng Yi" 西域置行省議 (A proposal to establish a province in the Western Regions). In *Huangchao Jingshi Wenbian* 皇朝經世文編 (Collected writings on statecraft of this august dynasty), edited by He Changling 駕長齡 and Wei Yuan 魏源, 81, 17a–23a. Preface 1827.

Gongzhong Dang (GZD) 宮中檔 (Palace memorials archive). National Palace Museum, Taibei.

Gongzhong Dang Qianlongchao Zouzhe (GZDQLCZZ) 宮中檔乾隆朝奏摺 (Secret palace memorials of the Qianlong period). Taibei: National Palace Museum, 1982–.

Goodrich, Chauncey S. "The Ancient Chinese Prisoner's Van." *T'oung Pao* 61, no. 4–5 (1975): 215–231.

Goodrich, L. C., and Fang, C-y. *Dictionary of Ming Biography, 1368–1644.* New York: Columbia University Press, 1976.

Guangxu Shuntianfu Zhi 光緒順天府志 (Guangxu period gazetteer of Shuntian prefecture), compiled by Miao Quansun 繆荃孫. 1886.

Guilun 桂輪. *Chang Wenxiang Gong Nianpu* 長文襄公年譜 (Chronological biography of Master Chang Wenxiang [Changling]). N.p.: Guicong Tang, 1841.

Guochao Hanxue Shicheng Ji 國朝漢學師承記 (Record of the models of Han learning in the reigning dynasty). Compiled by Jiangfan 江潘. 1886.

Guochao Qixian Leizheng Chubian 國朝耆獻類徵初編 (Classified biographical records of venerable persons of the reigning dynasty, first series). Compiled by Li Huan 李桓. Privately published by the Li family of Xiangyin, 1884–1890.

Guoshi Guan Dang 國史館檔 (Archive of the National History Office). National Palace Museum, Taibei.

Guy, Kent. *The Emperor's Four Treasuries: Scholars and the State in the Late Ch'ien-lung Era.* Cambridge: Harvard University Press, 1987.

Hami Zhi 哈密志 (Gazetteer of Hami). Compiled by Zhong Fang 鍾方 1846. Reprint. Beijing: Yugong Xuehui, 1937.

Hong Beijiang Xiansheng Yiji 洪北江先生遺集 (Bequeathed writings of Mr. Hong Beijiang). Shoujing Tang, 1877–1878.

Hong Liangji 洪亮吉. "Bairi Cihuan Ji" 百日賜還集 (Collection relating to my recall after one hundred days). In *Hong Beijiang Xiansheng Yiji*, 16. Shoujing Tang, 1877–1878.

———. "Gengshengzhai Shi" 更生齊詩 (Poems of the Gengsheng studio). In *Hong Beijiang Xiansheng Yiji*, 16–17. Shoujing Tang, 1877–1878.

———. "Gengshengzhai Wen Jiaji" 更生齊文甲集 (First collection of writings from the Gengsheng studio). In *Hong Beijiang Xiansheng Yiji*, 14. Shoujing Tang, 1877–1878.

———. "Gengshengzhai Wen Yiji" 更生齊文乙集 (Second collection of writings from the Gengsheng studio). In *Hong Beijiang Xiansheng Yiji*, 15. Shoujing Tang, 1877–1878.

———. "Ili Riji" 伊犁日記 (Ili Diary). In *Xiaofanghuzhai Yudi Congchao* 小方壺齊輿地叢鈔 (The little square vase studio geographical series), 8. Shanghai, 1891–1897.

———. "Qianshu Ili Riji—Fu Chusai Jiwen" 遣戍伊犁日記一附出賽記聞 (Diary of exile to Ili—Further to what I recorded and heard beyond the borders). In *Gujin Shuobu Congshu* 古今說部叢書 (Collectanea of ancient and modern writings), 25. Compiled by Wang Wenru 王文濡. Shanghai, 1910.

———. "Saiwai Lu" 賽外錄 (Records from beyond the borders). In *Hong Beijiang Xiansheng Yiji*, 24. Shoujing Tang, 1877–1878.

———. "Tianshan Kehua" 天山客話 (A visitor's chats on the Tianshan). In *Gujin Shuobu Congshu* (Collectanea of ancient and modern writings), 26. Compiled by Wang Wenru 王文濡. Shanghai, 1910.

———. "Wanli Hege Ji" 萬里荷戈集 (Collection concerning my ten thousand mile exile). In *Hong Beijiang Xiansheng Yiji*, 16. Shoujing Tang, 1877–1878.

Hsu Dau-lin, "Crime and Cosmic Order." *HJAS* 30 (1970): 111–125.

Huang Liuhong. *A Complete Book concerning Happiness and Benevolence: A Manual for Local Magistrates in Seventeenth-Century China*. Translated and edited by Djang Chu. Tucson: University of Arizona Press, 1984.

Huang Liuhong 黃六鴻. *Fuhui Quanshu* 福惠全書 (A complete book concerning happiness and benevolence), author's preface 1694. Compiled in a new edition by Yamane Yukio 山根幸夫, following edition by Obata Yukihiro 小畑行蘭. Kyoto, 1974.

Huang, Philip C. C. *The Peasant Economy and Social Change in North China*. Stanford, Calif.: Stanford University Press, 1985.

Huangchao Jingshi Wenbian 皇朝經世文編 (Collected writings on statecraft of this august dynasty). Edited by He Changling 駕長齡 and Wei Yuan 魏源. Preface 1827.

Huangchao Xingfa Zhi 皇朝刑法志 (Annals of penal law of our august dynasty). National Palace Museum, Taibei.

Hubu Zeli. See *Qinding Hubu Zeli*.

Hucker, Charles. *A Dictionary of Official Titles in Imperial China*. Stanford, Calif.: Stanford University Press, 1985.

Hughes, Robert. *The Fatal Shore: The Epic of Australia's Founding*. New York: Knopf, 1987.

Huidian. See *Qinding Daqing Huidian*.

Huijiang Tongzhi 回疆通志 (Comprehensive gazetteer of the Muslim provinces). Compiled by Hening 和寧. ca. 1809. Reprint. Taibei: Wenhai, 1966.

Hulsewé, A. F. P. "Ch'in and Han Law." In *CHC* vol. 1, edited by Denis C. Twitchett and Michael Loewe, 520–544. Cambridge: Cambridge University Press, 1986.

———. *Remnants of Ch'in Law: An Annotated Translation of the Ch'in Legal and Administrative Rules of the 3rd Century B.C. Discovered in Yün-meng Prefecture, Hu-Pei Province, in 1975*. Leiden: E. J. Brill, 1985.

———. *Remnants of Han Law. Vol. 1, Introductory Studies and an Annotated Translation of Chapters 22 and 23 of the History of the Former Han Dynasty*. Leiden: E. J. Brill, 1955.

Hummel, Arthur. *Eminent Chinese of the Ch'ing Period (ECCP)*. Washington, D.C.: United States Government Printing Office, 1943.

Ji Yun 紀昀. *Ji Xiaolan Jiashu* 紀曉嵐家書 (Family letters of Ji Xiaolan). Shanghai: Zhongyang Shuju, 1936.

———. *Su Wenzhong Gong Shi Ji* 蘇文忠公詩集 (Collected poems of Master Su Wenzhong). Preface 1771.

———. *Yuewei Caotang Biji* 閱微草堂筆記 (Notes from the Yuewei Hall). Beijing, 1800.

———. "Wulumuqi Zashi" 烏魯木齊雜詩 (Miscellaneous poems from Ürümqi). In *Jieyue Shanfang Huichao* 借月山房彙鈔 (Collections from the Jieyue Mountain House), 113. Reprint. Taibei: Yiwen, 1967.

Jiaobu Dang 剿捕檔 (Archive of suppression and arrest). National Palace Museum, Taibei.

Jixin Dang 寄信檔 (Archive of court letters). National Palace Museum, Taibei.

Johnson, Wallace. *The T'ang Code. Vol. 1, General Principles*. Princeton, N.J.: Princeton University Press, 1979.

Junji Dang (JJD) 軍機檔 (Archives of the Grand Council). National Palace Museum, Taibei.

Kahn, Harold. *Monarchy in the Emperor's Eyes: Image and Reality in the Ch'ien-Lung Reign*. Cambridge: Harvard University Press, 1971.

Karlgren, Bernhard. "The Book of Documents." In *Bulletin of the Museum of Far Eastern Antiquities, Stockholm* 22 (1950): 1–81.

Kawakubo Teirō 川久保悌郎. "Shindai ni okeru henkyō e no zaito hairyū ni tsuite: Shinchō no ryūkei seisaku to henkyō, sono ichi" 清代に於ける辺疆への罪徒配流について：清朝の流刑政策と辺疆，その一 (On the punishment of exile to the frontiers in the Qing: The Qing exile policy and the frontiers, part one). In *Hirosaki Daigaku Jinbun Shakai* 弘前大学人文社会 vol. 15, Shigaku hen 史学編 (Historical studies), no. II: 27–60.

————. "Shindai Manshū no henkyō shakai: Shinchō no ryūkei seisaku to henkyō, sono ni 清代満洲の辺疆社会: 清朝の流刑政策と辺疆, その二 (Frontier society in Manchuria during the Qing period: The exile policy and the frontiers during the Qing, part two)." *Hirosaki Daigaku Jinbun Shakai* vol. 27, Shigaku hen, no. IV: 57–82.

Keenan, David L. "The Secret Life of Ghosts: Chi Yün and the *Yüeh Wei Ts'ao T'ang Pi Chi*." Paper presented at the annual meeting of the Association for Asian Studies, Washington D.C., March 1989.

Kennan, George. *Siberia and the Exile System*. 2 vols. New York: Russell & Russell/The Century Co.: 1891.

Kessler, Lawrence D. "Ethnic Composition of Provincial Leadership during the Qing period." *JAS* 29, no. 3 (1969): 489–511.

Kierman, Frank A., Jr., and Fairbank, John K., eds. *Chinese Ways in Warfare*. Cambridge: Harvard University Press, 1974.

Kuhn, Philip A. *Rebellion and Its Enemies in Late Imperial China: Militarization and Social Structure, 1796–1864*. Cambridge: Harvard University Press, 1970.

————. "Political Crime and Bureaucratic Monarchy: A Chinese Case of 1768." *LIC* 8, no. 1 (June 1987): 80–104.

Lamley, Harry. "Subethnic Rivalry in the Ch'ing Period." In *The Anthropology of Taiwanese Society*, edited by Emily Ahern and Hill Gates, 282–318. Stanford, Calif.: Stanford University Press, 1981.

Lattimore, Owen. *Inner Asian Frontiers of China*. New York: American Geographical Society, 1940.

Lee, James. "Migration and Expansion in Chinese History." In *Human Migration—Patterns and Policies*, edited by William H. McNeill and Ruth S. Adams, 20–47. Bloomington: University of Indiana Press, 1978.

————. "State and Economy in Southwest China, 1400–1800." Cambridge: Harvard University Press, forthcoming.

Lee, Joseph J. *Wang Ch'ang-ling*. Boston: Twayne, 1982.

Lee, Robert H. G. *The Manchurian Frontier in Ch'ing History*. Cambridge: Harvard University Press, 1970.

Li Luanxuan 李鑾宣. "Di Shu" 抵戍 (Arriving in exile). In "Hege Ji" 荷戈集 (Exile collection), pt. 2, 13b. In *Jianbaishi Zhai Shi Ji* 堅白石齊詩集 (Collected poems from the Jianbaishi Studio), *juan* 9.

————. "Hege Ji" 荷戈集 (Exile collection). In *Jianbaishi Zhai Shi Ji* 堅白石齊詩集 (Collected poems from the Jianbaishi Studio). Preface 1819 by Jiang Yupu 蔣予蒲.

————. "Kou Zhan Er Duan Ju" 口占二斷句 (Two improvised sentences). In "Hege Ji," pt. 2, 8b. In *Jianbaishi Zhai Shi Ji, juan* 9.

————. "Sihuan Zashi" 司圜雜詩 (Miscellaneous prison poems). In *Qingshiduo* 清詩鐸 (Anthology of poems from the Qing dynasty), compiled by Zhang Yingchang 張應昌, 276–277. Preface 1857. Reprint. Beijing: Zhonghua Shuju, 1960. (Original title: *Guochao Shiduo* 國朝詩鐸).

———. "Xiangfeng Xing" 相逢行 (Poem on meeting). In *Sanzhou Jilüe* 三州輯略 (A summary compilation on three areas), compiled by Hening 和寧, *juan 9*, 336. 1805. Reprint. Taibei: Chengwen, 1968.

Li Yunyi 李云逸. *Wang Changling Shizhu* 王長齡詩注 (Annotated poetry of Wang Changling). Shanghai: Shanghai Guji Chubanshe, 1984.

Lin Enxian 林恩顯. "Qingdai Xinjiang Zhouxian Zhidu zhi Yanjiu" 清代新疆州縣制度之研究 (A study of the system of *Zhou* and *Xian* in Xinjiang during the Qing). *Renwen Xuebao* 人文學報 2 (1976): 18–45.

Lin Yutang. *The Gay Genius: The Life and Times of Su Tung-po*. New York: John Day, 1947.

Lin Zexu 林則徐. "Hege Jicheng" 荷戈紀程 (Journey into exile). In *Xiaofanghuzhai Yudi Congchao* 小方壺齊輿地叢鈔 (The little square vase studio geographical series), 2. Shanghai, 1891–1897.

———. *Lin Zexu Jiashu* 林則徐家書 (Lin Zexu's family letters). Shanghai: Zhongyang Shudian, 1935.

———. "Riji" 日記 (Diary). In *Lin Zexu Ji* 林則徐集 (Works of Lin Zexu), edited by Zhongshan University History Department. Beijing: Zhonghua Shuju, 1962. Reprint. Zhonghua Shuju, 1984.

Lin Zexu Shujian 林則徐書簡 (Lin Zexu's letters). Edited by Yang Guozhen 楊國楨. Fujian: Fujian Renmin Chubanshe, 1981.

"Linqing Jiao'an" 林清教案 (The sectarian case at Linqing). In *Gugong Zhoukan* 故宮週刊 (Palace Museum weekly), 223. Taibei: National Palace Museum, 1931–1933.

Lipman, Jonathan. "The Border World of Gansu, 1895–1935." Ph.D. diss., Stanford University, 1980.

Liu Xuanmin 劉選民. "Qingdai Dong San Sheng Yimin Yu Kaiken." 清代東三省移民與開墾 (Immigration and colonization in the three eastern provinces [Manchuria] during the Qing). *Shixue Nianbao* 史學年報 2, no. 5 (1938): 67–120.

Loewe, Michael. "The Structure and Practice of Government." In *CHC* vol. 1, edited by Denis C. Twitchett and Michael Loewe, 463–490. Cambridge: Cambridge University Press, 1986.

Lombard-Salmon, Claudine. *Un Exemple d'acculturation chinoise: La Province du Gui Zhou au XVIIIe siècle*. Paris: Ecole française d'extreme-orient, 1972.

Lü Kun 呂坤. *Shizheng Lu* 實政錄 (Record of true administration). 1872 edition.

Luo Ergang 羅爾綱. *Lüyingbing Zhi* 綠營兵志 (An account of the Green Standard Army). Chongqing: Commercial Press, 1945. Reprint. Beijing: Zhonghua Shuju, 1984.

Luo Yunzhi 羅運治. *Qing Gaozong Tongzhi Xinjiang Zhengce de Tantao* 清高宗統治新疆政策的探討 (An inquiry into the Qianlong Emperor's Xinjiang policy). Taibei: Liren Shuju, 1983.

Luo Zhengjun 羅正鈞. "Zuo Wenxiang Gong Nianpu" 左文襄公年譜 (Chronological biography of Master Zuo Wenxiang [Zuo Zongtang]). In *Zuo Wenxiang Gong Quanji* 左文襄公全集 (Complete works of Master Zuo Wenxiang). 1888–1897. Reprint. Taibei: Wenhai, 1964.

McElderry, Andrea. "Frontier Commerce: An Incident of Smuggling." *American Asian Review* 5, no. 2 (Summer 1987): 47–62.

Mackerras, Colin P. *The Rise of the Peking Opera, 1770–1870: Social Aspects of the Theatre in Manchu China.* Oxford: Clarendon Press, 1972.

McKnight, Brian. "Punishments in Traditional China: From Family to the Group to the State." Paper presented at the Conference on Punishment: Meanings, Purposes, Practices—A Critical Interdisciplinary Exploration, Columbia Society of Fellows in the Humanities, New York, May 1990.

———. *The Quality of Mercy: Amnesties and Traditional Chinese Justice.* Honolulu: University Press of Hawaii, 1981.

Mann, Susan. *Local Merchants and the Chinese Bureaucracy, 1750–1950.* Stanford, Calif.: Stanford University Press, 1987.

Mann Jones, Susan. "Hung Liang-chi (1746–1809): The Perception and Articulation of Political Problems in Late Eighteenth-Century China." Ph.D. diss., Stanford University, 1971.

Mann Jones, Susan, and Kuhn, Philip. "Dynastic Decline and the Roots of Rebellion." In *CHC* vol. 10, pt. 1, edited by John K. Fairbank, 107–162. Cambridge: Cambridge University Press, 1978.

Mazour, Anatole G. *The First Russian Revolution, 1825: The Decembrist Movement, Its Origins, Development, and Significance.* Stanford: Stanford University Press, 1961.

Meijer, Marinus. "The Autumn Assizes in Ch'ing Law." *T'oung Pao* 70 (1984): 1–17.

———. "Homosexual Offences in Ch'ing Law." *T'oung Pao* 71 (1985): 109–133.

———. *The Introduction of Modern Criminal Law in China.* Jakarta: Koninklijke Drukkerij de Unie Batavia, 1949.

———. "Slavery at the End of the Ch'ing Dynasty." In *Essays on China's Legal Tradition*, edited by Jerome A. Cohen, R. Randle Edwards, and Fu-mei Chang Chen, 327–358. Princeton, N.J.: Princeton University Press, 1980.

Meskill, Johanna Menzel. *A Chinese Pioneer Family: The Lins of Wu-feng, Taiwan, 1729–1895.* Princeton, N.J.: Princeton University Press, 1979.

Metzger, Thomas A. *Escape from Predicament: Neo-Confucianism and China's Evolving Political Culture.* New York: Columbia University Press, 1977.

———. *The Internal Organization of Ch'ing Bureaucracy: Legal, Normative and Communications Aspects.* Cambridge: Harvard University Press, 1973.

"Miji Dang" 密記檔 (Archive of secret accounts). In *Wenxian Congbian* 文獻叢編 (Collected historical documents), 6. Peiping: Palace Museum, 1930–1943.

Ming Shi 明史 (The history of the Ming). Beijing: Zhonghua Shuju, 1984.

Mingqing Shiliao 明清史料 (Historical materials of the Ming and Qing dynasties). Shanghai and Nangang: Academia Sinica, 1930–1957.

Morse, H. B. *The Chronicles of the East India Company Trading to China, 1635–1834.* 5 vols. Oxford: Clarendon Press, 1926.

Murray, Dian Hechtner. *Pirates of the South China Coast 1790–1810.* Stanford, Calif.: Stanford University Press, 1987.

Naquin, Susan. "Connections between Rebellions: Sect Family Networks in Qing China." *Modern China* 8, no. 3 (July 1982): 337–360.

———. *Millenarian Rebellion in China: The Eight Trigrams Uprising of 1813.* New Haven: Yale University Press, 1976.

———. *Shantung Rebellion: The Wang Lun Uprising of 1774.* New Haven: Yale University Press, 1981.

———. "True Confessions: Criminal Interrogations as Sources for Ch'ing History." *National Palace Museum Bulletin* 11, no. 1 (March–April 1976): 1–17.

Naquin, Susan, and Rawski, Evelyn. *Chinese Society in the Eighteenth Century.* New Haven: Yale University Press, 1987.

Nayancheng 那彥成. *A Wencheng Gong Nianpu* 阿文成公年譜 (Chronological biography of Master A Wencheng [Agui]). 1813. Reprint. Taibei: Wenhai, 1971.

Ng, Vivien. "Ch'ing Laws concerning the Insane: An Historical Survey." *CSWT* 4, no. 4 (December 1980): 55–89.

———. "Ideology and Sexuality: Rape Laws in Qing China." *JAS* 46, no. 12 (February 1987): 57–70.

———. "Insanity and the Law in Ch'ing China." Ph.D. diss., University of Hawaii, 1980.

Niida Noboru 仁井田陞. *Chūgoku Hōsei-shi Kenkyū* 中國法制史研究 (A study of Chinese legal history). 4 vols. Tokyo: Tokyo University Press, 1959–1964.

Nivison, David S. "Ho-shen and His Accusers: Ideology and Political Behavior in the Eighteenth Century." In *Confucianism in Action*, edited by David S. Nivison and Arthur F. Wright, 209–243. Stanford, Calif.: Stanford University Press, 1960.

Nouvelles Lettres édifiantes et curieuses écrites des missions de la Chine. Lyon, 1818.

Ocko, Jonathan K. "I'll Take It All the Way to Beijing: Capital Appeals in the Qing." *JAS* 47, no. 2 (May 1988): 291–315.

Overmyer, Daniel. *Folk Buddhist Religion: Dissenting Sects in Late Imperial China.* Cambridge: Harvard University Press, 1976.

Perdue, Peter C. *Exhausting the Earth: State and Peasant in Hunan, 1500–1850.* Cambridge: Harvard University Press, 1987.

———. "The Qing State and the Gansu Grain Market, 1739–1864." Paper presented at Conference on Economics and Qing History, Oracle, Arizona, 1988.

———. "The West Route Army and the Silk Road: Grain Supply and Qianlong's Military Campaigns in Northwest China (1735–1760)." Paper presented at the Columbia Seminar in Modern Chinese History, New York, February 1989.

Polachek, James. "The Inner Opium War." C. V. Starr Library, Columbia University. Manuscript, 1983.

———. "Literati Groups and Literati Politics in Early Nineteenth-Century China." Ph.D. diss., University of California at Berkeley, 1980.

Qi Qingshun 齐清順. "Qingdai Xinjiang Qianfan Yanjiu" 清代新疆遺犯研究 (Researches into the Xinjiang exiles of the Qing period). *Zhongguo Shi Yanjiu* 中國史研究 2 (1988): 83–97.

———. "Qingdai Xinjiang Qianyuan Yanjiu" 清代新疆遺員研究 (Researches into officials banished to Xinjiang in the Qing period). *Xinjiang Shehui Kexue Yanjiu* 新疆社会科学研究 (1986): 1–11.

Qi Shiyi 七十一 (Chunyuan Qi Shiyi 椿園七十一). "Xiyu Ji" 西域記 (Record of the Western Regions). In *Xiyu Zongzhi* 西域總志 (General gazetteer of the Western Regions). Preface 1777. Wuning, 1814.

Qi Yunshi 干罶迊. "Wanli Xingcheng Ji" 萬里行程記 (Record of a journey of ten thousand li). In *Wenyinglou Yudi Congshu* 問影樓輿地叢書 (The Wenying Mansion geographical series), vol. 5. Compiled by Hu Sijing 胡思敬. Beijing, 1908.

———. "Xichui Yaolüe" 西陲要略 (A summary of important aspects of the Western Regions). In *Xiaofanghuzhai Yudi Congchao* 小方壺齊輿地叢鈔 (The little square vase studio geographical series), 2. Shanghai, 1891–1897.

———. "Xichui Zhuzhi Ci" 西陲竹枝詞 (Bamboo Spray Words on the Western Regions). 1808.

———. "Xiyu Shidi" 西域釋地 (Explanation of the Western Regions). In *Xiaofanghuzhai Yudi Congchao* 小方壺齊輿地叢秒, 7. Shanghai, 1891–1897.

Qin Hancai 秦翰才. *Zuo Wenxiang Gong Zai Xibei* 左文襄公在西北 (Master Zuo Wenxiang (Zuo Zongtang) in the Northwest). Chongqing, 1945. Reprint. Changsha: Yuelu Shushe, 1984.

Qinding Daqing Huidian 欽定大清會典. (Imperially authorized collected institutes of the Qing). 1818.

Qinding Daqing Huidian. 1899. Reprint. Taibei: Xinwenli, 1976.

Qinding Daqing Huidian Shili (HDSL) 欽定大清會典事例 (Imperially authorized collected institutes and precedents of the Qing). 1818.

Qinding Daqing Huidian Shili (HDSL). 1899. Reprint. Taibei: Xinwenli, 1976.

Qinding Huangyu Xiyu Tuzhi 欽定皇輿西域圖志 (Imperially authorized illustrated gazetteer of the imperial dominions in the Western Regions). Compiled by Fuheng 傅恆. 1782. Reprint. Taibei: Wenhai, 1966.

Qinding Hubu Zeli 欽定戶部則例 (Imperially authorized regulations of the Board of Revenue). 1865.

Qinding Jiaobu Linqing Nifei Jilüe 欽定剿捕林清逆匪紀略 (Imperially authorized account of the suppression of the rebels at Linqing). 1781.

Qinding Liubu Chufen Zeli 欽定六部處分則例 (Imperially authorized regulations of the six boards). 1892. Reprint. Taibei: Wenhai, 1969.

Qinding Pingding Jiaofei Jilüe (JFJL) 欽定平定教匪紀略 (Imperially authorized account of the pacification of the religious rebels). 1816.

Qinding Pingding Zhunke'er Fanglüe Xubian 欽定平定準噶爾方略(續編) (Imperially authorized account of the suppression of the Zunghars [Continuation]). Compiled by Fuheng 傅恆. 1772.

Qinding Xinjiang Shilüe 欽定新疆識略 (Outline of knowledge about Xinjiang). Compiled by Songyun 松筠. Beijing: Wuyingdian, 1821.

Qinding Zhongshu Zhengkao 欽定中樞政考 (Imperially authorized regulations of the Board of War). ca. 1825. Reprint. Taibei: Xuehai, 1968.

Qing Shi Gao 清史稿 (Draft history of the Qing). 1928. Reprint. Beijing: Zhonghua Shuju, 1977.

Qing Shi Gao Xingfa Zhi Zhujie 清史稿刑法志註解 (Treatise on law from the draft history of the Qing, with annotations). Beijing: Law Publishing Company, 1957.

Qingchao Wenxian Tongkao (QCWXTK) 清朝文獻通考 (A comprehensive study of the historical institutions of the Qing dynasty). Shanghai: Commercial Press, 1936.

Qingchao Xu Wenxian Tongkao (QCXWXTK) 清朝續文獻通考 (Continued comprehensive study of the historical institutions of the Qing dynasty). Shanghai: Commercial Press, 1936.

Qingdai de Kuangye. 清代的礦業 (Mining in the Qing dynasty). Compiled by People's University Qing History Research Institute, Archives Department. Beijing: Zhonghua Shuju, 1983.

Qingdai Jiaqing Waijiao Shiliao 清代嘉慶外交史料 (Historical materials concerning foreign relations of the Jiaqing Emperor). Peiping: National Palace Museum, 1933.

Qingdai Wenzi Yu Dang 清代文字獄檔 (Archives of the Qing literary inquisition). Peiping: Palace Museum, 1931–1934. Reprint. Taibei: Huawen, 1969.

Qingdai Xuezhe Xiangzhuan 清代學者象傳 (Illustrated biographies of Qing dynasty scholars). Compiled by Ye Yanlan 葉衍蘭. Shanghai: Commercial Press, 1930.

Qingshi Liezhuan 清史列傳 (Biographies from Qing history). Shanghai: Zhonghua Shuju, 1928.

Roth, Gertraude. "The Manchu-Chinese Relationship 1618–1636." In *From Ming to Ch'ing*, edited by Jonathan D. Spence and John E. Wills, Jr., 1–38. New Haven: Yale University Press, 1979.

Rowe, William. *Hankow: Commerce and Society in a Chinese City, 1796–1889.* Stanford, Calif.: Stanford University Press, 1984.

———. *Hankow: Conflict and Community in a Chinese City, 1796–1885.* Stanford, Calif.: Stanford University Press, 1989.

Rudé, George. *Protest and Punishment: The Story of the Social and Political*

Protesters Transported to Australia, 1788–1868. Oxford: Clarendon Press, 1978.

Saguchi Tōru 佐口透. *Jūhachi–jūkyūseiki Higashi Torukisutan shakaishi kenkyū* 18–19 世紀東トルキスタン社会史研究 (Study of the social history of Eastern Turkestan in the eighteenth and nineteenth centuries). Tokyo: Yoshikawa Kobunkan, 1963.

Sanfasi Archives 三法司 (Archives of the three Judicial Offices). Institute of History and Philology, Academia Sinica, Taiwan.

Sanjdorj, M. *Manchu Chinese Colonial Rule in Northern Mongolia*. New York: St Martin's Press, 1980.

Sanzhou Jilüe 三州輯略 (A summary compilation on three areas). Compiled by Hening 和寧. 1805. Reprint. Taibei: Chengwen, 1968.

Schafer, Edward. *The Vermilion Bird*. Berkeley and Los Angeles: University of California Press, 1967.

Schneider, Lawrence. *A Madman of Ch'u: The Chinese Myth of Loyalty and Dissent*. Berkeley and Los Angeles: University of California Press, 1980.

Shangyu Dang (*SYD*) 上諭檔 (Imperial edicts record books). First Historical Archives, Beijing; National Palace Museum, Taibei.

Shaw, A. G. L. *Convicts and the Colonies: A Study of Penal Transportation from Great Britain and Ireland to Australia and Other Parts of the British Empire*. London: Faber and Faber, 1966.

Shen Jiaben 沈家本. "Chongjun Kao" 充軍考 (A study of military exile). In *Shen Jiyi Xiansheng Yishu, Jiabian* 沈寄簃先生遺書, 甲編 (Bequeathed writings of Mr. Shen Jiaben, first series). Beijing, ca. 1929. Reprint. Beijing, ca. 1985.

———. "Xingfa Fenkao" 刑法分考 (Separate studies of the punishments). In *Shen Jiyi Xiansheng Yishu, Jiabian*. Beijing, ca. 1929. Reprint. Beijing, ca. 1985.

———. "Zongkao" 總考 (General studies). In *Shen Jiyi Xiansheng Yishu, Jiabian*. Beijing, ca. 1929. Reprint. Beijing, ca. 1985.

Shepherd, John Robert. "Plains Aborigines and Chinese Settlers on the Taiwan Frontier in the Seventeenth and Eighteenth Centuries." Ph.D. diss., Stanford University, 1981.

Shiga Shuzo. "Criminal Procedure in the Ch'ing Dynasty, with Emphasis on Its Administrative Character and Some Allusion to Its Historical Antecedents (Part 1)." *Memoirs of the Research Department of the Tōyō Bunko, Tokyo* 32 (1974): 1–45.

Shiliao Xunkan 史料旬刊 (Historical materials issued every ten days). Peiping: Palace Museum, 1930–1931.

"Shuci Kuangbei Bizhao Dani Yuanzuo Renfan Qingdan" 書詞狂悖比照大逆緣坐人犯清單 (List of criminals in literary sedition cases sentenced by analogy to [the laws on] collective responsibility in rebellion [cases]). In *Wenxian Congbian* 文獻叢編 (Collected historical documents), 15. Peiping: Palace

Museum, 1930–1943.

Shujing, The Shoo King. Translated by James Legge. Vol. 3 of *The Chinese Classics.* Oxford: Clarendon Press, 1865.

Smith, A. E. *Colonists in Bondage: White Servitude and Convict Labor in 1607–1776.* Raleigh: University of North Carolina Press, 1947.

Smith, Kent. "Ch'ing Policy and the Development of Southwest China: Aspects of Ortai's Governor-Generalship." Ph.D. diss., Yale University, 1970.

Sogabe Shizuo 曾我部静雄. "Sōdai no shihai ni tsuite" 宋代の刺配について (On exile in the Song). *Bunka* 29, no. 1 (Spring 1965): 1–23.

Spence, Jonathan D. "Opium Smoking in Ch'ing China." In *Conflict and Control in Late Imperial China,* edited by Frederic Wakeman, Jr., and Carolyn Grant, 143–173. Berkeley and Los Angeles: University of California Press, 1975.

————. *The Search for Modern China.* New York: Norton, 1990.

Starn, Randolph. *Contrary Commonwealth: The Theme of Exile in Medieval and Renaissance Italy.* Berkeley and Los Angeles: University of California Press, 1982.

Sun, E-tu Zen. *Ch'ing Administrative Terms.* Cambridge: Harvard University Press, 1961. Reprint. Taibei: Nantian, 1978.

————. "Mining Labor in the Ch'ing Period." In *Approaches to Modern Chinese History,* edited by Albert Feuerwerker, Rhoads Murphey, and Mary C. Wright, 45–67. Berkeley and Los Angeles: University of California Press, 1967.

Tao Xisheng 陶希聖. *Qingdai Zhouxian Yamen Xingshi Shenpan Zhidu ji Chengxu* 清代州縣衙門刑事審判制度及程序 (The criminal justice system and procedure in district administration in the Qing dynasty). Taibei: Shihuo, 1972.

Taylor, Romeyn. "Yuan Origins of the *Wei-so* System." In *Chinese Government in Ming Times: Seven Studies,* edited by Charles O. Hucker, 23–40. New York: Columbia University Press, 1969.

Torbert, Preston. *The Ch'ing Imperial Household Department: A Study of Its Organization and Principal Functions, 1662–1796.* Cambridge: Harvard University Press, 1977.

Tu Wei-ming. *Neo-Confucian Thought in Action: Wang Yang-ming's Youth (1472–1509).* Berkeley and Los Angeles: University of California Press, 1976.

Twitchett, Denis C. "Hsüan-tsung." In *CHC* vol. 3, edited by Denis C. Twitchett and John K. Fairbank, 333–463. Cambridge: Cambridge University Press, 1979.

Vogel, Hans Ulrich. "Ch'ing Central Monetary Policy, 1644–1800." *LIC* 8, no. 2 (December 1987): 1–52.

Wakeman, Frederic, Jr. *The Great Enterprise: The Manchu Reconstruction of Order in Seventeenth-Century China.* Berkeley and Los Angeles: University of California Press, 1985.

Waldron, Arthur. "The Great Wall Myth: Its Origins and Role in Modern China." *Yale Journal of Criticism* 2, no. 1 (1988): 67–104.

Waley, Arthur. "China's Greatest Writer." In *The Secret History of the Mongols and Other Pieces*. London: George Allen and Unwin, 1963.

Waley-Cohen, Joanna. "The Stranger Paths of Banishment: Exile to the Xinjiang Frontier in Mid-Qing China." Ph.D. diss., Yale University, 1987.

Wang Xilong 王希隆. "Qingdai Shibian Xinjiang Shulüe" 清代实边新疆述略 (The consolidation of the Xinjiang frontier in the Qing). *Xibei Shidi* 西北史地, 1985, no. 4: 62–71.

Wang Yi-t'ung. "Slaves and Other Comparable Social Groups during the Northern Dynasties (386–618)." *HJAS* 16 (1953): 293–364.

Watson, Burton. *Records of the Grand Historian of China, Translated from the Shih Chi of Ssu-ma Ch'ien*. 2 vols. New York: Columbia University Press, 1961.

Watt, John. *The District Magistrate in Late Imperial China*. New York: Columbia University Press, 1972.

Wei Qingyuan 魏庆远, Wu Qiyan 吴奇衍, and Lu Su 鲁素. *Qingdai Nubi Zhidu* 清代奴婢制度 (The slavery system of the Qing dynasty). Beijing: People's University Press, 1984.

Wei Yuan 魏源. *Shengwu Ji* 聖武記 (Record of military achievements). ca. 1842. Reprint. Shanghai: Zhonghua Shuju 1936.

Whitbeck, Judith. "The Historical Vision of Kung Tzu-chen (1792–1841)." Ph.D. diss., University of California, Berkeley, 1980.

———. "Kung Tzu-chen and the Redirection of Literati Commitment in Early Nineteenth-Century China." *CSWT* 4, no. 10 (December 1983): 1–32.

Wilbur, C. Martin. *Slavery in China during the Former Han Dynasty*. Chicago Field Museum of Natural History, Anthropological Series, vol. 34. Chicago: Field Museum of Natural History, 1943.

Will, Pierre-Etienne. *Bureaucratie et famine en Chine au dix-huitième siècle*. Paris: Mouton and École des hautes études en sciences sociales, 1980.

Wright, Arthur F. *The Sui Dynasty*. New York: Knopf 1978.

Wu Yixian 吳翼先. *Xinjiang Tiaoli Shuolüe (XJTLSL)* 新疆條例說略 (A summary of the laws on Xinjiang). 1795. Preface 1788.

Wu Yuanfeng 吳元丰. "Qing Qianlong Nianjian Ili Tuntian Shulüe" 清乾隆年間伊犁屯田述略 (A summary of the military agricultural colonies at Ili in the Qianlong period of the Qing dynasty). *Minzu Yanjiu* 民族研究, 1987, no. 5: 92–100.

Xichui Zongtong Shilüe 西陲總統事略 (General outline of affairs of the Western Regions). Compiled by Songyun 松筠. 1808. Reprint. Taibei: Wenhai, 1965.

Xie Guozhen 謝國禎. *Qingchu Liuren Kaifa Dongbei Shi* 清初流人開發東北史 (A history of the opening of the northeast by exiles in the early Qing). Shanghai: Kaiming, 1948.

Xing'an Huilan (*XAHL*) 刑案滙覽 (Conspectus of penal cases). Compiled by Zhu Qingqi 祝慶祺 and Bao Shuyun 鮑書芸. Preface 1834.

Xingke Qiushen Tiben (*XKTB Qiushen*) 刑科秋審題本 (Routine memorials of the Board of Punishments concerning the autumn assizes). Genealogical Library, Church of Jesus Christ of Latter-Day Saints, Salt Lake City, Utah.

Xingke Tiben (*XKTB*) 刑科題本 (Routine memorials of the Board of Punishments). First Historical Archives, Beijing.

Xinjiang Tuzhi 新疆圖志 (Illustrated gazetteer of Xinjiang). Compiled by Wang Shunan 王樹枏. 1923. Reprint. Taibei: Wenhai, 1965.

Xiqing 西清. "Heilongjiang Waiji" 黑龍江外記 (Unofficial account of Heilongjiang). Ca. 1810. In *Xiaofanghuzhai Yudi Congchao*, 小方壺齊輿地叢鈔 (The little square vase studio geographical series), 1. Shanghai, 1891–1897.

Xu Bofu 徐伯夫. "Qingdai Qianqi Xinjiang Dichu de Mintun" 清代前期新疆地区的民屯 (Civilian colonies in Xinjiang in the early Qing). *Zhongguo Shi Yanjiu* 中國史研究 (May 1985): 85–95.

Xu Song 徐松. "Hanshu Xiyu Zhuan Buzhu" 漢書西域傳補注 (Notes on the chapters on the Western Regions in the Han dynastic history). 1829. Reprint. Taibei: Guangwen, 1968.

——. "Xinjiang Fu" 新疆賦 (Poem on Xinjiang). In *Qingchao Fanshu Yudi Congshu* 清朝藩屬輿地叢書 (Geographical series on Qing protectorates). 1824. Reprint. Taibei: Guangwen, 1968.

——. "Xiyu Shuidao Ji" 西域水道記 (Record of the waterways of the Western Regions). In *Qingchao Fanshu Yudi Congshu* 清朝藩屬輿地叢書 (Geographical series on Qing protectorates). 1824. Reprint. Taibei: Guangwen, 1968.

Xue Yunsheng 薛允升. *Duli Cunyi* (*DLCY*) 讀例存疑 (Concentration on doubtful matters while perusing the substatutes). Beijing: Hanmaozhai, 1905. Reprint. Taibei: Chengwen, 1970.

Yang Bin 楊賓. *Liubian Jilüe* 柳邊紀略 (Notes from the Willow Frontier), ca. 1690. In *Xiaofanghuzhai Yudi Congchao* 小方壺齊輿地叢鈔 (The little square vase studio geographical series), 1. Shanghai, 1891–1897.

Yang Chang 楊場 and Sun Yuchang 孫與常. "Mingdai Liuren Zai Dongbei" 明代流人在東北 (Exiles in the northeast during the Ming dynasty). In *Lishi Yanjiu* 歷史研究, 1985, no. 4: 54–66.

Yao Yongpu 姚永樸. "Jiu Wen Sui Bi" 舊聞隨筆 (Random notes on old tales). Beijing. 1919. Reprint. Taibei: Wenhai, 1968.

Yates, Robin D. S. "Slavery in Ancient China in Comparative and Historical Perspective." Paper prepared for Ancient China and Social Science Generalizations, Conference at Airlie House, Virginia, June 1986.

——. "Social Status in the Ch'in: Evidence from the Yün-meng Legal Documents. Part One: Commoners." *HJAS* 47, no. 1 (June 1987): 197–238.

Yü Ying-shih. "Han Foreign Relations." In *CHC* vol. 1, edited by Denis C.

Twitchett and Michael Loewe, 377–462. Cambridge: Cambridge University Press, 1986.

Yuehaiguan Zhi 粤海関志 (Gazetteer of the customs in Guangdong). Compiled by Liang Tingnan 梁廷枏. Reprint. Taibei: Chengwen, 1968.

Yutianxian Zhi 玉田縣志 (Gazetteer of Yutian district). 1889.

Zelin, Madeleine. *The Magistrate's Tael: Rationalizing Fiscal Reform in Eighteenth-Century Ch'ing China*. Berkeley and Los Angeles: University of California Press, 1984.

———. "The Rights of Tenants in Mid-Qing Sichuan: A Study of Land-Related Lawsuits in the Baxian Archives." *JAS* 45, no. 3 (May 1986): 499–526.

Zeng Wenwu 曾問五. *Zhongguo Jingying Xiyu Shi* 中國經營西域史 (A history of China's management of its Western Regions). Shanghai: Commercial Press, 1936.

Zhang Jinfan 張晉藩. "Qing Lü Chu Tan" 清律初探 (A first approach to the laws of the Qing). In *Zhongguo Falü Shilun* 中国法律史論 (On the history of China's laws). Beijing: Falü Chubanshe, 1982.

Zhang Tiegang 張铁纲. "Qingdai Liufang Zhidu Chutan" 清代流放制度初探 (A first approach to the exile system of the Qing). In *Lishi Dangan* 历史档案, 1989, no. 3: 80–86.

Zhang Weiren 張偉仁 (Chang Wejen). *Qingdai Fazhi Yanjiu* 清代法制研究 (An investigation into the legal system of the Qing dynasty). Taibei: Academia Sinica Institute of History and Philology, 1983.

Zhao Lisheng 赵俪生. "Xibeixue de Tahuangzhe zhi yi" 西北学的拓荒者之一 (One of the trailblazers of northwest studies). *Xibei Shidi*, 1985, no. 1: 9–12.

Zhao Yi 趙翼. *Huangchao Wugong Jisheng* 皇朝武功紀盛 (Record of the great military achievements of this imperial dynasty). Reprint. Taibei: Wenhai, 1966.

———. *Oubei Shichao* 甌北詩鈔 (Oubei's selected poems). Shanghai: Commercial Press, 1939.

Zhongguo Fazhi Shi Lunwen Xuan 中國法制史論文選 (Selected articles on the history of the legal system in China). Beijing: Law and Politics University, 1984.

Zhongshu Zhengkao. See *Qinding Zhongshu Zhengkao*.

Zhupi Zouzhe (ZPZZ) 硃批奏摺 (Imperially endorsed palace memorials). First Historical Archives, Beijing.

"Zuo Wenxiang Gong Nianpu." See Luo Zhengjun.

Index

Adeodato, 97–98

Adis, 197

Agui: and colonization policy, 71, 73; mentioned, 13, 82, 197; pays fine for Gui Jingzhao, 204

Aibida, 89n

Aksu: as exile destination, 68; exiles at, 165; mentioned, 23, 68n; positions reserved for *feiyuan* at, 141n

Amnesties: for banished officials, 195–196; discussed, 193–196; exclusions, 194; for exiles, 194; mentioned, 188; under Song, 45–46; when proclaimed, 193

An Lushan Rebellion, 42

Anxi: cost of grain at, 125, 126, 128n; as exile destination, 66–67; exiles pass through, 105, 127n; supplies obtained at, 120

Archery, 141n, 144

Asiha: awarded rank, 139; exiled, 89n

Assizes, 63–64

Bai Juyi, 44

Balikun: as exile destination, 61, 67, 170, 206n; exiles pass through, 107; government issue at, 173, 178–179; mentioned, 105n, 127n, 143; settled, 26; taxation at, 171

Banished officials: accommodation for, 150; archery taught by, 141n, 144; Chinese language skills used, 143; composition, 89–93; contribute to frontier development, 146; duration of punishment, 191–193, 228; employment, 4, 140–146; families, 70–71; food, 153; funding, 139–140; gambling, 154; horticulture, 152–153; influence on perceptions of frontiers, 4, 158–162; leisure, 152–154; life, 146–155; literary activity, 152, 156–157; numbers, 31, 70; post-exile careers, 205–211; provinces from which banished, 93; recall procedure, 192–193; restrictions on, 149–150, 152; rollcalls, 149–150; sex, 150, 154; and statecraft movement, 159–161; status, 146–148; teaching, 144; theater, 153, 154, 179–180; treatment, 147–150. *See also* Chen Huai; *Feiyuan* in Manchuria; Hong Liangji; Ji Yun; Journey; Qi Yunshi; Xu Song

Banishment. *See* Exile

Banishment to Manchuria: for collective responsibility, 58, 59, 207, 223; as commutation, 57, 223; distinguished from banishment to Xinjiang, 32; in early Qing, 57; for ineptitude, 58; in Ming, 49; for political reasons, 58

Sun Shiyi, 80–81
Suzhou (Gansu): travel passes obtained at, 105

Taifeiyin: exile, 89n; why exiled, 81–82; transfer to China proper, 202
Taiwan: migration to, 18–19; not used as exile destination, 54; as source of exiles, 91–93
Tang dynasty, 41–44
Tang La, 169
Tarbagatai, 143n, 170
Tattoos: administered by coroner, 117–118; for changees, 112n; for collectively responsible exiles, 117n; of destination, 114–115; exemptions, 115–116, 117n; forms, 114–115, 116; removal, 117–118; significance, 117; size, 112; for Song exiles, 45
Ten great evils. See Shi e
Tian Baiyan, 150n
Tiebao: exiled, 89n; postexile career, 208, 209n
Trade between Xinjiang and China proper, 28
Transport, 120–121
Travel passes: cost, 105n; obtained at Suzhou, 105; for travel to Xinjiang, 165
Tuntian (military agricultural colonies): under Han, 38; in Xinjiang, 27–30, 160, 162n, 170–174
Turfan: administration, 24; exiles pass through, 107; under Han, 38, 39; mentioned, 105n, 127n; under Tang, 42

Uncertainty: and assizes system, 63; and benevolence, 35; involved in exile, 7, 77, 138–139, 140, 189, 211, 215, 222; concerning treatment of pirates, 99
Ürümqi: administration, 24; Bi Yuan visits, 149; civil-military balance at, 140; corruption case at, 85n, 145; distance from Beijing, 131; emancipation at, 211; examination quotas at, 144; exile colonies at, 170–172; as exile destination, 67–70, 95, 170, 208, 210; grain prices, 28n; life at, 152–155; mining at, 174, 190; posts reserved for feiyuan at, 141n; schools at, 144. See also Banished officials; Convicts in Xinjiang; Exile colonies; Xinjiang

Ush: as exile destination, 68–70; mentioned, 23; positions reserved for feiyuan at, 141n; uprising at, 175

Waiqian. See Frontier banishment
Wang Baixin, 162n
Wang Changling, 155
Wang Danwang, sons, 85, 197. See also Gansu case
Wang Liyuan, 144n
Wang Tingkai, 146
Wang Yangming: exiled, 50; mentioned, 158, 215, 217; views on exile and self-renewal, 50
Wang Yuanshu, 158
Wang Zichong: in exile, 165; mother, 164
Water: for cartwheels, 121; on journey, 120
Wei Keyu, 103, 133
Wei Peijin, 111, 142
Wei Yuan: draws on Ji Yun, 156; influence concerning Xinjiang, 162; links to exiles, 161; on Xinjiang, 161
Wei Zhiyi, 44
Weishibu, 89n
Weisuo, 48
Wenfu: founds schools, 144; lenient attitude, 147; provides Ji Yun with lodging, 150; suppresses convicts' riot, 185
Wenning, 89n
Wenshou: and self-imposed fines, 204n; exiled, 89n; why exiled, 81
White Lotus. See Reasons for exile: religious sect participation
Wine, availability in Xinjiang, 153–154
Women: apply to make contributions on son's behalf, 203; in exile, 6, 23, 71, 72, 169, 179, 184; exiled, 96–97n, 101, 122, 130, 136–137; left without support, 97n, 164, 200, 201; mentioned, 197; and monetary redemption, 73, 75n; as "outer" relatives, 198, 222; outnumbered in exile, 179; in prison, 64; special treatment, 130, 223–224; status in exile, 169
Wu Chengxu, 200
Wu Shigong: exiled, 89n; return, 206n
Wu Xiongguang: exiled, 89n; postexile career, 206; why exiled, 86
Wu Yasan, 113–114
Wu Yulin, 145